The Design of Digital Systems

McGRAW-HILL SERIES IN ELECTRONIC SYSTEMS

John G. Truxal and Ronald A. Rohrer, Consulting Editors

The Design of Digital Systems

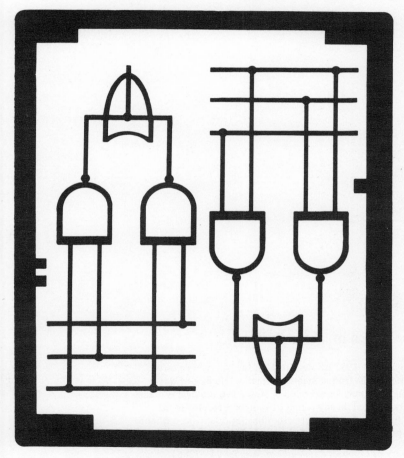

John B. Peatman

Professor of Electrical Engineering   The Georgia Institute of Technology

McGRAW--HILL BOOK COMPANY

New York   St. Louis   San Francisco   Düsseldorf   Johannesburg   Kuala Lumpur   London

Mexico   Montreal   New Delhi   Panama   Rio de Janeiro   Singapore   Sydney   Toronto

The Design of Digital Systems

Library of Congress Catalog Card Number 74-172661
07-049136-4

890KPKP7987654

To
Marilyn and to
Lisa, Katy, and Bob

CONTENTS

PREFACE

This book is intended for the engineer interested in obtaining an overview of the digital mode of operation. It opens the door to the many applications of digital techniques. It differs from many books in that it develops design capability while keeping this breadth of application in mind.

An effective digital systems designer requires at least three distinct capabilities. First, he must have a fundamental understanding of the operation of the components available to him, including not only the *gates* and *flipflops* of formal switching circuit theory but also memory devices, information-gathering devices, and devices whereby the digital system can inform or control. Furthermore, to be an effective designer, his understanding must extend beyond the framework of only simplified and idealized devices. For example, since the proper use of flipflops requires careful observance of timing considerations, the designer is aided by having systematic ways to design with flipflops so as to insure the automatic observance of these timing considerations.

Second, the designer must understand thoroughly the algorithmic processes involved in his system problem. For example, if he is operating on the pulse rates being generated by a turbine flow meter, then a fundamental understanding of pulse-rate algorithms will lead to systems designs which exhibit good error characteristics.

Third, the designer must understand how to implement those functions and systems which are too complicated to be tackled directly with a single, formal design technique. In this sense, designing almost any system is not unlike jumping from boulder to boulder to cross a stream. Each boulder may represent a specific formal design technique which may or may not be used in carrying out the system design. In addition to studying boulders, the designer must pay attention to how streams are crossed. For example, the whole area of *serial* versus *parallel* modes of operation can be thought of as providing alternative routes across the stream.

This book attempts to organize and unify the development of these three capabilities to understand and use digital components, exploit powerful algorithmic processes, and realize an effective system organization from a desired system specification.

From another point of view, this book is directed toward a specific goal of engineering studies—the development of creative design capability. The digital area provides a beautiful opportunity to develop this capability under rather ideal conditions: the specifications for system performance can be made both real and unambiguous; only a few types of building blocks are needed to design a wide variety of complex systems; and the availability of a simple cost criterion permits the student to carry out design while subject to a specific, real measure of the quality of his design. To take advantage of this opportunity, most chapters close with a broad variety of problems having a design flavor.

The book will typically be used in a one-semester or two-quarter course in introductory digital systems design at the senior level or at the junior level if it is deemed worthwhile to trade off the increased engineering experience of seniors for the opportunity to follow this course with other design-oriented courses. Although the context of the book is electrical, each component is sufficiently explained to permit the book to be used in a variety of curricula as an introduction to digital systems design. The incentive to so use the book lies in the diverse applications of digital techniques, many of which are described in the first chapter.

An attempt has been made to make many parts of the book self-contained. Consequently, one way in which the book might be used is to study the "bare bones" of each chapter in order to obtain an accelerated route toward the overall systems design picture. The remaining sections of each chapter can be studied at a later time as the need arises or in a subsequent course. Such an accelerated route through the *switching circuit design* portion of the book can be followed by omitting the latter halves of Chapters 2, 3, and 4 as well as Sections 5-5 to 5-9 and 5-12. Similarly, a quick view of overall systems design can be obtained from Sections 6-1, 6-2, and 6-5, while input-output considerations can be sensed through a study of Sections 7-1 and 7-3. The nature of a variety of algorithmic processes might best be obtained by considering one example from each of several sections of Chapter 8. Finally, the appendixes can be used either to support specific sections of the text or to obtain a quick overview of some peripheral topics.

It was my good fortune to study digital systems design under Dr. Harry W. Mergler of Case Western Reserve University. In every sense this book is a reflection of his influence. I am deeply indebted to my students at Georgia Tech who, through their design problem work, have also been my teachers. Indebtedness is also acknowledged to Joseph W. Mehaffey, Jr., of the Lockheed-Georgia Company for our many discussions and for his viewpoint on automatic malfunction detection expressed in Appendix A5. For insight into pipeline systems organization, I am grateful to L. Wayne Cotten of the National Security Agency.

I have been fortunate to have had the counsel and support of two able administrators while at Georgia Tech: Drs. Benjamin J. Dasher and Demetrius T. Paris. The development of my digital systems courses was wholeheartedly

supported by the former, while the opportunity to devote myself completely
to the preparation of this book was made possible by the latter. Finally, I am
grateful to my wife, Marilyn, for her single-minded devotion to the preparation of this book, including the typing of the complete manuscript.

John B. Peatman

The Design of Digital Systems

1

A Rationale for Designing Digital Systems

1-1 MERITS OF OPERATION IN THE DIGITAL MODE

Rare is the field of engineering endeavor which has not felt the impact of digital technology. This is due to the broad range of opportunities which the digital mode of operation makes available. In this section, we shall consider the nature of these opportunities, together with examples of systems which capitalize upon them.

Many systems take advantage of the *accuracy and resolution* which can be attained digitally. Data can be represented and manipulated *within* a digital system to any desired degree of accuracy. Furthermore, the digital system can *obtain* this data with astounding accuracy and resolution.

The optical tracking mount shown in Fig. 1-1 is a system used by NASA to track and obtain position data on satellites. It directs a laser beam toward a satellite. The satellite uses optical *corner reflectors* to return the beam in the exact direction from which it came. Then a telescope picks up the returned beam. By locking the laser-beam–telescope combination on to the satellite, the satellite's direction can be determined by making angular measurements on the optical tracking mount itself. These angular measurements are made, with a

1

Fig. 1-1   Optical tracking mount. (*National Aeronautics and Space Administration.*)

Fig. 1-2   Eighteen-bit optical shaft-angle encoder. (*Itek Corp./Wayne-George Division.*)

resolution of better than 5 s of arc, using optical shaft-angle encoders. One of these is illustrated in Fig. 1-2. It divides the angular position around one axis of the optical tracking mount into $2^{18} = 262,144$ parts and says which one of these parts corresponds to the position of the mount.

Another example of a system which uses the digital mode to obtain high accuracy and resolution is the quartz thermometer shown in Fig. 1-3. By building an oscillator around a quartz crystal mounted in the temperature probe, a frequency is obtained which is proportional to temperature. Using digital counters, this frequency is converted to a temperature display. It has the unusually fine resolution of $0.0001°C$, which is useful for monitoring small temperature changes. Its absolute accuracy of $0.1°C$ is very good in so convenient a measuring instrument.

Digital systems often capitalize on having a *compatible data base*. This is exemplified by a large and complex process-control system in which temperatures, pressures, flow rates, and chemical composition are all converted into numbers. No matter what input is considered, its value ends up in the system as a number. In this form, it can be added, multiplied, integrated, or otherwise processed. The processing is constrained only by the equations governing the physical processes involved and not by the fact that one number represents a temperature while another represents a flow rate.

The *error-control* possibilities opened up by digital operation are a key factor in its choice for many systems. This capability arises in several ways. Consider the simplicity with which data are stored in the small ferrite cores used in magnetic core memories and shown in Fig. 1-4. Fundamentally, all that is asked of each of these cores is that it remain magnetized in either a clockwise or counterclockwise direction. We never ask any one core to represent information

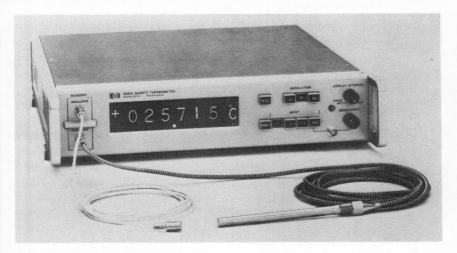

Fig. 1-3   Quartz thermometer. (*Hewlett-Packard Co.*)

Fig. 1-4 Ferrite cores used for digital data storage. (*Electronic Memories Inc.*)

using more than these two states. Yet, we can represent the value of a physical quantity to any desired accuracy by using groups of these ferrite cores. For example, with 10 cores, we can represent its value with an accuracy of 0.1 percent; with 20 cores, 0.0001 percent.

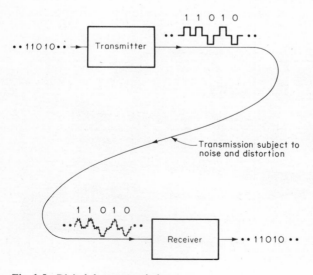

Fig. 1-5 Digital data transmission.

Another example whereby information with tight tolerances can be represented using combinations of things having loose tolerances occurs in digital communication. Here information can be represented with a sequence of 1s and 0s to any desired accuracy. In transmission, each 1 might be represented by a positive pulse, each 0 by a negative pulse. Any distortion which occurs to the waveform in transmission is irrelevant—as long as upon reception each positive and negative pulse is recognized as such. The receiver can then *reconstruct* the sequence of 1s and 0s, as illustrated in Fig. 1-5.

In addition to the error control afforded by the simplicity with which information is represented, the digital mode provides the opportunity to introduce error-detection and error-correction capability into this representation. For example, Fig. 1-6 shows some eight-channel perforated tape. Each *8-bit character* has an odd number of holes. If a single error occurs during the reading of any character, it will be detected. The erroneous character will appear to have an even number of holes.

More generally the digital mode provides error control in the following sense. A large, complex system can be designed and built to do a certain job.

Fig. 1-6 Eight-channel perforated tape. (*Digitronics Corp.*)

Fig. 1-7 Automated warehouse. (*Euclid Crane Co.*)

Once a working system is achieved, "carbon copies" of this working system can be built and they will do the same job equally faithfully. Unlike an analog system, there is no need to "tweak" the performance of the system (by adjusting potentiometers throughout the system) in order to have it meet the system specifications. In the digital system, as each element does its simple job, the combination of many of these elements will perform the complex system job.

In many circumstances it is the *data storage* capability of the digital mode which is of prime value to a system. Unlike various analog modes of data storage (such as the voltage on a capacitor in an analog computer), the digital mode is not subject to the slow deterioration of information as time passes. This is true whether the information is stored as a pattern of holes in perforated tape, as the magnetization of discrete ferrite cores in a magnetic core memory, or as the magnetization of separate infinitesimal spots on the rotating disc of a magnetic disc memory.

An example of a system which capitalizes on this merit is the automated warehouse shown in Fig. 1-7. The stacking crane stores and retrieves material in any of the thousands of storage locations available. Unlike a normal warehouse, there is absolutely no need to store all items of the same type together in order to keep track of them. Each item stored is characterized in coded form by numbers stored in a small computer. Then, to retrieve a specific item, it can be located by sorting through numbers stored in the computer in a fraction of a second. Because this permits the random storage of materials, an automated warehouse is conveniently used right up to its maximum capacity—an ideal which is usually only poorly approached in a conventional warehouse.

The digital mode allows the convenient *manipulation of the time variable* under a variety of circumstances. The digital mode offers the opportunity to sample a signal and convert each sample to digital form. In this form, *time* is no more constrained than any other characteristic of the signal. For example, time can be *compressed*. Thus, when sonar signals are picked up by a submarine over an interval of a few seconds, they can be compressed and repeatedly processed or displayed every few milliseconds. As another example, the time variable can be repeatedly folded back on itself as is done in signal averaging. Thus, the waveform of a weak periodic signal buried in noise can be enhanced by overlaying successive segments of the noisy signal, where the segment length equals the period of the signal. Then the signal will reinforce itself while the noise tends to cancel out. A third example is provided by the variety of systems

Fig. 1-8   Numerically controlled milling machine. (*Cincinnati Milacron Inc.*)

which collect large segments of radar signals or seismic signals and which then obtain a Fourier transform of these data in order to view it in the frequency domain.

The automatic *sequencing of operations* is another powerful attribute of operation in the digital mode. The countdown sequence before the lift-off of a space vehicle or missile represents one example. The startup sequence for a large power-generating facility represents another. A third, shown in Fig. 1-8, is provided by a numerically controlled milling machine. Here, the sequence of operations may include milling, drilling, reaming, and tapping—all directed by the sequence of operations read into the machine's controller from a perforated tape. The machine changes tools automatically upon command. Then it moves the workpiece, carrying out the required operation. In a similar vein, the automatic wire-wrap machine shown in Fig. 1-9 will automatically wire the backplane of a complex digital system. Each wire is programmed with a single

Fig. 1-9   Automatic wire-wrap machine. (*Gardner-Denver Co.*)

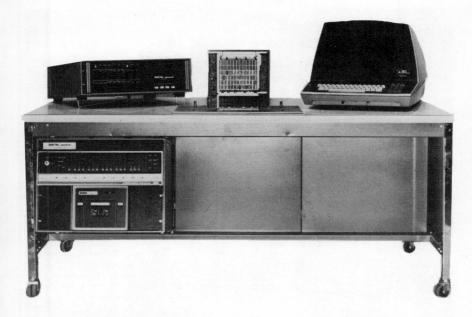

Fig. 1-10 Computer-based diagnostic test system. (*Digital/General Corp.*)

punched card, which specifies the two terminals to be interconnected and the routing of the wire between them.

In each of the above examples, the sequence of operations is specified beforehand. Often it is desirable to go further. A common and potent application of small computers is to carry out sequencing of operations where the sequence depends upon measured responses obtained along the way. Thus, a diagnostic test system, such as that shown in Fig. 1-10, might be used to test a certain piece of digital equipment upon completion of its final assembly. The first tests might determine whether each subsystem as a whole works correctly. Any subsystem which does not work can then be subjected to further tests, which are chosen to narrow down the source of trouble. By basing the test sequence on the results obtained, this diagnostic test routine can single out the source of trouble quickly.

Computing flexibility in the digital mode offers many opportunities. The optical and radio telescopes used by astronomers provide one example. The huge 200-in. telescope at Mt. Palomar, California, is dwarfed by its *equitorial* mount, as shown in Fig. 1-11. The mount has an equitorial axis which is aligned with the earth's axis and which rotates at earth's rate in the opposite direction. Consequently, the telescope, when once positioned on a star, will remain fixed upon that star. Today, the same telescope could be mounted in a much simpler *azimuth-elevation* mount and still achieve the same purpose. Such a mount

Fig. 1-11 World's largest optical telescope and its even larger equitorial mount at Palomar Observatory. (*Hale Observatories.*)

points the telescope at a specified elevation angle and a specified angle about its azimuth, or vertical, axis. Using a computer-controlled translator, the operator of the telescope could be given a control panel identical to that which he would expect, and like, for an equitorial mount. His inputs to this control panel would be translated by the computer into appropriate inputs to the control systems which drive the actual "az-el" mount about its two axes.

Another example which makes good use of computing flexibility is the system used on some airplanes for loading cargo. This system, built into the airplane, measures the weight exerted by the airplane on each of the three wheel assemblies. These three weights are combined appropriately to provide the gross weight of the airplane and the position of its center of gravity (both along the length of the airplane and laterally). These are the parameters of direct concern when an airplane is being loaded, and yet they can not be measured directly.

Examples of systems which can derive useful data by combining several measurements in this way extend into practically every type of engineering activity. An inertial guidance system measures accelerations and integrates these to obtain the position of a vehicle. A seismic oil-exploration system measures the earth's response to explosive charges and derives a map of the layered structure beneath the earth's surface. An oil refinery trims its controls automatically to achieve that proportion of products (jet fuel, gasoline, fuel oil, kerosene, etc.) which will maximize total profit when these products are sold. This last procedure is an exciting example of a system with built-in sensitivity and responsiveness to the fluctuations in the marketplace.

Often the digital mode is used because it provides *compatibility with desirable input or output devices*. The quartz thermometer of Fig. 1-3 exemplifies this on both the input and the output. The quartz-crystal oscillator on the input provides a frequency proportional to temperature which can be handled conveniently in a digital counter. On the output, the only way possible to obtain a direct reading, considering the range and resolution involved, is with a digital display.

The stepping motor is another output device which provides exceptionally useful characteristics when driven by a digital system. The unit shown in Fig. 1-12 steps 800 steps per revolution at a maximum rate of 1,200 steps per second. This means that every 833 μs the motor can be given a command to step one step in either direction (or not to step). By keeping track of these steps, the *position* of a shaft can be accurately controlled.

One final reason why many systems are designed digitally is the *availability of low-cost, high-performance digital integrated circuits*. These features of integrated circuits stem from the high degree of mass production in the manufacturing processes, as illustrated in Fig. 1-13. Some of these integrated circuits are illustrated in Fig. 1-14. The packaging protects the small circuit inside and provides a convenient means for interconnection with other ICs.

As we close this section, it should be apparent that the many merits of designing digitally have initiated, and will continue to initiate, the use of the digital mode in a variety of applications. The engineer best able to undertake

Fig. 1-12 High-resolution, fast-response stepping motor. (*USM Corp., Gear Systems Division.*)

Fig. 1-13   Facility for mass producing integrated circuits. (*Motorola Semiconductor Products Inc.*)

Fig. 1-14   Integrated circuits.

these new applications is the one who is thoroughly immersed in both their opportunities and their pitfalls.

1-2 APPROACHES TO DIGITAL-SYSTEM ORGANIZATION

The structures which are used to implement digital systems can be conveniently divided into three classes:

1. Special-purpose structures in which the structure is dictated directly by the system requirements.
2. Structures organized around a *dedicated* general-purpose digital computer. (Dedication means that the programming (software) is prepared to meet the requirements of one specific application.)
3. Large timeshared computing facilities. Here major emphasis is placed upon providing low-cost computational power to a variety of users.

   Special-purpose structures have been used in a variety of systems. The quartz thermometer of Fig. 1-3 represents an example in which only a relatively small amount of digital logic is needed to achieve the system function. Because of this, the system function has been most economically achieved with a special-purpose structure. Many other types of instrumentation equipment are designed using special-purpose structures for this same reason. Figure 1-15 illustrates a digital multimeter organized in this way.

   On a larger scale, the controller used by a numerical control system, such as that shown in Fig. 1-8, has traditionally been organized as a special-purpose

Fig. 1-15 Digital multimeter. (*Data Technology Corp.*)

Fig. 1-16   Large special-purpose structure for digital spectrum analysis.
(*Raytheon Co.*)

structure. Its function is to translate the commands it receives on perforated tape into the mechanical motions of the milling machine. With the swiftly descending costs of small computers, the time has passed when such a special-purpose structure is the most economical solution to this problem.

On a larger scale, Fig. 1-16 illustrates a special-purpose structure which can carry out digital spectrum analysis on extremely wideband radar signals. Its structure is dictated by the necessity of processing huge amounts of data with a fixed but extensive algorithm—the fast Fourier transform algorithm. Its *pipeline* structure (discussed in Sec. 6-3) permits a drastic increase in the rate of processing data over that which can be achieved with even the fastest general-purpose computers. Thus, it accepts a steady flow of radar data at a rate of 3 million bits/s, Fourier-transforms these data, and emits the transformed output at the other end of the pipeline structure.

More and more, engineered structures are being organized around general-purpose digital computers. The growth in the small-computer industry (where *small* might be used, somewhat arbitrarily, to indicate computers costing less than $20,000) is largely a reflection of the growth in the use of computers dedicated to a specific job. Much of this growth has been fostered by the *original equipment manufacturers* (OEMs) who build small computers into their equipment. The diagnostic test system of Fig. 1-10 represents one example. The computer built into that system is dedicated to the specific job of diagnostic testing. The payoff from the software development which goes into making the computer useful in this system is multiplied many times as the system is reproduced for many customers.

One large manufacturer of small computers estimates that 50 percent of their small-computer sales are OEM sales. A large share of the remaining sales go into individual systems which are likewise tailored to a specific purpose. Consequently, it has been estimated that 80 to 85 percent of all small computers are dedicated to special-purpose systems.

At the other end of the general-purpose-computer spectrum, we find the large-computer systems used on a timeshared basis by a variety of users. Here the emphasis of the computer design is quite different from that for the small computer. With a variety of users, it becomes important to be able to move user programs in and out of the computer at high rates of speed. Providing an efficient structure for sharing the computer thus becomes a critical issue.

In light of this distinction between three very different types of digital-system structures, it is pertinent to question what the emphasis of this book will be. We shall develop the background, insight, and capability to design systems which serve one function. In terms of the three kinds of structures outlined at the beginning of the section, this means that we shall be involved with the design of special-purpose structures and structures organized around a dedicated small computer. We shall not consider those aspects of digital design which are peculiar to the design of large timeshared computing facilities.

2
Preliminary Considerations

2-1 THE DESIGN PROCESS

The design of any digital system can be broken down into a succession of manageable steps. This is an essential characteristic of the design process. And, to the extent that the designer consciously subdivides the design task into these steps, he is able to bring a variety of potent design tools to bear on the problem. In contrast, a designer who tends to think of digital design as consisting fundamentally of one or two of these formal steps, together with a hodgepodge of miscellaneous tricks, will miss significant opportunities for achieving a low-cost, smoothly organized system design. Some of these steps are:

1. Assessing how the system inputs and outputs constrain the system design (e.g., how fast do inputs change; how are inputs coded; what form of output is required?).
2. Deciding how much time is available to carry out the required data manipulations. This determines whether specific algorithms will be implemented in parallel (for speed) or serially (for economy). It also determines whether a specific logic line is fast enough to do the job.

3. Deciding how various types of information within the system should be coded. Some of this will be dictated by the required coding of information on the input or output, unless a code conversion is deemed worthwhile. For other internally generated and used information, the coding will be dictated by the way in which the information is used.
4. Studying the operations involved in order to develop an algorithm which is particularly well suited to the problem. An arithmetic operation like multiplication or a data manipulation like sorting can be organized in a variety of ways. Often the greatest opportunities for simplifying a system design reside in this area of algorithm development.
5. Specifying a system structure of well-defined, interconnected subsystems which will meet the system requirements.
6. Implementing the subsystems. In a complex system, the design procedure may begin all over again in order to implement a well-defined but still complicated subsystem.

2-2 QUANTIZATION AND CODING

Often a continuous variable, such as a voltage or an angular position, must be represented digitally. The process of breaking up a continuous variable into discrete quanta is called *quantization*. If these quanta are all of equal size, we might say that the continuous variable has been *linearly* quantized.† Thus in Fig. 2-1a, the continuous voltage range between 0 and 10 mV has been linearly quantized into 5 quanta. In contrast, it is sometimes useful to quantize a continuous variable *nonlinearly* using quanta of unequal size. This might be done, for example, in making a digital fuel gauge for an airplane's fuel tank. If the gauge actually gives a measure of the depth of fuel in the tank and if the

†Actually this is not completely appropriate terminology since quantization is inherently a nonlinear process. However, the nonlinearity introduced by the quantization process itself is often of negligible significance when the size of each quantum is small.

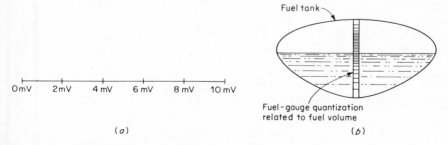

(a)   (b)

Fig. 2-1 Quantization. (a) Linear quantization; (b) nonlinear quantization.

volume is related to the depth by a nonlinear function, then by using nonlinear quantization this nonlinearity can be effectively removed. Each quantum can be made to represent the same volume of fuel as that of any other quantum, as in Fig. 2-1*b*.

If *quantization* is the term used to describe the dividing of a continuous variable into discrete parts, then *coding* is the term used for naming these parts. Various possibilities exist. If we quantize population by age using a rough nonlinear quantization, we might use *code words* like infants, children, teenagers, young adults, adults, and "golden-agers." Or using a finer linear quantization we might use code words like one year olds, two year olds, three year olds, etc. In quantizing a neighborhood into individuals we use code words like Ben Sutton and "Doc" Williams.

For digital purposes each of the above examples could represent an excellent scheme of quantization. However, none of the above represents a good *coding* scheme for these same digital purposes. In systems, we shall be representing all information in terms of *binary* or *Boolean* variables which take on either of only two values. Physically these two values could be represented by:

A hole (or its absence) in punched paper tape
The clockwise or counterclockwise magnetization of a ferrite core in a computer memory
A pulse (or its absence) at a certain time on a certain wire
A voltage of +5 or 0 V on a wire

However, in all these cases we shall represent the two values of a Boolean variable by the values 1 and 0.

This is all very well if we never want to do more than quantize variables into 2 quanta. In this case we can code the 2 quanta with one variable A, letting $A = 0$ represent 1 quantum while letting $A = 1$ represent the other. To code more quanta we must use combinations of Boolean variables. Using two Boolean variables A and B, we can code 4 quanta, using the four combinations

$$\begin{array}{cccc} A = 0 & A = 0 & A = 1 & A = 1 \\ B = 0 & B = 1 & B = 0 & B = 1 \end{array}$$

With three Boolean variables we get eight combinations—by taking each combination above together with $C = 0$ to get four combinations

$$\begin{array}{cccc} A = 0 & A = 0 & A = 1 & A = 1 \\ B = 0 & B = 1 & B = 0 & B = 1 \\ C = 0 & C = 0 & C = 0 & C = 0 \end{array}$$

plus each combination again but with $C = 1$ to get four more combinations

$A = 0$	$A = 0$	$A = 1$	$A = 1$
$B = 0$	$B = 1$	$B = 0$	$B = 1$
$C = 1$	$C = 1$	$C = 1$	$C = 1$

We can generalize this to say that with n Boolean variables we can code 2^n quanta.

Use of the code reduces to identifying each quantum with a specific integer, followed by the representation of this integer by the corresponding combination of Boolean variables.

2-3 COMMONLY USED CODES FOR POSITIVE INTEGERS

The most commonly used code for positive integers is *binary* code. The binary code shown in Fig. 2-2 uses four Boolean variables, or *bits*, to code the integers from zero to fifteen.

Binary code is one example of an *analytic* code. This means that the integers coded can be related to the values of the bits by

$$I = \sum_i K_i b_i + K_0$$

where the weight K_i associated with each bit b_i must be a constant, as must be K_0, the bias constant. The 4-bit binary code satisfies the analytic relation

$$I = 8b_8 + 4b_4 + 2b_2 + b_1$$

Analytic codes, as we shall see subsequently, are especially well suited for

I	b_8	b_4	b_2	b_1
0	0	0	0	0
1	0	0	0	1
2	0	0	1	0
3	0	0	1	1
4	0	1	0	0
5	0	1	0	1
6	0	1	1	0
7	0	1	1	1
8	1	0	0	0
9	1	0	0	1
10	1	0	1	0
11	1	0	1	1
12	1	1	0	0
13	1	1	0	1
14	1	1	1	0
15	1	1	1	1

Fig. 2-2 Binary code.

carrying out arithmetic operations. In contrast, a nonanalytic code will tend to give us extra troubles if we use it to implement these same arithmetic operations.

Finding the decimal equivalent of a binary number or vice versa consists of employing the analytic relationship in one direction or the other.

Example 2-1   Find the decimal equivalent of the binary number 0110101.

Applying the analytic relationship gives

$$
\begin{aligned}
I &= 64 \times 0 + 32 \times 1 + 16 \times 1 + 8 \times 0 + 4 \times 1 + 2 \times 0 + 1 \times 1 \\
  &= \quad 0 \ + \ 32 \ + \ 16 \ + \ 0 \ + \ 4 \ + \ 0 \ + \ 1 \\
  &= \quad 53
\end{aligned}
$$

Example 2-2   Find the binary equivalent of the decimal number 83.

Since we will be expressing 83 as the summation of various powers of two, we can begin by finding the largest power of two less than 83, which is 64. Then

$$83 = 64 \times 1 + \text{remainder}$$

Repeating this over and over again gives

$$
\begin{aligned}
83 &= 64 \times 1 + 19 \\
   &= 64 \times 1 + 32 \times 0 + 16 \times 1 + 3 \\
   &= 64 \times 1 + 32 \times 0 + 16 \times 1 + 8 \times 0 + 3 \\
   &= 64 \times 1 + 32 \times 0 + 16 \times 1 + 8 \times 0 + 4 \times 0 + 3 \\
   &= 64 \times 1 + 32 \times 0 + 16 \times 1 + 8 \times 0 + 4 \times 0 + 2 \times 1 + 1 \\
   &= 64 \times 1 + 32 \times 0 + 16 \times 1 + 8 \times 0 + 4 \times 0 + 2 \times 1 + 1 \times 1
\end{aligned}
$$

Consequently

$$(83)_{\text{decimal}} = (1010011)_{\text{binary}}$$

An example of a code which is closely related to binary code, which is nonanalytic, and yet which has its own useful properties is *Gray* code. This code, shown in Fig. 2-3, is useful because it is a *unit-distance* code which can easily be converted to binary code. The unit-distance property means that in going from the coding for any integer I to the coding for $I + 1$ only 1 bit changes regardless of the value of I. This is a property which is usefully employed in conjunction with shaft-angle encoders, which quantize and code the angular position of a rotating shaft. In Chap. 7 we shall describe this use of Gray code more fully. The conversion from Gray to binary code will be illustrated later in this chapter.

The general structure of Gray code for n bits can be described in terms of the following points:

1. Except for the beginning and ending of the code,
      bit g_1 alternates two 1s, two 0s, two 1s, two 0s, etc.,
      while bit g_2 alternates four 1s, four 0s, four 1s, four 0s, etc.,

I	g_8	g_4	g_2	g_1
0	0	0	0	0
1	0	0	0	1
2	0	0	1	1
3	0	0	1	0
4	0	1	1	0
5	0	1	1	1
6	0	1	0	1
7	0	1	0	0
8	1	1	0	0
9	1	1	0	1
10	1	1	1	1
11	1	1	1	0
12	1	0	1	0
13	1	0	1	1
14	1	0	0	1
15	1	0	0	0

Fig. 2-3   Gray code.

and bit g_4 alternates eight 1s, eight 0s, eight 1s, eight 0s, etc.,
and bit g_k alternates $2K$ 1s, $2K$ 0s, $2K$ 1s, $2K$ 0s, etc.

2. The first transition from 0 to 1 for bit g_{2K} occurs right in the middle of the first string of 1s for bit g_k.

To illustrate that Gray code is nonanlytic, consider the case of a 2-bit Gray code:

I	g_2	g_1
0	0	0
1	0	1
2	1	1
3	1	0

If this is analytic, it must satisfy an equation of the form

$$I = K_2 g_2 + K_1 g_1 + K_0$$

Substituting in $I = 0$, $g_2 = 0$, and $g_1 = 0$ yields $K_0 = 0$. Now, using $I = 1, g_2 = 0$, and $g_1 = 1$ yields $K_1 = 1$. Next, using $I = 2, g_2 = 1$ and $g_1 = 1$ yields $K_2 = 1$. But then there is a contradiction as we substitute $I = 3$, $g_2 = 1$, and $g_1 = 0$, which says $3 \overset{?}{=} 1$. Because of this contradiction, the required analytic relationship is not satisfied and the code is therefore nonanalytic.

Another class of useful codes are the *binary coded decimal* (BCD) codes. BCD codes code each decimal digit of an integer as a separate entity. Because the conversion to or from a BCD code is much simpler than to or from binary code, the BCD code is particularly useful in a system which must accept decimal data from people or which must present such data to people. The most commonly used BCD code is 8421 BCD code, in which each decimal digit is coded as a 4-bit binary number. The name *8421 BCD* is derived from the weights associated with these 4 bits.

Example 2-3 Express $(396)_{decimal}$ in 8421 BCD code.

$$(396)_{decimal} = \underbrace{(0011}_{3} \quad \underbrace{1001}_{9} \quad \underbrace{0110)}_{6}{}_{8421\ BCD}$$

This is another example of an analytic code, with weights of 800, 400, 200, 100, 80, 40, 20, 10, 8, 4, 2, and 1 for the three-digit version.

A less frequently used BCD code but one which is superior to 8421 BCD code in at least one major respect is *excess-three BCD* (XS-3) code. Again, each digit of the corresponding decimal number is coded separately, but now the coding for each digit is that shown in Fig. 2-4. Note that if three were added to each number I and then it was converted to its 4-bit binary equivalent, we would end up with the coding shown. Hence the name *excess-three*.

Example 2-4 Express $(396)_{decimal}$ in excess-three BCD code.

$$(396)_{decimal} = \underbrace{(0110}_{3} \quad \underbrace{1100}_{9} \quad \underbrace{1001)}_{6}{}_{XS-3}$$

Being as similar as it is to 8421 BCD code, it might be suspected that this code is analytic also. Indeed, this turns out to be the case with the code satisfying the analytic relation (for a two-digit version of the code):

$$I = 80e_{80} + 40e_{40} + 20e_{20} + 10e_{10} + 8e_8 + 4e_4 + 2e_2 + e_1 - 33$$

The bias constant of -33 can be checked by inserting the coding for $I = 0$ into this relation. What is the corresponding value of the bias constant for a three-digit excess-three BCD code?

I	e_8	e_4	e_2	e_1
0	0	0	1	1
1	0	1	0	0
2	0	1	0	1
3	0	1	1	0
4	0	1	1	1
5	1	0	0	0
6	1	0	0	1
7	1	0	1	0
8	1	0	1	1
9	1	1	0	0

Fig. 2-4 Excess-three BCD coding of the 10 digits.

Excess-three BCD code is an example of a *self-complementing* code. For a three-digit number I this means that $999 - I$ can be obtained simply by changing all 0s to 1s and all 1s to 0s. That the code is self-complementing can be seen in Fig. 2-4. Note that if for the coding of any integer I all 0s are changed to 1s while all 1s are changed to 0s, the result will be the coding for $9 - I$. And since this is true for each digit, it follows that it is true for an n-digit number. This simple forming of the *nine's complement* of a number is useful in implementing both addition and subtraction with only an adder. It permits us to do the coded equivalent of the following example.

Example 2-5 Subtract 261 from 842 using nine's complementing plus an addition process.

First note that

$$842 - 261 = 581$$

is equivalent to

$$842 + (\overbrace{999 - 261}^{738}) + 1 - 1,000 = 581$$

Thus we carry out the operation as follows:

$$
\begin{array}{ccc}
 & & 1 \\
842 & & 842 \\
\underline{-261} & \xrightarrow{\text{9s comp}} & \underline{738} \\
 & & \cancel{1}581
\end{array}
$$

A major disadvantage of these BCD codes lies in their wastefulness in the number of quanta they can code with a given number of bits. For example, given 12 bits we can code any three-digit number with a BCD code; that is, we can code 1,000 quanta. If instead we use binary code, these 12 bits are capable of coding 4,096 quanta.

2-4 COMMONLY USED CODES FOR SIGNED NUMBERS

Often we wish to code both positive and negative integers. We shall use a *sign bit* of 1 to indicate when a number is negative and a sign bit of 0 to indicate when it is either zero or positive. (The opposite definition is possible but will not be used in this book since it leads to a slight complication in the implementation of some arithmetic operations.)

To obtain a signed-number code based on binary code, two possibilities are commonly used, as illustrated in Fig. 2-5. *Sign plus binary magnitude* is the binary extension of what we do when we express positive and negative numbers decimally: where we use a sign, the code uses a sign bit; where we use the decimal magnitude, it uses the binary magnitude. This code has no strong features to recommend it. Being an extension of binary code, its interpretation

Integer coded	Sign plus binary magnitude							Sign plus two's complement						
	s	b_{32}	b_{16}	b_8	b_4	b_2	b_1	s	b_{32}	b_{16}	b_8	b_4	b_2	b_1
+63	0	1	1	1	1	1	1	0	1	1	1	1	1	1
⋮														
+9	0	0	0	1	0	0	1	0	0	0	1	0	0	1
+8	0	0	0	1	0	0	0	0	0	0	1	0	0	0
+7	0	0	0	0	1	1	1	0	0	0	0	1	1	1
+6	0	0	0	0	1	1	0	0	0	0	0	1	1	0
+5	0	0	0	0	1	0	1	0	0	0	0	1	0	1
+4	0	0	0	0	1	0	0	0	0	0	0	1	0	0
+3	0	0	0	0	0	1	1	0	0	0	0	0	1	1
+2	0	0	0	0	0	1	0	0	0	0	0	0	1	0
+1	0	0	0	0	0	0	1	0	0	0	0	0	0	1
0	0	0	0	0	0	0	0	0	0	0	0	0	0	0
−1	1	0	0	0	0	0	1	1	1	1	1	1	1	1
−2	1	0	0	0	0	1	0	1	1	1	1	1	1	0
−3	1	0	0	0	0	1	1	1	1	1	1	1	0	1
−4	1	0	0	0	1	0	0	1	1	1	1	1	0	0
−5	1	0	0	0	1	0	1	1	1	1	1	0	1	1
−6	1	0	0	0	1	1	0	1	1	1	1	0	1	0
−7	1	0	0	0	1	1	1	1	1	1	1	0	0	1
−8	1	0	0	1	0	0	0	1	1	1	1	0	0	0
−9	1	0	0	1	0	0	1	1	1	1	0	1	1	1
⋮														
−63	1	1	1	1	1	1	1	1	0	0	0	0	0	1

Fig. 2-5 Signed number codes based on binary code.

by people is relatively difficult. Furthermore, an arithmetic operation such as addition requires the checking of the sign bits followed by an addition or a subtraction of the magnitudes, depending upon both the signs and the magnitudes. This is a direct result of the code not being analytic.

Figure 2-5 also illustrates *sign plus two's complement* code. This code looks the same as sign plus binary magnitude for positive integers. For negative numbers it looks strange! It is formed, for negative numbers, with a 1 for the sign bit and with the *two's complement* of the magnitude for the remaining bits. This two's complement is formed by subtracting the n-bit binary magnitude of the negative number from 2^n. Thus the 6-bit two's complement of 000001 is

$$\begin{array}{r} 1000000 \\ - 000001 \\ \hline 111111 \end{array}$$

and this, preceded by a sign bit of 1, yields the 7-bit sign plus two's complement coding of −1 shown in the table (Fig. 2-5).

In contrast to sign plus binary magnitude code, sign plus two's complement code is analytic. For the 7-bit code, the analytic relation is given by

$$I = -64s + 32b_{32} + 16b_{16} + 8b_8 + 4b_4 + 2b_2 + b_1$$

A direct result of this code being analytic is that numbers can be added together without regard to their signs as if they were positive numbers and the result will be correct, provided any overflow is neglected.

Example 2-6 Add +5 and −2 together in sign plus two's complement code.

```
(+5)  ──────▶      0000101
+(−2) ──────▶   + |1111110
(+3)  ──────▶   X|0000011
                ↗
              Neglect
```

Example 2-7 Add −5 and +2 together in sign plus two's complement code.

```
(−5)  ──────▶      1111011
+(+2) ──────▶   +  0000010
(−3)  ──────▶      1111101
```

Example 2-8 Add −5 and −2 together in sign plus two's complement code.

```
(−5)  ──────▶      1111011
+(−2) ──────▶   + |1111110
(−7)  ──────▶   X|1111001
                ↗
              Neglect
```

Example 2-9 Add +63 and +63 together in the same 7-bit sign plus two's complement code and represent the result in the same 7-bit code.

This is impossible; +126 cannot be coded with anything less than an 8-bit sign plus two's complement code. In any system we design we must ensure that such an actual overflow never will arise or we must design circuitry which will detect its occurrence and provide some appropriate course of action.

Two other signed-number codes are illustrated in Fig. 2-6. These are the 8421 BCD code analogies of the two codes we have just been discussing. The *sign plus 8421 BCD magnitude* code is a useful code for systems which must interact directly with people since a decimal input or display can be obtained directly from this code. However, it has the feature, again, of being nonanalytic. Consequently arithmetic operations implemented in this code have an extra degree of complexity. In contrast, *sign plus ten's complement (8421 BCD)* code is analytic, and numbers expressed in this code can be added directly in an adder designed for positive 8421 BCD code numbers without concern over their signs. The *ten's complement* in the name of the code means that the 9-bit coding of −1 has a 1 in the sign bit and 100 − 1 = 99 (expressed in 8421 BCD code) for the remaining bits.

Integer coded	Sign plus 8421 BCD magnitude									Sign plus ten's complement (8421 BCD)								
	s	d_{80} d_{40}	d_{20} d_{10}	d_8 d_4	d_2 d_1					s	d_{80} d_{40}	d_{20} d_{10}	d_8 d_4	d_2 d_1				
+99	0	1	0	0	1	1	0	0	1	0	1	0	0	1	1	0	0	1
⋮																		
+11	0	0	0	0	1	0	0	0	1	0	0	0	0	1	0	0	0	1
+10	0	0	0	0	1	0	0	0	0	0	0	0	0	1	0	0	0	0
+9	0	0	0	0	0	1	0	0	1	0	0	0	0	0	1	0	0	1
+8	0	0	0	0	0	1	0	0	0	0	0	0	0	0	1	0	0	0
+7	0	0	0	0	0	0	1	1	1	0	0	0	0	0	0	1	1	1
+6	0	0	0	0	0	0	1	1	0	0	0	0	0	0	0	1	1	0
+5	0	0	0	0	0	0	1	0	1	0	0	0	0	0	0	1	0	1
+4	0	0	0	0	0	0	1	0	0	0	0	0	0	0	0	1	0	0
+3	0	0	0	0	0	0	0	1	1	0	0	0	0	0	0	0	1	1
+2	0	0	0	0	0	0	0	1	0	0	0	0	0	0	0	0	1	0
+1	0	0	0	0	0	0	0	0	1	0	0	0	0	0	0	0	0	1
0	0	0	0	0	0	0	0	0	0	0	0	0	0	0	0	0	0	0
−1	1	0	0	0	0	0	0	0	1	1	1	0	0	1	1	0	0	1
−2	1	0	0	0	0	0	0	1	0	1	1	0	0	1	1	0	0	0
−3	1	0	0	0	0	0	0	1	1	1	1	0	0	1	0	1	1	1
−4	1	0	0	0	0	0	1	0	0	1	1	0	0	1	0	1	1	0
−5	1	0	0	0	0	0	1	0	1	1	1	0	0	1	0	1	0	1
−6	1	0	0	0	0	0	1	1	0	1	1	0	0	1	0	1	0	0
−7	1	0	0	0	0	0	1	1	1	1	1	0	0	1	0	0	1	1
−8	1	0	0	0	0	1	0	0	0	1	1	0	0	1	0	0	1	0
−9	1	0	0	0	0	1	0	0	1	1	1	0	0	1	0	0	0	1
−10	1	0	0	0	1	0	0	0	0	1	1	0	0	1	0	0	0	0
−11	1	0	0	0	1	0	0	0	1	1	1	0	0	0	1	0	0	1
⋮																		
−99	1	1	0	0	1	1	0	0	1	1	0	0	0	0	0	0	0	1

Fig. 2-6 Signed number codes based on 8421 BCD code.

This brief description of a few codes and their properties will provide the background needed for discussing many related matters throughout the book. In addition, since the subject of codes and code properties is a broad one, it will arise again in quite a few sections of the book where the technique being discussed is intimately related to some specific code.

2-5 LOGICAL CONNECTIVES

In order to express Boolean variables as functions of other Boolean variables, we need to define several logical connectives. The role which these serve in Boolean algebra is analogous to the role served by connectives such as addition and multiplication for ordinary algebra.

Consider first the AND connective as it relates to two Boolean variables A and B. Figure 2-7a illustrates two ways to express the algebraic ANDing of A and B. The *truth table* in Fig. 2-7b has nothing to do with truth or falsehood but

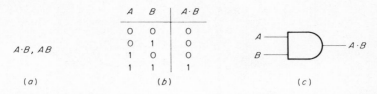

A	B	A·B
0	0	0
0	1	0
1	0	0
1	1	1

A·B, AB

(a)   (b)   (c)

Fig. 2-7 The AND connective. (a) Algebraic representations; (b) truth table; (c) graphic symbol.

rather is simply a listing of the four possible combinations A and B and the corresponding values of $A \cdot B$. Note that $A \cdot B = 1$ if and only if $A = 1$ and $B = 1$. The commonly used graphic symbol† is shown in Fig. 2-7c. For three (or more) Boolean variables, the function $A \cdot B \cdot C = 1$ if and only if $A = 1$ *and B = 1 and C = 1*.

The OR connective, or, more properly the INCLUSIVE-OR connective, is illustrated in Fig. 2-8. Note that $A + B = 1$ if $A = 1$ or if $B = 1$ or both. It is the inclusion of this *or both* condition which leads to the name INCLUSIVE-OR. For three (or more) variables $A + B + C = 1$ if and only if any one or more of the variables $A, B,$ or C are equal to 1.

The EXCLUSIVE-OR connective, illustrated in Fig. 2-9, excludes the *or both* case described in the last paragraph. Consequently, for two variables, the function $A \oplus B = 1$ if and only if either input = 1 while the other input = 0. The extension to three variables is not immediately obvious. However, it can be derived by considering the sequence of operations

$$(A \oplus B) \oplus C$$

The first column of the truth table in Fig. 2-9d illustrates the function $A \oplus B$, while the second column is an EXCLUSIVE-ORing between this and the variable

†See *Military Standard—Graphic Symbols for Logic Diagrams*, MIL-STD-806B, February 26, 1962. This may be obtained by writing Naval Publications and Forms Center, 5801 Tabor Ave., Philadelphia, Pa. 19120.

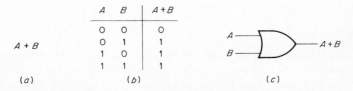

A	B	A+B
0	0	0
0	1	1
1	0	1
1	1	1

A + B

(a)   (b)   (c)

Fig. 2-8 The OR connective. (a) Algebraic representation; (b)truth table; (c) graphic symbol.

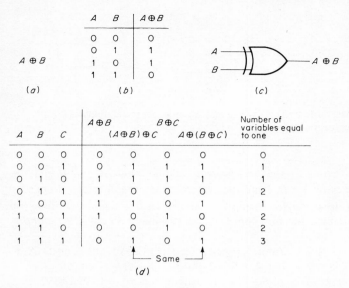

Fig. 2-9   The EXCLUSIVE-OR connective. (*a*) Algebraic representation; (*b*) truth table; (*c*) graphic symbol; (*d*) derivation of properties of $A \oplus B \oplus C$.

C. A proper question is whether

$$(A \oplus B) \oplus C \stackrel{?}{=} A \oplus (B \oplus C)$$

The third and fourth columns develop the truth table for $A \oplus (B \oplus C)$. Since the second and fourth columns are identical in all cases, we have proven this *Boolean identity*

$$(A \oplus B) \oplus C = A \oplus (B \oplus C)$$

Consequently, since the order of operations makes no difference, it makes sense to express the operation without parentheses:

$$A \oplus B \oplus C$$

The meaning of this function is not as obvious as an ANDing or an ORing of three variables. However, if we count the number of variables (A, B, and C) equal to one in each row of the truth table, as has been done in the fifth column, we note that

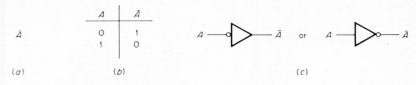

Fig. 2-10 The NOT operator. (*a*) Algebraic representations; (*b*) truth table; (*c*) graphic symbols.

$$A \oplus B \oplus C = \begin{cases} 1 & \text{if an odd number of variables equals 1} \\ 0 & \text{if an even number of variables equals 1} \end{cases}$$

The extension of this analysis to the general case for any number of variables gives

$$A \oplus B \oplus C \oplus D \oplus \cdots = \begin{cases} 1 & \text{if an odd number of variables equals 1} \\ 0 & \text{if an even number of variables equals 1} \end{cases}$$

As a consequence, the EXCLUSIVE-OR connective is a *parity*-determining (that is, oddness-evenness-determining) connective.

An operator for which we shall find a recurrent need is the NOT operator, illustrated in Fig. 2-10. We shall describe

$$\overline{A}$$

with any of the words "not *A*," "*A* not," or "the complement of *A*." The device, represented graphically with either symbol in Fig. 2-10*c*, is called an *inverter*. The inversion is indicated, symbolically, by the little circle on either the input or the output. (Without the circle, the symbol would represent a noninverting amplifier.)

The NOR connective, illustrated in Fig. 2-11, is simply the OR connective followed by an inversion. The symbol indicates this by being formed from the

A	B	A + B	$\overline{A + B}$
0	0	0	1
0	1	1	0
1	0	1	0
1	1	1	0

$\overline{A + B}$,   *A* NOR *B*

A NOR *B*

(*a*)   (*b*)   (*c*)

Fig. 2-11 The NOR connective. (*a*) Algebraic representations; (*b*) truth table; (*c*) graphic symbol.

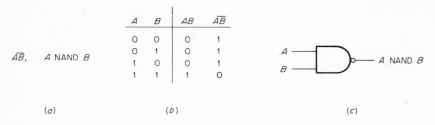

$\overline{AB}$,   *A* NAND *B*

A	B	AB	$\overline{AB}$
0	0	0	1
0	1	0	1
1	0	0	1
1	1	1	0

(*a*)   (*b*)   (*c*)

Fig. 2-12 The NAND connective. (*a*) Algebraic representations; (*b*) truth table; (*c*) graphic symbol.

OR symbol plus the modification of a small circle on the output. The NAND connective, illustrated in Fig. 2-12, is likewise formed from the AND connective followed by an inversion.

We have defined quite a few logical connectives, and, at this point, it is reasonable to ask whether all of these are necessary. To answer, our design techniques will largely center around the use of ANDs, ORs, and NOTs. However, the devices we have for implementing our circuits are often NAND and NOR gates. Then we shall find that some jobs just naturally call for the oddness-evenness characteristic inherent in an EXCLUSIVE-OR function. Furthermore, we can implement these with readily available integrated-circuit EXCLUSIVE-OR gates.

2-6 LOGICAL PROBLEM FORMULATION

If we are given the word statement for a problem in which some Boolean variable is a "wordy" function of some other Boolean variables, we can make sense out of these words by reexpressing them in a truth-table relationship between independent and dependent variables. First, however, we must define the variables more explicitly. The potency of this technique of first defining the variables and then the function with a truth table is that we avoid becoming overwhelmed with the problem. Rather, we break it down into small, easily manageable steps.

Example 2-10 Obtain a logical description of the common situation found in house wiring where a light in a stairwell can be turned on or off from a switch at the bottom of the stairs or from a switch at the top of the stairs.

Our first step is to define the variables precisely. This can be done rather arbitrarily. Although the results we obtain will depend on these definitions, they can be interpreted in light of the definitions. Suppose we define a variable *L* to indicate whether the light is on or off. More precisely, suppose we let

$$L = \begin{cases} 1 & \text{when the light is on} \\ 0 & \text{when the light is off} \end{cases}$$

If we let T represent the position of the switch at the top of the stairs, then we might define

$$T = \begin{cases} 1 & \text{when the switch at the top of the stairs is up} \\ 0 & \text{when the switch at the top of the stairs is down} \end{cases}$$

Similarly,

$$B = \begin{cases} 1 & \text{when the switch at the bottom of the stairs is up} \\ 0 & \text{when the switch at the bottom of the stairs is down} \end{cases}$$

With these definitions, we are almost ready to make the truth table. However, we need one further piece of information. Let us suppose that when both switches are down, the light is off. This gives the first row in our truth table:

T	B	L
0	0	0
0	1	
1	0	
1	1	

Now, although we might not be able to see the "big picture" and fill in this truth table all at once, we do not need to have this ability. We only need to be able to resolve one row at a time. For example, if we leave the top switch down ($T = 0$) but change the bottom switch to up ($B = 1$), then the light should change and turn on ($L = 1$). Thus we have the second row:

T	B	L
0	0	0
0	1	1 ←
1	0	
1	1	

Proceeding in this fashion, we finally arrive at

T	B	L
0	0	0
0	1	1
1	0	1
1	1	0

This looks like the EXCLUSIVE-OR connective we discussed in the previous section.

In general, this procedure will take us from an ill-defined function to a well-defined function—defined with a truth table. In Chap. 3, we shall learn how to implement the arbitrary functions which arise as we use this procedure on aribtrary problems.

2-7 IMPLEMENTING LARGE SYSTEMS WITH INTERCONNECTED SUBSYSTEMS

As indicated in Sec. 2-1, one of the major steps in the design of any system is the specification of a system structure. This step is almost invariably an intuitive one. As such, it is one of the most puzzling. However, it also represents the most promising opportunity for drastically reducing the cost and the complexity of the final system implementation. The formal techniques of combinational circuit design discussed in Chap. 3 (which tend to whittle down already small problems) might arm the good designer with the ability to cut the cost of a system by 10 to 20 percent over that achieved by a poor designer. In contrast, the selection of a good system structure may lead to a saving of 25 to 50 percent over that achieved through a less optimum system structure!

What tools are available to aid in this process of breaking down a large system into appropriate subsystems? Or a large subsystem into appropriate sub-subsystems? There are several:

1. It is helpful to study generally useful subsystems, such as arithmetic circuitry, analog-to-digital converters, and stepping motors. This we shall do in Chaps. 7 and 8 and Appendix A3.
2. It is useful to examine the extremes of highly parallel system structures (where many things are done all at once) and highly serial system structures (where many things are done one at a time) and to study the extent to which these can be applied in general. This will be the subject of Chap. 6.
3. Another area of study is the development of new algorithms. A far-reaching example of this has been the development of the fast Fourier transform by Cooley and Tukey. They have developed an algorithm which has drastically changed the way in which many real engineering problems are tackled.

    Almost any area of study, be it signal processing or the numerical control of machine tools, has its own set of problems and its opportunities for algorithm development. Given a worthwhile area and an unsatisfactorily resolved problem, we have the breeding ground for the development of a vital new algorithm.
4. A final area of study is that of *iterative circuits*, that is, circuits in which a common block of circuitry is used over and over again. We shall find that such circuits are the natural outgrowth of many algorithmic processes, particularly the arithmetic algorithms of Chap. 8. The last six sections of this chapter are devoted to iterative circuits. This study will permit us to take easy advantage of the several alternative implementations which an iterative circuit offers.

2-8 INFORMATION DISTRIBUTED IN SPACE AND TIME

Before studying iterative circuits, we need to develop the idea that information—the same information—can be represented in different ways. For the moment, assume that logical 1 is represented by a voltage of +5 V while logical 0 is represented by a voltage of 0 V. Then the term *information distributed in space* means that at a specific moment in time one Boolean variable A may be represented by the voltage on one wire while at that same moment in time another variable B is represented by the voltage on another wire. This is to be contrasted with the situation in which we look at one wire at two different times. If the voltage on the wire when we first look represents the value of A whereas the voltage on the wire some short time later represents the value of B, then we say that we have *information distributed in time.*

Information may come into a system in either form. For example, if toggle switches are used to give the system voltage levels corresponding to positions of the switches and if these positions are not changed, then the outputs of these switches exemplify information distributed in space. On the other hand, when digital data are received by a ground station from a satellite, the voltage on the output of the receiver will represent one Boolean variable at one instant and another Boolean variable a moment later. In fact, the steady stream of data received is simply put out by the receiver as one voltage level after another, representing one Boolean variable after another. This is a good example of information distributed in time.

Within a system we may take pains to convert the representation of information to one form from the other to facilitate ease of manipulation. For example, all of our combinational circuit design techniques, which will be developed in Chap. 3, are ways of generating Boolean functions of Boolean variables *which are distributed in space.* The general problem of doing this as simply as possible and subject to various constraints has long been a main current of research in digital systems. The corresponding problem of generating Boolean functions of information distributed in time and using such techniques to advantage has been studied much less extensively, except in the context of one-dimensional iterative circuits, which will be discussed in the next section. However, this last case is sufficiently significant to warrant its wide use under a variety of circumstances.

2-9 ONE-DIMENSIONAL ITERATIVE CIRCUITS

Earlier in this chapter we discussed the Gray code and mentioned that it can be converted easily to binary code. Because this conversion can be expressed as an iterative process, it will serve as an excellent example for our discussions here. In Fig. 2-13, a 4-bit Gray code is listed along with the 4-bit binary equivalent. Notice that b_8 is the same as g_8; that is,

$$b_8 = g_8$$

Next, looking at b_4, we see that b_4 is the same as g_4 as long as $b_8 = 0$; however, if $b_8 = 1$, we note that b_4 is the same as the complement of g_4. That is,

	Gray code				Binary code			
I	g_8	g_4	g_2	g_1	b_8	b_4	b_2	b_1
0	0	0	0	0	0	0	0	0
1	0	0	0	1	0	0	0	1
2	0	0	1	1	0	0	1	0
3	0	0	1	0	0	0	1	1
4	0	1	1	0	0	1	0	0
5	0	1	1	1	0	1	0	1
6	0	1	0	1	0	1	1	0
7	0	1	0	0	0	1	1	1
8	1	1	0	0	1	0	0	0
9	1	1	0	1	1	0	0	1
10	1	1	1	1	1	0	1	0
11	1	1	1	0	1	0	1	1
12	1	0	1	0	1	1	0	0
13	1	0	1	1	1	1	0	1
14	1	0	0	1	1	1	1	0
15	1	0	0	0	1	1	1	1

Fig. 2-13 Gray code and conversion to binary.

$$b_4 = \begin{cases} g_4 & \text{if } b_8 = 0 \\ \overline{g_4} & \text{if } b_8 = 1 \end{cases} \tag{2-1}$$

This can be reexpressed, using the EXCLUSIVE-OR connective, as

$$b_4 = g_4 \oplus b_8$$

which can be shown to be the same as Eq. (2-1) by reexpressing Eq. (2-1) as a truth table. Similarly we see that b_2 is the same as g_2 if $b_4 = 0$ and is equal to $\overline{g_2}$ if $b_4 = 1$. This leads to the Boolean equation

$$b_2 = g_2 \oplus b_4$$

A similar analysis leads to the final relation

$$b_1 = g_1 \oplus b_2$$

In the case of an n-bit Gray code we have the general conversion algorithm to binary code:

$$b_{2^{n-1}} = g_{2^{n-1}} \qquad \text{for the most significant bit}$$

and   (2-2)

$$b_k = g_k \oplus b_{2k} \qquad \begin{array}{l} \text{for the remaining bits, where} \\ k = 2^{n-2}, \ldots, 8, 4, 2, 1 \end{array}$$

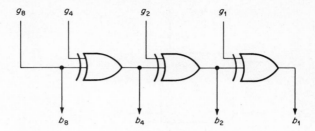

Fig. 2-14   Gray-to-binary converter iterated in space.

The 4-bit converter is shown *iterated in space* in Fig. 2-14. By iteration in space we mean that the iterative block (in this case a two-input EXCLUSIVE-OR gate) is repeated over and over again. Furthermore, we imply that all inputs are available at the same time and that all outputs are generated simultaneously.

This converter is a specific example of the class of *one-dimensional iterative circuits*, for which a general case iterated in space is illustrated in Fig. 2-15. The circuit is one-dimensional because the iterated blocks repeat each other in one direction only. This block B can be thought of as a group of AND gates, OR gates, and inverters interconnected appropriately to implement the required Boolean functions

$$y_k = y_k(x_k, f_{k-1})$$

$$f_k = f_k(x_k, f_{k-1})$$

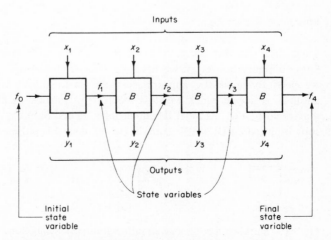

Fig. 2-15   General one-dimensional iterative circuit iterated in space.

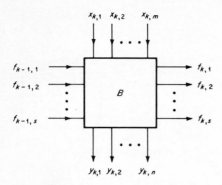

Fig. 2-16 The most general one-dimensional iterative block.

This iterative circuit illustrates the general case in which the desired output y_k is generated bit by bit. On occasion, an iterative circuit may have as its only purpose the generation of the final state variable. The reason for developing the problem as an iterative circuit in this case, as always, is to simplify the implementation of the function.

The term *state variable* is used to point up the role of f_2, for example, to describe only as much information as is needed about the inputs f_0, x_1, and x_2 in order to generate the subsequent outputs y_3, y_4, and f_4. Looking back on the Gray-to-binary converter in Fig. 2-14, we see that this *concept of state* plays a significant role. The state variable b_4 (which also happens to be an output) is all that is needed to describe g_8 and g_4 in order to generate the subsequent outputs b_2 and b_1. We shall have more to say about state concepts in Sec. 2-11.

For the most general one-dimensional iterative circuit, we can have any number of iterative blocks and each block B might have m circuit input variables, s state input and output variables, and n circuit output variables, as illustrated in Fig. 2-16.

As an alternative to having a one-dimensional iterative circuit iterated in space, it is possible for it to be iterated *in time*. In order to do this for the Gray-to-binary converter, we need just one two-input EXCLUSIVE-OR gate and we need to cause the appropriate variables to appear at its inputs one after another. A device which we shall use for this purpose is the *1-bit shift register*, illustrated in Fig. 2-17a. If IN equals 0 (or 1) just before a pulse is applied to the shift input, then OUT will equal 0 (or 1) after this pulse and until a subsequent

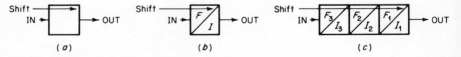

Fig. 2-17 Shift registers. (*a*) One-bit shift register; (*b*) symbolism for indicating the initial and final values contained in a one-bit shift register; (*c*) symbolism for a three-bit shift register showing initial and final values.

pulse is applied to the shift input. In using 1-bit shift registers in conjunction with an algorithmic process like Gray-to-binary conversion, initially we shall load the 1-bit shift register with one of our input bits (somehow), apply a certain number of shift pulses, and then be interested in the resulting, or final, bit of information stored in this 1-bit shift register. These initial and final values, which will be the inputs and outputs of the process, will be symbolized as shown in Fig. 2-17b. Finally we may take the output of one 1-bit shift register and feed it directly into the input of another. Figure 2-17c illustrates a convenient symbology to depict this situation for three 1-bit shift registers, resulting in one 3-bit shift register.

To iterate the Gray-to-binary-conversion algorithm in time, consider the circuit illustrated in Fig. 2-18. The shift registers are loaded initially with g_8, g_4, g_2, and g_1. By comparing with Fig. 2-14, note that the inputs to the EXCLUSIVE-OR gate are initially equal to g_4 and g_8 and therefore that its output is initially equal to b_4. The output g_8 (which is equal to b_8) of the bottom 1-bit shift register, $SRB0$, is initially "waiting at the gate" at the input of the top-most shift register bit $SRB1$. When the first of the three shift pulses occurs, the output of $SRB1$ changes from g_1 to b_8 while at the same time the output of $SRB2$ changes from g_2 to g_1, $SRB3$ changes from g_4 to g_2, and $SRB0$ changes from g_8 to b_4. This new condition is illustrated in Fig. 2-19a. After another shift pulse, the condition of the circuit is shown in Fig. 2-19b. Finally, after the third and final shift pulse, the condition of the circuit is depicted in

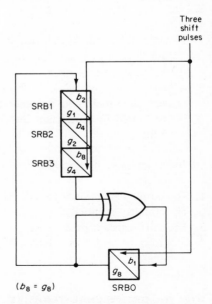

Fig. 2-18 Gray-to-binary converter iterated in time.

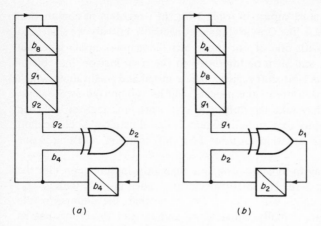

Fig. 2-19 Intermediate results in the Gray-to-binary conversion. (*a*) After first pulse; (*b*) after second pulse.

Fig. 2-18 with b_8, b_4, b_2, and b_1 in $SRB3$, $SRB2$, $SRB1$, and $SRB0$, respectively.

This example illustrates the trade-offs available between iterating in space and iterating in time. By iterating in time:

1. The iterative block (which is only a two-input EXCLUSIVE-OR gate in this case but which can be quite complicated in general) needs to be implemented only once.
2. Advantage may be taken of those circumstances where the input is already available distributed in time. If the output is likewise required to be distributed in time, then the 3-bit shift register is not needed, but only $SRB0$.

On the other hand, by iterating in space:

1. The outputs are available as fast as possible and all at once.
2. The circuitry required to generate shift pulses is avoided.
3. The shift registers are avoided.
4. The iterative block may be inexpensively available as an MSI (medium-scale integration) circuit.

2-10   TWO-DIMENSIONAL ITERATIVE CIRCUITS

Some algorithmic processes give rise to two-dimensional iterative circuits, exemplified generally in Fig. 2-20. Examples of such processes are binary multiplication, binary division, and binary-to-BCD-code conversion. Such a circuit can be implemented in any of the following five ways:

1. Entirely in space (as in Fig. 2-20)
2. Horizontally in space and vertically in time
3. Vertically in space and horizontally in time
4. Entirely in time and fast iteration horizontally
5. Entirely in time and fast iteration vertically ·

To iterate vertically in space and horizontally in time, as shown in Fig. 2-21, it is necessary to leave only one column of iterative blocks intact and then use shift registers to feed the appropriate inputs into these blocks and store the corresponding outputs.

To iterate entirely in time we need a circuit which we shall designate as a *serial switch*, illustrated in Fig. 2-22. This circuit, which can be implemented with a few of the gates discussed previously in Sec. 2-5, satisfies the Boolean equation

$$\text{OUT} = \begin{cases} I_1 & \text{if } S = 1 \\ I_0 & \text{if } S = 0 \end{cases}$$

To iterate entirely in time, fast iteration vertically, we use one iterative block and present inputs to it so that in effect we go through the array, one block at a time, in the order in which the blocks are numbered in Fig. 2-20. At the end of each column the serial switch is needed to start off the new column correctly. This is illustrated in Fig. 2-23. The timing diagram shows when each shift register gets its shift pulses as well as when the serial switch's S input is at one level or the other.

One of the real-life complications of iterating a two-dimensional iterative process in time results when the array is not rectangular but has a trapezoidal shape. Another complication arises when the inputs do not enter the array in the simple manner of Fig. 2-20. Both of these situations arise in the multiplication of two 4-bit binary numbers, as illustrated in Fig. 2-24. To iterate such a problem in time it helps to:

1. Draw out the circuit iterated in space
2. Number the blocks in the order in which they will be used
3. Set up shift registers to hold intermediate results
4. Set up shift registers to hold inputs and outputs
5. Insert serial switches as needed to switch the flow of data from one source to another
6. Construct a timing diagram for the various shift signals and serial switches' S inputs

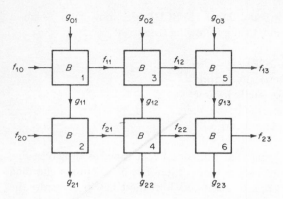

Fig. 2-20 General two-dimensional iterative circuit iterated in space.

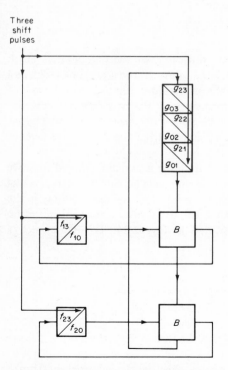

Fig. 2-21 Circuit iterated vertically in space,
horizontally in time.

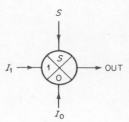

Fig. 2-22 Serial switch.

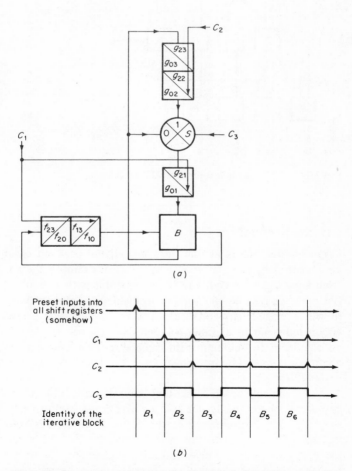

(a)

(b)

Fig. 2-23 Circuit iterated entirely in time and fast iteration vertically. (a) Iterative circuit; (b) timing diagram.

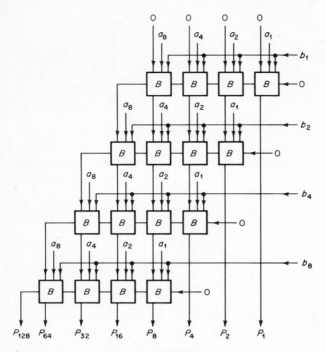

Fig. 2-24   Binary multiplication iterated in space.

2-11 STATE CONCEPTS

Given all the inputs at one time, *any* digital problem can be solved entirely combinationally (i.e., entirely in space). For example, the algorithm to convert from Gray to binary code can be implemented with a circuit in which each input (i.e., each Gray-code bit) must be available at a separate point in the circuit and in which each binary-code output is also available at a separate point in the circuit independent of time. Another example occurs in the implementation of an algorithm for obtaining the square root of a number. A general-purpose computer does this by iterating in time, but the algorithm could be implemented entirely in space.

   In general, recognizing that any digital problem can be implemented entirely combinationally, we seek to partition a problem so as to cut it down in size. If this partitioning takes the form of an iterative circuit, then we can immediately implement the problem in any of the several ways discussed previously. We want to investigate the requirements on the algorithm for such a partition to exist, as well as several design techniques which will yield simplifications in the implementation. However, we shall limit ourselves to

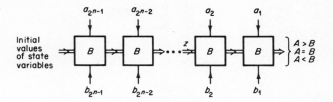

Fig. 2-25 Comparator iterated in space.

one-dimensional iterative circuits, as is done in the extensive literature on this subject. The extension to two-dimensional iterative circuits represents relatively unexplored territory.

Consider the iterative circuit for converting from Gray to binary code. We could treat the problem as one of implementing the n Boolean functions

$$b_{2k} = f(g_1, g_2, g_4, \ldots, g_{2n-1}) \quad \text{for } k = 0, 2, 1, \ldots, n-1$$

However, it is better to recognize the structure of the algorithm, which allows a circuit having the form of Fig. 2-14.

As another example, consider the comparison of two n-bit binary numbers

$$A = a_{2n-1} a_{2n-2} \cdots a_1$$

and

$$B = b_{2n-1} b_{2n-2} \cdots b_1$$

in order to determine whether A is greater than, equal to, or less than B. This comparison can be carried out by comparing corresponding bits, starting with the most significant bits, as illustrated in Fig. 2-25. The arrow between blocks is shown as a double line to indicate that more than one Boolean variable may be needed here. The question is how many *states* are needed at point z in order to represent the information to the left of point z as far as generating the output to the right? One state would indicate that up to point z, $A = B$; that is, $a_i = b_i$ for all blocks to the left of z. Another state would indicate that the issue has already been decided and that $A > B$. A third state would indicate that the comparison has already been decided but with $A < B$. How many Boolean variables are needed to code these three states?

2-12 FLOW DIAGRAMS

The function of a flow diagram is to give a graphic view of what happens in the iterative block B of an iterative circuit. It describes the output state and any

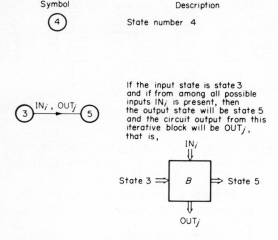

Fig. 2-26 Symbology for flow diagrams.

circuit outputs emanating from block B as a function of the input state and the circuit inputs. Our symbology for flow diagrams is shown in Fig. 2-26.

Example 2-11 Construct the flow diagram for the iterative block used in Gray-to-binary conversion.

The iterative block is redrawn in Fig. 2-27a. If we define *state 0* as representing when $b_j = 0$ and *state 1* as representing when $b_j = 1$ (where b_j represents either the input or the output state variable), then the flow diagram becomes that shown in Fig. 2-27b.

To check this, consider the following example: If the input state is 0 (that is, $b_{2k+1} = 0$) and if the circuit input is 1 (that is, $g_{2k} = 1$), then the circuit output is 1 (that is, $b_{2k} = 1$) and the output state is 1 (again $b_{2k} = 1$). This is represented in the flow diagram by the arrow going from states 0 to 1.

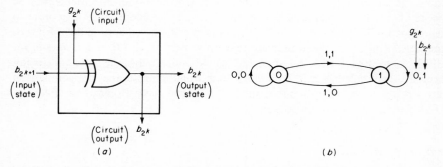

Fig. 2-27 Flow-diagram development for Gray-to-binary conversion. (a) Iterative block; (b) flow diagram.

2-13 ELIMINATION OF REDUNDANT STATES BY OUTPUT GROUPING

Once an iterative block has been represented by a flow diagram, it is useful to ask whether any states are redundant, that is, whether the circuit outputs can be correctly generated using fewer states to describe the state information. After all, we do not want to use 20 states if we can actually get by with only 10, properly defined.

The procedure for eliminating redundant states is an ideal design technique in the sense that it always works to reduce the number of states to the minimum number possible. The procedure begins with a *flow table*, which is just a tabulation of the same information available in the flow diagram but in tabular form. An example of a flow diagram and its corresponding flow table is shown in Fig. 2-28.

Now, if any states are eliminated, it will be done by discovering that two or more states can be combined into a new state, thus eliminating one or more states without affecting any circuit outputs. Certainly a prerequisite for states to be combined is that for the same circuit input the outputs must be the same. Thus as a tentative start, we can group states 1 and 3 together (because their circuit outputs are the same) and then we can group states 2, 4, and 5 together:

$$(1, 3) \quad (2, 4, 5)$$

At this point, we are hoping that the five original states can be combined into just two new states, as indicated by the parentheses. However we must check for a contradiction, as in the table in Fig. 2-29a. This table indicates that no contradiction arises for the states in the first group but that one contradiction does arise in the second group. This situation can be resolved by trying to break up the states into three groups, where the third group consists of the original state 5:

$$(1, 3) \quad (2, 4) \quad (5)$$

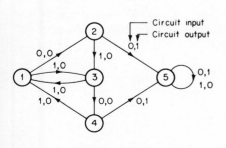

Input state	Output state and circuit output	
	Input = 0	Input = 1
1	2,0	3,0
2	5,1	3,0
3	4,0	1,0
4	5,1	1,0
5	5,1	5,0

Output state   Circuit output

Fig. 2-28 Flow diagram and its flow table.

Input state	Output state Input = 0	Input = 1
First group { 1	2 } Same	3 } Same
{ 3	4 } group	1 } group
Second group { 2	5 }	3 } Same group } Different
{ 4	5 } Same group	1 } group
{ 5	5 }	5 } group

(a)

Input state	Output state Input = 0	Input = 1
First group { 1	2 } Same	3 } Same
{ 3	4 } group	1 } group
Second group { 2	5 } Same	3 } Same
{ 4	5 } group	1 } group
Third group { 5	5	5

(b)

Fig. 2-29 Elimination of redundant states. (*a*) (1, 3) (2, 4, 5) grouping; (*b*) (1, 3) (2, 4) (5) grouping.

The new flow table is shown in Fig. 2-29*b*. This time the grouping leads to no contradictions. As a result of this simplification, states 1 and 3 can be replaced by a new state X, states 2 and 4 can be replaced by a new state Y, and state 5 can be renamed Z, yielding the new flow diagram shown in Fig. 2-30. Again, this flow diagram is as valid a description of the iterative block as the original flow diagram because circuits built on the basis of both diagrams will generate the same circuit outputs.

This procedure yields the minimum number of states needed because we started with only enough groups to differentiate between different output conditions and added a new state only to resolve a contradiction.

2-14 STATE ASSIGNMENT

Once an iterative block has been described in terms of the minimum number of states involved, then the problem arises of how to *code* these states. This coding of the states is commonly referred to as the *state-assignment problem*. The "problem" arises because one possible state assignment may yield a simpler implementation of the iterative block than another assignment. Unfortunately there is no standard design technique for obtaining a good state assignment. However, there are several approaches.

First, if the number of states is four or less, then all possible state assignments can be tried. As we shall see, even for coding four states with two Boolean variables, this will require our checking of only three assignments—all others being essentially similar to these three.

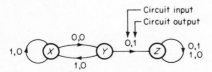

Fig. 2-30 Simplified flow diagram with redundant state removed.

Other than checking all possible essentially different state assignments, the literature on the subject leaves us only with guidelines for selecting a good state assignment. We will speak of two state assignments as being essentially similar if one can be obtained from the other by:

1. Interchanging variables
2. Complementing a variable
3. Combining the above two steps

These steps are equivalent to renaming the variables in the implementation of the iterative block.

Consider now the state assignment problem for four states 1, 2, 3, and 4. We shall need at least two Boolean variables to distinguish between four things. For a specific problem, it might be an advantage to use more than two variables, but for now let us consider the problem of using just two variables. First, we can code one state, say, state 1, with $X = 0$ and $Y = 0$, where X and Y are the two state variables. Note that by using the rules for essentially similar state assignments, any other assignment can be operated upon in any of several ways so that state 1 is coded with $X = 0$ and $Y = 0$. Now the one other state whose coding cannot be changed by these rules is the state coded by $X = 1$ and $Y = 1$. Consequently there are only the three essentially different state assignments shown in Fig. 2-31a. The x's in these three alternative state assignments signify that these assignments can be used to code the remaining states arbitrarily since the assignments will be essentially similar. For example, consider Fig. 2-31b and note that assignment No. 1b can be obtained from No. 1a by interchanging the variables X and Y.

For the general state-assignment problem with n states, where n is greater than four, obtaining a state assignment which is significantly better than "average" is a matter of luck, insight, and the employment of some of the guidelines available in the literature on this problem. However, as designers we are armed for combat reasonably well just by recognizing that the state

Coding X Y	State Assignment No.1	State Assignment No. 2	State Assignment No. 3	Coding X Y	State Assignment No.1a	State Assignment No.1b
0 0	1	1	1	0 0	1	1
0 1	x	x	x	0 1	3	4
1 0	x	x	x	1 0	4	3
1 1	2	3	4	1 1	2	2
		(a)				(b)

Fig. 2-31 State assignment possibilities for four states. (a) Three essentially different state assignments; (b) two essentially similar state assignments.

assignment selected affects the cost of implementing the iterative block. We probably shall not blithely assume an arbitrary state assignment and move on without checking an alternative or two.

PROBLEMS

2-1   Quantization   Do the divisions on the fuel gauge of your car quantize fuel linearly or nonlinearly? How can you check? If they are quite nonlinear, do you suppose this is intentional? Explain.

2-2   Quantization   Logarithmic quantization is a form of nonlinear quantization which will put quantum boundaries at $k \cdot FS$, $k^2 \cdot FS$, $k^3 \cdot FS$, $k^4 \cdot FS$, ..., where FS represents the full-scale value and $0 < k < 1$ (with its value closer to 1 for finer quantization).

(*a*)   Where might logarithmic quantization be usefully employed?

(*b*)   If the voltage range between 1 and 10 V is logarithmically quantized, with both 1 and 10 V being quanta boundaries, then what value of k will quantize this range into 100 quanta?

(*c*)   Using this same value of k, how many quanta are needed to logarithmically quantize the range between 0.1 and 10 V?

2-3   Coding   How many Boolean variables are needed to code 1,000 quanta? 1 million quanta?

2-4   Binary code   Find the decimal equivalents of the following binary numbers:

(*a*)	01000111	(*d*)	1101000
(*b*)	10101101	(*e*)	0110100
(*c*)	00101100	(*f*)	0011010

2-5   Binary code   Find the binary equivalents of the following decimal numbers:

(*a*)	22	(*d*)	7
(*b*)	44	(*e*)	70
(*c*)	88	(*f*)	700

2-6   Binary code   To count down in decimal, we count the 1s digit down one every time, the 10s digit down one whenever the 1s digit counts down from 0 to 9, etc. Using the analogous procedure to count down in binary, write the numbers from 1111 down to 0000. Is there any way to check your results?

2-7   Binary code   By using a process analogous to what you do when you add decimal numbers together, add the following binary numbers together. Check your results by converting the binary numbers to their decimal equivalents.

(*a*)	10100	(*c*)	0111
	00011		0001
(*b*)	1010	(*d*)	0111
	0011		0011

2-8   Binary code   Knowing what you do about subtracting decimal numbers by forming the nine's complement of the subtrahend and using an adder, figure out an analogous procedure for subtracting binary numbers using the *one's complement* of the subtrahend (whatever that must be) plus a binary adder. How do you form the one's complement? (Assume that only numbers which will yield a positive result are to be subtracted.)

2-9 Codes Compare the number of bits needed to code each of the following ranges with 8421 BCD code and with binary code:

(a) $0 - 9$ (c) $0 - 999$
(b) $0 - 99$ (d) $0 - 9999$

2-10 Signed-number codes If I is equal to each number below, then express $I + 1$. Assume, first, that the numbers are expressed in sign plus binary magnitude code and then in sign plus two's complement code.

(a)   01000   (c)   11000
(b)   00011   (d)   10011

2-11 Signed-number codes. If I is equal to each number below, then express $I + 1$. Assume, first, that the numbers are expressed in sign plus 8421 BCD magnitude code and then in sign plus ten's complement (8421 BCD) code.

(a)   000111001   (c)   100111001
(b)   001010000   (d)   101010000

2-12 Codes Express the number 87 as an 8-bit number in each of the following codes:

(a)   Binary
(b)   8421 BCD
(c)   Excess-three BCD

2-13 Signed-number codes Express both +43 and −43 as a 9-bit number in each of the following codes:

(a)   Sign plus binary magnitude
(b)   Sign plus two's complement
(c)   Sign plus 8421 BCD magnitude
(d)   Sign plus XS-3 BCD magnitude
(e)   Sign plus ten's complement (8421 BCD)
(f)   Sign plus ten's complement (XS-3 BCD)

2-14 Analytic codes Is the following an analytic encoding of the integers 0 to 4? If your answer is no, explain. If your answer is yes, then express I as an analytic function of ABC.

I	A	B	C
0	0	0	1
1	1	1	0
2	1	1	1
3	1	0	0
4	1	0	1

2-15 Analytic codes If the integer 0 is encoded with all 0s in an analytic code, then what do you know about the value of the bias constant?

2-16 Analtyic codes Is the following coding for the integers 0 to 4 analytic? If not, then explain. If yes, then express I analytically.

I	A	B	C
0	0	0	0
1	0	0	1
2	0	1	1
3	1	1	0
4	1	0	0

2-17 Analytic codes Is the *1-out-of-10 BCD* code listed below analytic? If not, then explain. If it is, then express N analytically.

N	A	B	C	D	E	F	G	H	I	J
0	0	0	0	0	0	0	0	0	0	1
1	0	0	0	0	0	0	0	0	1	0
2	0	0	0	0	0	0	0	1	0	0
3	0	0	0	0	0	0	1	0	0	0
4	0	0	0	0	0	1	0	0	0	0
5	0	0	0	0	1	0	0	0	0	0
6	0	0	0	1	0	0	0	0	0	0
7	0	0	1	0	0	0	0	0	0	0
8	0	1	0	0	0	0	0	0	0	0
9	1	0	0	0	0	0	0	0	0	0

2-18 Analytic codes Which of the codes below are analytic codes?

(*a*)   Sign plus binary magnitude
(*b*)   Sign plus two's complement
(*c*)   Sign plus 8421 BCD magnitude
(*d*)   Sign plus ten's complement (8421 BCD)

2-19 Coding For some purposes, it is convenient to code numbers with a *binary coded ternary* code (where *ternary* means *base 3*, just as *binary* means *base 2* and *decimal* means *base 10*). How many Boolean variables are needed, as a minimum, to code each ternary digit?

2-20 Coding (*a*) A shaft-angle encoder with an 8-bit binary output breaks its total range up into how many quanta?

(*b*) On the other hand, an encoder with an 8-bit 8421 BCD code output breaks its total range up into how many quanta?

2-21 Boolean identities Using a truth table, determine whether each of the following is a true Boolean identity:

(*a*) $A + \bar{A} \overset{?}{=} 1$ (*e*) $\overline{A + B} \overset{?}{=} \bar{A}\bar{B}$

(*b*) $A\bar{A} \overset{?}{=} 0$ (*f*) $\overline{AB} \overset{?}{=} \bar{A} + \bar{B}$

(*c*) $(A + B)C \overset{?}{=} AC + BC$ (*g*) $\overline{A + B} \overset{?}{=} \bar{A} + \bar{B}$

(*d*) $AB + C \overset{?}{=} (A + C)(B + C)$ (*h*) $\overline{AB} \overset{?}{=} \bar{A}\bar{B}$

2-22 EXCLUSIVE-OR connective

(*a*) $1 \oplus 0 \oplus 1 \oplus 0 \oplus 1 \oplus 0 \oplus 0 \oplus 0$ = ?
(*b*) $1 \oplus 0 \oplus 1 \oplus 0 \oplus 1 \oplus 0 \oplus 0$ = ?

2-23 Boolean identities Using a truth table and the definitions of the gates (where a circle represents an inversion), are any of the gates in the Fig. P 2-23 equivalent to each other? In other words, does F_1 have the same truth table as F_2? or F_3? or F_4? and so forth?

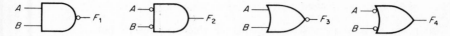

Fig. P 2-23

2-24 Problem formulation Given the two 2-bit binary numbers

$$A = a_2 a_1 \quad \text{and} \quad B = b_2 b_1$$

construct a truth table for the function F such that $F = 1$ if and only if $A \geqslant 2B$.

2-25 Problem formulation Define the *programmed gate* shown with a truth table in Fig. P 2-25. The output can be considered to be a Boolean function of the inputs A and B which changes as a function of the control inputs X and Y. The circuit is

(a)   An AND gate if $X = 1$ and $Y = 1$
(b)   An EXCLUSIVE-OR gate if $X = 0$ and $Y = 1$
(c)   An OR gate if $X = 1$ and $Y = 0$ or if $X = 0$ and $Y = 0$

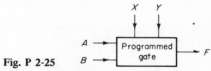

Fig. P 2-25

2-26 Problem formulation Is it possible to define an L function for a light which can be operated from any of *three* switches, analogous to Example 2-10 in the text? If so, show the truth table. If not, explain. Assume the light is off when all three switches are down.

2-27 Iterative circuits Construct the truth tables for the two outputs of the general iterative block shown in Fig. P 2-27 if the function of the iterative circuit is to take a binary number

$$A = a_{16} a_8 a_4 a_2 a_1$$

and generate another binary number

$$F = f_{16} f_8 f_4 f_2 f_1$$

such that

(a) $F = A + 1$ $\qquad\qquad\qquad$ (b) $F = A - 1$

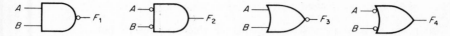

Fig. P 2-27 (a) Iterative circuit; (b) general iterative block.

2-28 Iterative circuits Construct the truth tables for the outputs of the general iterative block shown in Fig. P 2-28 if the function of the iterative circuit is to compare two binary numbers

$$A = a_8 a_4 a_2 a_1 \quad \text{and} \quad B = b_8 b_4 b_2 b_1$$

for $A > B$, $A = B$, or $A < B$. Assume the state variables are defined as follows:

$$x = 1 \quad \text{if and only if } A > B$$
$$y = 1 \quad \text{if and only if } B > A$$

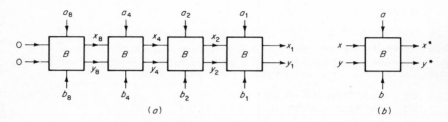

Fig. P 2-28 (a) Iterative circuit; (b) general iterative block.

2-29 Iterative circuits (a) With a truth table, define the five outputs of the *doubler* circuit shown in Fig. P 2-29, for which

$$D = d_8 d_4 d_2 d_1 \quad \text{and} \quad D^* = d_8^* d_4^* d_2^* d_1^*$$

are each an 8421 BCD code digit. The circuit must implement the equation

$$10c^* + D^* = 2D + c$$

where $c^* = 0$ if and only if $2D + c$ is less than 10.

(b) Can three of these doublers be interconnected to form an iterative circuit which will double a three-digit number expressed in 8421 BCD code? If so, show the circuit. If not, explain. (Doublers are useful for iteratively carrying out binary-to-decimal conversion, as we shall see in Chap. 8.)

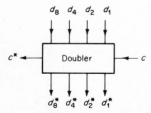

Fig. P 2-29

2-30 Iterative circuits (a) In this problem, similar to the last one, define the five outputs of the *halver* circuit shown in Fig. P 2-30 with a truth table. Again, D and D^* are each an 8421 BCD code digit. The circuit must implement the equation

$$10r + D = 2D^* + r^* \quad \text{or} \quad \frac{10r + D}{2} = D^* + \frac{r^*}{2}$$

(*b*) Can this circuit be used iteratively to halve a three-digit number expressed in 8421 BCD code? If so, show the circuit. If not, explain. (Halvers are useful for iteratively carrying out decimal-to-binary conversion.)

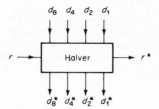

Fig. P 2-30

2-31 Iteration in time Show the circuit of Prob. 2-27*a* iterated in time, including initial and final values stored in the shift-register bits. Also indicate the number of shift pulses used. This circuit is a *serial binary counter.*

2-32 Iteration in time Show the circuit of Prob. 2-28 iterated in time, including initial values stored in the shift-register bits and the location of x_1 and y_1 at completion. Indicate the number of shift pulses used. This circuit is a *serial comparator.*

2-33 Two-dimensional iterative circuits For the iterative process defined by Fig. 2-20, show the process iterated horizontally in space and vertically in time.

2-34 Two-dimensional iterative circuits Again, for the iterative process defined by Fig. 2-20, show the process iterated entirely in time and fast iteration horizontally. Include a timing diagram.

2-35 Two-dimensional iterative circuits Using as few shift-register bits as possible, implement the iterative process defined in Fig. P 2-35 by iterating horizontally in space and vertically in time. At the completion, all six outputs $h_6, \ldots, h_1$ must be available.

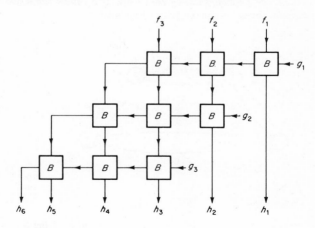

Fig. P 2-35

2-36 Two-dimensional iterative circuits Again, using as few shift-register bits as possible, implement the iterative process of Prob. 2-35 by iterating entirely in time, with fast iteration horizontally. All six outputs must be available at completion. Show the timing diagram.

2-37 State concepts Can the comparison of two binary numbers for equality be carried out iteratively, bit by bit? If not, explain. If so, then how many states are needed to represent the information between adjacent iterative blocks and what does each state designate?

2-38 State concepts Can the comparison of two binary numbers A and B for detecting $A > B$, $A = B$, or $A < B$ be carried out iteratively, bit by bit, least-significant bit first, as shown in Fig. P 2-38? If not, explain. If so, then how many states are needed to represent the information between adjacent iterative blocks and what does each state designate?

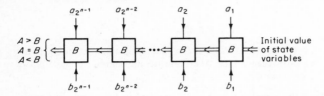

Fig. P 2-38

2-39 Flow diagrams (a) Define the states and then construct the flow diagram for the circuit of Prob. 2-27a.

  (b) Does Prob. 2-27b have the same flow diagram?

2-40 Flow diagrams Define the states and then construct the flow diagram for the comparator shown in Fig. 2-25.

2-41 Flow diagrams Repeat Prob. 2-40 for the comparator of Prob. 2-38. Should the resulting flow diagram be the same as for Prob. 2-40? Explain.

2-42 Elimination of redundant states Can the flow diagram shown in Fig. P 2-42 be simplified? Explain, showing your work. If it can be simplified, what significance does this have for the corresponding iterative circuit?

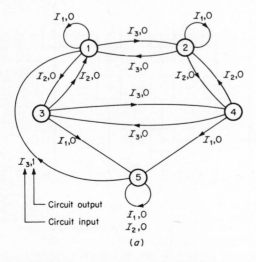

Input	Output state and circuit output		
state	I_1	I_2	I_3
1	1,0	3,0	2,0
2	2,0	4,0	1,0
3	5,0	1,0	4,0
4	5,0	2,0	3,0
5	5,0	5,0	1,1

(a)   (b)

Fig. P 2-42 (a) Flow diagram; (b) its flow table.

2-43 Elimination of redundant states Can the flow diagram shown in Fig. P 2-43 be simplified? Explain, showing your work.

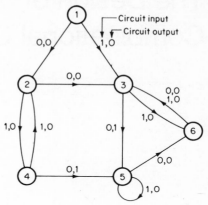

Fig. P 2-43

2-44 State assignment (*a*) The comparator discussed in conjunction with Fig. 2-25 in Sec. 2-11 included no attempt at making a specific state assignment. On the other hand, Prob. 2-28 makes a specific state assignment for this same problem. What is this state assignment? Make a truth table for the output state variables as functions of the input state variables plus the circuit inputs for the iterative block.

(*b*) Repeat this problem using the state assignment

X	Y	
0	0	$A = B$ so far
1	1	
1	1	$A > B$
0	1	$A < B$

plus the constraint that if the input and output states both represent "$A = B$ so far" then $x^* = \overline{x}$ and $y^* = \overline{y}$ (where x^* is the output state variable while x is the input state variable).

(*c*) Are the truth tables obtained in (*a*) and (*b*) the same? Explain. What implication does this have for implementing the comparator?

REFERENCES

An excellent discussion of a variety of codes, together with their arithmetic properties, can be found in Y. Chu, "Digital Computer Design Fundamentals," Chaps. 1 and 2, McGraw-Hill, New York, 1962.

Iterative circuits, their properties and implementations, are thoroughly developed in F. C. Hennie, "Finite-state Models for Logical Machines," chaps. 1 and 10, Wiley, New York, 1968.

For a clear, concise development of approaches to the state assignment problem, see H. C. Torng, "Logical Design of Switching Systems," chap. 14, Addison-Wesley, Reading, Mass., 1964.

3
The Design of
Combinational Circuitry

3-1   THE ROLE OF INTUITION IN THE DESIGN PROCESS

As was indicated in Sec. 2-7, one of the most difficult jobs in digital design is the process of breaking down a large system into a group of subsystems. This is difficult because the really good breakdown is likely to be found intuitively. However, it is worth the effort because of the opportunities usually available for significantly reducing cost and system complexity.

While this reliance on intuition is of paramount importance at the system level, it also can play a significant role at the other end of the spectrum of digital design—in the design of *combinational circuitry*. By combinational circuitry we mean circuitry where all information is distributed in space and where all outputs are Boolean functions of inputs.

As an example of this role which intuition can play in the design of combinational circuitry, consider the following problem. Suppose we have two 2-bit binary numbers

$$A = a_2 a_1 \qquad B = b_2 b_1$$

and a 1-bit binary number

$$C = c_1$$

We wish to add these three binary numbers together to get the resulting binary number

$$S = s_4 s_2 s_1$$

which will be the binary coding for some number between 0 and 7. By closing our eyes to the use of intuition and instead using the formal techniques given in this chapter, we have the problem of implementing three functions (s_4, s_2, and s_1) of five variables (a_2, a_1, b_2, b_1, and c_1). These formal techniques lead to a *simplest sum-of-products* form for each of these three functions. These can then be implemented entirely with the NAND gates and inverters of Sec. 2-5. We might use as a measure of the cost of this implementation the total number of *gate leads*,† defined as the sum of the inputs and outputs for all the gates (e.g., a gate having two inputs costs three gate leads—two gate leads for the two inputs plus one gate lead for the output). For this circuit, implemented in this way, the cost is somewhere around two hundred gate leads.

As an alternative approach, using intuition, we can try to break the problem down into smaller parts. Adding the numbers together bit by bit leads to a circuit of the form shown in Fig. 3-1*a*, as we shall see in Sec. 3-3 when we discuss binary addition more fully and define the *full adders* shown here. Going still further, intuitively, it turns out that the full adder can be implemented with

†Counting *gate leads* provides a reasonable measure of cost in several senses. First, integrated-circuit manufacturers tend to set prices proportional to the number of gate leads. Second, the manufacturing costs of assembling combinational circuits are likely to be proportional to the number of gate leads.

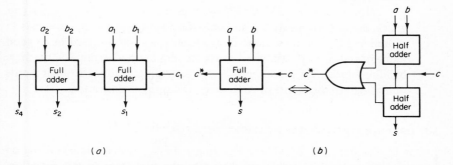

(*a*)   (*b*)

Fig. 3-1 Breaking a big problem down into smaller problems. (*a*) Solution using full adders; (*b*) an equivalence.

two *half-adders* plus an extra OR gate, as shown in Fig. 3-1*b*. At this stage all of the techniques of design plus intuition can be brought to bear on the little half-adder circuit, a circuit having just two inputs and two outputs. Implemented entirely with NAND gates, the total circuit now requires only 54 gate leads, or roughly *one-quarter* of the complexity of the circuit designed by formal techniques alone!

3-2 THREE STEPS IN THE DESIGN PROCESS

The design of combinational circuitry can be broken down to the following steps:

1. Define the combinational problem, perhaps with a truth table listing dependent variables as functions of independent variables.
2. Using intuition, try to break down the problem into interconnected smaller problems, as was done in Sec. 3-1. As a general rule, if a function of *five* or more variables is to be implemented, the problem probably should be broken down to smaller interconnected problems. This approach is likely to lead to a less costly implementation than tackling the original problem directly.

    One consequence of this is that computerized versions of the graphical techniques discussed in this chapter really do not buy us very much. Their power lies mainly in allowing us to tackle problems which are so large (more than four variables) that we should not be tackling them directly anyway.
3. Using design techniques appropriate to the logic elements we have available, implement the function as simply as possible. We shall find that our design techniques are very appropriate as long as we have AND gates, OR gates, and inverters available. Furthermore, by making a simple translation of these results we can use these same techniques to design with NOR or NAND gates.

    However, given EXCLUSIVE-OR gates and MAJORITY gates (for which the output equals 1 if and only if a majority of the inputs equals 1) as building blocks, these same design techniques will not lead us to good implementations. If we were going to do much designing with these building blocks, we would need design techniques attuned to their merits rather than to the merits of AND gates, OR gates, and inverters.

3-3 OBTAINING AN IMPLEMENTATION FOR A FUNCTION

In the last section, we talked about getting a simple, low-cost implementation for a function. In this section we shall take the first steps in this direction. Consider the problem of adding two 4-bit binary numbers. Figure 3-2 illustrates

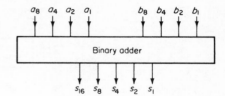

Fig. 3-2 Overall problem of binary addition.

the overall problem, where the two binary inputs are

$$A = a_8 a_4 a_2 a_1 \quad \text{and} \quad B = b_8 b_4 b_2 b_1$$

and where the sum is

$$S = A + B = s_{16} s_8 s_4 s_2 s_1$$

Tackled directly, the problem becomes one of implementing five functions (s_{16}, s_8, s_4, s_2, and s_1) of eight variables ($a_8, \ldots, b_1$). Those eight variables cause us to ask whether we can break the problem down, and indeed we can.

We can aid our intuition by considering, first, what we do when we add decimal numbers:

1. We add the numbers a digit at a time beginning with the unit's digit.
2. In any of these additions, if we ever get a result which is 10 or greater, we add 1 to the next digit. This is illustrated with an example in Fig. 3-3a.

To add binary numbers we need only to carry out an analogous procedure, as illustrated in Fig. 3-3b. This suggests that we organize the combinational circuit into blocks, each of which adds together 1 bit of A, 1 bit of B, and perhaps a carry bit from the addition of bits just to the right. This block generates 1 bit of S plus perhaps a carry bit to be added in to the bits just to the left. This structure is shown in terms of the Boolean variables involved in Fig. 3-4a. The corresponding circuit is shown in Fig. 3-4b. The iterative block is the commonly

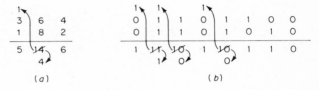

Fig. 3-3 Examples of decimal and binary addition. (a) Decimal addition, illustrating the generation of a carry; (b) binary addition, illustrating the generation of a carry.

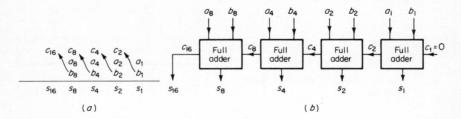

Fig. 3-4 Binary-adder circuit. (*a*) Definition of variables for the binary adder; (*b*) iterative circuit implementation.

used circuit—the *full adder*, referred to in Sec. 3-1. It is so commonly used that it is available commercially as an MSI (medium-scale integration) circuit.

The full adder can be formally defined with a truth table. To do this we might first consider each of the eight possible additions of three 1-bit numbers, as in Fig. 3-5*a*. If we write the sum as a 2-bit number, the least significant bit is the sum bit while the most significant bit is the carry bit of the full adder. For a general full adder, we designate the general inputs a, b, and c and the general outputs s and c^*. The truth table is shown in Fig. 3-5*b*.

Where the full adder adds three 1-bit numbers together to produce a sum bit and a carry bit, a *half-adder* adds two 1-bit numbers, again producing a sum bit and a carry bit as in Fig. 3-6*a*. Its truth table is shown in Fig. 3-6*b*. That the sum bit s of a full adder can be implemented with two half adders connected as in Fig. 3-7*a* can be demonstrated by noting that this simply forms s with a two-step process of first adding a and b together and then adding the least significant bit of the result to c. Alternatively, this can be demonstrated with the truth table in Fig. 3-7*b*, where s_1 is formed using the truth table in Fig. 3-6*b* (with $x = a$ and $y = b$). Next, the same truth table is used again but with $x = s_1$ and $y = c$ to yield the function s. By comparing this with the truth table in Fig. 3-5*b*, we see that indeed the circuit is valid.

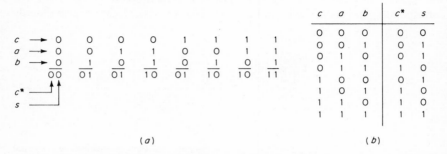

Fig. 3-5 Development of the truth table of a full adder. (*a*) Eight possible summations of three 1-bit numbers; (*b*) truth table for a full adder.

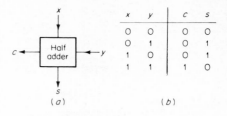

Fig. 3-6 Half adder. (*a*) General representation; (*b*) truth table.

We can explore the generation of the carry output bit of the full adder using the half-adder circuit of Fig. 3-7*a* as a starting point. Working in this direction, we can first construct the truth table for c_1 by using the truth table for the half-adder, again with $x = a$ and $y = b$. Then the truth table for c_2 can be obtained by again referring to the truth table for the half-adder and substituting $x = s_1$ and $y = c$. Finally, the *desired* function, the carry output of the full adder (c^*), is taken from Fig. 3-5*b* and repeated in Fig. 3-7*b*. We note that every time c^* is supposed to be equal to 1, either c_1 or c_2 is equal to 1. Furthermore, neither c_1 nor c_2 is ever equal to 1 except when c^* is equal to 1. Therefore we can obtain c^* with

$$c^* = c_1 + c_2$$

as was shown and taken for granted in Fig. 3-1*b*.

We thus have reduced the implementation of the 4-bit binary adder down to the problem of implementing the half-adder. If our building blocks are AND gates, OR gates, and inverters, then we note that the carry function of the half adder is simply

$$c = a \cdot b$$

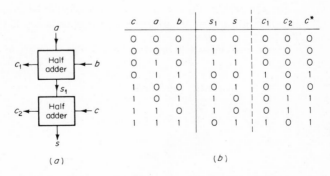

Fig. 3-7 Development of full adder from two half adders. (*a*) Generation of the *s* function of a full adder using two half adders; (*b*) truth table.

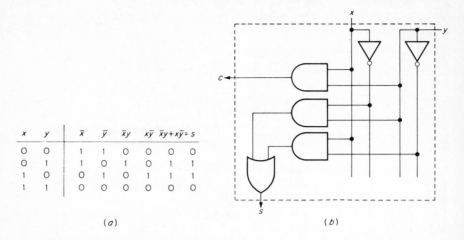

x	y	$\bar{x}$	$\bar{y}$	$\bar{x}y$	$x\bar{y}$	$\bar{x}y+x\bar{y}=s$
0	0	1	1	0	0	0
0	1	1	0	1	0	1
1	0	0	1	0	1	1
1	1	0	0	0	0	0

(*a*)   (*b*)

Fig. 3-8 Half-adder. (*a*) Derivation of a Boolean expression for *s*; (*b*) implementation of the half-adder.

To implement the output *s*, consider the truth table in Fig. 3-8*a*. The functions $\bar{x}$ and $\bar{y}$ are shown in order to lend credence to the fact that the function in the third column is indeed $\bar{x}y$. We are interested in this function because it has a single 1 and three 0s and because the 1 is in a row corresponding to one of the 1s in the desired function shown on the right. Similarly the fourth column shows a function having a single 1 corresponding in position to the other 1 in the desired function *s*. Again, it can be verified that this function is $x\bar{y}$. By ORing these two functions together, we get a 1 wherever either of the ORed functions has a 1. Consequently

$$s = \bar{x}y + x\bar{y}$$

The complete implementation of the half adder is shown in Fig. 3-8*b*.

We can obtain this kind of a *sum-of-products*† implementation for any Boolean function. For example, Fig. 3-9 gives a truth table for an arbitrary

†The term *sum of products* is derived from referring to ORing as a sum and ANDing as a product.

A	B	C	F	$\bar{A}B\bar{C}$	$A\bar{B}\bar{C}$	$A\bar{B}C$
0	0	0	0	0	0	0
0	0	1	0	0	0	0
0	1	0	1	1	0	0
0	1	1	0	0	0	0
1	0	0	1	0	1	0
1	0	1	1	0	0	1
1	1	0	0	0	0	0
1	1	1	0	0	0	0

Fig. 3-9 Derivation of a sum-of-products expression for an arbitrary function *F*.

Boolean function F, together with the functions which will be ORed together to implement it in sum-of-products form. Note that a function (such as $\overline{A}B\overline{C}$) having a single 1 in its truth table can be expressed as an ANDing of all the variables, either in *asserted form* (A,B,C) or *negated form* $(\overline{A},\overline{B},\overline{C})$. Furthermore, the variables which are in negated form are those which equal 0 in the row where the function equals 1. Thus $\overline{A}B\overline{C}$ equals 1 in the row where $A = 0$, $B = 1$, and $C = 0$. The resulting sum-of-products expression for F is

$$F = \overline{A}B\overline{C} + A\overline{B}\,\overline{C} + A\overline{B}C$$

At this stage we have a way of implementing *any* Boolean function with AND gates, OR gates, and inverters. The emphasis of the next few sections will be on obtaining simpler, less costly implementations.

3-4 KARNAUGH MAPS

The basis for the simplification technique discussed in the next two sections is one Boolean identity

$$ABC + AB\overline{C} = AB \tag{3-1}$$

That this is so is demonstrated in Fig. 3-10. In order to use this, we want to recognize when we have two ANDings of the same variables in which *only one* of the variables appears in asserted form in one ANDing while appearing in negated form in the other. For example, we would like to recognize that

$$A\overline{B}E \quad \text{and} \quad A\overline{B}\overline{E}$$

include the same variables $(A, B,$ and E in one form or the other) and that only the form of E differs in the two expressions. Consequently, in place of the function

$$A\overline{B}E + A\overline{B}\overline{E}$$

A	B	C	ABC	AB$\overline{C}$	ABC+AB$\overline{C}$	AB
0	0	0	0	0	0	0
0	0	1	0	0	0	0
0	1	0	0	0	0	0
0	1	1	0	0	0	0
1	0	0	0	0	0	0
1	0	1	0	0	0	0
1	1	0	0	1	1	1
1	1	1	1	0	1	1

└─Same─┘

Fig. 3-10 Demonstration of a fundamental Boolean identity.

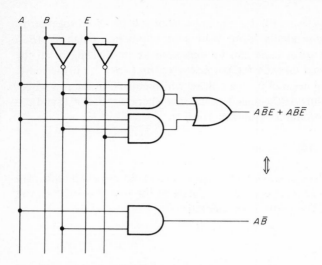

Fig. 3-11   Basic simplification.

we can use the simpler function

$$A\bar{B}$$

The circuit simplification is demonstrated in Fig. 3-11.

A *Karnaugh map* represents an excellent way for recognizing all such simplifications for functions of four variables or less. For functions of more variables, this graphic technique is not only difficult to apply but it is also not usually appropriate to apply. It is generally far better to break such a large problem down intuitively, as discussed previously.

A Karnaugh map provides a way of representing a Boolean function which is similar to a truth table in that the value of the function is tabulated for all possible combinations of inputs. It contains no more and no less information than is available in the truth table. However, the information is presented in a form which greatly aids the simplification process. Figure 3-12 illustrates three functions (F_2, F_3, and F_4), their truth tables, and their corresponding Karnaugh maps. There is *one square* in the Karnaugh map corresponding to *one row* in the truth table. The value of the function for this row of the truth table is represented by the 1 or 0 in the corresponding square of the Karnaugh map.

In order to understand which square corresponds to which row, consider the Karnaugh map in Fig. 3-12a. The bottom two squares correspond to the two rows where $A = 1$, while the top two squares correspond to the other two rows where $A = 0$. This information is signified, cryptically, by the letter A, together with the bracket beside the bottom row of squares. Really what is meant by this is that $A = 1$ for this bottom row of squares. (This is also indicated, somewhat redundantly, by the 1 inside the bracket.) The fact that the top row of squares is where $A \neq 1$ means that that is where $A = 0$. The 0s and 1s along the outside edges of the Karnaugh map are useful for going from each row of a truth table to the corresponding square in the Karnaugh map. For example, in Fig. 3-12a, the second row of the truth table represents the condition under which $A = 0$ and $B = 1$. The value $A = 0$ picks out the two squares in the top row of the Karnaugh map, while the value $B = 1$ picks out the square on the right. Note that $F_2 = 0$ under this condition of A and B and that a 0 appears in the top-right square to signify this.

As another example, consider the four-variable function in Fig. 3-12c. The eleventh row of the truth table, where $A = 1$, $B = 0$, $C = 1$, and $D = 0$, corresponds to the square in the Karnaugh map where $AB = 10$ (bottom row) and where $CD = 10$ (column on the right), thus picking out the square in the lower-right-hand corner. The value of the function $F_4 = 1$ in this case is represented by the 1 in this lower-right-hand square.

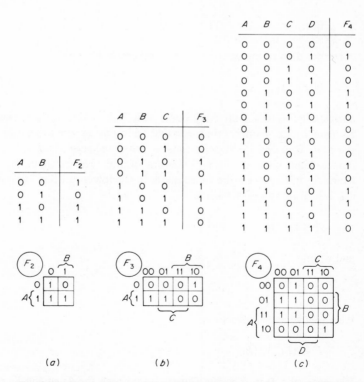

Fig. 3-12 Truth tables and their Karnaugh maps. (a) Two variables; (b) three variables; (c) four variables.

A	B	C	F	$A\bar{B}\bar{C}$	$A\bar{B}C$	$A\bar{B}$
0	0	0	0	0	0	0
0	0	1	0	0	0	0
0	1	0	0	0	0	0
0	1	1	0	0	0	0
1	0	0	1	1	0	1
1	0	1	1	0	1	1
1	1	0	0	0	0	0
1	1	1	0	0	0	0

Fig. 3-13 Recognizing a simplification with a Karnaugh map.

Notice that the numbers along the top edge of the four-variable Karnaugh map do *not* proceed

        00   01   10   11

corresponding to increasing binary numbers, but rather

        00   01   11   10

corresponding to a 2-bit Gray code. This is related to the key characteristic of a Karnaugh map, namely, that *in going from one square to an adjacent square (in the same row or column) the value of only one variable changes*. This is used to detect when we have a simplification of the type provided by Eq. (3-1). For example, in Fig. 3-13, the two squares in the lower-left-hand corner each contain a 1 indicating that $F = 1$ when

        $A = 1$ $B = 0$ and $C = 0$

and when

        $A = 1$ $B = 0$ and $C = 1$

We know we can express F as

        $F = A\bar{B}\bar{C} + A\bar{B}C$

However, the fact that the squares containing the 1s in the Karnaugh map are adjacent to each other says that a simplification is available. The variable which differs between the two squares (*C*) drops out, leaving

$$F = A\bar{B}$$

We shall speak of these two squares forming a *two-square implicant*. The term implicant is used because $A\bar{B} = 1$ implies that $F = 1$. The Karnaugh map is an outstanding tool for quickly and easily recognizing all such two-square implicants for functions of four or less variables. Any pair of 1s which are adjacent to each other in the same row or column form a two-square implicant. However, two 1s at the opposite ends of a row (or column) differ in only one variable. Consequently, we should think of these as being adjacent to each other. It is as if opposite edges of the Karnaugh map touched each other, as they would if we cut out the map and made a cylinder out of it, matching up the opposite edges. Figure 3-14 illustrates some examples of two-square implicants. Notice, again, that a two-square implicant always drops out exactly one of the variables and that it is the variable which changes in going from one of the adjacent squares to the other.

This simplification can be extended to the case where two 2-square implicants are adjacent to each other, forming a *four-square implicant*. This will

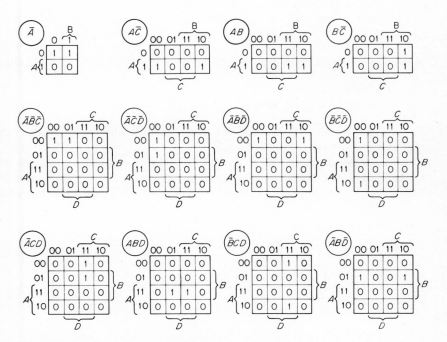

Fig. 3-14 Examples of two-square implicants.

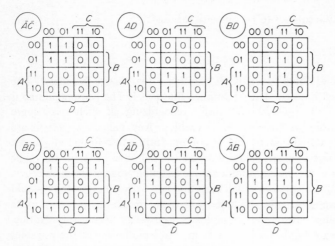

Fig. 3-15 Examples of four-square implicants.

drop out two variables corresponding to the algebraic simplification:

$$F = AB\overline{C}\overline{D} + ABC\overline{D} + AB\overline{C}D + ABCD$$
$$= (AB\overline{C}\overline{D} + ABC\overline{D}) + (AB\overline{C}D + ABCD)$$
$$= \qquad AB\overline{D} \qquad + \qquad ABD$$
$$= \qquad\qquad AB$$

A four-square implicant can be recognized on a Karnaugh map as four 1s either

1. Forming a square or
2. In line, filling one row or column

Fig. 3-15 illustrates some possibilities. Note the difficult case to visualize—the four corners, forming the implicant $\overline{B}\overline{D}$.

An *eight-square implicant* consists of eight 1s grouped together in two adjacent rows or columns, as shown in Fig. 3-16. It drops out three variables. This use of Karnaugh maps to identify implicants is a key step in the procedure

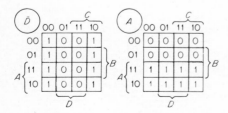

Fig. 3-16 Examples of eight-square implicants.

for simplifying the implementation of a Boolean function presented in the next section.

3-5 SIMPLEST SUM-OF-PRODUCTS FORM OF A FUNCTION

In Sec. 3-3, we developed means for obtaining a sum-of-products expression for a function. In looking back, we can see that the resulting expression will not generally lead to a particularly simple implementation. Each *product* includes every variable (in either asserted or negated form), and none of these products have been combined into the implicants discussed in the last section. In this section we shall develop a method for obtaining as simple an implementation as is possible, subject to the constraint that it have the sum-of-products form. We shall develop the procedure by means of a series of examples.

Example 3-1 Obtain a simplest sum-of-products implementation for the function F_1 given by the truth table in Fig. 3-17a.

   The first step of the procedure is to *make a Karnaugh map of the function*, as in Fig. 3-17b. Next, *encircle all implicants which are not included completely in a larger implicant*. Thus, for example, the two-square implicant $\overline{BC}$ is *not* encircled because it is included completely within the larger four-square implicant $\overline{B}$. On the other hand, the two-square implicant AC is encircled rather than the *one-square implicant ABC* because the latter is included completely within the former.

   Now F_1 can be expressed as an ORing of these two implicants

$$F_1 = \overline{B} + AC$$

That this is valid is shown in Fig. 3-17c, where the proof consists of checking the equality square by square. For example, the upper-left-hand corners of the three maps (corresponding to the input condition $A = 0, B = 0$, and $C = 0$), say,

$$1 = 1 + 0$$

which is certainly valid. As another example, consider the upper-right-hand corners. Here we have

$$0 = 0 + 0$$

again a valid statement. Finally, consider the case where $A = 1, B = 0$, and $C = 1$. Here we have

$$1 = 1 + 1$$

which is again valid. The final implementation is shown in Fig. 3-17d.

Example 3-2 Obtain a simplest sum-of-products expression for the function given by the Karnaugh map of Fig. 3-18a.

   Again all implicants which are not included completely within a larger implicant are encircled. This gives one 4-square implicant BD and four 2-square

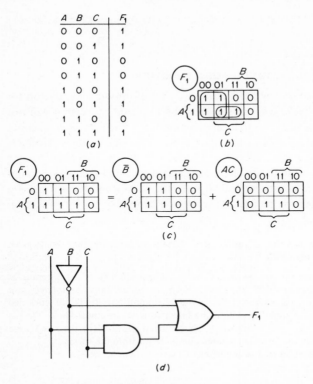

Fig. 3-17 Solution steps for Example 3-1. (*a*) Truth table of
F_1 ; (*b*) Karnaugh map of F_1 ; (*c*) verification of the equation
$F_1 = \overline{B} + AC$; (*d*) implementation.

implicants. The resulting expression is

$$F_2 = BD + \overline{AB}\,\overline{C} + \overline{A}CD + ABC + A\overline{C}D$$

If the circuit corresponding to this equation were wired together, it would be found

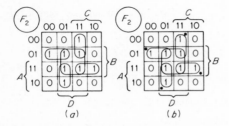

Fig. 3-18 Karnaugh maps for Example 3-2.
(*a*) Karnaugh map with implicants encircled;
(*b*) essential implicants marked with a dot.

to generate F_2 correctly for all possible combinations of inputs. Interestingly enough, the AND gate implementing BD can be removed from the circuit and the circuit will *still* be found to generate F_2 correctly for all possible combinations of inputs. That this is so results because the implicant BD covers only 1s which already are covered by the other implicants. Consequently, its presence is redundant. It should be removed, simplifying the implementation.

To recognize which implicants are needed, another step is added to our procedure: *Mark all essential implicants with a dot.* An implicant is defined to be an *essential* implicant if at least one 1 in the function is covered by this implicant alone. The dot should be put in *one* of these squares which make the implicant essential. This is shown, for this example, in Fig. 3-18b. Finally, since the essential implicants cover all the 1s of F_2, we can write

$$F_2 = \overline{AB}\overline{C} + \overline{A}CD + ABC + A\overline{C}D$$

Example 3-3 Obtain a simplest sum-of-products expression for the function given by the Karnaugh map of Fig. 3-19.

Again the implicants are encircled, and the two essential implicants are marked with dots. However, we now note that the two essential implicants do not cover all the 1s in F_3. Thus we come to the fourth and final step of our procedure: *Express the function as an ORing of all of the essential implicants plus a combination of some of the remaining implicants so as to cover all of the 1s in the function as simply as possible. Simply* here means to minimize an appropriate cost criterion, such as the number of gate leads, defined in Sec. 3-1.

In this example this step says to implement F_3 as either

$$F_3 = \overline{W}X\overline{Y} + WYZ + X\overline{Y}Z$$

or

$$F_3 = \overline{W}X\overline{Y} + WYZ + WXZ$$

but *not* as

$$F_3 = \overline{W}X\overline{Y} + WYZ + X\overline{Y}Z + WXZ$$

In this problem we have no good reason to prefer one of the acceptable implementations over the other. They both yield the same number of gate leads.

With these examples, we have dealt with all possible contingencies. Reiterating this general procedure for obtaining a simplest sum-of-products expression for a function, we have the following four steps:

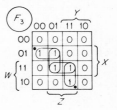

Fig. 3-19 Karnaugh map for Example 3-3.

1. Make a Karnaugh map of the function.
2. Encircle all implicants which are not included completely in a larger implicant.
3. Mark all essential implicants with a dot.
4. Express the function as an ORing of all of the essential implicants plus a combination of some of the remaining implicants so as to cover all of the 1s in the function as simply as possible.

3-6 "DON'T CARE" CONDITIONS

If a combinational circuit is to be designed in which some combination of inputs will never occur, then these combinations are called *don't care* conditions and can be considered to be either 0s or 1s, whichever helps the simplification the most.

Example 3-4 Design a combinational circuit which will detect whenever an 8421 BCD code digit is divisible by 3.

For 8421 BCD code, the combinations corresponding to binary 10, 11, 12, 13, 14, and 15 never occur. Therefore they are don't care conditions. Each one is indicated in the Karnaugh map for the function in Fig. 3-20 with an X. The encircled X's are used as 1s; the remaining X's are treated like 0s, yielding

$$F = d_8 d_1 + d_4 d_2 \overline{d}_1 + \overline{d}_4 d_2 d_1 + \overline{d}_8 \overline{d}_4 \overline{d}_2 \overline{d}_1$$

Notice that the X's are used to make implicants (which include one or more 1s) as large as possible. However, implicants which include *only* X's are not encircled.

3-7 IMPLEMENTATION OF A FUNCTION VIA $\overline{F}$

In addition to simplifying the implementation of a function F by obtaining the simplest sum-of-products expression for F, often a simpler implementation can be found by obtaining a simplest sum-of-products expression for $\overline{F}$ and then inverting the output to obtain F.

Example 3-5 Implement the function F_x defined by the Karnaugh map in Fig. 3-21*a* as simply as possible. Assume all inputs are available in both asserted and negated form (i.e., that we have not only A, B, C, and D available but also $\overline{A}$, $\overline{B}$, $\overline{C}$, and $\overline{D}$).

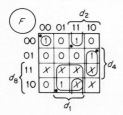

Fig. 3-20 Simplification of a function having "don't care" conditions.

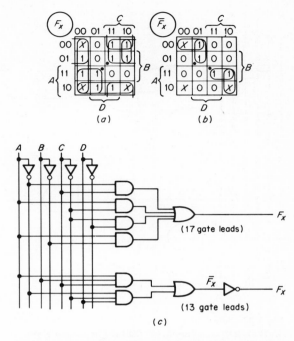

Fig. 3-21 Simplification and implementation of F_x. (a) Karnaugh map of F_x; (b) Karnaugh map of $\overline{F}_x$; (c) two implementations.

A simplest sum-of-products expression for F_x is

$$F_x = \overline{A}C + A\overline{C} + \overline{C}\overline{D} + A\overline{B}$$

The implementation is shown at the top of Fig. 3-21c and costs 17 gate leads.

To proceed with the implementation via $\overline{F}_x$, first a Karnaugh map must be constructed, as in Fig. 3-21b. Note that the don't care conditions of F_x are still don't care conditions for $\overline{F}_x$. The simplest sum-of-products expression for $\overline{F}_x$ is

$$\overline{F}_x = ABC + \overline{A}\overline{C}D$$

and the implementation is shown at the bottom of Fig. 3-21c. It costs only 13 gate leads.

If the inputs had not been available in *both* asserted and negated form but in asserted form only, then we would have had to include the cost of the inverters needed on the inputs. This would increase the cost of the implementation obtained via F_x to 25 gate leads while increasing the cost of the implementation obtained via $\overline{F}_x$ to only 17 gate leads.

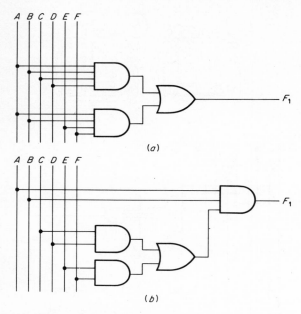

Fig. 3-22   Alternative implementations of F_1. (a) Sum-of-products implementation; (b) factored implementation.

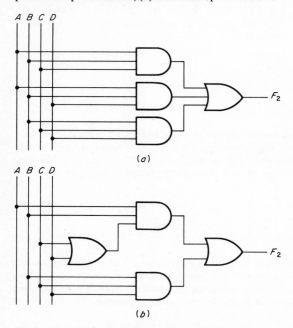

Fig. 3-23   Alternative implementations of F_2. (a) Sum-of-products implementation; (b) factored implementation.

3-8 ALGEBRAIC FACTORING

After the simplest sum-of-products form for a function F (or its complement $\overline{F}$) has been found, there is another rather straightforward step which may reduce the cost of the implementation further. It consists of factoring the result, as permitted by the Boolean theorem

$$ABCD + ABEF = AB(CD + EF)$$

which can be verified with a truth-table proof. However, this factoring *does not necessarily* reduce cost. For example, using the cost criterion of gate leads, the function

$$F_1 = ABCD + ABEF$$

shown in Fig. 3-22*a* costs 13 gate leads. In comparison, the factored expression

$$F_1 = AB(CD + EF)$$

shown in Fig. 3-22*b* also costs 13 gate leads.

Factoring tends to help when one or more of the terms within brackets is a single variable. For example, the implementation of the function

$$F_2 = ABC + ABD + BCD$$

is shown in Fig. 3-23*a* and costs 16 gate leads. A factored form of the same function

$$F_2 = AB(C + D) + BCD$$

is shown in Fig. 3-23*b* and costs 14 gate leads.

As a final example, consider the following case where factoring actually results in a more costly implementation. If

$$F_3 = ABC + ADE + BDF$$

then this circuit can be implemented directly, as shown in Fig. 3-24*a*, costing 16 gate leads. The factored form

$$F_3 = A(BC + DE) + BDF$$

is shown in Fig. 3-24*b* and costs 19 gate leads.

As can be seen from these examples, factoring can, on occasion, yield further simplification of an already good circuit. However, it must be used with

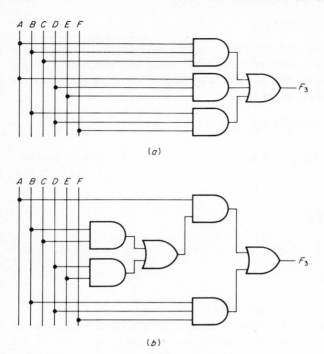

Fig. 3-24 Alternative implementations of F_3. (a) Sum-of-products implementation; (b) factored implementation.

care since it can also result in a more costly implementation than the original unfactored form.

3-9 DESIGN WITH NAND AND NOR GATES

The design techniques developed up to this point have led to implementations in terms of AND gates, OR gates, and inverters. However, the gates available for implementing digital systems are often NAND or NOR gates.

Consider the circuit shown in Fig. 3-25a. This circuit configuration is available in integrated-circuit form as a series 54/74† TTL (transistor-transistor-logic) gate. The inputs A and B and the output F will be either at a *high* level (+2.0 to +5.0 V) or at a *low* level (0 to +0.8 V).

If either input goes low, point X is pulled low, turning off Q_2 and hence Q_4, while R_2 turns on Q_3. Thus F goes high (and does so with an extremely low output impedance—typically 140 Ω). In contrast, with both inputs high, point X

---

†Series 54/74 is a popular form of TTL logic created by Texas Instruments, Inc., and second-sourced by almost everybody.

is pulled up, turning on Q_2 and hence Q_4. Point Y is pulled low by Q_2, and Q_3 turns off. Thus F goes low (and does so again with an extremely low output impedance—typically 12 Ω). These conditions are summarized in Fig. 3-25b where H and L signify high and low voltages, respectively.

In Chap. 2, we introduced a symbology which is a military standard commonly accepted by industry. This symbology uses the *shape* of a gate to distinguish between whether it is to be thought of as an AND gate or an OR gate. It uses a small circle (or its absence) to indicate whether a signal is to be thought of as being negated or not. One further point of symbology to which we will adhere is concerned with our labeling of variables and functions on logic diagrams. *Any labeled variable or function will be considered to be equal to 1 when the voltage is high; conversely, it will be equal to 0 when the voltage is low.* This is commonly known as *positive-true* definition. (The opposite is known as *negative-true* definition.)

With this definition, the voltage truth table for the TTL gate in Fig. 3-25b is translated into the logic truth table in Fig. 3-25c. Consequently, this TTL gate is a NAND gate. Figure 3-26 shows two equivalent symbolic representations of the NAND gate. That these are equivalent can be demonstrated in several ways. One way is to prove the Boolean identity†

$$\overline{AB} = \overline{A} + \overline{B} \tag{3-2}$$

and then to recognize that Fig. 3-26a is the circuit equivalent of the left side of this equation while Fig. 3-26b is the circuit equivalent of the right side of the equation. We shall refer to this as the INVERT-OR representation of the gate.

† Known in Boolean algebra as DeMorgan's theorem.

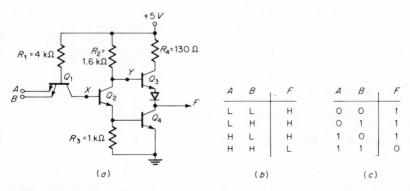

Fig. 3-25 TTL Gate and its truth tables. (a) Series 54/74 TTL gate configuration; (b) its voltage truth table; (c) its logic truth table.

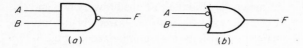

Fig. 3-26 Two equivalent representations of the NAND gate. (*a*) NAND representation; (*b*) INVERT-OR representation.

To implement any function with NAND gates, it is only necessary to use these two symbols wherever ORs and ANDs are needed and to keep the inversions straight. Note that if a variable F is inverted twice, the result will be the variable again; that is,

$$F = \overline{\overline{F}}$$

Example 3-6 Implement the two solutions to the problem of Example 3-5 with NAND gates (and inverters). The two AND-OR-NOT implementations are shown in Fig. 3-21c.
The first function is

$$F_x = \overline{A}C + A\overline{C} + \overline{C}\overline{D} + A\overline{B}$$

Its NAND-gate implementation is shown in the top of Fig. 3-27. Note the good fortune of having inversions on both the output of the NAND gate and the input to the INVERT-OR gate; by inverting twice the same result is achieved as if there were no inversions at all. Also note the labeling of each function on the output of each NAND gate; because of the inversion, these are properly labeled (if they are labeled at all) as

$$\overline{\overline{A}C} \quad \overline{A\overline{C}} \quad \overline{\overline{C}\overline{D}} \quad \overline{A\overline{B}}$$

where the bar over each expression accounts for the inversion indicated by the small circle on the output of each NAND gate.
It might be argued that this is not a NAND-gate implementation because of the use of the INVERT-OR symbol. However, since the INVERT-OR and NAND symbols are completely equivalent, this is perfectly acceptable; furthermore, the use of the two types of gate symbols results in a circuit which *looks* like the AND-OR-NOT implementation, providing ease of understanding.
The second function is

$$\overline{F}_x = ABC + \overline{A}CD$$

and is shown implemented in the bottom of Fig. 3-27.

Example 3-7 Implement the function

$$F_y = AB + AC$$

as simply as possible using NAND gates (and inverters). Assume the inputs are available in asserted form only.

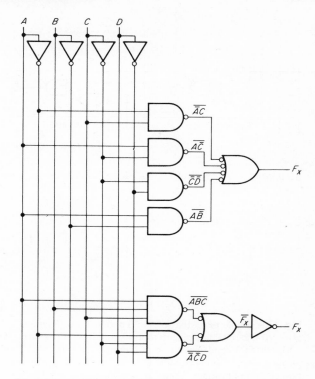

Fig. 3-27 NAND-gate implementations of the two solutions of Example 3-5.

Consider implementing this in two forms: the sum-of-products form given and also the factored form

$$F_y = A(B + C)$$

If we were given AND gates, OR gates, and inverters, we would get the two implementations shown in Fig. 3-28a and b. We would prefer the factored form of Fig. 3-28b. On the other hand, our problem asks for NAND-gate implementations. These are shown in Fig. 3-28c and d. Now, because of the inverters which creep into the implementation of the factored form, we prefer the sum-of-products form. However, note that if the inputs had been available in both asserted and negated form, we would prefer the implementation of the factored form (which would cost eight gate leads, as compared with nine gate leads for the sum-of-products form).

Thus far in this section we have dealt solely with NAND gates. However, not all devices are NAND gates. For example, the RTL (resistor-transistor-logic) gate shown in Fig. 3-29a has the voltage truth table and logic truth table shown in Fig. 3-29b and c. This is the logic of a NOR gate.

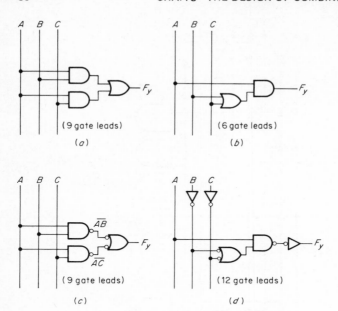

Fig. 3-28 Implementations of the function F_y of Example 3-7. (a) AND-OR-NOT implementation of sum-of-products form; (b) AND-OR-NOT implementation of factored form; (c) NAND implementation of sum-of-products form; (d) NAND implementation of factored form.

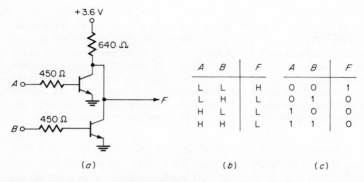

Fig. 3-29 RTL gate and its truth table. (a) Circuit configuration; (b) voltage truth table; (c) logic truth table.

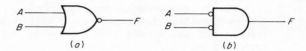

Fig. 3-30   Two equivalent representations of the NOR gate. (*a*) NOR representation; (*b*) INVERT-AND representation.

In order to design with NOR gates, it is helpful to use the equivalent representations shown in Fig. 3-30. That these are equivalent can be verified by noting that they implement the two sides of the Boolean identity†

$$\overline{A + B} = \bar{A}\bar{B} \tag{3-3}$$

Example 3-8   Implement

$$F_y = AB + AC = A(B + C)$$

as simply as possible using NOR gates (and inverters). Assume the inputs are available in asserted form only.

†This is another form of DeMorgan's theorem.

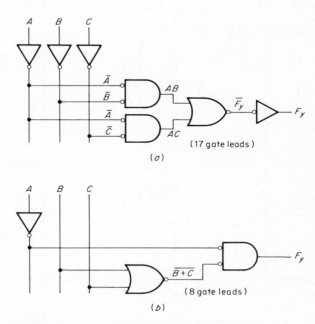

Fig. 3-31   Implementations of the function F_y. (*a*) NOR implementation of sum-of-products form; (*b*) NOR implementation of factored form.

     The two implementations are shown in Fig. 3-31a and b, with the lower-cost implementation being the factored form of 3-31b. If the inputs had been available in *both* asserted and negated form, this would still have been the lower-cost implementation.

3-10 DOT-AND/ORING

Generally speaking, outputs of gates are meant to go to the inputs of other devices. However, with some types of gates, a logical meaning can be associated

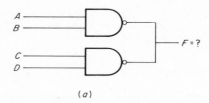

(a)

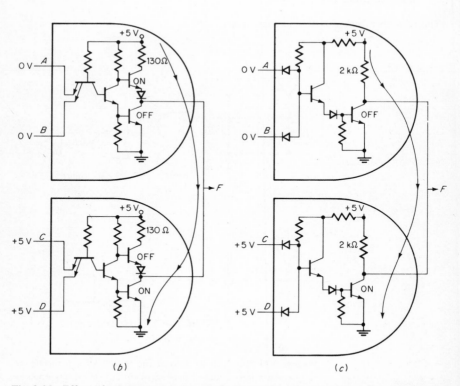

(b)   (c)

Fig. 3-32 Effect of tying gate outputs together. (a) Tying outputs of two gates together; (b) not recommended for TTL gates; (c) fine for DTL gates.

with tying the outputs of two gates together, as in Fig. 3-32a. With other types of gates, such tying of outputs together is not recommended. An example of the latter situation is the TTL gate of Fig. 3-25a. In Fig. 3-32b, the outputs of two of these gates are shown tied together. If the top gate is trying to force the output high while the bottom gate is trying to force the output low, then a low-impedance path arises in these integrated circuits with 5 V across it and perhaps 30 to 40 mA through it—too much power to be dissipating in microscopic circuits! On the other hand, the circuit of Fig. 3-32c illustrates a powerful use of DTL (diode-transistor-logic) NAND gates. If either output transistor is turned on, the output is pulled low. No harm is done to the gates because this is what the output transistor in a gate standing alone does anyway. (However, it *is* common to omit one of the 2-kΩ load resistors when outputs are tied together, using a gate with an *open-collector* output.)

Having seen that DTL-NAND-gate outputs can be tied together, we might now ask how the output F in Fig. 3-32a is related to the inputs A, B, C, and D. Since F is pulled low if the output transistor in either gate is turned on and since the output transistor of a gate will be turned on if and only if both inputs to the gate go high, we have

$$F = \overline{AB + CD}$$

In other words, if A AND B both go high OR if C AND D both go high, then the output will go low. It is this OR which leads to the expression for this circuit, the *dot-OR*† connection. It is conventionally symbolized as in Fig. 3-33, where OC means *open collector*.

The above relationship gives rise to the equivalences shown in Fig. 3-34. And because of our previous equivalence between the NAND and the INVERT-OR symbols, Fig. 3-34 can be reexpressed as in Fig. 3-35. Note the *dot-AND* symbolism used here.

These equivalences lead to the following *dot-AND/OR simplification procedure*, which is applicable to any circuit implemented with logic having dot-AND/OR capability:

1. Design the circuit, forgetting about the dot-AND/OR capability.

†Also referred to as the *wired-OR* connection.

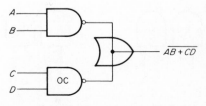

Fig. 3-33 Symbolism for dot-ORing.

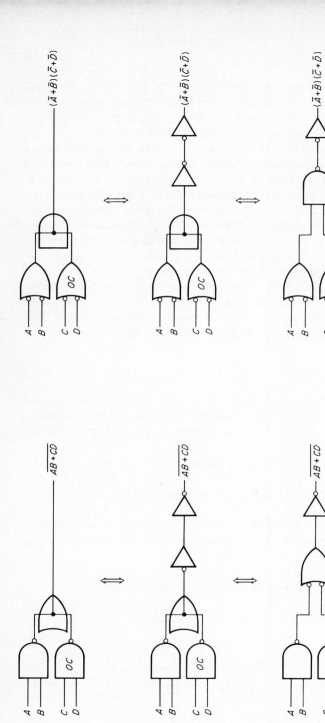

Fig. 3·35 An equivalent equivalence.

Fig. 3·34 An equivalence.

2. Look at the resulting circuit. Anywhere there are two or more gates whose outputs go *only* into one gate, a dot-AND/OR simplification is possible. Tie the outputs of these gates together, and replace the gate they feed with an inverter.
3. Remove any inverter pairs which result, provided the circuit does not use the signal between the inverters.

Example 3-9   Simplify the circuit of Fig. 3-36*a* implemented with DTL NAND gates.

Since DTL NAND gates possess dot-AND/OR capability, we can apply the procedure, as shown in Fig. 3-36*b* and *c*.

Dot-AND/ORing is the almost universally used way of getting information from peripheral equipment into small computers through an *input bus*, as

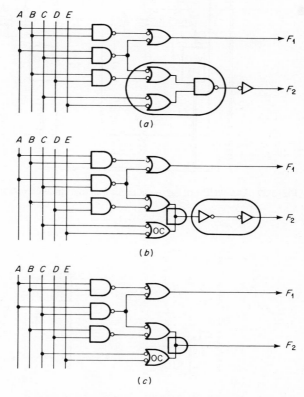

Fig. 3-36 Applying the dot-AND/OR simplification procedure. (*a*) Initial circuit; (*b*) circuit after dot-ANDing; (*c*) final circuit after removing inverter pair.

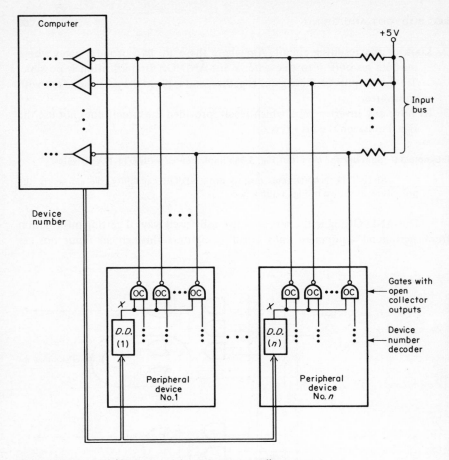

Fig. 3-37   Dot-AND/ORing on an input bus to a small computer.

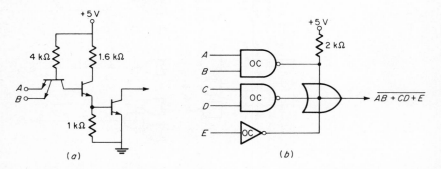

Fig. 3-38   Modified TTL gate with open-collector output. (*a*) Its structure; (*b*) its use.

illustrated in Fig. 3-37. The computer will send out a *device number*, which goes to all of the peripheral devices. When this device number picks out device No. 1, that device decodes this device number so that the x input to each of the gates shown goes high. If the other input on any gate is also high, then the output goes low, pulling that bus line low. Meanwhile, the inputs to the bus lines from all the other peripheral units are disabled because their x inputs are all low (preventing the turn-on of their output transistors). By ORing the m inputs from each of n peripherals in this way, the number of input wires to the computer is reduced from $m \times n$ to just m.

Because of the power of dot-AND/ORing, TTL logic lines like series 54/74 provide modified NAND gates or inverters having the open-collector output illustrated in Fig. 3-38a. Their use is illustrated in Fig. 3-38b and also in Fig. 3-37.

3-11 MULTIPLE-OUTPUT CIRCUITS

The problem of implementing a single, isolated Boolean function is a rarity. More often, the designer is faced with the problem of implementing several functions of the same group of variables. Of course, it is possible to proceed by implementing each function as if the problem of implementing the others did not exist. However, we always wish not only to implement but to do so with low cost.

The *common-implicants* approach proceeds by obtaining a simplest sum-of-products expression for each function and its complement and then recognizing that any implicants common to two functions need only be implemented once. In looking at a *single* function, it always pays to obtain the largest implicants possible. Here it may pay to take a smaller implicant for one function because it is common to another function. The easiest place to see such a possibility is in the Karnaugh maps.

Example 3-10 Implement F_1 and F_2, defined by the Karnaugh maps of Fig. 3-39a, as simply as possible using NAND gates not having dot-AND/OR capability. Assume all inputs are available in both asserted and negated form.

Express each function F_1, $\overline{F}_1$, F_2, and $\overline{F}_2$ in simplest sum-of-products form:

$$F_1 = A\overline{D} + A\overline{B} \qquad\qquad 9 \quad \text{GL}\dagger$$

$$\overline{F}_1 = \overline{A} + BD \qquad\qquad 8\ddagger \text{ GL}$$

or $\qquad\qquad\qquad$ —————*Note*

$$\overline{F}_1 = \overline{A} + \overline{(ABD)} \qquad\qquad 9\ddagger \text{ GL}$$

$$F_2 = B\overline{C}D + A\overline{B}C + \overline{(ABD)} \qquad 12 \quad \text{GL given } \overline{F}_1$$
$$\qquad\qquad\qquad\qquad\qquad\qquad 16 \quad \text{GL otherwise}$$

$$\overline{F}_2 = \overline{B}\overline{C} + B\overline{D} + \overline{A}C \qquad\qquad 15\ddagger \text{ GL}$$

†Gate leads.
‡Counting inverter on output.

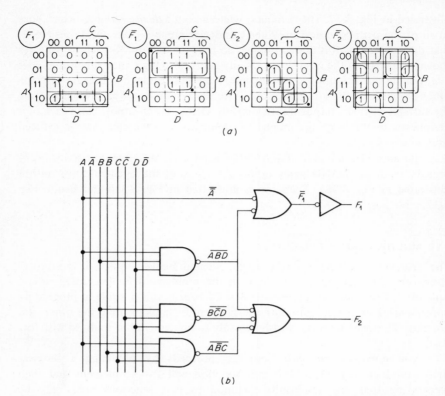

(a)

(b)

Fig. 3-39 Design and implementation of Example 3-10. (a) Karnaugh maps; (b) implementation.

Comparing alternatives leads to the choice of implementing via $\overline{F}_1$ and F_2 as in Fig. 3-39b for 21 gate leads.

Example 3-11 Repeat Example 3-10 assuming the NAND gates *do* have dot-AND/OR capability.

As soon as we begin to use dot-AND/ORing, we forego the opportunity of using common implicants since dot-AND/ORing kills the individual output functions of each gate. Consequently, we do best to compare the 21-gate-lead solution already found (which is still available to us) with another solution in which dot-AND/ORing is used on all functions. Note that the functions to be considered will be the same as in the last example, but that the costs will be different. Using the procedure of the last section to obtain the implementations, these costs are found to be:

$$F_1 = A\overline{D} + A\overline{B} \qquad\qquad \text{8 GL}$$
$$\overline{F}_1 = \overline{A} + BD \qquad\qquad \text{5 GL}$$
$$F_2 = B\overline{C}D + A\overline{B}C + ABD \qquad \text{14 GL}$$
$$\overline{F}_2 = \overline{B}\overline{C} + B\overline{D} + \overline{A}C \qquad \text{9 GL}$$

The implementation via $\overline{F}_1$ and $\overline{F}_2$ is shown in Fig. 3-40 and costs only 14 gate leads. Dot-ORing provides the cheapest solution. Note the addition of the inverter implementing the $\overline{A}$ term in $\overline{F}_1$. If the input A had been used instead of $\overline{A}$ followed by an inverter, it would have been A no longer. In addition, if A had come from a switch instead of a gate, the dot-ORing would not have been a valid operation.

3-12 BRIDGING

The availability of low-cost integrated-circuit EXCLUSIVE-OR gates or MAJOR-ITY gates raises the question of how they can be incorporated into the design of arbitrary Boolean functions. We shall study a technique which is not so much a self-contained design procedure as it is a way to bend the characteristics of the EXCLUSIVE-OR and MAJORITY functions to the design procedures we have already studied. This procedure takes three steps:

1. Study the *patterns* made by EXCLUSIVE-OR and MAJORITY functions on Karnaugh maps.
2. Match one of these functions as closely as possible to the function to be implemented. That is, select an EXCLUSIVE-OR or a MAJORITY function which has a Karnaugh map almost identical to that of the function to be implemented.

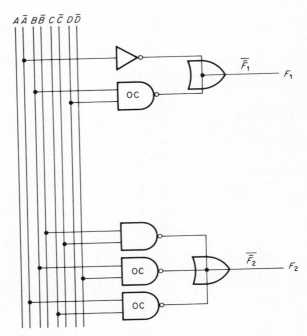

Fig. 3-40 Implementation of Example 3-11.

3. By using the technique of *bridging* (discussed below), implement the desired function from the EXCLUSIVE-OR or MAJORITY function.

A variety of the patterns which EXCLUSIVE-OR functions can make on a Karnaugh map are shown in Fig. 3-41. Notice the "checkerboard" nature of these functions and that there are always half 1s and half 0s in each map. In addition, the expression for each function can be changed to something equivalent just by complementing an even number of variables or by complementing the entire function together with an odd number of variables. For example:

$$\overline{A} \oplus B \oplus C = A \oplus \overline{B} \oplus C = A \oplus B \oplus \overline{C} = \overline{A} \oplus \overline{B} \oplus \overline{C} = \overline{A \oplus B \oplus C}$$

The patterns which result from a three-input MAJORITY function, shown in Fig. 3-42, also have the property of always giving half 1s and half 0s. However

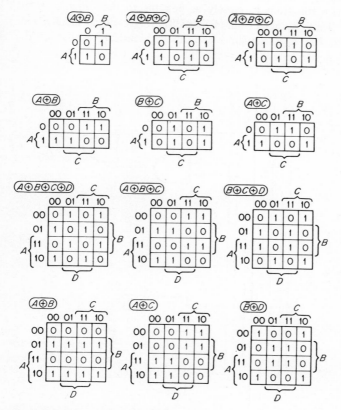

Fig. 3-41 Some EXCLUSIVE-OR functions.

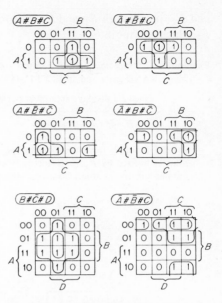

Fig. 3-42 Some MAJORITY functions.

instead of the checkerboard pattern, the **MAJORITY** function gives a "clumped" pattern—all the 1s are clumped in one bunch and all the 0s in another. The expression

$$A \mathbin{\#} B \mathbin{\#} C$$

is equal to 1 if and only if two or three of the variables equal 1, that is, if a majority of the variables equal 1. Notice that the Karnaugh map for an arbitrary **MAJORITY** function such as

$$\overline{A} \mathbin{\#} \overline{B} \mathbin{\#} C$$

is equal to 1 where $\overline{A}\overline{B}C = 1$ and at all adjacent squares. Also notice that if a function F is a **MAJORITY** function, then so too is $\overline{F}$.

The technique of *bridging* constructs a desired function F_2 out of a given function F_1, using the following form:

$$F_2 = F_1 G_1 + G_2$$

where G_1 and G_2 are chosen so as to "bridge" between F_1 and F_2. More generally, it may be convenient to bridge between $\overline{F}_1$ and F_2, or between $\overline{F}_1$

and $\overline{F}_2$, or between F_1 and $\overline{F}_2$. The role of G_1 is to *eliminate* the effect of 1s in F_1 which are not in F_2.

Example 3-12 Implement the function F_2 shown in Fig. 3-43a using the bridging technique with NAND gates and an EXCLUSIVE-OR or a MAJORITY gate.

Since F_2 displays an almost perfect checkerboard pattern, select

$$F_1 = A \oplus B \oplus C \oplus D$$

as the function from which to bridge. This function, shown in Fig. 3-43b, contains all the 1s needed by F_2. It is necessary only to eliminate the effect of the two 1s in the upper-left-hand corner. Consequently, the bridging takes the form

$$F_2 = F_1 G_1$$

where, as is shown in Fig. 3-43c, the function G_1 must have 1s where both F_2 and F_1

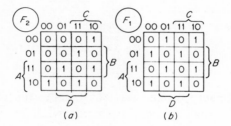

(a)   (b)

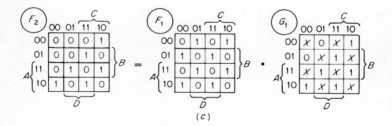

(c)

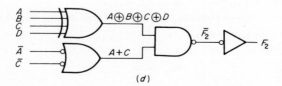

(d)

Fig. 3-43 Design and implementation of Example 3-12. (a) Desired function; (b) function from which to bridge; (c) bridging; (d) implementation.

have 1s, must have 0s where F_2 has 0s while F_1 has 1s, and can have either 1s or 0s where F_1 has 0s. The result is

$$G_1 = A + C$$

and the total implementation is shown in Fig. 3-43d. To count cost (in order to compare it with the cost of an implementation using *only* NAND gates), we need to know a cost of the EXCLUSIVE-OR gate relative to that of a NAND gate. If the price of a four-input EXCLUSIVE-OR gate is three times as much as that of a NAND gate, then we might derive some equivalent number of gate leads for the EXCLUSIVE-OR gate in the range

$$5 \leqslant \text{Equivalent gate leads} \leqslant 15$$

depending on how we wish to weight the relative cost of assembly (assuming this is proportional to the five *actual* gate leads) vs. the cost of components (assuming this is proportional to the $3 \times 5 = 15$ *equivalent* gate leads).

This last example illustrated a case where F_2 could be obtained by bridging from F_1 simply by eliminating the effect of some 1s in F_1. On the other hand, if the bridging problem consists solely of *adding* some 1s to F_1, we have

$$F_2 = F_1 + G_2$$

Example 3-13 Implement the function F_2 of the previous example by bridging using the equation

$$\overline{F}_2 = F_1 + G_2$$

where F_1 must be redefined appropriately. Implement with NAND gates and an EXCLUSIVE-OR gate.

The bridging technique is outlined in Fig. 3-44a, where

$$F_1 = \overline{A} \oplus B \oplus C \oplus D = \overline{A \oplus B \oplus C \oplus D} = \text{etc.}$$

and where G_2 must have 1s where $\overline{F}_2$ has 1s while F_1 has 0s, must have 0s where $\overline{F}_2$ and F_1 have 0s, and can have either 1s or 0s where $\overline{F}_2$ and F_1 have 1s. This leads to

$$G_2 = \overline{A}\overline{C}$$

and the implementation is shown in Fig. 3-44b. Notice that this is exactly the same implementation as in the previous example. Only the *representation* of the NAND gates has been changed.

The general problem of bridging requires both the addition of some 1s and the deletion of other 1s in going from F_1 to F_2. The next example illustrates the procedure.

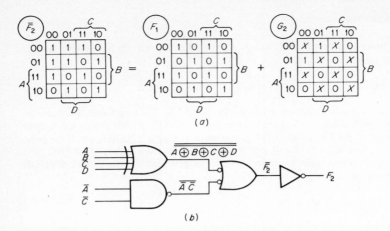

Fig. 3-44 Design and implementation of Example 3-13. (*a*) Bridging; (*b*) implementation.

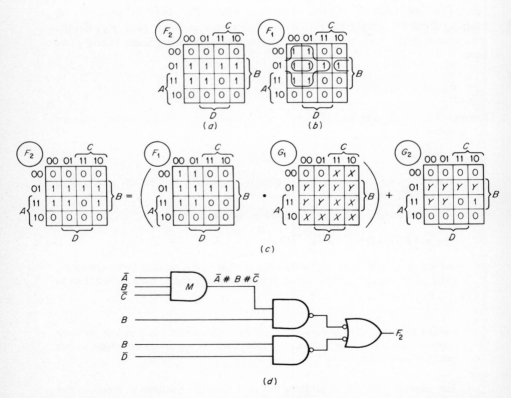

Fig. 3-45 Design and implementation of Example 3-14. (*a*) Desired function; (*b*) function from which to bridge; (*c*) bridging; (*d*) implementation.

Example 3-14 Implement the function F_2, shown in Fig. 3-45a, using the bridging technique with NAND gates and an EXCLUSIVE-OR gate or a MAJORITY gate.

Since the 1s are more or less clumped together, we shall bridge from the MAJORITY function

$$F_1 = \overline{A} \, \# \, B \, \# \, \overline{C}$$

shown in Fig. 3-45b. The bridging requires the deletion of two 1s and the addition of one 1. The Karnaugh maps for the functions G_1 and G_2 must satisfy the equation

$$F_2 = F_1 G_1 + G_2$$

square by square. This leads to the following requirements

F_2	F_1	G_1	G_2
0	0	X	0
0	1	0	0
1	0	X	1
1	1	Y	Y

where X's represent don't care conditions while the Y's represent the constraint that either G_1 or G_2, or both, must equal 1. The maps for G_1 and G_2 are shown in Fig. 3-45c. Notice that because of the Y's many trade-off possibilities exist. For example, if all of the Y's in G_1 are set equal to 0, then $F_2 = G_2$ and bridging has not done a thing. On the other hand,

$$G_1 = B$$

leads to

$$G_2 = B\overline{D}$$

and the implementation shown in Fig. 3-45d.

The final implementation of this example has led to a sufficiently complex solution to warrant our asking whether we might not have done as well or better implementing this problem directly with NAND gates. And, indeed, such is the case, for the expression

$$\overline{F}_2 = \overline{B} + ACD$$

leads to a nine-gate-lead implementation. The moral here is the same as that for algebraic factoring: While the design technique may appear to be well suited to the problem, there is no guarantee that it will lead to a better solution than is available through some other means.

Generally speaking, bridging is a potent technique for functions which are almost EXCLUSIVE-OR functions. It is less powerful for functions which are almost **MAJORITY** functions. Also, if bridging requires only the adding of 1s or requires only the elimination of the effects of some 1s, it tends to be a more competitive technique because then only one of the G functions is required.

In addition to its application in the design of circuits taking advantage of **EXCLUSIVE-OR** or **MAJORITY** functions, bridging is also useful in the design of multiple-output circuits. Once one output has been implemented, it can be used to bridge to another output.

3-13 SYMMETRIC FUNCTIONS

Symmetric functions arise in a variety of contexts and often lead to complex implementations if handled directly. These are functions which remain invariant under permutations of the variables so that, for example,

$$f(a,b,c,d) = f(b,d,c,a)$$

A symmetric function can be specified by saying how many 1s it takes on the inputs to generate a 1 on the output. It is often symbolized as indicated by the following example:

$$F = S_{(2,3)} \{x_1, x_2, x_3, x_4\}$$

This describes a symmetric function F of the four variables x_1, x_2, x_3, and x_4 which equals 1 if and only if two or three of the variables equal 1. Some familiar functions, expressed in this terminology, are:

$$ABC = S_{(3)} \{A,B,C\}$$
$$A + B + C = S_{(1,2,3)} \{A,B,C\}$$
$$A \oplus B \oplus C = S_{(1,3)} \{A,B,C\}$$
$$A \# B \# C = S_{(2,3)} \{A,B,C\}$$

The purpose of this section is not only to describe symmetric functions but also to indicate an approach to their implementation which takes advantage of the full adders available as MSI circuits. The full adders are arranged to count the number of inputs equal to 1 and to generate this count as a binary number. Then output gating is used to generate the symmetric function output from this binary number. The procedure will be developed through an example.

Example 3-15 Implement $F = S_{(2,3,6)} \{x_1, \ldots, x_7\}$.

The *form* of the solution is shown in Fig. 3-46a. The full adders are arranged so as to add the seven 1-bit binary numbers $x_1, \ldots, x_7$, yielding the binary sum $b_4 b_2 b_1$. The output gating then serves to decode this into the required symmetric

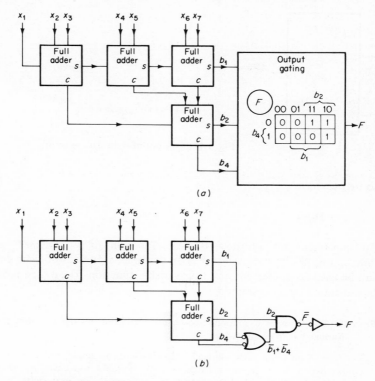

Fig. 3-46 Design and implementation of Example 3-15. (*a*) Form of solution; (*b*) complete implementation.

function with the equation

$$F = \overline{b}_4 b_2 + b_2 \overline{b}_1 = b_2 (\overline{b}_4 + \overline{b}_1)$$

The implementation with NAND gates plus full adders is shown in Fig. 3-46*b*.

3-14   IMPLEMENTING A FUNCTION WITH AN MSI DATA SELECTOR

The medium-scale integrated-circuit *data selector,* shown in Fig. 3-47, offers a completely different approach to the implementation of an arbitrary Boolean function. This circuit selects one of the eight input lines $D0, \ldots, D7$ and (in effect) connects it to the output F. Which line is selected is determined by the number

$$N = 4S_4 + 2S_2 + S_1$$

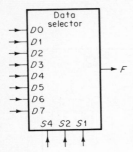

Fig. 3-47 One-out-of-eight data selector.

so that we have

$$F = D(N)$$

To implement an arbitrary Boolean function of n variables, we need a "one-out-of-2^{n-1}" data selector. For example, a one-out-of-eight data selector can be used to implement any four-variable function. The design procedure will be illustrated by an example.

Example 3-16 Obtain a minimum-cost implementation of the function shown in the Karnaugh map of Fig. 3-48a.

Which approach will lead to a minimum-cost implementation depends on the relative costs of the various logic circuits available. For example, the data selector approach developed here might be compared in cost with a NAND-gate implementation.

The key design tool for this approach is not the Karnaugh map but rather the truth table shown in Fig. 3-48b. Three of the input variables A, B, and C will be used as the data selector variables S_4, S_2, and S_1. Consequently, the values of A, B, and C will make the output F of the data selector equal to one of the eight inputs $D0, \ldots, D7$. Now for each value of A, B, and C there are two values of F, one corresponding to $D = 0$ and one to $D = 1$. There are four possible pairs of values that F can take on. Corresponding to each, we can express F with the Boolean function shown below:

If $\begin{Bmatrix} \text{when } D = 0, F = 0 \\ \text{when } D = 1, F = 0 \end{Bmatrix}$ then $F = 0$

If $\begin{Bmatrix} \text{when } D = 0, F = 1 \\ \text{when } D = 1, F = 1 \end{Bmatrix}$ then $F = 1$

If $\begin{Bmatrix} \text{when } D = 0, F = 0 \\ \text{when } D = 1, F = 1 \end{Bmatrix}$ then $F = D$

If $\begin{Bmatrix} \text{when } D = 0, F = 1 \\ \text{when } D = 1, F = 0 \end{Bmatrix}$ then $F = \overline{D}$

This leads to the truth table shown in Fig. 3-48b. Note the inclusion of (N), which is equal to $4A + 2B + C$, and of $D(N)$, the Nth input to the data selector, determined from the four relations just given since this value of $D(N)$ becomes F. The implementation is shown in Fig. 3-48c.

3-15 LOADING RULES

When implementing combinational logic with hardware, not only is it important to know how to simplify functions but also it is vital to understand the characteristics of the logic line being used to carry out the implementation. In this chapter we have discussed design with various gate types (for example, NAND gates) and with gates having dot-AND/OR capability.

Another design consideration is the constraint of *loading rules* imposed by the logic line. For example, with series 54/74 TTL, a gate having the standard totempole output† will drive up to 10 gate inputs. Such a gate is said to have a *fan-out* of 10. If more than 10 gates are driven by the output of any gate, then

†With both the pull-up and pull-down transistors shown in Fig. 3-25.

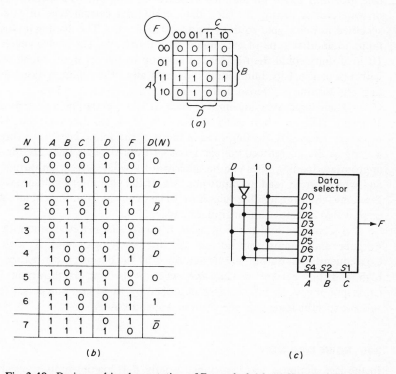

Fig. 3-48 Design and implementation of Example 3-16. (a) Karnaugh map; (b) truth table; (c) implementation.

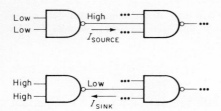

Fig. 3-49 Source and sink loads.

when the gate output is supposed to be high, the output voltage may dip below the minimum voltage level guaranteed by the manufacturer. Alternatively, when the gate output is supposed to be low, the output voltage may rise above the maximum voltage level guaranteed by the manufacturer. It is these *guaranteed voltage levels* which provide guaranteed amounts of noise immunity and which thus determine whether a combinational logic design will perform reliably.

Often loading rules are specified in terms of arbitrarily defined *load units*. *One load unit* might be the load imposed by an input to a specific type of gate on whatever is driving it. Then the output of a certain type of gate might be specified as being able to drive up to 10 load units. The loading imposed by the input to another type of gate might be 2 load units. The device which can drive 10 load units could then be loaded with up to five of these 2-load-unit inputs, with ten of the 1-load-unit inputs, or with any other combination which keeps the total loading at 10 load units or less.

When logic lines are mixed, such as when designing a system using both TTL and DTL or when using an MSI circuit in another logic line, it is often necessary to specify loading rules in terms of the actual currents involved. Then, as long as the guaranteed voltage levels of the two logic lines are the same, the appropriate loading rules can be described by what current an output can drive and what current load an input imposes. If the guaranteed voltage levels are not the same, then the loading rules have to be deduced from the circuits themselves or provided by one of the manufacturers.

A complication arises because the currents involved on both the gate outputs and inputs depend on whether the logic level is high or low. Consequently, an output will be described by the current it can *source* when it is high and the current it can *sink* when it is low, as shown in Fig. 3-49. Correspondingly, an input is also described by these two currents. (The loading rules of specific logic lines are given in Appendix A1.)

3-16   NOISE IMMUNITY

In the last section it was mentioned briefly that loading limitations are made in order to maintain guaranteed minimum and maximum voltage levels. In this section we shall explore the relationship between these guaranteed levels and noise immunity. For the sake of clarity, we shall use the characteristics and specifications corresponding to a specific logic line—series 54/74 TTL.

First, we shall define a *threshold voltage* for a NOR gate, NAND gate, or inverter as *that voltage which when applied to all the inputs produces the same voltage on the output*. Figure 3-50 illustrates a two-input NAND gate with the two inputs tied together. If the voltage applied to these inputs slowly changes as shown, then as long as V_{IN} is less than V_1, the output will be unaffected by V_{IN}. As V_{IN} increases above V_1, the output voltage V_{OUT} will decrease until finally for V_{IN} greater than V_2, the output no longer changes. We define $V_{threshold}$ as *that voltage at which* $V_{OUT} = V_{IN}$. If all gates in a combinational circuit have exactly this same threshold voltage and if we call a voltage "high" or "low" depending on whether it is above or below the threshold, then no matter how closely the inputs may be to the threshold voltage, the outputs will be the expected voltages, as defined by the Boolean equations which the gates implement.

For an actual logic line, the threshold voltage may vary somewhat from gate to gate or for the same gate at different temperatures or different supply voltages. Nevertheless, the variation is sufficiently small and the concept sufficiently useful for manufacturers to specify an approximate threshold voltage for a logic line. Thus for series 54/74 TTL, the threshold voltage is approximately 1.5 V.

Going from a loose intuitive definition of the switching characteristics of a logic line to a rigid, guaranteed specification, a manufacturer will list a *maximum*

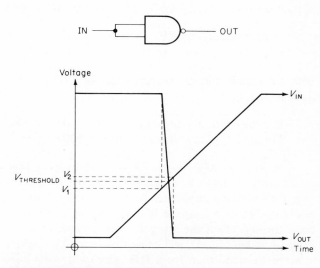

Fig. 3-50 Definition of threshold voltage.

logical 0 output (0.4 V for series 54/74 TTL) and a *minimum logical 1 output* (2.4 V for series 54/74 TTL) for gates under all conditions. The manufacturer will then state the corresponding minimum and maximum input voltages which will *guarantee* that the output voltage will be better than these worst-case values. Thus for series 54/74 TTL an input voltage greater than 2.0 V is guaranteed to force the output below 0.4 V (providing the loading rules are observed). Similarly, an input voltage less than 0.8 V is guaranteed to force the output above 2.4 V. These series 54/74 TTL guaranteed characteristics are summarized in tabular form below:

Gate input	*Gate output*
Less than 0.8 V	Greater than 2.4 V
Greater than 2.0 V	Less than 0.4 V

When a manufacturer refers to this logic line as having *400 mV of guaranteed noise immunity in both states*, it is simply saying that even if 400 mV (0.4 V) of noise is picked up on the wire running from the output of one gate to the input of another, that input voltage will still be within the limits tabulated above. For example, if the output of a gate is actually 2.5 V, then a peak amplitude of 400 mV of noise will carry that output up as high as 2.9 V and down as low as 2.1 V. In either case, the input to another gate attached to this output will never drop below the 2.0 V specified and, in fact, will not drop below 2.1 V.

In general, we have a *typical noise immunity* much greater than this guaranteed 400 mV suggests. Typical gate outputs for series 54/74 TTL are

$$\text{Logical } 1_{\text{typical}} = 3.3 \text{ V}$$
$$\text{Logical } 0_{\text{typical}} = 0.2 \text{ V}$$

With a threshold voltage of approximately 1.5 V, we have the following typical noise immunities:

Logical 1 typical noise immunity = 3,300 − 1,500 = 1,800 mV
Logical 0 typical noise immunity = 1,500 − 200 = 1,300 mV

Specifying noise immunity with voltages in this way does not tell the whole story. If noise is capacitively coupled into the wire between two gates, then the lower the impedance from that wire to ground, the smaller will be the resulting *RC* time constant of the coupling circuit and less noise *energy* will come through. Thus the low gate output impedance of a TTL gate, even in the logical-1 state (140 Ω), will cause that logic to be much less susceptible to being affected by noise than for a DTL gate (where the logical-1 output impedance might be 2,000 Ω).

3-17   SPEED CONSTRAINTS ON COMBINATIONAL DESIGN

So far we have discussed combinational design from the point of view of minimizing cost. We have assumed that the time it takes for changes on the inputs to propagate through the circuitry and cause changes on the outputs is unimportant. In many applications, this is a fair assumption, particularly in the design of special-purpose systems which are tied in to electromechanical devices or to people since their response times are so slow that the logic, by comparison, probably looks infinitely fast. In other systems, this propagation delay between changes on inputs and the resulting changes on outputs is a critical matter. In Chap. 5, we will discuss the interrelationship between the *clock rate* of a system and the maximum allowable propagation delay permissible in the combinational logic.

By specifying a maximum propagation delay for all gates in a system, this speed constraint can be reinterpreted as the maximum allowable number of levels of gating in the combinational circuitry. A circuit is said to have *n levels of gating* if the *worst-case propagation delay* between any input and any output is

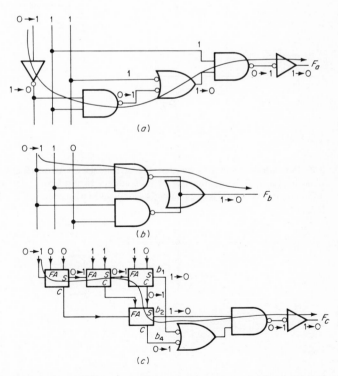

Fig. 3-51   Levels of gating. (*a*) Five levels of gating; (*b*) one level of gating; (*c*) twenty levels of gating.

determined by the changing-signal's passage through n gates. Figure 3-51a and b illustrate two examples. Another interesting example is provided by the implementation of the symmetric function shown in Fig. 3-46b. If the full adder is an MSI circuit in which the carry output is generated in three levels of gating while the sum output is generated in five levels, then the entire circuit has twenty levels of gating, as demonstrated in Fig. 3-51c. The worst-case propagation delay occurs with the inputs shown. The change on the far-left input propagates through all four full adders and changes b_1, b_2, and b_4. The worst-case signal path is shown.

PROBLEMS

3-1 Half-adder Using truth tables, demonstrate that the circuit shown is a *half-adder*, that is, that its outputs satisfy the truth table of Fig. 3-6.

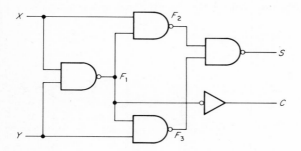

Fig. P 3-1

3-2 Full adder Demonstrate that the circuit shown is a *full adder*, satisfying the truth table of Fig. 3-5. Note the use of half adders to implement the full adders. (This is the implementation which leads to the 54-gate-lead implementation of the problem discussed in Sec. 3-1.)

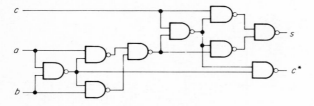

Fig. P 3-2

3-3 Structuring a problem solution Consider the problem of generating the eight *threshold functions* $T_1, \ldots, T_8$ of eight variables $x_1, \ldots, x_8$, where

$T_i = 1$ if i or more variables equal 1

(a) Can the problem be broken down as in Fig. P 3-3a? If so, define the iterative block.

(b) Can the problem be broken down as in Fig. P 3-3b? If so, define the iterative block.

(c) Can you break the problem down in any other way? If so, show and define your breakdown.

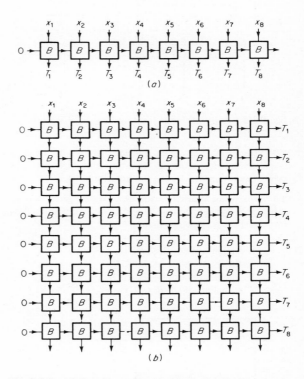

Fig. P 3-3 (a) One-dimensional iterative circuit; (b) two-dimensional iterative circuit.

3-4 Structuring a problem solution (a) What binary number can be added to a digit expressed in 8421 BCD code in order to convert it to XS-3 BCD code?

(b) What binary number can be added to a digit expressed in XS-3 BCD code in order to convert it to 8421 BCD code (neglecting any fifth bit generated in the addition)?

(c) Using the 4-bit binary adder shown in Fig. P 3-4 (assumed to be available as an MSI circuit), if $I = 0$, then convert $a_8 a_4 a_2 a_1$ expressed in 8421 BCD code to $b_8 b_4 b_2 b_1$ expressed in XS-3 BCD code. If $I = 1$, then convert XS-3 BCD to 8421 BCD. Your job is to express the inputs $(c_8, c_4, c_2,$ and $c_1)$ as functions of I so as to accomplish this.

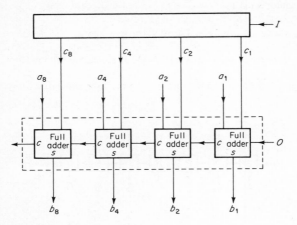

Fig. P 3-4

3-5 Structuring a problem solution Given a 10-bit number expressed in sign plus binary magnitude code, show an iterative structure for converting it to a sign plus two's complement number. Define the iterative block.

3-6 Structuring a problem solution We are given four 3-bit binary numbers $A = a_4 a_2 a_1$, $B = b_4 b_2 b_1$, $C = c_4 c_2 c_1$, and $D = d_4 d_2 d_1$. We wish to design a circuit which will sort these four numbers as shown so that

$W = $ largest of (A, B, C, D)
$X = $ next largest of (A, B, C, D)
$Y = $ next largest of (A, B, C, D)
$Z = $ smallest of (A, B, C, D)

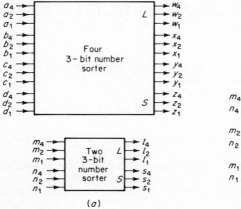

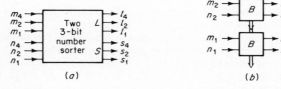

(a)

(b)

Fig. P 3-6

(a) If you had some of the number-sorters shown in Fig. P 3-6a for two 3-bit binary numbers, could you combine them to sort the four numbers above? If so, show the connection. If not, how would you break this big problem down into smaller problems?

(b) Can the *two 3-bit number-sorter* be broken down to an interconnection of smaller circuits which sort the numbers bit by bit iteratively as shown in Fig. P 3-6b? If so, then define states and show the flow diagram for the iterative block. If not, then explain how you might break the problem down.

3-7 Karnaugh maps Construct Karnaugh maps for the two outputs of a full adder.

3-8 Karnaugh maps Why is a Karnaugh map labeled as shown in Fig. P 3-8a rather than as in Fig. P 3-8b? Does it really make any difference? Explain.

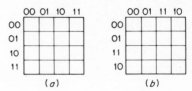

Fig. P 3-8 (a) (b)

3-9 Karnaugh maps (a) In the five-variable Karnaugh map shown in Fig. P 3-9, can you recognize all two-square implicants (such as $\overline{A}BDE$)?

(b) Can you recognize all four-square implicants (which can be thought of simply as two 2-square implicants adjacent to each other)?

(c) Can you recognize all eight-square implicants?

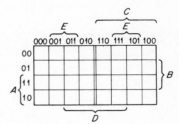

Fig. P 3-9

3-10 Simplest sum of products Find a simplest sum-of-products expression for each function shown in Fig. P 3-10.

3-11 Don't care conditions Two three-valued functions are represented by

$$A = a_2 a_1 = 00, 01, \text{ or } 10$$
$$B = b_2 b_1 = 00, 01, \text{ or } 10$$

Construct a Karnaugh map in the form shown in Fig. P 3-11 for a function F which equals one whenever the binary number A is equal to or greater than the binary number B and is zero otherwise.

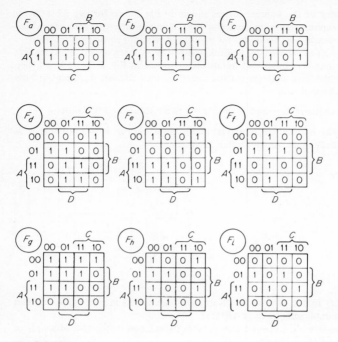

Fig. P 3-10

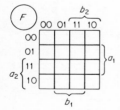

Fig. P 3-11

3-12 Don't care conditions Using a Karnaugh map of the form shown in Prob. 3-11, define a function F which will compare two 2-bit binary numbers (00, 01, 10, 11) and which will equal 1 if and only if $A \geqslant B$. By the nature of the application $|A - B| \leqslant 1$.

3-13 Don't care conditions Find a simplest sum-of-products expression for each function shown in Fig. P 3-13.

3-14 Don't care conditions Find a simplest sum-of-products expression for the complement of each function in Fig. P 3-13.

3-15 Algebraic factoring Compare the number of gate leads involved in implementing each of the following functions directly, and after carrying out algebraic factoring, using AND and OR gates.

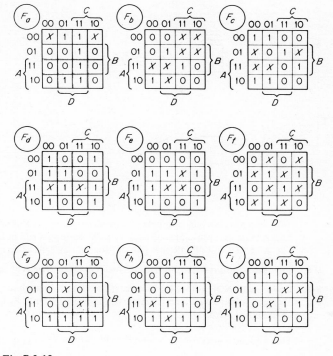

Fig. P 3-13

(a)	$F_a = AB + AC = A(B + C)$
(b)	$F_b = AB + AC + BD = A(B + C) + BD$
(c)	$F_c = AB + AC + AD = A(B + C + D)$
(d)	$F_d = AB + AC + AD + E = A(B + C + D) + E$
(e)	$F_e = ABC + ADE = A(BC + DE)$
(f)	$F_f = ABC + ADE + F = A(BC + DE) + F$
(g)	$F_g = ABC + ADE + AFG = A(BC + DE + FG)$

3-16 Relationships between circuits If AND gates and inverters are connected as shown in Fig. P 3-16, will the voltage represented by F_x equal the voltage represented by F_y for all combinations of A and B? Justify your answer in some way.

3-17 Graphical representations of a logic circuit Can a logic circuit with the following voltage truth table

A	B	F
L	L	L
L	H	L
H	L	H
H	H	L

be symbolized as

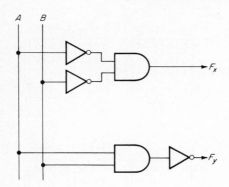

Fig. P 3-16

(a) An AND gate plus appropriate inversions on inputs and outputs?
(b) An OR gate plus appropriate inversions on inputs and outputs?
(c) An EXCLUSIVE-OR gate plus appropriate inversions on inputs and outputs?

If so, show the appropriate symbol, using small circles to represent inversions.

3-18 Design with NOR gates   (a) Construct the eight Karnaugh maps (W, X, Y, Z, $\overline{W}$, $\overline{X}$, $\overline{Y}$, and $\overline{Z}$) for a combinational circuit which will convert an 8421 BCD code digit $ABCD$ to its nine's complement $WXYZ$:

$$(WXYZ)_{8421\ BCD} = \text{Nine's complement of } (ABCD)_{8421\ BCD}$$

(b) Implement this circuit with NOR gates (which do not have dot-AND/OR capability). Assume all inputs are available in both asserted and negated form. Minimize the total number of gate leads.

3-19 Design with NAND gates Simplify the circuit shown in Fig. P 3-19 as much as possible using NAND gates (which do not have dot-AND/OR capability). Minimize gate leads. Assume the following input combinations will never occur:

$$(A, B, C, D) = (0, 0, 0, 1) \text{ and } (1, 1, 1, 1)$$

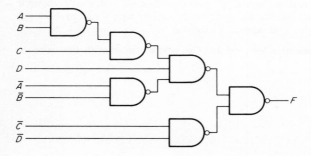

Fig. P 3-19

3-20 Design with NAND gates Assuming all inputs are available in both asserted and negated form, implement each function shown in Fig. P 3-20 as simply as possible using NAND gates (which do not have dot-AND/OR capability). Minimize gate leads.

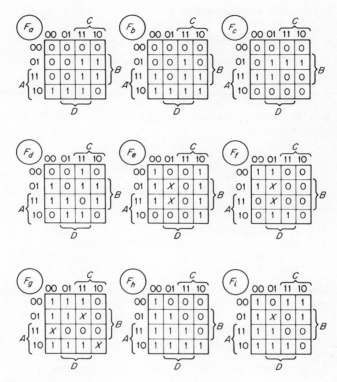

Fig. P 3-20

3-21 Design with NOR gates Repeat Prob. 3-20 using NOR gates (which do not have dot-AND/OR capability).

3-22 Dot-AND/ORing Minimizing gate leads, assuming inputs are available in asserted form only, and doing everything possible to minimize cost, implement

$$F = A(B + CD)$$

using

     (a)   NAND gates not having dot-AND/OR capability
     (b)   NAND gates having dot-AND/OR capability
     (c)   NOR gates not having dot-AND/OR capability
     (d)   NOR gates having dot-AND/OR capability

3-23 Dot-AND/ORing   Given two 2-bit binary numbers

$$A = a_2 a_1 \quad \text{and} \quad B = b_2 b_1$$

Implement as simply as possible the function F such that

$$F = 1 \quad \text{if and only if } A \geqslant 2B$$

Use NAND gates having dot-AND/OR capability. Assume inputs are available in both asserted and negated form.

3-24 Dot-AND/ORing   Repeat Prob. 3-20 using NAND gates having dot-AND/OR capability.

3-25 Multiple-output circuit   Use of Karnaugh maps to obtain simplest sum-of-products expressions has yielded

$$F_1 = B\bar{C}D + A\bar{B}C + ABD \qquad F_2 = A\bar{D} + A\bar{B}$$
$$\bar{F}_1 = \bar{B}C + B\bar{D} + \bar{A}C \qquad \bar{F}_2 = \bar{A} + ABD$$

Assuming inputs are available in both asserted and negated form and minimizing gate leads, implement F_1 and F_2 using

    (a)   NAND gates not having dot-AND/OR capability
    (b)   NAND gates having dot-AND/OR capability
    (c)   NOR gates not having dot-AND/OR capability
    (d)   NOR gates having dot-AND/OR capability

3-26 Multiple-output circuit   Do everything you can to minimize the total number of gate leads while implementing F_1 and F_2 shown in Fig. P 3-26 using NAND gates

    (a)   Without dot-AND/OR capability
    (b)   With dot-AND/OR capability

Assume all inputs are available in both asserted and negated form.

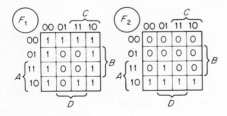

Fig. P 3-26

3-27 EXCLUSIVE-OR and MAJORITY functions   Express F_a and F_b shown in Fig. P 3-27 either as an EXCLUSIVE-OR function or as a three-input MAJORITY function.

3-28 Full subtractor and circuit equivalences   (a) By using the analogy to decimal subtraction, considering examples, and making a truth table, define the *full subtractor* shown in Fig. P 3-28a, four of which are used for subtracting one binary number ($s_8 s_4 s_2 s_1$) from another ($m_8 m_4 m_2 m_1$). Assume the minuend is equal to or greater than the subtrahend.

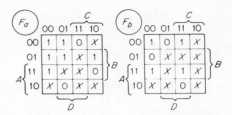

Fig. P 3-27

(b) Compare the result with the truth table for a full adder in Fig. 3-5. Can a full subtractor be constructed by putting inverters in on some of the inputs and outputs of a full adder and defining these derived inputs and outputs appropriately? Explain.

(c) If inverters are put on *all* inputs and outputs of a full adder, is the resulting circuit a full adder, as shown in Fig. P 3-28b?

(d) Answer part (c) for a full subtractor.

(e) Given a full adder, show all the ways it can be represented as a full adder or a full subtractor with assorted inputs and outputs inverted.

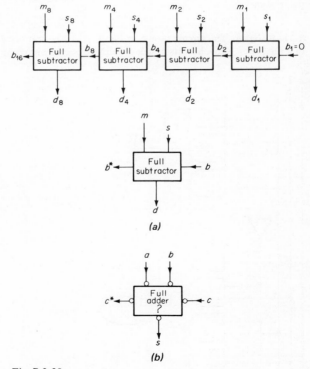

(a)

(b)

Fig. P 3-28

3-29 EXCLUSIVE-OR and MAJORITY functions Consider the Karnaugh maps for the outputs of a

(*a*)   Full adder
(*b*)   Full subtractor

By comparing with Figs. 3-41 and 3-42, can you express these outputs as EXCLUSIVE-OR or MAJORITY functions? If so, do so.

3-30 Bridging Use bridging to implement each function shown in Fig. P 3-30 with an EXCLUSIVE-OR gate or a MAJORITY gate plus NAND gates (not having dot-AND/OR capability). Assume all inputs are available in both asserted and negated form. Minimize gate leads for each function.

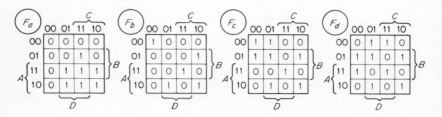

Fig. P 3-30

3-31 Bridging The circuit shown in Fig. P 3-31 has been used as an MSI implementation of a full adder. Show how its design could have been achieved by bridging.

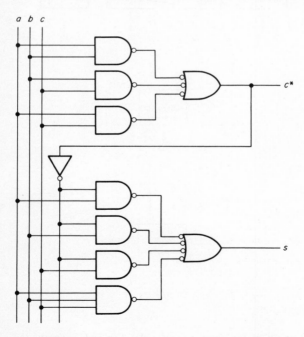

Fig. P 3-31

3-32 Symmetric function (*a*) Show an interconnection of full adders which will count the number of 1s among 15 Boolean variables and which will emit a 4-bit binary number $b_8 b_4 b_2 b_1$ equal to this number.

(*b*) Using the circuit in (*a*) plus NAND gates which do not have dot-AND/OR capability, obtain minimum-cost implementations of each of the following functions:

F_1 = 15-input MAJORITY function
$F_2 = S_{(7,11)} \{x_1, \ldots, x_{15}\}$
$F_3 = S_{(0,4,8,12)} \{x_1, \ldots, x_{15}\}$

3-33 Designing with a data selector Implement each of the functions shown in Fig. P 3-33 with a one-out-of-four data selector. Is there any way to avoid using an inverter?

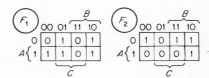

Fig. P 3-33

3-34 Designing with a data selector Implement each of the functions shown in Fig. P 3-34 with a one-out-of-eight data selector.

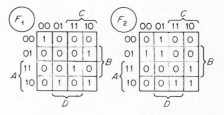

Fig. P 3-34

3-35 Loading rules A series 54/74 TTL gate has the specs shown in Fig. P 3-35*a*. A 930 series DTL gate with a 2-kΩ load resistor has the specs shown in Fig. P 3-35*b*. If the guaranteed voltage levels of Sec. 3-15 and 3-16 are to be maintained, then how many

(*a*)   TTL gate inputs will a TTL gate drive?
(*b*)   DTL gate inputs will a DTL gate drive?
(*c*)   TTL gate inputs will a DTL gate drive?
(*d*)   DTL gate inputs will a TTL gate drive?

In each part, show a circuit corresponding to the limiting case.

3-36 Levels of gating Compare the number of levels of gating in a 10-bit binary adder made with

(*a*)   The full adders of Prob. 3-2
(*b*)   The full adders of Prob. 3-31

In each case, show the input conditions and the signal path which leads to the worst-case propagation delay.

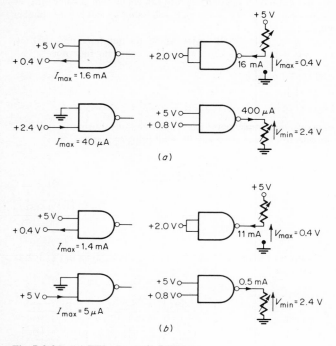

Fig. P 3-35 (*a*) TTL specs; (*b*) DTL specs.

REFERENCES

The subject of combinational circuits and their simplification is discussed in many books on switching circuits and switching theory. For example, several useful additions to the topics developed here are discussed in R. E. Miller, "Switching Theory," vol. 1, "Combinational Circuits," pp. 102–115 (symmetric and threshold functions), pp. 117–125 (functional decomposition), pp. 184–188 (Quine-McCluskey method), chap. 4 (multiple-output circuits), Wiley, New York, 1965.

The use of Karnaugh maps for more than four variables is described in M. P. Marcus, "Switching Circuits for Engineers," pp. 106–109, Prentice-Hall, Englewood Cliffs, N.J., 1962, 1967.

Characteristics of specific logic types, the description of available MSI circuits, and a wealth of application ideas are available in the integrated-circuits catalogs and application notes of leading integrated-circuit manufacturers, such as Texas Instruments, Motorola, and Fairchild.

4
Memory Devices

Up to this point, our concern has been solely with combinational circuits, that is, with circuits whose outputs are Boolean functions of the circuit inputs. This study has provided us with the power to specify and design a circuit which will carry out an arbitrary manipulation on data if these data are all available at the same time. In fact, given any problem in which all input data are available, *any* function of these data can be obtained using only combinational gating. That this is not often done can be attributed to the cost effectiveness and to the versatility of carrying out operations sequentially. For example, to sum together six 10-bit binary numbers, the circuitry could take the form of six 10-bit combinational adders (each consisting of 10 full adders). Each 10-bit adder feeds into the input of the next to form a two-dimensional array of 60 full adders (assuming the sum can be expressed as a 10-bit number). On the other hand, if the six numbers can be inserted into the circuit one after another, if intermediate results can be stored, and if each addition is carried out bit by bit, then only one full adder is needed.

In this section, we shall define the other main building block of digital systems—the *flipflop*. What is a flipflop? A wall switch is an example of a mechanical flipflop because it satisfies the two properties:

1. It must be able to reside in either of two distinct states without external influences holding it there.
2. It must have one or more inputs which can force it to either of these two states.

Flipflops serve a variety of functions in a digital system. They store data; for example, the intermediate results in the addition problem described above. They cause information to appear in sequence, as desired for entering the six numbers, bit by bit, in that same problem. Flipflops can also make a digital circuit do one thing with its inputs at one time and quite another thing at another time. That is, the circuit outputs may be a function not only of its inputs but also of the states of some flipflops in the circuit. An extreme example of this is a binary counter in which the outputs change each time a pulse occurs on a single input.

These three functions—storing data, sequencing data, and altering circuit behavior on the basis of flipflop states—represent the three common uses of flipflops. However, to take advantage of the versatile flipflop, we need one other device—a *clock*. Whereas a digital system will generally consist of many gates and many flipflops, it usually will have only a single clock.

4-2   THE FUNCTION OF A CLOCK

In its most rudimentary form, a *clock* is just a circuit which serves as a single source of pulses. It may be an oscillator which emits a string of pulses or a square wave such as the unijunction relaxation oscillator of Fig. 4-1*a* (if the frequency is not critical) or the crystal oscillator of Fig. 4-1*b* (for tighter frequency tolerance). On the other hand, it may be the amplified and squared-up output of the timing track of a magnetic disc memory selected as the system clock so that all of the remaining information in the disc memory will be synchronized to the clock in spite of any variation in the speed of the disc. Perhaps the system clock is derived from the 60-Hz ac power line, as in Fig. 4-1*c*, so as to yield a relatively slow but stable frequency. Whatever the source, the clock serves as the heart of a system, synchronizing the operation of every flipflop to its steady train of pulses.

One way of viewing a digital system is shown in Fig. 4-2. Between clock pulses the flipflops are unchanging, and the outputs are functions of the inputs together with the flipflop states. In addition to generating outputs, the circuit also generates new inputs to control the flipflops. However, the flipflops all wait to change, if the inputs say to change, until a signal arrives from the clock. This

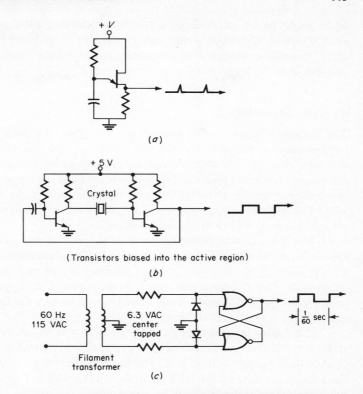

Fig. 4-1   Some clock circuits. (*a*) Unijunction relaxation oscillator; (*b*) crystal oscillator; (*c*) clock derived from the ac power line.

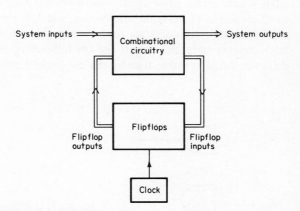

Fig. 4-2   General view of any digital system.

signal might be the negative-going transition occurring once per period of the clock's output. Thus the system can be thought of as being marched by the clock through a sequence of combinational problems. Each combinational problem lasts for the duration of one clock period.

4-3 THE LATCH CIRCUIT

The simplest flipflop circuit consists of two gates tied back to back in the configuration of Fig. 4-3. The two inputs are denoted as *direct inputs* because they are sensitive only to the direct, or dc, level of the voltage there. For this *NAND gate latch*, the preset and clear inputs are normally equal to 1. Because of the inversion on the INVERT-OR gate representation, these 1 inputs do not affect the latch. Consequently, it will remain in either of two stable states: the *set* state (when $Q = 1$) or the *cleared* state (when $Q = 0$).

This latch can be preset by making the preset input go to 0, which will force the output of the upper gate to go to 1. Then, assuming the clear input is 1, as it normally is, the lower gate will have two inputs of 1, causing its output to go to 0. This 0 output will remain at the input of the upper gate after the preset input goes to 1 again. Consequently, even though the latch is no longer being preset, it remains in the set state.

If the clear input should go to 0, the latch will be forced into the cleared state. If the latch is simultaneously preset and cleared by making preset = clear = 0, then both outputs will go to 1. The last input to return to 1 will determine the subsequent state of the latch. If both inputs return to 1 simultaneously, the subsequent state of the latch will be ambiguous.

This latch circuit (or its NOR-gate equivalent) is important in its own right and also because more complicated flipflops are constructed around it. It has one further property of value in its operation. A careful stability study of the latch would reveal three conditions of equilibrium; the two stable states and a third condition of unstable equilibrium, which is passed through as the latch is set or cleared from one state to the other. As a consequence of this, when the latch changes state, the output rise (or fall) time is limited only by the inherent delays in the gates rather than by the rise (or fall) time of the direct input.

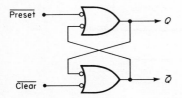

Fig. 4-3 Latch circuit.

4-4   FLIPFLOP STRUCTURES AND THE RACE PROBLEM

The representation of an arbitrary digital system in Fig. 4-2 highlights a problem which must be solved in one way or another. For successful operation we assumed that upon reception of a signal from the clock (perhaps its negative-going transition) all flipflops that are supposed to change state do so simultaneously. If this occurs, then the inputs which determine whether or not a flipflop will change state can be functions of any of the other flipflops in the system. However, if all of the flipflops do not change state simultaneously, then a late-changing flipflop may respond to the changed state of an earlier-changing flipflop rather than to its previous state. When flipflops are assumed to change state simultaneously but for one reason or another do not, we speak of a potential *race* condition being present, which may give rise to ambiguous performance.

This race problem is avoided in different ways with different lines of logic. Each way employs a *clock input* to control the time at which the flipflop will change state. This clock input has associated with it a *set* and a *clear* input, which control *what* the flipflop will do *when* the clock input occurs. In contrast to the direct preset and clear inputs of the last section, these set and clear inputs require the clock input in order to affect the flipflop. The name *ac input* will be used to denote this clock input, together with its associated set and clear inputs.

Some high-speed general-purpose digital computers use latches plus *gated clock pulses* for flipflops in order to keep the complexity and hence the delay between input and output as slight as possible. Figure 4-4a illustrates this approach. The set and clear inputs, which gate the clock pulse, are generally derived by gating from the outputs of other flipflops. Since the latch tries to follow the set and clear inputs during the time that the clock input equals 1, this clock pulsewidth must be extremely short. Otherwise, as the flipflops in a system change state, they will lead to *new* set and clear inputs. An excessively long clock pulse will cause the flipflops to respond not only to the initial set and clear inputs but also to these changed set and clear inputs. On the other hand, the clock pulse must be long enough for the latch to react to a narrow pulse on either of its inputs. Consequently, such a system imposes stringent requirements on the clock pulsewidth.

In contrast, Fig. 4-4b illustrates an approach used in many integrated-circuit flipflops and commonly referred to as a *master-slave flipflop*. It is developed here with NAND gates, but the circuit is identical, except for input and output labeling, with the corresponding NOR-gate implementation. Variants of this circuit are the common flipflop configuration used in most DTL and TTL integrated circuits. In this circuit, when the clock input equals 1, the set and clear inputs are permitted to set or clear the master latch but the slave latch is isolated from the master latch. Then as the clock input goes to 0, first the master latch is isolated from the set and clear inputs and then the slave latch is

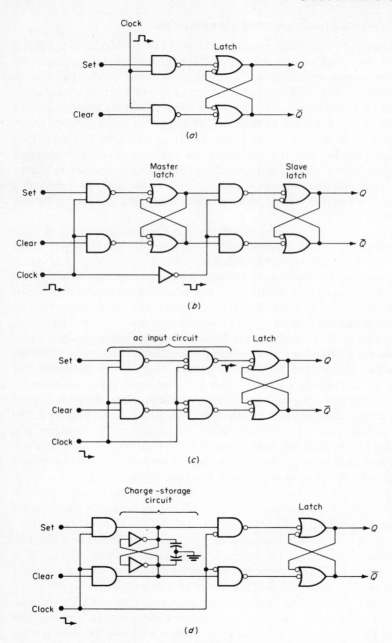

Fig. 4-4 Approaches to avoid the race problem. (*a*) Latch circuit + input gating + narrow clock pulse; (*b*) master-slave flipflop; (*c*) edge-triggered flipflop;
(*d*) charge-storage flipflop.

connected to the master latch. Note that externally this flipflop appears to be sensitive to the negative-going transition of the clock since it is during this transition that the output changes, if it changes at all. Note also that the master latch is opened to the set and clear inputs all the time the clock input equals 1 and not just during the negative-going transition of the clock.

A third approach toward resolving the race problem is exemplified by the *edge-triggered flipflop* circuit in Fig. 4-4c. A variation of this circuit is used in RTL integrated circuits. Note that the resistors and transistors in this flipflop are configured mostly but not entirely into NAND gates. The *ac input circuit* will take a 1 input on either the set or the clear input, together with a negative-going transition on the clock input, and will generate a narrow negative pulse into the latch. It does so by taking advantage of the inherent delay, measured in nanoseconds, between a change in the clock signal entering the gates on the far left and the resulting change on the output of either of these gates. This slight delay is enough to make both inputs to one of the INVERT-NAND gates go negative momentarily following the negative-going transition of the clock.

Another version of the edge-triggered flipflop is the *charge-storage flipflop* of Fig. 4-4d. The charge-storage circuit causes the outputs of the gates on the far left to remain unchanged somewhat longer than the gate propagation delay alone would do. Variations of this circuit are used in some TTL integrated circuits.

As we shall find in the next chapter, the use of edge-triggered flipflops offers some advantage over master-slave flipflops for designing systems which must be clocked at a high rate. The changes which occur in the signals throughout a system are initiated by each clock transition. As shown in Fig. 4-5a, these changes must all settle out by the time the clock signal again goes high if the system is designed around master-slave flipflops. A longer settling

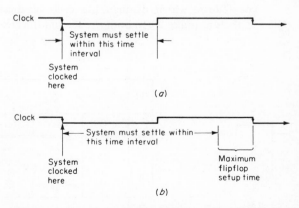

Fig. 4-5 Effect on system use of different flipflops. (*a*) Settling time restrictions on master-slave flipflops; (*b*) settling time restrictions on edge-triggered flipflops.

time is permitted if edge-triggered flipflops are used, as shown in Fig. 4-5b. Here it is only necessary for the system changes to settle out enough before the next clock transition to allow the flipflops to "setup" to their new input conditions.

In this section and in the next, we are concentrating attention upon the ac input to a flipflop. Often a flipflop will have both an ac input and the direct preset and clear inputs discussed in the previous section. The design of circuitry which utilizes both of these will be treated in the next chapter.

4-5 TYPES OF FLIPFLOPS

In the previous section we typed flipflops according to the way in which they deal with the race problem. In this section, we shall type flipflops according to the manner in which they respond to set, clear, or other ac inputs when the clock pulse (or clock transition) occurs. The symbol for a flipflop having a set and a clear input in addition to the clock input is illustrated in Fig. 4-6a. The small circle on the clock input indicates that the flipflop changes state as the clock goes to 0 rather than when it goes to 1. In Fig. 4-6b, the subscripts n and n + 1 associated with input and output variables refer to the value of the variables before and after the 1 to 0 clock transition occurs. Thus for the *RS flipflop*, if the set and clear inputs both equal 0 during the nth clock period, then the output Q_{n+1} during the n + 1th clock period will be equal to the output Q_n during the nth clock period; that is, the output will not change between the nth and the n + 1th clock periods. If, on the other hand, the set input equals 1 and the clear input equals 0 during the nth clock period, then the flipflop will be set; that is, the output Q_{n+1} during the n + 1th clock period will be 1. If during the nth clock period the clear input equals 1 while the set input equals 0, then the flipflop will be cleared, yielding $Q_{n+1} = 0$.

The feature which distinguishes each of these flipflop types from the others is their response when both the set and the clear inputs equal 1 and a 1 to

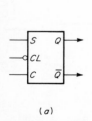

Flipflop type →		RS	JK	Set overrides clear	Clear overrides set
S_n	C_n	Q_{n+1}	Q_{n+1}	Q_{n+1}	Q_{n+1}
0	0	Q_n	Q_n	Q_n	Q_n
0	1	0	0	0	0
1	0	1	1	1	1
1	1	Ambiguous	$\overline{Q}_n$	1	0

(*a*)   (*b*)

Fig. 4-6 Four flipflop types employing set-clear inputs. (*a*) Flipflop symbolism; (*b*) truth tables for four types of flipflops.

0 transition occurs on the clock input. An *RS* flipflop will respond ambiguously, requiring the digital designer to prevent this condition from ever occurring. Referring back to Fig. 4-4 and considering the operation of each of the flipflop configurations when the set and clear inputs equal 1 simultaneously, we recognize that all four are *RS* flipflops.

In contrast to the operation of an *RS* flipflop, a *JK flipflop* will change state, or *toggle*, when both the set and clear inputs equal 1 and the clock transition occurs. This is indicated by the equation

$$Q_{n+1} = \overline{Q}_n$$

A *set-overrides-clear flipflop* will set when both set and clear inputs equal 1, whereas the *clear-overrides-set flipflop* will clear. Notice that a set-overrides-clear flipflop can be turned into a clear-overrides-set flipflop simply by redefining inputs and outputs. Another type of flipflop in common use is the *1-bit shift register* already discussed in Chap. 2. This is also often called a *delay flipflop* because the output during the $n + 1$th clock period is identical to the input during the nth clock period. It is shown and defined in Fig. 4-7a.

We shall also find it convenient to define the *switched-input delay flipflop*, shown in Fig. 4-7b. This is defined with the equivalence shown in terms of the standard delay flipflop and the serial switch (a combinational circuit defined in Sec. 2-10). It can be implemented in the same way; however, we shall find it sufficiently useful to warrant its construction as a standard integrated circuit. (A standard delay flipflop with direct preset and clear inputs is often used to serve this same function, but it requires special timing signals and gating to do so.)

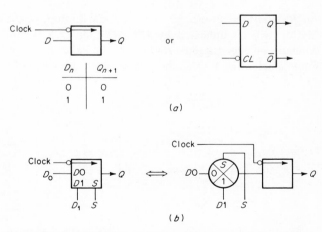

Fig. 4-7 Delay flipflops. (*a*) Standard delay flipflop; (*b*) switched-input delay flipflop.

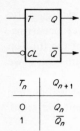

T_n	Q_{n+1}
0	Q_n
1	$\bar{Q}_n$

Fig. 4-8   Toggle flipflop.

One final flipflop type, shown in Fig. 4-8, is the *toggle flipflop*. It changes state if the toggle input equals 1 when the clock 1 to 0 transition occurs; otherwise, the state remains unchanged.

4-6 ACTUAL FLIPFLOPS AND THEIR GRAPHIC REPRESENTATION

As was mentioned previously, a flipflop will often include direct inputs as well as the ac input, as shown in Fig. 4-9*a*. The small circles on the direct preset and direct clear inputs indicate that the flipflop will be preset, or cleared, when one of these inputs equals 0. Conversely, the flipflop is unaffected when the direct preset and clear inputs equal 1. The direct preset input is distinguished from the direct clear input in the symbol by its adjacency to the ac set input.

Characteristics which we shall *imply* with this symbology are that

1. The flipflop is a *JK* flipflop.
2. It has the master-slave configuration.

An *RS* flipflop, set-overrides-clear (*SOC*) flipflop, or clear-overrides-set (*COS*) flipflop will be indicated by *RS, SOC,* or *COS* within the flipflop symbol. Similarly, an edge-triggered flipflop will be indicated by (*E-T*) within the symbol. For example, Fig. 4-9*b* symbolizes an edge-triggered *RS* flipflop.

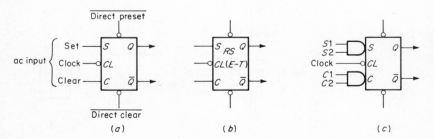

Fig. 4-9   Representation of some actual flipflops. (*a*) Master-slave-configured *JK* flipflop; (*b*) edge-triggered *RS* flipflop; (*c*) flipflop with ANDed set and clear inputs.

Often a flipflop has several ac set (or clear) inputs which must all equal 1 for the flipflop to set (or clear). These are indicated symbolically in Fig. 4-9c.

4-7 LONG SHIFT REGISTERS

Because of its natural application to the serially organized systems to be discussed in Chap. 6 and because of the inherent simplicity of its input-output structure, the *long shift register* has been implemented in several ways, employing a variety of technologies. By a long shift register, we mean a shift register with anywhere from 100 to 100,000 bits and having the configuration shown in Fig. 4-10, with a single logic input (IN), a single output (OUT), and a clock input.

One approach to the implementation of a long shift register has been as an LSI[†] device. The use of MOS (metal oxide semiconductor) technology is particularly promising in this application. A typical unit is illustrated in Fig. 4-11. By using microscopic interconnections and circuits which are optimized for small size, many bits can be built into one device. Some of the devices built this way are *dynamic* shift registers, which means that the clock rate must be maintained continuously and at a frequency above some minimum (for example, 1 kHz) or errors will occur in the bits stored. We will find that for serially organized processes or systems this is not a handicap.

Because of its low cost and high reliability, the traditional way to implement the long shift register has been with the combination of a wire[‡] or glass delay line plus input-output circuitry. This I/O circuitry, manufactured and packaged with the delay line, makes the combination look identical to a *clocked* long shift register, that is, a long shift register in which the frequency of the shift input must be precisely controlled or errors in the data will arise. For example, a 10,000-bit clocked shift register having a 1-MHz clock rate might require a tolerance on this 1-MHz rate of something like 20 parts per million over the temperature range of interest. A small, low-cost, commercially available crystal oscillator, such as that shown in Fig. 4-12, will have a frequency tolerance of 10 parts per million over a 0 to 50°C temperature range and a square-wave output

†Large-scale integration.
‡Also called a *magnetostrictive delay line*.

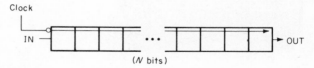

Fig. 4-10 Long shift register.

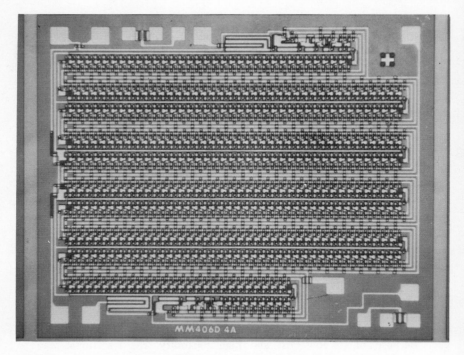

Fig. 4-11   Dual 100-bit dynamic shift register. (*National Semiconductor Corp.*)

and may be powered by the same 5-V supply needed for TTL or DTL logic. With this clock-rate-tolerance requirement satisfied, the delay line plus I/O circuitry will provide a highly reliable long shift register.

A long shift register implemented with a wire delay line plus I/O circuitry, as shown in Fig. 4-13, can be manufactured having any number of bits between 500 and 20,000. Since the manufacturer determines the exact number of bits simply by snipping a wire, the cost is independent of this exact number of bits.

Fig. 4-12   Temperature-compensated crystal oscillator. (*Motorola Communications and Electronics Inc.*)

Fig. 4-13 Wire delay line plus I/O circuitry with cover removed. (*Andersen Laboratories, Inc.*)

The clock rate must also be specified and must be between approximately 0.5 to 2.0 MHz. Again, the exact rate is easily met regardless of its value in this range since the manufacturer of a crystal oscillator, like that in Fig. 4-12, is set up to trim the frequency anyway.

When implemented with a glass delay line plus I/O circuitry, as shown in Fig. 4-14, the clocked long shift register has similar characteristics, except that the number of bits obtainable is approximately 500 to 4,000 and the clock rate is between 5 and 50 MHz. The constraint of a fixed clock rate is no handicap in many systems applications and can be designed around in others. For example, in one of the problems at the end of the chapter, we shall see how to design circuitry which will allow the clock period to be any integral multiple of that required by the delay line plus its I/O circuitry. The result will be a long shift register which, to the system designer, looks as if it can be clocked at almost any arbitrary clock rate.

One characteristic of the implementations of long shift registers which we have discussed and which has a bearing on their applications is the *volatility* of their data storage. If power is momentarily lost and then restored, the data in the shift register are lost. For many applications, particularly real-time applications, this volatility is of little importance providing the data in the long

Fig. 4-14 Glass delay line plus I/O circuitry. (*Corning Electronics*)

shift register are updated fairly often. With the resumption of power, the system is simply reinitialized. For other applications, the development of a magnetic LSI technology holds the promise of providing long, nonvolatile shift registers.

4-8 MAGNETIC DISC AND DRUM MEMORIES

Two devices which provide nonvolatile storage for anywhere from 50,000 to 50,000,000 bits of data (on a single disc or drum) are magnetic discs and magnetic drums plus their I/O circuitry. These two devices are very similar in both operation and performance characteristics. Because of this similarity and because of the trend away from drums and toward discs, we shall discuss magnetic disc memories with the understanding that the discussion also applies to magnetic drum memories.

The disc of a magnetic disc memory constantly rotates beneath a group of *recording heads*, each head defining one *track* on the disc. Since the heads fly on an air cushion approximately 0.0001 in. above the disc, each track can be used to store somewhere between 300 to 1,000 bits/in. along the track. Consequently, storage capability is a function of the diameter of the disc and the number of tracks used.

The cost of the disc memory, including the I/O circuitry, depends also on how the I/O circuitry is configured. For example, Fig. 4-15 illustrates a disc memory which is produced with 16, 32, 64, or 128 tracks, depending on the required storage capacity. However, the cost of this memory is kept down by providing I/O access to only 1 bit at a time. Internally this permits the use of only one *data write amplifier* and one *data read amplifier*, which are gated to or from the selected track.

Although cost is saved with this procedure, the rate at which data are read into or out of the disc memory is limited to the rate at which bits pass under one recording head. This, in turn, depends on how the data are structured (since the turning rate of the disc is fixed at 3,540 rpm). If a track is divided up into 16-bit data words (corresponding to the common word size of many small computers) and if the number of data words is made equal to a power of 2 (in order to

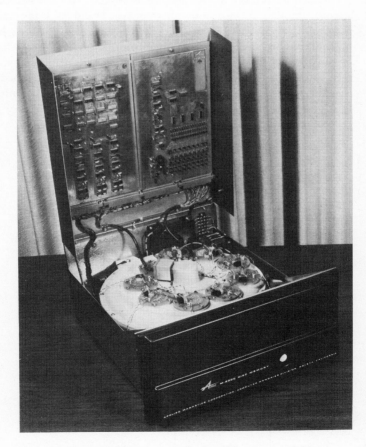

Fig. 4-15 Low-cost disc memory having I/O access to 1 bit at a time. (*Applied Magnetics Corp.*)

simplify drastically the addressing of data), then 1,024 words can be stored on one track. This leads to a data rate of about 1 million bits/s. If the disc memory configured in this way is interfaced to a small computer which accepts or puts out one 16-bit word at a time, this means that transfer of data will proceed at a 62,000 word/s rate. This may be perfectly satisfactory for many applications, but it is an order of magnitude or more below the maximum possible transfer rate of many small computers. To the user, this disc memory (with 64 tracks of data) might be represented more or less as shown in Fig. 4-16. The *bit clock* and the *origin clock* are timing signals derived from two extra tracks on the disc which are permanently stored for reading only. The *bit clock* provides a steady pulse-rate output and identifies the position of each new bit of data on each track of the disc. The *origin clock* is a pulse which occurs between two bit clock pulses, providing one pulse per revolution.

Each bit of data on the disc is addressed by its track address and by its bit address. Its *track address*, a number between 0 and 63, is selected by the binary number $T_{32} T_{16} T_8 T_4 T_2 T_1$. Within the selected track, the *bit address* is formed by counting bit clock periods starting from bit address zero, which is identified by the origin clock.

An anomaly of the disc memory occurs when changing the track address or changing between reading data out of the disc and writing data into the disc. Since

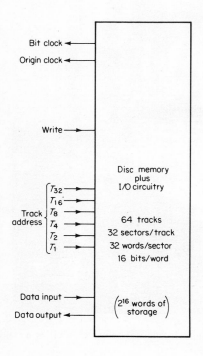

Fig. 4-16 Organization of disc memory.

these changes require several bit times, each track is divided up into *sectors* and the first bit positions in each sector are used not to store data but simply to provide time for these changes to be made. In using the disc memory, the track address and the write input are permitted to change only at the beginning of a sector. Thus, whereas the disc memory of Fig. 4-16 indicates that each sector stores thirty-two 16-bit words, it might actually take up 33 x 16 bits of the sector to allow for the response time to the track address and write input changes.

The constraints imposed upon the user by this anomaly are that writing into the disc must be done in multiples of 32 words. Furthermore, the smooth flow of data is broken every 32 words to allow for the one-word gap at the beginning of each sector. These constraints present an inconvenience, but not much more, to the user. In practice, each word on a track can be addressed using a *sector and word address counter* (see Prob. 5-27, at the end of Chap. 5). It is only necessary to avoid reading out of or writing into the first word of each sector. Each data word in the entire disc memory might be addressed with the 16-bit number

$$T_{32} T_{16} T_8 T_4 T_2 T_1 S_{16} S_8 S_4 S_2 S_1 W_{16} W_8 W_4 W_2 W_1$$

where T_i, S_j, and W_k indicate the physical location of each word. Another bit (W_d in Prob. 5-27) can be used to indicate the first word of each sector, which should be ignored. With this addressing scheme, the addresses appear in sequence as increasing binary numbers.

To *read* data out of the disc memory starting at the arbitrary address

0011010110000101

we must set

$$T_{32} T_{16} T_8 T_4 T_2 T_1 = 001101 \quad \text{and} \quad \text{write} = 0$$

and then wait for the sector and word address counter to reach 01100 00101. Then, as data is read out, each time the sector and word address counter rolls over from 11111 11111 to 00000 00000, we must increase the track address by 1. The bits of each word appear on the *data output* one after another, synchronized to the bit clock. (Since these bits change halfway between the bit-clock pulses, the data output can be looked at on either the leading or the trailing edge of the bit-clock pulse). This readout is *nondestructive*, which means that the data, in addition to being read out, are still stored on the disc and have not been disturbed.

To *write* data on to the disc, it is necessary to begin the write operation at the beginning of a complete sector. For example, if we wish to begin writing at address

010001 00011 00000

then we must set

$$T_{32} T_{16} T_8 T_4 T_2 T_1 = 010001$$

and wait for the sector and word address counter to reach 00011 00000, at which time the write input must be changed from "Write = 0" to

Write = 1

Now, whatever is on the *data input* will be stored on the disc bit by bit (except for the first 16 bits of each sector, which must be skipped over). When writing is completed, the write input must be changed back to 0 at the end of a sector. If power is ever lost on a disc memory and then restored, the origin clock will automatically resynchronize the sector and word address counter to the data locations on the disc (see Prob. 5-27).

For a specific application, it might be desired to speed up the transfer rate of data into and out of the disc memory by, say, a factor of 16. In this case the manufacturer must design the I/O circuitry so as to have 16 data input lines and 16 data output lines handling 16-bit words. Then, if there are 64 tracks of data on the disc, these will be grouped into four 16-bit words. Instead of addressing each of the 64 tracks, now the I/O circuitry addresses one of the four words.

4-9 MAGNETIC CORE MEMORIES

Magnetic core memories have several features which recommend them for many applications. As with a magnetic disc memory, the data storage is nonvolatile; that is, it is not lost if power is lost. But the dominating characteristic which distinguishes core memories from either long shift registers or disc memories is their *random-access* feature; any word of data can be accessed as fast as any other word. This feature is of overwhelming usefulness for the main memory of a computer and accounts for the virtually complete demise of magnetic drum memories in this application. Today, core memories are available not only as an integral part of a small or large computer system but also as free-standing units. These can either be built into a special-purpose digital system, organized to help implement some function peripheral to a general-purpose computer, or used simply as an adjunct to the memory of the computer. One of the exciting evolutions in core memories, from an applications point of view, has been the development of small core memories mounted entirely on one printed circuit board, as exemplified in Fig. 4-17. The unit shown is organized into one-thousand twenty-four 8-bit words for a total of 8,192 bits of data storage. The board includes everything but the power supplies needed to energize it. It

Fig. 4-17 1024 × 8 magnetic core memory. (*Sanders Associates, Inc.*)

can transfer 8-bit words of data into or out of storage at a rate of 660,000 words/s. Figure 4-18 illustrates a larger memory and its power supply. It is organized into 4,096 (4K) 24-bit words. It can transfer 24-bit words at a rate of 1 million words/s. Both of these memories include power-failure protection which insures that if and when power is lost, the I/O circuitry will not inadvertently change some of the stored data.

To a user, a magnetic core memory is a remarkably simple device. Although the I/O configuration and the timing requirements for inputs will vary somewhat from one manufacturer's core memory to another's, these differences are minor. The I/O configuration of Fig. 4-19 and the timing of these inputs and outputs, as shown in Fig. 4-20, apply in actuality to the core memory shown in Fig. 4-17. If the user of the core memory generates inputs having the timing shown, then the following characteristics will be realized:

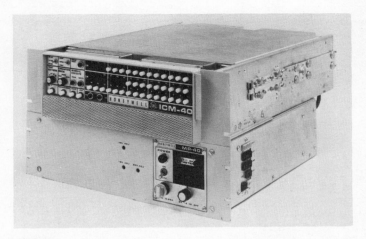

Fig. 4-18 $4K \times 24$ magnetic core memory. (*Honeywell, Inc., Computer Control Division.*)

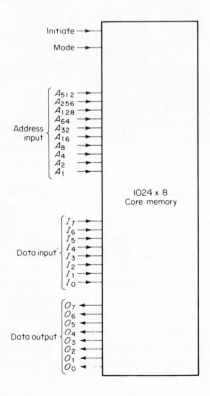

Fig. 4-19 I/O configuration of a core memory.

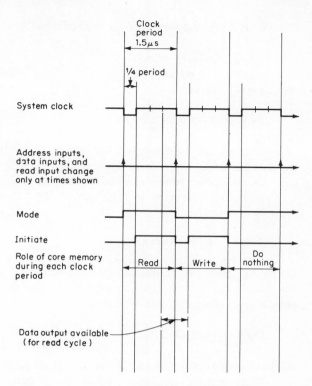

Fig. 4-20 Core memory timing diagram.

1. The system clock period of 1.5 μs permits one 8-bit word of data to be written into or read out of the core memory during each clock period.
2. Changes in the *address input, data input*, and *mode input* are assumed to be synchronized to the negative-going transitions of the system clock. (However, the core memory does not actually look at these until one-quarter of a cycle into the clock period.)
3. To read or to write, an *initiate* pulse can be generated by ANDing the system clock pulse with a *read or write* signal, which is also synchronized to the negative-going transitions of the clock.
4. When reading out of the core memory, the *data output* is available to the system by the end of the clock period.

Consequently, *the use of the core memory simplifies to the generation and use of signals and data which are all synchronized to the negative-going transitions of the clock.*

What must be done to *write* a word of data (binary number 13)

$$I_7 I_6 I_5 I_4 I_3 I_2 I_1 I_0 = 00001101$$

into memory address six

$$A_{512} \cdots A_1 = 0000000110$$

of the core memory? During one clock period, these numbers must be applied to the data input and the address input, while the mode input is made equal to 0 (to write rather than to read) and an initiate pulse is generated.

What must be done to *read* out of the core memory the contents of memory address five:

$$A_{512} \cdots A_1 = 0000000101$$

During one clock period, this address must be applied to the address input, while the mode input is made equal to 1 (to read rather than to write) and an initiate pulse is again generated. The 8-bit output

$$O_7 O_6 O_5 O_4 O_3 O_2 O_1 O_0$$

will be available before the end of the same clock period.

While reading out this 8-bit word of data, the core memory must momentarily erase the eight cores which stored this data. However, this information is automatically written back into these eight cores so that, to the user, it looks as though the data has not been disturbed. This feature is characteristic of virtually all magnetic core memories and accounts for the short *access* time (0.45 μs for the memory described here) between the beginning of the initiate pulse and when the data output is available. This access time plus the time required to restore the data back into the cores accounts for the longer *cycle* time of the core memory (1.5 μs for this memory).

4-10 SEMICONDUCTOR RANDOM-ACCESS MEMORIES

Using various LSI technologies, semiconductor memories are built having the same random-access characteristic as magnetic core memories. In fact, the I/O description of Fig. 4-19 and the timing description of Fig. 4-20 give a reasonable description of a semiconductor memory.

The specific LSI circuits which form the heart of such a semiconductor memory may differ slightly in one respect or another from this description. For example, one circuit has no read input. Instead, it constantly presents the addressed data on the data output. Another circuit requires an extra *strobe* pulse which begins slightly after the read or the write pulse begins and terminates slightly before the read or write pulse terminates. By building a semiconductor memory out of an array of these LSI circuits, together with some extra circuitry, a fair-sized memory can be obtained. In addition, any timing problems can be resolved internally so that the user is provided with an easily used memory.

The promise of semiconductor memories over magnetic core memories lies in their high speed, small size, and progressively decreasing cost. To counteract these advantages, the user of a semiconductor memory has the volatility of its data storage with which to contend.

4-11 READ-ONLY MEMORIES

Read-only memories (ROMs) are used in a variety of applications. Some computers and desk calculators take advantage of the exceptional speed capability of ROMs to *microprogram* special routines such as floating-point arithmetic and trigonometric functions. They are also used to provide low-cost, highly reliable means of storing the fixed program for a small computer dedicated to a specific task.

Another application of ROMs is to implement a set of arbitrary Boolean functions, as shown in Fig. 4-21. The n outputs $O_1, \ldots, O_n$ can be thought of as being Boolean functions of the m inputs $I_1, \ldots, I_m$. Looked at in this way, a read-only memory provides a means of implementing any combinational circuit. It provides a versatile technology whereby a semiconductor manufacturer can satisfy the requirements of a customer who wants an LSI combinational circuit built to meet his own needs. For example, a key item in a major product of a certain customer might be a two-dimensional iterative circuit having a fairly complex iterative block. This block can be implemented as a low-cost ROM and packaged in a standard integrated-circuit package, as shown in Fig. 4-22. The customer now can implement the iterative circuit entirely in space because the cost is no longer prohibitive and the added speed pays off in his application.

LSI circuits represent only one of several approaches which are being applied to ROM manufacture. Another technology utilizes wires routed either through or around ferrite cores to represent each one or zero. Each ferrite core provides inductive coupling between all input combinations and 1 bit of the output. This approach makes possible the production of ROMs having hundreds

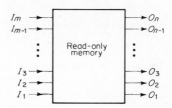

Fig. 4-21   ROM implementation of Boolean functions.

of thousands of bits of storage, which are manufactured with punched-card controlled, automatic wire-routing machines.

Fig. 4-22   An 8-bit input, 4-bit output ROM. (*Texas Instruments Inc.*)

PROBLEMS

4-1 Clocks Using a guide to products and manufacturers like *EEM* or *Electronics Buyers Guide*, determine reasonable ranges of values for

    (*a*)   The resonant frequency of a crystal oscillator
    (*b*)   The resonant frequency of a tuning fork oscillator

4-2 Latch circuit Using NOR gates, show an implementation of a latch circuit and label inputs and outputs. Is the latch sensitive to 1s or to 0s on the inputs?

4-3 Latch circuit Given two gates in the laboratory which are connected together as a latch circuit, how might you determine the conditions (i.e., voltages) corresponding to the state of unstable equilibrium referred to at the end of Sec. 4-3?

4-4 Flipflop structure If the clock input in Fig. 4-4*c* slowly changes from 1 to 0, perhaps with a fall time of 1 ms, will the flipflop change state? Must your answer be qualified in any way?

4-5 Flipflop structure Answer Prob. 4-4 for the circuit of Fig. 4-4*b*.

4-6 Flipflop structure Given an integrated-circuit flipflop in the lab, how might you go about experimentally determining whether it is a master-slave flipflop or an edge-triggered flipflop?

4-7 Flipflop types The numbers labeled on the flipflop shown in Fig. P 4-7 represent integrated-circuit lead numbers. With the small circles and the input labeling shown, this is a *JK* flipflop.

    (*a*) How many other ways can the flipflop leads be defined yielding a *JK* flipflop? Show them.

    (*b*) Is there any way to define so as to yield a set-overrides-clear flipflop? Illustrate or explain your answer.

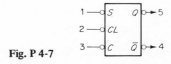

Fig. P 4-7

4-8 Flipflop types If Fig. P 4-7 represented a set-overrides-clear flipflop, as labeled, how might it be redefined to yield a clear-overrides-set flipflop? Show all possibilities.

4-9 Actual flipflops Show the modification necessary in the edge-triggered flipflop of Fig. 4-4*c* in order to provide direct preset and clear inputs. Label these inputs "Preset," "Preset," "Clear," or "Clear" as appropriate.

4-10 Actual flipflops Modify the flipflop of Fig. 4-4*b* in order to provide direct presetting and clearing capability. Is it necessary to go into both latches in order to insure the desired operation? (Consider presetting only the slave latch immediately followed by a clock pulse. Then consider presetting only the master latch and the state of the output if a clock pulse should be a long time in occurring.)

4-11 Actual flipflops Modify the circuitry of Fig. 4-4*c* in order to yield a *JK* flipflop. Note that this can be done by using three-input gates for the set and clear inputs, by putting a 0 into the *set* gate when the flipflop is already set and by putting a 0 into the *clear* gate when the flipflop is already cleared.

4-12 Actual flipflops Modify the circuitry of Fig. 4-4*b* in order to yield a *JK* flipflop.

4-13 Actual flipflops Modify the circuitry of Fig. 4-4*c* in order to yield a set-overrides-clear flipflop.

4-14 Actual flipflops· Modify the circuitry of Fig. 4-4*b* in order to yield a set-overrides-clear flipflop.

4-15 Actual flipflops By adding an inverter, modify the circuitry of Fig. 4-4*b* or *c* in order to yield a delay flipflop (that is, a 1-bit shift register with a single input *D*).

4-16 Clocked shift register In this problem we want to explore the circumstances under which a clocked shift register (clocked at a fixed frequency) can be made to look like a shift register clocked at a different frequency. The circuit shown in Fig. P 4-16 employs a serial switch (defined in Sec. 2-10), together with a 5-bit shift register. Assume that while the shift register is clocked with the C_0 waveform shown, the rest of the system is clocked with one

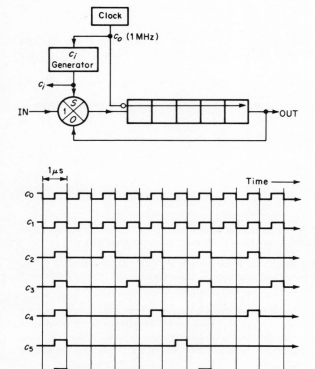

Fig. P 4-16

of the waveforms C_i (where $i = 1, 2, 3, 4, 5, 6$) shown so that this system only cares what the shift-register output OUT is at the moment just before C_i goes from 1 to 0.

(a) Using $C_i = C_1$, is it not true that $OUT_{k+5} = IN_k$ with an effective clock period of 1 μs?

(b) With $C_i = C_2$, does $OUT_{k+5} = IN_k$ with an effective clock period of 2 μs?

(c) Repeat for $C_i = C_3 ; C_4 ; C_5 ; C_6$.

4-17 Clocked shift register Repeat Prob. 4-16 using a 6-bit shift register. For some values of i, the circuit looks like a 6-bit shift register shifting at a slower clock rate. For other values of i, the circuit looks like a shift register having fewer than 6 bits.

(a) How are the values of i which lead to a 6-bit shift register related numerically to the number 6?

(b) Given an n-bit shift register and a derived clock rate C_m (defined as in Fig. P 4-16), how must n and m be related in order to obtain, in effect, an n-bit shift register clocked at a rate of $1/m$ MHz?

(c) Are there *any* values of n such that using an n-bit shift register, together with any C_m for $1 \leqslant m < n$, the result will be an n-bit shift register clocked at a rate of $1/m$ MHz? What characterizes such values of n?

4-18 Long shift registers A group of k m-bit shift registers can be made to look like a k x m-bit shift register simply by tying the output of each one to the input of the next. This serial connection offers the designer a way to achieve an arbitrarily long shift register. On the other hand, the *parallel* connection shown in Fig. P 4-18, although somewhat more complicated, permits slow and fast shift registers to be combined to obtain a long, fast shift register. The shift register on the right, $SR5$, is intended to illustrate a 4-bit shift register in which each bit is the switched-input delay flipflop described in conjunction with Fig. 4-7b of the text.

(a) Develop a timing diagram for C_0, C_{0A}, and C_{0B} so that $OUT_{n+24} = IN_n$ with an effective clock rate equal to that of C_0.

(b) If $SR1$, $SR2$, $SR3$, and $SR4$ possess a maximum clock rate of 1 MHz, then what should be the clock rate of $SR0$ and $SR5$ in order that $SR1, \ldots, SR4$ can be shifted at 1 MHz? What will be the effective clock rate of the resulting 24-bit shift register?

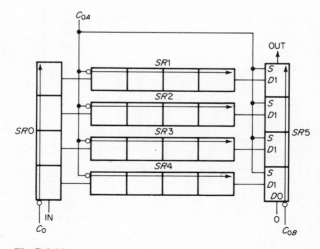

Fig. P 4-18

4-19 Magnetic disc memories The organization of the disc memory of Fig. 4-16 is convenient for use in conjunction with a small computer. Another organization might be more useful for this or other applications and is represented in Fig. P 4-19. On each track, every 16-bit data word is alternated with an 8-bit blank, providing a 24-bit sector length. For the same $32 \times 32 = 1,024$ data words per track, this requires more bits per track (24,576), but it still does not exceed the manufacturer's maximum (26,624).

With this organization, the system is clocked with equally spaced pulses C_{0A} (at a rate of 0.062 MHz). At each of these C_{0A} pulses, the system can decide whether it wants to write $I_{15} \cdots I_0$ into the disc or read $O_{15} \cdots O_0$ out of the disc during the next C_{0A} period. The words on each track are addressed by counting the 1,024 C_{0A} pulses per revolution.

(a) Develop a timing diagram for C_0, C_{0A}, C_{0B}, and S. Show C_0 as a narrow positive pulse and each C_{0A} and C_{0B} pulse as a narrow positive pulse aligned with a C_0 pulse. Should the 8-bit blank go at the beginning of each C_{0A} period, at the end, or doesn't it matter?

(b) We have assumed that since the system is clocked with C_{0A}, then both the write and the track address inputs will change only in synchronism with C_{0A}. Is this really necessary? Explain.

(c) If the output of the disc memory $O_{15} \cdots O_0$ is correct at the moment when the system is clocked with C_{0A}, does it matter to the system that it is shifted (with C_{0B}) during the 16 μs between C_{0A} pulses? Explain.

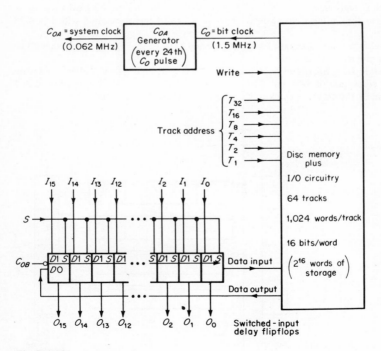

Fig. P 4-19

4-20 Magnetic core memories The core memory system shown and described in Figs. 4-17, 4-19, and 4-20 was discussed there assuming the system clock period would be set equal to the core memory cycle time of 1.5 μs. Figure P 4-20 gives the actual timing specifications for this core memory system. In this problem, assume the system clock period will be 2.0 μs. Divide the system clock period into as few equal intervals as are necessary to meet the following characteristics:

(*a*) Assume that changes in the address input, data input, and mode input are synchronized to the negative-going transitions of the system clock.

(*b*) The initiate pulse starts somewhat later in the clock period and changes only on the subdivisions of the clock period described above.

(*c*) The data output must be available sometime before the end of the clock period. Show a timing diagram, analogous to Fig. 4-20, which meets these requirements.

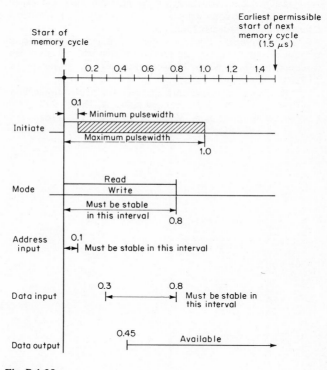

Fig. P 4-20

4-21 Magnetic core memories With the 1.5-μs clock period of the system described in the chapter, could the clock period have been divided into fewer than the four equal intervals shown and still meet the characteristics required in Prob. 4-20? If so, show a timing diagram which uses as few equal intervals as possible. If not, then explain.

4-22 Read-only memories How many bits of read-only storage are needed and how must they be organized to implement a full adder?

4-23 Read-only memories Consider implementing the *doubler* described in Prob. 2-29 with a read-only memory. How must it be organized?

4-24 Read-only memories Can a 6-bit input, 4-bit output ROM be used to implement two *distinct* full adders? Explain.

REFERENCES

The most up-to-date information on specific flipflops, their circuit configurations, and performance characteristics is available through the spec sheets and application notes of integrated-circuit manufacturers (like Texas Instruments, Fairchild, and Motorola) and manuals provided by logic card manufacturers (like Digital Equipment Corp., EECo., and Honeywell's 3C Division).

An excellent discussion of the characteristics and capabilities of wire, glass, and quartz delay lines is presented by J. H. Eveleth, Serial Buffer Stores Using Delay Lines, *Computer Design*, August 1968, pp. 52–57.

A technology which may come to dominate the field of very long shift registers because of very small size and low cost is that which leads to the *magnetic domain devices* described by H. R. Karp, Magnetic Bubbles—A Technology in the Making, *Electronics*, September 1, 1969, pp. 83–87.

Read-only memories and the features of various technologies used to implement them are discussed by J. Marino and J. Sirota, There's a Read-Only Memory That's Sure to Fit Your Needs, *Electronics*, March 16, 1970, pp. 112–116.

5

The Design of
Sequential Circuitry

5-1 SYNCHRONOUS SEQUENTIAL CIRCUITS

In Chap. 3, we developed a design technique for defining Boolean functions and minimizing their implementation with the aid of Karnaugh maps. In this chapter, we shall develop an analogous technique for defining and minimizing the implementation of synchronous sequential circuits.

A *sequential circuit* is any circuit containing both flipflops and gates. It is called this because its operation sequences through a succession of states during successive clock periods. In so doing, it breaks a complex problem down into a sequence of simpler problems, leading eventually to the desired result.

A sequential circuit is *synchronous* if all of the clock inputs on all of the flipflops in the circuit are tied together to a common clock source. Furthermore, synchronous sequential circuit design is carried out by making use of only the ac inputs to the flipflops. Often, after a sequential circuit is designed synchronously, it will be modified by using the direct preset and clear inputs on the flipflops to preset information into the circuit. The result is no longer synchronous, but the design problem has been broken down into two steps which makes the avoidance of race problems straightforward.

Later in this chapter, we shall consider the more general problem of asynchronous sequential circuit design. There we shall permit the clock inputs on some of the flipflops to come from the outputs of other flipflops rather than only from the system clock. We shall do this in the interests of simplifying the resulting circuitry. The price we pay for any increased simplicity in an asynchronous circuit is that the maximum clock rate at which the asynchronous circuit can be run reliably is slower than that for the corresponding synchronous circuit.

The class of circuits which can be grouped together as synchronous sequential circuits can all be depicted as in Fig. 5-1. Note that, in addition to the requirement on the flipflop clock inputs, we shall also assume that all of the circuit inputs are synchronized to the clock. This means that they might come from flipflops, or gates, in another part of the system but that these flipflops also receive their clock inputs directly from the system clock. This requirement insures that the level inputs to the flipflops in the synchronous sequential circuit under consideration will be unchanging just before the clock transition occurs. When changes do occur, they will happen just after the clock transition.

What are some of the kinds of circuits which we wish to be able to design with synchronous sequential circuits? The following represent several classes:

1. Counters with no circuit inputs and with circuit outputs being the same as flipflop outputs. These might be binary, 8421 BCD, or arbitrarily coded counters.
2. Up-down counters in which a circuit input determines whether the counter will count up or down for each clock transition. Again, the flipflop outputs are the circuit outputs.

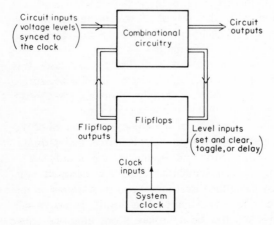

Fig. 5-1 Arbitrary synchronous sequential circuit.

3. Gated counters which count if a circuit input is in one state when the clock transition occurs and which do not count otherwise.
4. Scalers with an arbitrary count sequence but a specified period. Often combinational circuitry is employed to generate circuit outputs derived from the states of the scaler.
5. Operational circuits for implementing arithmetic operations serially, for example, a serial adder which adds two binary numbers bit by bit during successive clock periods.

5-2 TRANSITION MAPS AND SYNCHRONOUS COUNTER DESIGN WITH *RS* FLIPFLOPS

Consider the design of a 2-bit Gray-code counter. This counter finds use in the drive circuitry for the stepping motors discussed in Chap. 7. Figure 5-2a and b illustrates a block diagram of this counter and the desired count sequence. The first two rows of the count sequence say that if $A = 0$ and $B = 0$, then, when the next clock transition occurs, these will change to $A = 0$ and $B = 1$.

This same information is contained in the upper-left-hand corner of the two Karnaugh maps in Fig. 5-2c. The subscript n indicates the present state of these variables, while the subscript $n + 1$ indicates the next state, or the state which will exist after the clock transition occurs. Thus the upper-left-hand square in the A_{n+1} map corresponds to the present state $A_n = 0$ and $B_n = 0$. The 0 in this square says that the next state of A, namely, A_{n+1}, will have a value of 0. The 1 in the upper-left-hand square of the B_{n+1} map says that the next state of B will be 1.

Notice that the Karnaugh map contains neither more nor less information than the count sequence. They both describe what the output of the counter must do. However, they present this description in two different formats. Similarly, the *transition map* of Fig. 5-3 presents exactly the same information in a third format. We shall find this third format eminently suitable for minimizing sequential circuits just as the Karnaugh map presented a format quite suitable for minimizing combinational circuits.

A transition map plots the *changes* in the state of one flipflop as a function of everything which affects it (i.e., its present state, the present state of

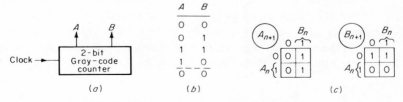

Fig. 5-2 Definition of a 2-bit Gray-code counter. (*a*) Block diagram; (*b*) count sequence; (*c*) Karnaugh maps.

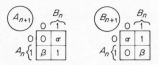

Fig. 5-3   Transition maps for the 2-bit Gray-code counter.

other flipflops, and the present state of any circuit inputs). Notice that any changes which occur in the output of a flipflop must be determined by the states of flipflops and circuit inputs as they exist *just before* the transition on the clock input occurs. In a synchronous sequential circuit, these states have been present during the entire clock period prior to the transition on the clock input. These changes are plotted as follows:

α indicates that the flipflop is to change from 0 to 1
β indicates that the flipflop is to change from 1 to 0
1   indicates that the flipflop is to go from 1 to 1
0   indicates that the flipflop is to go from 0 to 0
X indicates a don't care condition

Thus in Fig. 5-3, the upper-left-hand square of the B_{n+1} map contains an α, indiating that when $A_n = 0$ and $B_n = 0$, then the B flipflop will change from 0 to 1 when the next clock transition occurs.

So far we have described only what the *outputs* of the flipflops must do. This information is independent of the kind of flipflop (*RS, JK*, delay, etc.) which we have for implementing the circuit. The next step in the design procedure requires the derivation of *generalized input equations* for the kind of flipflop to be used. These equations describe the level inputs (e.g., set and clear inputs) required to produce the various flipflop output changes.

For an *RS* flipflop, the top figure in Fig. 5-4 illustrates the input conditions required in order that the flipflop will make an α transition, that is, go from 0 to 1. The third row of Fig. 5-4 illustrates that if the flipflop output is set and is to remain set (that is, go from 1 to 1), then there are two possible combinations of set and clear inputs which will achieve this. In either case, the clear input must be 0, but it does not matter whether the set input is 0 or 1.

Considering the set input for these six possible cases, we see that it *must* be enabled (i.e., made equal to 1) for all present states in which the transition map displays an α and that it *may* be enabled for all present states where a 1 appears in the transition map. In all other cases, the set input must be disabled (i.e., made equal to 0). These facts are stated by the generalized input equations

$$S = \alpha \qquad DC_S = 1, X$$

which say we *must* set on the α's in the transition map whereas 1s and X's form don't care conditions for the set input.

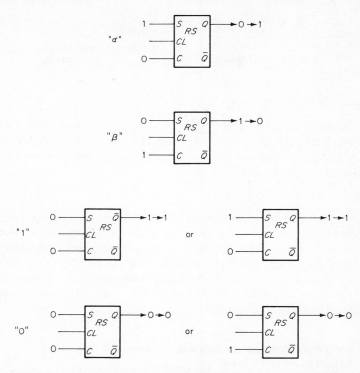

Fig. 5-4   Derivation of the generalized input equations for an RS flipflop.

We shall now examine how these generalized input equations are used to interpret the transition map. We shall translate the A_{n+1} transition map into a S_A Karnaugh map for the function which must be used to set the A flipflop in order to implement the 2-bit Gray-code counter. Figure 5-5 illustrates this map. Note that the α in the transition map has been translated into a 1, the 1 into an X, and the 0 and β into 0s as required by the generalized input equations for setting an RS flipflop. The maps for S_A and S_B give

$$S_A = B \qquad S_B = \overline{A}$$

Reconsidering Fig. 5-4 with the clear input in mind results in the generalized input equations for the clear input to an RS flipflop:

Fig. 5-5   Karnaugh maps for deriving the set input equations for implementing the 2-bit Gray-code counter with RS flipflops.

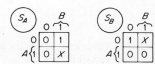

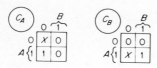

Fig. 5-6   Karnaugh maps for the clear inputs for the 2-bit Gray-code counter.

$$C = \beta \qquad DC_C = 0, X$$

Again these say that β's must be cleared whereas 0s and X's are don't care conditions for the clear input. From the maps in Fig. 5-6, which were obtained from the transition maps for our counter using these generalized input equations, we obtain

$$C_A = \overline{B} \qquad C_B = A$$

Our design procedure has resulted in the specific input equations needed to implement the Gray-code counter with RS flipflops. It has taken advantage of those instances where the flipflop inputs *may* be enabled in order to simplify the implementation. The final circuit is shown in Fig. 5-7. Note the small circle on the clock inputs of the flipflops and the corresponding waveform shown, which serves as an additional reminder that these flipflops change state on a negative-going clock transition.

5-3 SYNCHRONOUS COUNTER DESIGN USING OTHER FLIPFLOP TYPES

In the last section, we developed the complete design procedure for implementing an arbitrary counter with RS flipflops. In this section, we shall

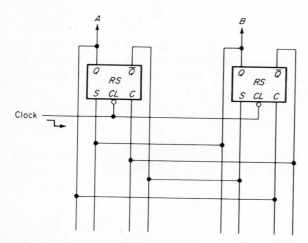

Fig. 5-7   Completed design for the 2-bit Gray-code counter implemented with RS flipflops.

examine the point at which the design procedure will be different for different flipflop types. Whereas the transition maps reflect only information associated with the count sequence of the counter to be designed, the specific input equations for the final circuit are dependent upon the type of flipflop being used. The generalized input equations represent the effect of different flipflop types upon the design procedure.

In order to derive the generalized input equations for a *JK* flipflop, we ask what the set and clear inputs must do corresponding to each possible entry in a transition map. These possibilities are shown in Fig. 5-8. Note that the set input to the flipflop *must* be enabled on all α's, *may* be enabled on β's and 1s (and, of course, on any *X*'s which appear in the map), but *must not* be enabled on 0s. These results can be expressed by

$$S = \alpha \qquad DC_S = 1, \beta, X$$

A similar analysis of the clear input yields

$$C = \beta \qquad DC_C = 0, \alpha, X$$

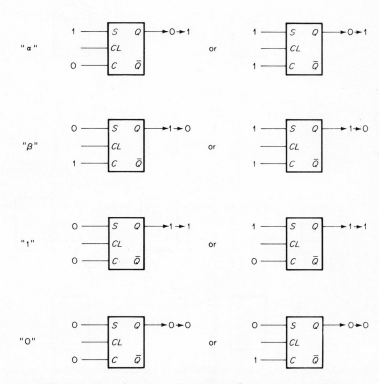

Fig. 5-8 Derivation of the generalized input equations for a *JK* flipflop.

In the case of a set-overrides-clear input, the results become somewhat more complicated. Considering Fig. 5-9, we see that the set input must be enabled on α's, that it may be enabled on 1s, but that it must not be enabled on β's or 0s. Turning now to the clear input, we see that it must be enabled on β's, that it may be enabled on α's and 0s and that it may also be enabled on 1s *if* the set input is also enabled. The generalized input equations may be written

$$S = \alpha \qquad DC_S = 1, X$$
$$C = \beta \qquad DC_C = 0, \alpha, 1_S, X$$

where 1_S represents those 1s for which it has been decided to enable the set input.

The results of these and similar analyses for all of the flipflop types discussed in Chap. 4 are tabulated in Fig. 5-10. In practice, a digital designer is usually constrained to one flipflop type, or perhaps two, and consequently his use of the appropriate generalized input equations becomes second nature to

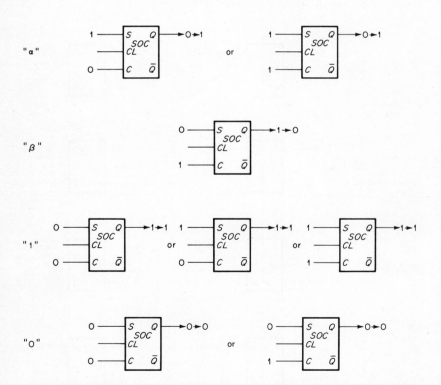

Fig. 5-9 Derivation of the generalized input equations for a set-overrides-clear flipflop.

Flipflop type	Generalized input equations	
RS	$S = \alpha$ $C = \beta$	$DC_S = 1, X$ $DC_C = 0, X$
JK	$S = \alpha$ $C = \beta$	$DC_S = 1, \beta, X$ $DC_C = 0, \alpha, X$
Set overrides clear	$S = \alpha$ $C = \beta$	$DC_S = 1, X$ $DC_C = 0, \alpha, 1_S, X$
Clear overrides set	$S = \alpha$ $C = \beta$	$DC_S = 1, \beta, 0_C, X$ $DC_C = 0, X$
Toggle	$T = \alpha, \beta$	$DC_T = X$
Delay	$D = \alpha, 1$	$DC_D = X$

Comments :

1_S Represents those ones for which the set input will be enabled

0_C Represents those zeros for which the clear input will be enabled

Fig. 5-10   Generalized input equations.

him. For example, some logic lines employ the *JK* flipflop exclusively. In this case the designer need only remember that he must set on α's and that everything else but 0s represents don't cares for setting. Similarly, he must clear on β's, and everything else but 1s represents don't cares for clearing.

Example 5-1 Using the flipflops of Fig. 4-9c (plus NAND gates, if needed) and minimizing cost, design the 3-bit counter with the arbitrary count sequence shown in Fig. 5-11b. (Presumably, if we can design a counter with an arbitrary and perhaps peculiar count sequence, then we can design any counter.)

The transition maps can be derived directly from the count sequence. For example, the first row in the count sequence and the upper-left-hand corner in the transition maps correspond to each other. When the counter is in the 000 state, then upon reception of the next clock transition, the F flipflop will go from 0 to 0 while the G and the H flipflops will both make α transitions. Correspondingly, the upper-left-hand corner of the three transition maps show 0, α, and α.

To obtain the input equations, we could use the six maps corresponding to S_F, C_F, S_G, C_G, S_H, and C_H. However, with a little experience, we can obtain the correct input equations directly from the transition maps. For example, since we are using *JK* flipflops, we can look at the F_{n+1} transition map and note that we must set on the α and avoid the 0s. Everything else represents don't care conditions for the set input. This leads to the function

$S_F = G$

shown in Fig. 5-11. The other input equations are obtained in similar fashion.

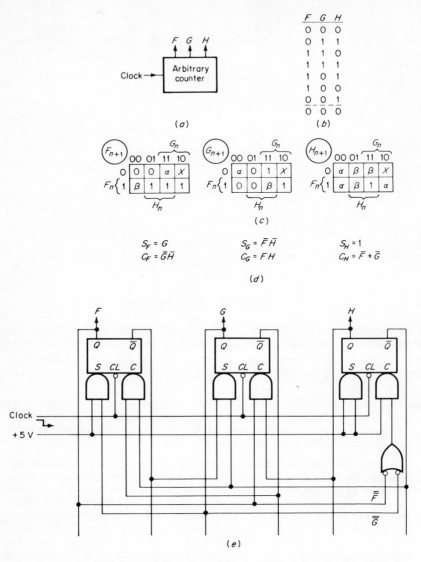

Fig. 5-11 Design of an arbitrary counter. (*a*) Block diagram; (*b*) count sequence; (*c*) transition maps; (*d*) input equations for *JK* flipflops; (*e*) implementation.

The final implementation makes good use of the extra set and clear inputs on the flipflops. If these were not available, then extra NAND gates and inverters would be used.

Example 5-2 Using set-overrides-clear flipflops with single set and clear inputs and using NOR gates, redesign the arbitrary counter of Example 5-1.

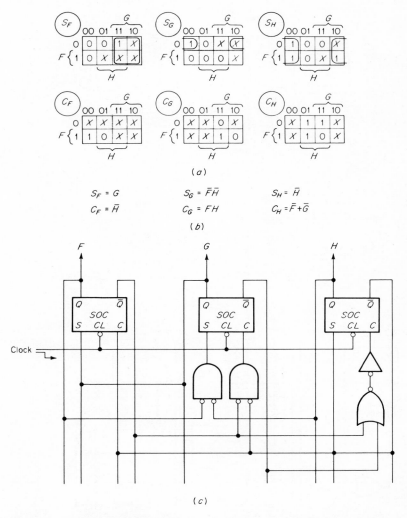

$$S_F = G$$
$$C_F = \bar{H}$$

$$S_G = \bar{F}\bar{H}$$
$$C_G = FH$$

$$S_H = \bar{H}$$
$$C_H = \bar{F} + \bar{G}$$

(b)

(c)

Fig. 5-12 Alternative implementation of an arbitrary counter. (a) Karnaugh maps for set and clear inputs using set-overrides-clear flipflops; (b) input equations for set-overrides-clear flipflops; (c) implementation with set-overrides-clear flipflops and NOR gates.

Referring back to the transition maps of Fig. 5-11, together with the generalized input equations of Fig. 5-10, we can construct Karnaugh maps for S_F, C_F, S_G, C_G, S_H, and C_H, as in Fig. 5-12a. By using $S_F = G$, we help ourselves in the implementation of the clear input function C_F. We know we have to clear on the β in the lower-left-hand corner and that we can use 0s and X's as don't cares.

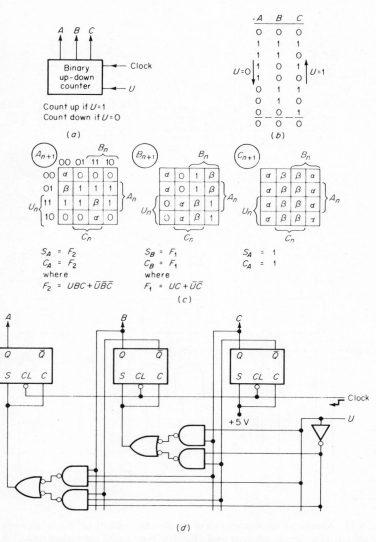

Fig. 5-13 Design of a binary up-down counter. (*a*) Block diagram; (*b*) count sequence; (*c*) transition maps and input equations; (*d*) implementation.

Furthermore, we can use any 1s as don't cares for which the set input is enabled. The two 1s in the lower-right-hand corner satisfy this condition. Consequently, we can implement $C_F = \overline{H}$, which represents an improvement over what could be attained previously with a JK flipflop. The complete set of input equations is shown in Fig. 5-12b, while the implementation is shown in Fig. 5-12c.

5-4 SYNCHRONOUS SEQUENTIAL CIRCUITS HAVING INPUTS

Up to this point, we have considered only the design of counters having no inputs (other than the clock). The only modification needed in our design procedure to handle circuit inputs is to include these as variables in the transition maps. This modification can be demonstrated with an example.

Example 5-3 Using the JK flipflops of Fig. 4-9a plus NAND gates, design a 3-bit binary up-down counter. Minimize cost.

The solution is developed in Fig. 5-13.

Another example of a sequential circuit is the shift register. A shift register is, in effect, just a string of delay flipflops. Its implementation with either RS or JK flipflops can be developed via the transition map of Fig. 5-14a for 1 bit which says

$$Q_{n+1} = I_n$$

A 4-bit implementation is shown in Fig. 5-14b.

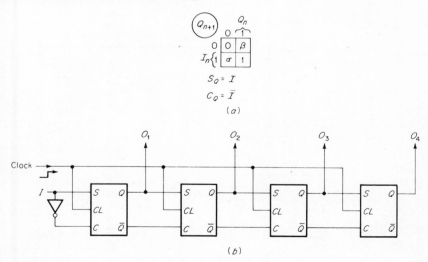

Fig. 5-14 Design of a shift register. (a) Transition map and input equations for a 1-bit shift register; (b) 4-bit shift register implemented with either RS or JK flipflops.

5-5 SCALER DESIGN

Often in designing the timing circuitry for a digital system there is a need for a counter having a specified period, or scale *p*. In such a case, the actual count sequence is often unimportant just so long as there are exactly *p* states in one cycle of the counter. The design of such *scalers* represents an intriguing problem in synchronous design.

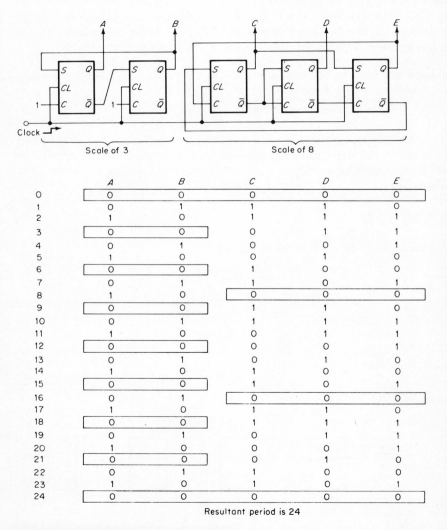

	A	B	C	D	E
0	0	0	0	0	0
1	0	1	1	1	0
2	1	0	1	1	1
3	0	0	0	1	1
4	0	1	0	0	1
5	1	0	0	1	0
6	0	0	1	0	0
7	0	1	1	0	1
8	1	0	0	0	0
9	0	0	1	1	0
10	0	1	1	1	1
11	1	0	0	1	1
12	0	0	0	0	1
13	0	1	0	1	0
14	1	0	1	0	0
15	0	0	1	0	1
16	0	1	0	0	0
17	1	0	1	1	0
18	0	0	1	1	1
19	0	1	0	1	1
20	1	0	0	0	1
21	0	0	0	1	0
22	0	1	1	0	0
23	1	0	1	0	1
24	0	0	0	0	0

Resultant period is 24

Fig. 5-15 Paralleled scalers using *JK* flipflops.

Recalling that our design procedure for a counter assumed that the count sequence was specified at the outset, we are immediately in a quandary as to how we might take advantage of this extra latitude in order to produce a simple implementation. In general, we can do several things. Using trial and error, we can build up a catalog of efficient scaler designs for small values of the period p. Appendix A3 contains such a catalog. It also develops a uniform approach which is useful for larger values of p.

Finally, we can note that if the periods of two scalers p_1 and p_2 are relatively prime,† then running these two scalers from the same clock source will yield a resultant scaler having a period $p_1 p_2$. An example of this is shown in Fig. 5-15. In order to illustrate the result, each time all zeros appear in either scaler these zeros are encircled. In the scale-of-three scaler, this occurs every three clock times. In the scale-of-eight scaler, it occurs every eight clock times. And in the resultant scaler, it occurs every 24 clock times, proving that a scale-of-24 scaler has been constructed.

5-6   MAXIMUM CLOCK RATE FOR A SYNCHRONOUS CIRCUIT

Thus far we have developed a general technique for carrying out synchronous sequential circuit design. In this section, we shall answer a related question: What is the *maximum clock rate* at which a synchronous circuit will operate reliably?

As we shall see, the maximum clock rate will be determined by the propagation delays of signals through gates and through flipflops. It will also be determined by the *setup time* of a flipflop, that is, the time which must be allowed after a set or clear input changes and before the clock transition occurs in order for the flipflop to react to this new value on the set or clear input. Consequently, before we can pin down the maximum clock rate of a system, we need to know the manufacturer's specifications on these timing characteristics of the logic.

The data shown in Fig. 5-16 give maximum propagation delays under worst-case conditions of loading for some typical logic elements in the series 54/74 TTL logic line. Rise times and fall times are not really as fast as depicted in Fig. 5-16. Consequently, the usual procedure for measuring the propagation delay for a logic element like a gate is to measure the time interval between input and output crossings of the nominal threshold voltage‡ for the logic line, as shown in Fig. 5-17.

The data given in Fig. 5-16 for a normal inverter illustrates the point that the propagation delay depends on whether the input makes a 0 to 1 or 1 to 0

---

†Two integers are said to be relatively prime if they have no common factor other than one. For example, 15 and 22 are relatively prime whereas 15 and 18 are not.
‡Defined in Sec. 3-16.

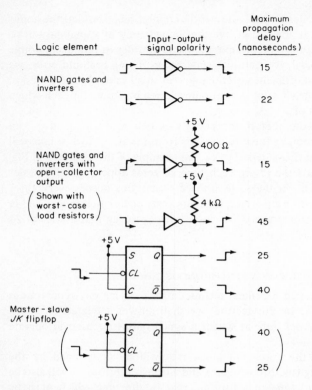

Logic element	Input-output signal polarity	Maximum propagation delay (nanoseconds)

NAND gates and inverters

NAND gates and inverters with open-collector output

(Shown with worst-case load resistors)

Master-slave *JK* flipflop

Fig. 5-16 Maximum propagation delays of series 54/74 TTL logic elements.

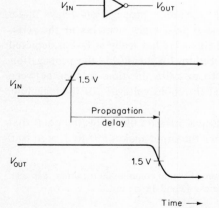

Fig. 5-17 Measurement of propagation delay of a TTL inverter. (Nominal threshold voltage for series 54/74 TTL is 1.5 V.)

transition. It also depends on the circuit used to measure propagation delay. For example, the test circuit used to specify this data includes a worst-case load. This is equivalent to 10 gate inputs plus the capacitive loading which might be encountered in wiring the output to these 10 gate inputs.

The data given for an inverter having an open-collector output (for dot-AND/ORing) illustrates the deterioration in the propagation delay (from 22 to 45 ns) when the output is pulled up with a 4-kΩ resistor rather than with the 140-Ω output impedance typical of the "totempole" output configuration of a normal TTL gate. On the other hand, this propagation delay can be reduced by using a load resistor of less than 4 kΩ.

The propagation delays for the flipflop, given in Fig. 5-16, represent the time between the negative-going transition on the clock input and the changes on the outputs. The difference between the two propagation delays occurs because the 0 to 1 output change *causes* the 1 to 0 output change (through the circuitry of the slave latch, much as in Fig. 4-4*b*).

In order to complete the specification for the ac input to a flipflop, we need a worst-case specification on *setup* and *release* times, as illustrated in Fig. 5-18. The left end of the ambiguity region occurring 20 ns before the clock transition is the *worst-case setup time*. This means that as long as a set or a clear input changes to a new value more than 20 ns before the clock transition occurs, the flipflop will be sure to set up to this new value (regardless of whether it is a 1 or a 0).

As indicated in Fig. 4-5*b*, for an edge-triggered flipflop, the worst-case setup time is unrelated to the width of the clock pulse. In contrast, for the master-slave flipflop discussed here, it is equal to the width of the clock pulse. As we shall see, the maximum clock rate for a system depends upon this worst-case setup time. Consequently, when using master-slave flipflops, it may be advantageous to use a clock waveform for which the clock pulses are as narrow as the flipflops will tolerate. This is what is shown in Fig. 5-18. On the other hand, it must be remembered that if the clock pulse is longer than this, then so, too, is the worst-case setup time for master-slave flipflops.

The other extreme of the ambiguity region, shown in Fig. 5-18, represents the *worst-case release time*. While for these flipflops this time happens to coincide with the clock transition, for other flipflop types this will not

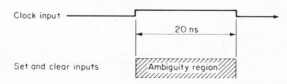

Fig. 5-18 Setup–release-time ambiguity region for a series 54/74 TTL master-slave *JK* flipflop.

necessarily be the case. If a set or clear input changes to a new value at any time to the right of the ambiguity region, the flipflop will not have released from the old value. Examples of various possibilities are shown in Fig. 5-19, where each example shows the clock input (at the top of the figure), the set input S, and the flipflop output Q. The maximum clock rate at which a system will perform reliably depends on these timing characteristics of the logic and also on the way in which the system is organized. For example, a synchronous circuit has the circuit configuration shown in Fig. 5-20.

In describing the combinational circuitry, we must characterize each gate in the circuit by a worst-case propagation delay. The consequence of being more conservative than reality requires, at this stage, will be to obtain a maximum clock rate which is lower than reality dictates. For example, if the combinational circuitry consists solely of TTL NAND gates (not having dot-AND/OR capability), we might specify the worst-case propagation delay of a NAND gate with an overly conservative 22 ns (the larger of the two values given in Fig. 5-16). On the other hand, as a signal propagates through NAND gating, it will

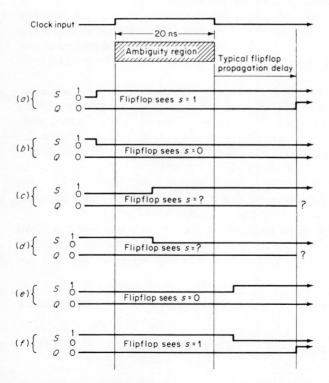

Fig. 5-19 Six examples of setup–release-time possibilities.

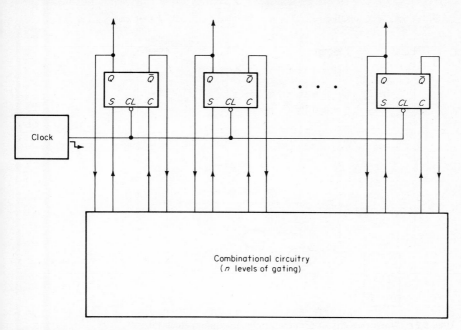

Fig. 5-20   Organization of a synchronous circuit.

give rise to alternating 0 to 1 and 1 to 0 transitions. Consequently, a more realistic worst-case propagation delay might be the average of 15 and 22 ns, or about 19 ns.

In characterizing the combinational circuitry of Fig. 5-20 as consisting of n levels of gating, we are recognizing that the circuit has a worst-case combination of inputs and input changes. For this combination, at least one signal change propagates through n gates in going from the output of one flipflop to the input of another.

The maximum clock rate for reliable operation is related to the minimum clock period as follows:

$$f_{\max \text{ (MHz)}} = \frac{1{,}000}{T_{\min \text{ (ns)}}} \tag{5-1}$$

The minimum clock period $T_{\min}$ is determined, as shown in Fig. 5-21, using

$$
\begin{aligned}
T_{\min} = \ &\text{Maximum flipflop propagation delay} \\
&+ n \times \text{maximum gate propagation delay} \\
&+ \text{worst-case flipflop setup time}
\end{aligned}
\tag{5-2}
$$

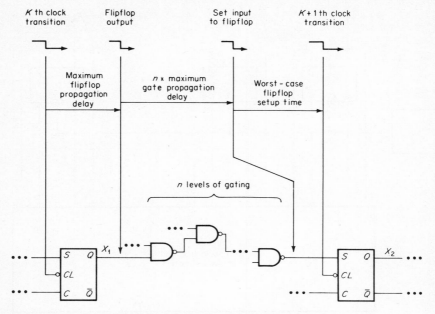

Fig. 5-21 Worst-case circuit for determining maximum clock rate.

This permits a flipflop (X_1 in Fig. 5-21) to change state in response to a clock transition, lets the change propagate through the combinational gating, and lets the flipflop X_2 set up to the new value which appears on its set input. Upon the completion of these things, the next clock transition can clock the flipflop X_2 (as well as X_1) and the system will do as it was designed to do.

Example 5-4 Determine the maximum clock rate of a synchronous circuit consisting of series 54/74 TTL master-slave *JK* flipflops and seven levels of NAND gates (not having dot-AND/OR capability).

First we determine T_{min}:

$$T_{min} = 40 + 7 \times 19 + 20 = 193 \text{ ns}$$

Then

$$f_{max} = \frac{1,000}{T_{min}} = \frac{1,000}{193} = 5.1 \text{ MHz}$$

This is close to the commonly used rule of thumb which says that the maximum system clock rate which can be achieved with a given logic line is equal to one-third the worst-case maximum *toggling rate*[†] of the flipflops being used. For these TTL

[†]The maximum toggling rate of a *JK* flipflop is the maximum rate at which clock pulses can be applied (with $S = C = 1$) such that the flipflop changes state reliably for each pulse.

flipflops, the maximum toggling rate is 15 MHz. Obviously this rule of thumb puts severe constraints on the design of a system; the entire system is almost necessarily synchronous, and no more than seven levels of logic are permitted.

For any clock rate slower than the maximum clock rate dictated by these considerations, the circuitry sits idly by for the latter portion of clock period (after T_{min} has transpired) waiting for the next clock transition to occur. Consequently, while we have a constraint on the maximum clock rate for the system, there is no corresponding constraint on the minimum clock rate.

The determination of the maximum clock rate for a system represents a good problem for computer-aided design. Not only can the computer be used to keep track of realistic gate and flipflop propagation delays (distinguishing between those corresponding to 0 to 1 and 1 to 0 transitions of outputs), but it can also pinpoint the worst-case signal propagation path. If the resulting maximum clock rate is not fast enough, the designer then knows where the circuit must be redesigned in order to reduce the number of levels of gating.

5-7 MAXIMUM ALLOWABLE CLOCK SKEW FOR A LOGIC LINE

When we speak of the *maximum allowable clock skew* for a given logic line, we are referring to the situation depicted in Fig. 5-22. Because of loading

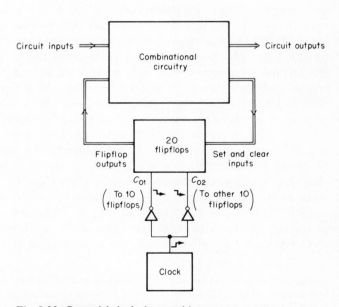

Fig. 5-22 Potential clock-skew problem.

considerations, the clock inputs to the 20 flipflops have been split into two groups, one group driven by C_{01} and the other by C_{02}.[†] Ideally these give negative-going transitions at exactly the same time since they are both generated by inverters having the same signal on their inputs. However, in reality any *difference* in propagation delay between these inverters will cause the negative-going transitions on C_{01} and C_{02} to occur at slightly different times. *Maximum allowable clock skew is the maximum time difference which can occur between almost-simultaneous clock transitions which the flipflops will treat as being simultaneous.* In other words, we design a circuit like that in Fig. 5-22 to work correctly when $C_{01} = C_{02} \equiv C_0$. If the circuit does not work correctly when the transition on C_{02} occurs 10 ns after that on C_{01}, then we say that this 10-ns difference has exceeded the maximum allowable clock skew. As in the case of determining the maximum clock rate of a system, to determine the maximum allowable clock skew for a logic line, we need to know the timing characteristics of that logic line's flipflops and gates.

In the last section, we found that the combinational circuitry in a synchronous circuit tends to hurt performance in the sense that the more levels of gating there are, the lower the maximum clock rate must be. In contrast, when discussing clock skew, these same levels of gating help performance. They help because they retard changes at the set and clear inputs to flipflops resulting from changing outputs on other flipflops. Consequently, a worst-case circuit configuration for discussing clock skew is the shift-register circuit shown in Fig. 5-23a. One result of this is that the maximum allowable clock skew for a logic line depends on the characteristics of the flipflop only—it is independent of the characteristics of the gate. If we investigate the clock-skew characteristics of a series 54/74 TTL edge-triggered JK flipflop, we need its timing characteristics, as given in Fig. 5-23b. Note that the worst-case release time is 5 ns. This means that the set and clear inputs must not change until at least 5 ns after the clock transition. If they change before this (say, at the same instant at which the clock transition occurs), then there will be ambiguity over whether the flipflop will respond to the old or new values on the set and clear inputs.

If in Fig. 5-23a we assume that the 0 to 1 transition occurs first on C_{01} and then on C_{02}, we can ask whether either flipflop is free of clock skew problems. And indeed flipflop A is all right because its inputs change even *later* than they would with synchronous inputs, where $C_{02} = C_{01} \equiv C_0$. The problem arises on the inputs to flipflop B, as depicted in Fig. 5-23c. After C_{01} occurs, the outputs of flipflop A may change as early as 10 ns later. Since these are the inputs to flipflop B, the worst-case release-time requirement dictates that the clock transition on flipflop B, namely, C_{02}, must occur at least 5 ns before this,

---

[†] Some logic lines permit any number of *clock drivers* (which are inverters or gates having a high fan-out) to be paralleled so as to drive the required load without clock skew problems. If this is not done, the consequences are those discussed here.

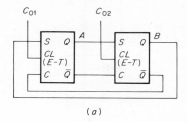

(a)

10 ns < flipflop propagation delay < 50 ns

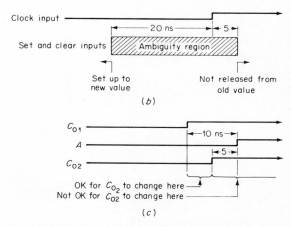

(b)

(c)

Fig. 5-23 Determination of maximum allowable clock skew. (a) Circuit; (b) series 54/74 TTL edge-triggered *JK* flipflop timing characteristics; (c) development of clock-skew constraint.

giving a maximum allowable clock skew of $10 - 5 = 5$ ns. In general, we have

Maximum allowable clock skew = minimum flipflop propagation delay

$$- \text{worst-case flipflop release time} \qquad (5\text{-}3)$$

The fact that the maximum allowable clock skew is not zero permits us to resolve the difficulty posed in Fig. 5-22. It also permits us to generate the *pseudosynchronous* clock signals which will be discussed in this chapter.

Inadvertently exceeding the maximum allowable clock skew represents a common error for a novice designer. One example comes about by mixing flipflop types within one system. For example, series 54/74 TTL logic includes

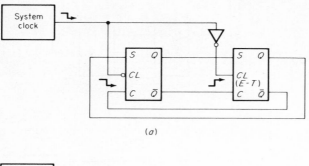

(a)

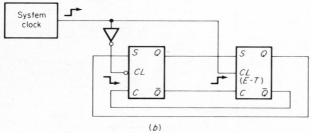

(b)

	Minimum propagation delay	Worst - case release time
Master – slave	10	0
Edge – triggered	10	5

(c)

Fig. 5-24 Mixing flipflop types. (a) Edge-triggered flipflop clock input delayed; (b) master-slave flipflop clock input delayed; (c) timing characteristics.

the master-slave *JK* flipflop of Fig. 5-16, which changes state on the 1 to 0 transition of the clock. It also includes the edge-triggered *JK* flipflop of Fig. 5-23, which changes state on the 0 to 1 transition of the clock. If *synchronous* design is attempted using both of these by inverting the clock input either to the master-slave flipflops or to the edge-triggered flipflops, then we end up with one of the two worst-case situations shown in Fig. 5-24. The maximum allowable clock skew in each case is equal to the minimum propagation delay of one flipflop minus the worst-case release time of the other. In the case of Fig. 5-24a, this gives 5 ns and in that of Fig. 5-24b, 10 ns. Consequently, the circuit of Fig. 5-24b will work satisfactorily providing the inverter has a propagation delay of less than 10 ns; otherwise, clock-skew problems may plague the circuit.

5-8 ASYNCHRONOUS COUPLING OF COUNTERS AND SCALERS

Early in this chapter, we developed a technique for designing synchronous counters using transition maps. This technique and the resulting counters share a problem which arose in the design of combinational circuitry: as the number of variables gets larger, both the design technique and the resulting implementations become increasingly unwieldy. This can be seen intuitively by considering the synchronous design of a 10-bit binary counter. The most significant bit changes state only twice during each complete cycle of the counter, which takes 1,024 clock pulses. Since every one of these pulses goes to the clock input on the flipflop for this most significant bit, the function of the set and clear inputs on this flipflop is to prevent it from changing state in response to 1,022 out of 1,024 of these clock pulses.

In comparison, asynchronous coupling permits each flipflop to receive its clock input only when it is supposed to do something. For example, consider the count sequence for a 4-bit binary counter, as shown in Fig. 5-25a. Assume we

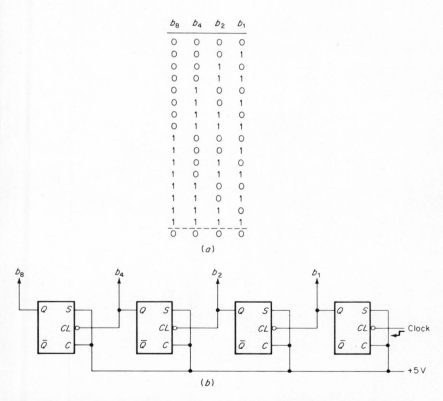

(a)

(b)

Fig. 5-25 Asynchronous binary counter. (a) Count sequence; (b) implementation.

wish to implement this counter using TTL *JK* flipflops which change state on 1 to 0 clock transitions. Since b_1 changes state every time, it can be implemented as shown in Fig. 5-25b with $S = C = 1$ and the clock connected to its clock input. Now notice that every time b_2 changes state, b_1 is changing from 1 to 0. Consequently, if, as in Fig. 5-25b, b_1 is used as the clock input on the b_2 flipflop and if $S = C = 1$ on this flipflop, then it will change state exactly when it

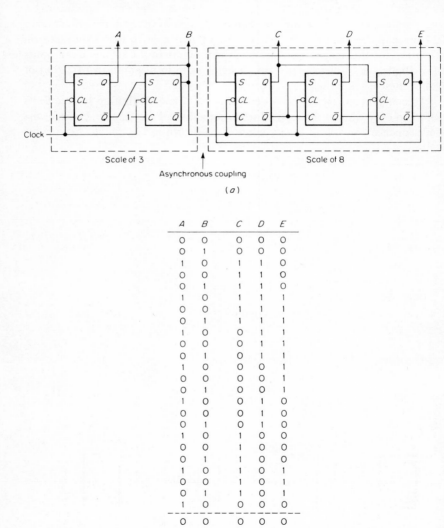

A	B	C	D	E
0	0	0	0	0
0	1	0	0	0
1	0	1	1	0
0	0	1	1	0
0	1	1	1	0
1	0	1	1	1
0	0	1	1	1
0	1	1	1	1
1	0	0	1	1
0	0	0	1	1
0	1	0	1	1
1	0	0	0	1
0	0	0	0	1
0	1	0	0	1
1	0	0	1	0
0	0	0	1	0
0	1	0	1	0
1	0	1	0	0
0	0	1	0	0
0	1	1	0	0
1	0	1	0	1
0	0	1	0	1
0	1	1	0	1
1	0	0	0	0
0	0	0	0	0

(*b*)

Fig. 5-26 Asynchronously coupled scalers. (*a*) Circuit; (*b*) count sequence.

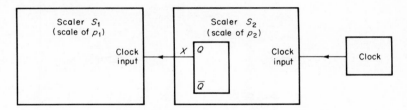

Fig. 5-27 General problem of asynchronously coupling scalers together.

should. A similar analysis of b_4 and b_8 leads to the complete implementation shown.

If this counter had been implemented with *JK* flipflops which change state on *0 to 1* clock transitions, it would only have been necessary to get the clock input for each flipflop from the $\overline{Q}$ output (instead of the Q output) of the previous flipflop. This would provide the necessary 0 to 1 clock transition when the previous flipflop's Q output makes a 1 to 0 transition.

The major advantage of designing a binary counter *synchronously* is that it is fast; after one flipflop propagation delay, all flipflops have settled out. In contrast, an asynchronous binary counter offers simplicity of circuitry at the expense of much slower settling under certain circumstances. For example, a 10-bit asynchronous binary counter will take 10 flipflop propagation delays to settle out as it counts up from all 1s to all 0s.

The more general application of asynchronous design occurs when coupling counters or scalers in series to obtain a long count cycle. For example, a scaler with a period of 24 can be implemented by coupling together the scale-of-three and scale-of-eight scalers of Fig. 5-15 asynchronously, as in Fig. 5-26*a*. The resulting count sequence is shown in Fig. 5-26*b*. Notice that since the flipflops shown have clock inputs sensitive to 1 to 0 transitions, the scale-of-eight scaler counts every time *B* changes from 1 to 0.

In order to apply this technique in general, consider coupling two scalers S_1 and S_2, as in Fig. 5-27, to obtain an asynchronous scaler with period $p = p_1 p_2$. This can be done providing there is one flipflop *X* in scaler S_2 which makes only one 0 to 1 transition (and one 1 to 0 transition) during one period of the scaler.

Example 5-5 Consider two scalers which have the count sequence shown in Fig. 5-28. Can a scale-of-42 scaler be constructed by asynchronouly coupling the clock input of scaler S_1 to an output of S_2 as in Fig. 5-28*b*?

No; neither flipflop *D*, nor *E*, nor *F* meets the required condition. If the clock input of scaler S_1 were connected to *D*, for example, then during one cycle of scaler S_2, scaler S_1 would count twice, not once. The resulting scaler would have a period of 21 instead of the desired 42.

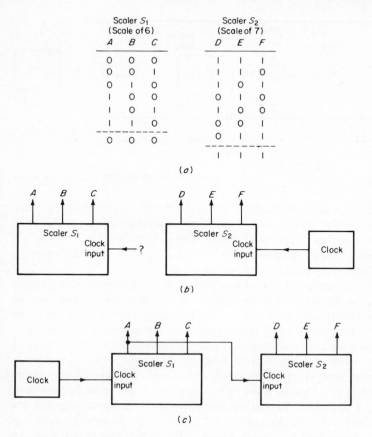

Fig. 5-28 Asynchronously coupling scalers together. (*a*) Count sequences; (*b*) trying to get the clock input for scaler S_1 from scaler S_2; (*c*) getting the clock input for scaler S_2 from scaler S_1.

Example 5-6 Again considering the scalers defined in Fig. 5-28*a*, can scaler S_2 be asynchronously coupled to S_1 to obtain a scale-of-42 scaler?

Yes; while neither flipflop B nor C meets the required condition, flipflop A does. Consequently, the connection shown in Fig. 5-28*c* will give a period of 42.

A more stringent set of requirements must be met if two *counters* are to be coupled asynchronously. In this case we must not only meet the previous condition, but, in addition, the flipflop X, which will be used as the source of transitions for the other scaler, must make a 0 to 1 or a 1 to 0 transition at the exact moment when the scaler should change state.

Example 5-7 Assuming two 8421 BCD decade counters have been implemented with flipflops whose clock inputs are sensitive to 0 to 1 transitions, construct an asynchronous two-decade 8421 BCD code counter.

      The count sequence for one decade is shown in Fig. 5-29a. Since the ten's decade must receive its clock input as the unit's decade rolls over from 9 to 0, we must look for a flipflop which changes state in going from 9 to 0. We see that both d_8 and d_1 meet this condition. However, d_1 changes back and forth many times in one cycle of the decade counter, and so it cannot serve as the source of clock transitions to the ten's decade. On the other hand, d_8 meets all requirements. Since d_8 changes from 1 to 0 when the ten's decade needs a clock input of 0 to 1, we connect the ten's decade to $\bar{d}_8$, as shown in Fig. 5-29b.

5-9 PSEUDOSYNCHRONOUS COUPLING OF COUNTERS AND SCALERS

In the last section we developed a technique which exchanged speed for simplicity in coupling counters or scalers together. In this section, we shall develop another technique which yields the speed of a synchronous circuit plus the simplicity that results from clocking each scaler or counter only when it should be counted.

      First, as will be explained below, we need gating of a form dictated by the flipflops used in the counters or scalers. If the flipflops change state on a 0

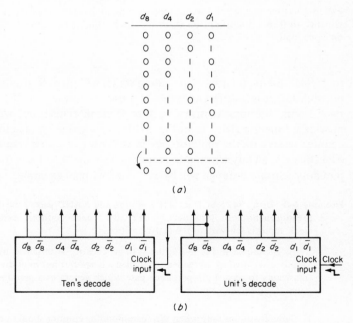

Fig. 5-29 Design of a two-decade 8421 BCD counter. (a) Count sequence for one decade; (b) implementation.

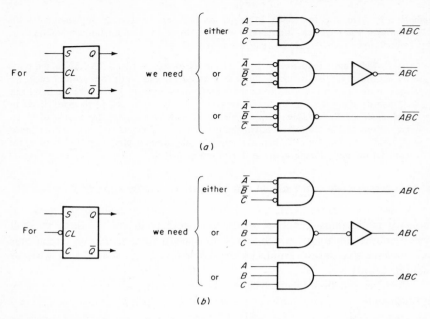

Fig. 5-30 Required gates for carrying out pseudosynchronous design. (*a*) Flipflops sensitive to 0 to 1 transitions on clock input; (*b*) flipflops sensitive to 1 to 0 transitions on clock input.

to 1 clock input, then we need gating which will provide a function $\overline{ABC}$. Three possibilities, using different types of gates, are shown in Fig. 5-30*a*. Alternatively, with flipflops sensitive to 1 to 0 clock transitions, we need gating to provide a function ABC, as in Fig. 5-30*b*. This gating on the clock input to each counter represents the only increase in the cost of a pseudosynchronous counter over that of an asynchronous counter. The use of this gating to carry out pseudosynchronous design will be explained with an example.

Example 5-8 Using 8421 BCD decade counters and NAND gates (and inverters), design a pseudosynchronous three-decade 8421 BCD code counter. Assume each decade's clock input is sensitive to a 0 to 1 transition.

As shown in Fig. 5-31, the system clock C_0 is obtained by inverting C^*, the output of a square-wave generator (called a *clock* but not used directly as a source of transitions to any flipflops). Each gate which generates a *pseudosynchronous* clock signal (C_0A and C_0B) must

1. Generate pulses only when the corresponding counter should be counted
2. Generate pulses whose *trailing edges* trigger the counter

The first requirement calls for ANDing things together, while the second requirement says that the result should be inverted to a 0. Then when the C^* input changes from 1 to 0, the gate output (C_{0A} or C_{0B}) will change from 0 to 1, triggering the counter.

We can think of the pseudosynchronous clock signals as being generated by gating the C^* clock. For proper operation, the ten's decade must receive a C_{0A} negative pulse for the last half of the clock period during which the unit's decade is in state 9. Then, as C_0 rises from 0 to 1, counting the unit's decade from nine to zero, C_{0A} will also rise from 0 to 1, counting the ten's decade. Similarly, the hundred's decade must receive a C_{0B} negative pulse for the last half of the clock period during which both the unit's decade and the ten's decade are in state 9. At the end of this clock period, as C^* drops to 0, all three inputs (C_0, C_{0A}, and C_{0B}) rise from 0 to 1 and the counter counts from 99 to 100.

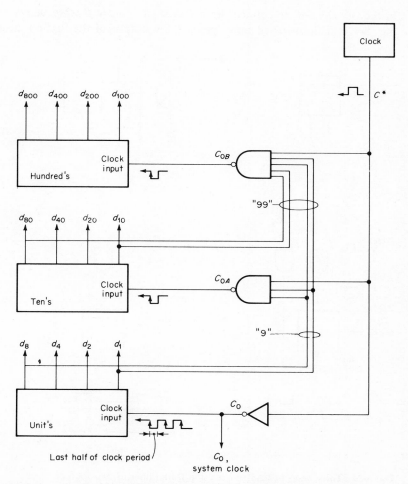

Fig. 5-31 Pseudosynchronous three-decade 8421 BCD code counter.

If the propagation delays for the gates generating C_0, C_{0A}, and C_{0B} are equal, then in counting from 99 to 100 *these pseudosynchronous signals trigger their respective counters at exactly the same time*—one propagation delay after the 1 to 0 transition on C^*. This occurs because C^* enables the gates during the *last half* of the clock period. It is the first thing to change from 1 to 0 as the pulses C_{0A} and C_{0B} are formed. (The other inputs change one flipflop propagation delay after the 0 to 1 transition on C_0.)

The final point in the design concerns the use of d_8 and d_1 to detect *nine* in each counter. Notice in the count sequence, shown in Fig. 5-29a, that state 9 is the only state in which $d_8 d_1 = 1$. In general, a Karnaugh map can be used to pick up such a simplification (instead of using $d_8 \bar{d}_4 \bar{d}_2 d_1 = 1$).

5-10 DIRECT PRESETTING OF FLIPFLOPS

In the last chapter we defined the *switched-input delay flipflop*, shown again in Fig. 5-32a. This switched input permits the output of the flipflop during one

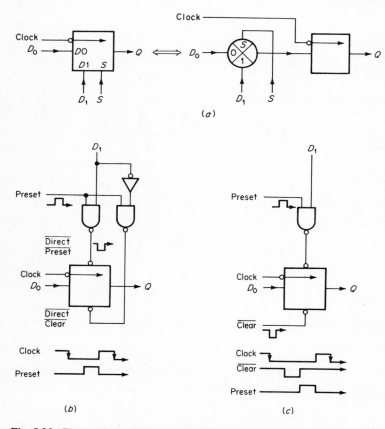

Fig. 5-32 Three ways of loading a flipflop from either of two sources D_0 or D_1. (a) Switched-input delay flipflop; (b) one-step presetting; (c) two-step presetting.

clock period to be the same as either of two inputs D_0 or D_1 during the previous clock period, the desired one being chosen by the *switch* input S. This function of making the output of a flipflop the same as either of two variables can be achieved using direct preset and clear inputs to a flipflop. There are two disadvantages of achieving the function by direct presetting rather than with switched-input delay flipflops:

1. The input must remain constant during the direct presetting operation.
2. Use of direct presetting in a system precludes the simplicity of a completely synchronous design.

The circuit shown in Fig. 5-32b illustrates *one-step presetting*. Since the flipflop will respond ambiguously if both ac and direct inputs occur simultaneously, the preset pulse must occur *between* clock transitions, as shown. Notice that if $D_1 = 1$ when the preset pulse occurs, the flipflop will be direct presetted. On the other hand, if $D_1 = 0$, then the flipflop will be direct cleared.

With regard to the disadvantages mentioned above, notice that if D_1 *changes* during the preset pulse, the flipflop will end up in the state corresponding to D_1 at the end of the pulse. One consequence and disadvantage of this is illustrated in Fig. 5-33a. Using the ac inputs, information can be shifted to the right bit by bit. However, if we attempt to shift the 2-bit number $X = X_2 X_1$ into A and A into B using one preset pulse, we will end up with $B = A = X$. This occurs because in going high, the preset pulse reads X into A. Then, with the preset pulse still high, A is read into B. If such vertical transfer of information must be made, we need to use *two* preset pulses, first presetting A into B and then presetting X into A.

In contrast, Fig. 5-33b illustrates the ease with which information can be shifted either horizontally or vertically using the switched-input delay flipflop. This circuit is completely synchronous. Its use in a system will result not only in a simpler system but also in a system that is simpler to design.

Two-step presetting of information into a flipflop is illustrated in Fig. 5-32c. This approach increases the timing complexity of presetting in order to simplify the input gating. Note that the flipflop is first cleared to 0. Then, if $D_1 = 1$, the flipflop is preset to 1. On the other hand, if $D_1 = 0$, the flipflop is left cleared.

Although these examples have illustrated the direct presetting of delay flipflops, the procedures are independent of the type of flipflop used. If we had the problem of designing a counter which will count down toward zero from a number preset into the counter, we might use *JK* flipflops. This would simplify the counter design. Then we could use direct presetting to load the number into the counter initially.

Sometimes we wish simply to preset a counter or shift register to zero or to some fixed number. In this case we can use a pulse going directly to the appropriate direct preset or clear inputs. For example, Fig. 5-34 illustrates an asynchronous binary counter which can be direct cleared to zero.

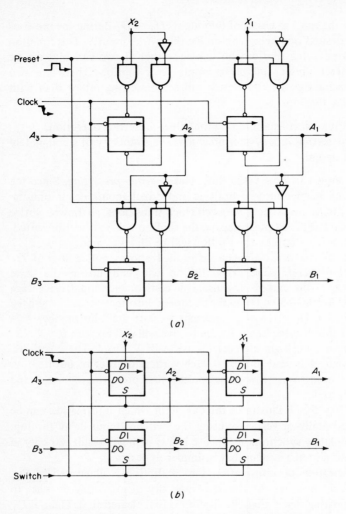

Fig. 5-33 Contrasting approaches to two-dimensional shifting. (*a*) Horizontal shifting OK; vertical shifting *not* OK; (*b*) horizontal and vertical shifting OK.

5-11 SYSTEM CLOCKING

Thus far in this book, our discussions have centered on the bits and pieces of digital systems: the combinational circuitry of a code converter, the sequential circuitry of a counter, or the input-output characteristics of a magnetic core memory. In this section, we shall consider a subject which imposes itself on

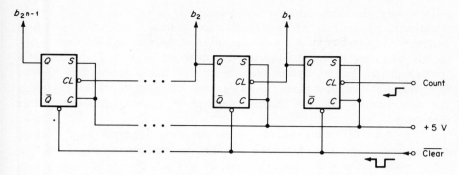

Fig. 5-34 Asynchronous binary counter which can be direct cleared to zero.

every part of a digital system. The *system clocking* in a digital system looks much like the circulatory system in a human body. They begin with the beat of a clock or a heart. And just as this beat distributes throughout the body causing blood to flow through each and every organ, so *clock signals* distribute to the clock input and presetting circuitry on every flipflop in every corner of a digital system.

System clocking can become a Pandora's box of problems if it is handled casually. Our goal is to insure that clock inputs on flipflops arrive *before* set and clear levels change. It is to insure that presetting operations do not interfere with each other or with ac inputs to flipflops. With the help of a few guidelines, we can handle system clocking in such a way that timing problems will not arise.

One approach to system clocking is to use *single-phase* clocking. This means that all changes in a system are synchronized to a single clock signal (but may occur asynchronously several propagation delays later), as in Fig. 5-35a.

In contrast, Fig. 5-35b illustrates *multiple-phase* clocking. Here, some flipflops may be synchronized to C_0 while others are synchronized to C_1 or C_2.

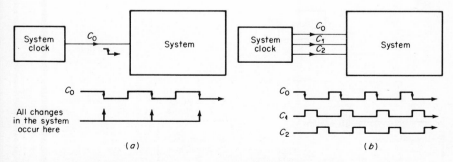

Fig. 5-35 Single- and multiple-phase system clocking. (a) Single-phase clocking; (b) multiple-phase clocking.

Alternatively, the clock inputs on all flipflops may be synchronized to C_0 while all presetting operations are synchronized to C_2. In any case, a multiple-phase system is characterized by this sequencing of operations through interlaced clock signals, all having the same frequency but differing in phase. Each phase of a multiple-phase clocking system can be treated like a single-phase system. Consequently, multiple-phase clocking can be thought of as extending the opportunities available through single-phase clocking into one further dimension.

In terms of timing considerations, the most straightforward clocking scheme is *single-phase synchronous clocking,* as illustrated in Fig. 5-36. This figure might represent two major subsystems in an entirely synchronous system. Alternatively, it might represent two small, synchronous subsystems in a larger asynchronous system. The point is that both subsystems are synchronous and clocked with the same signal. Consequently, there are no flipflop or gate outputs in subsystem A or B which change *before* any flipflop in A or B is clocked. Therefore in carrying out the design, not only can the set and clear inputs to each flipflop in subsystem B be functions of any flipflop and gate outputs in B, but they can be functions of the flipflop and gate outputs in A as well. Similarly, the flipflops in A can have set and clear inputs which are functions of anything in subsystem B. In other words, the two synchronous subsystems form a synchronous system, and in a synchronous system anything can look at anything.

The next, more complex clocking scheme is *single-phase asynchronous clocking.* In the general case, where there are two asynchronous subsystems, as in Fig. 5-37*a*, neither subsystem can safely use the flipflop and gate outputs of the other subsystem to derive flipflop set and clear inputs. A flipflop may receive its clock input asynchronously several propagation delays after the transition on the system clock C_0. Consequently, it cannot derive its set and clear inputs from an indiscriminate choice of flipflop and gate outputs without

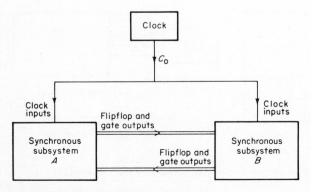

Fig. 5-36 Single-phase synchronous clocking.

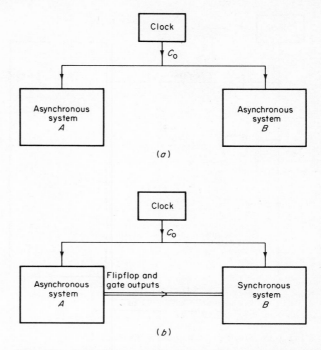

Fig. 5-37 Single-phase asynchronous clocking. (*a*) Both sub-systems asynchronous; (*b*) one subsystem asynchronous, one synchronous.

running the risk of having one of these change *just before* the clock input transition occurs, leading to an ambiguous output state.

One commonly used special case of single-phase asynchronous clocking is illustrated in Fig. 5-37*b*. In this case, one subsystem is synchronous. Many system designs use simple asynchronous *timing circuitry* in this way. Since this timing circuitry is just a series of counters which derive *timing signals* by counting clock pulses, it has no need to refer to other subsystems. On the other hand, if the rest of the system is synchronous, it can safely derive set and clear inputs from anything in the system, including these asynchronous timing signals.

An approach to single-phase system clocking which is an extension of the pseudosynchronous ideas discussed in Sec. 5-9 is *single-phase pseudosynchronous clocking,* illustrated in Fig. 5-38. The gates used to generate the pseudosynchronous clock signals C_0, C_{0A}, and C_{0B} must be chosen to correspond to the clock input sensitivity of the system flipflops, as was discussed in conjunction with Fig. 5-30. This will insure that the pseudosynchronous pulses all occur during the second half of the clock period of C_0, the system clock.

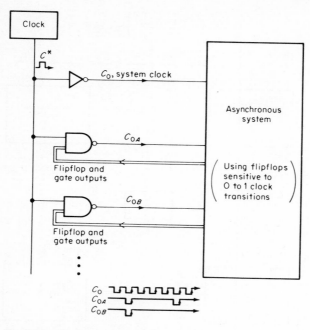

Fig. 5-38 Single-phase pseudosynchronous clocking.

The use of pseudosynchronous design with a general asynchronous system requires two further constraints not discussed in Sec. 5-9. First, all signals which are used with C^* to form the pseudosynchronous clocking signals must settle out in less than one-half a clock period. Otherwise, when C^* goes high, there may be a moment when all other inputs also go high, forming a *spurious clock pulse*. The flipflops which receive this pulse for a clock input will respond to it as if it were a true clock signal, giving rise to faulty system performance.

The other constraint on pseudosynchronous clocking concerns the pulse outputs of the gates used to generate the pseudosynchronous clocking signals. Although one output might exhibit some clock skew relative to the other outputs, this must be less than the maximum allowable clock skew for the flipflops in the system. If this constraint is met, then the set and clear inputs on any flipflop using one of these signals as its clock input can derive its set and clear inputs from *any* flipflop or gate output in the system. In order to satisfy this requirement, it may be necessary to implement these few gates in a system with some which have been matched for propagation delay. Alternatively, a faster line of logic might be used for these gates (such as series 54H/74H TTL if the system is implemented with series 54/74 TTL). These will exhibit not only lower propagation delay but also proportionally lower *differences* in propagation delay than the slower line of logic used in the rest of the system.

The power of using this pseudosynchronous approach to system clocking lies in the freedom it gives to the designer in gating the clock signals to any component in a system. For example, the clock input to a shift register can be gated on or off with impunity. While it is gated off, another pseudosynchronous clock signal might be gated on and used to direct clear the shift register to zero.

Multiple-phase system clocking is used, typically, to solve some specific problem in designing a system. One of these is to provide a general approach for using both the ac inputs and the direct presets and clears on the flipflops in a system, depicted in Fig. 5-39. Four clock phases are generated, of which only three are used. The ac inputs on all flipflops in a system are synchronized to C_0. Then the C_1 phase, which is not used, provides one-quarter clock period of leeway between ac and direct inputs on the flipflops. The C_2 and C_3 phases can be ANDed with appropriate timing signals in the system and used to generate direct preset and clear pulses which do not interfere with the ac operation of any flipflop.

An example of two-phase clocking occurs in any master-slave flipflop. One phase is generated by inverting the clock input and is used internally to connect master to slave. The other phase, the clock input, is used externally to connect the slave outputs back to the master inputs (through the flipflop input gating).

A third way in which multiple clock phases are used is represented by Fig. 5-40. Perhaps the major portion of a system includes asynchronous circuitry and is represented by subsystem A. Subsystem B may take data from A, operate on it for a while, and then feed the results back into A. In order to simplify its circuitry, it is also designed asynchronously. The required bilateral transfer of data between these two asynchronous subsystems can be effected by using two

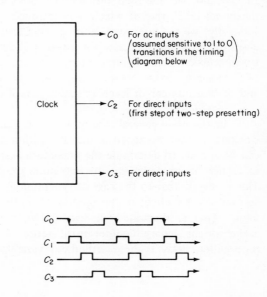

Fig. 5-39 Multiple-phase clocking for ac and direct inputs to flipflops.

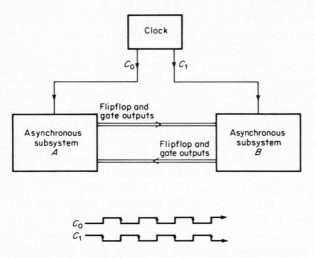

Fig. 5-40 Interconnecting two asynchronous subsystems by using two clock phases.

clock phases. Then when A is looking at B (on the C_0 transition), B is not changing. Conversely, when B is looking at A (on the C_1 transition), A is not changing.

5-12 MAXIMUM CLOCK RATE FOR A DIGITAL SYSTEM

In Sec. 5-6, we discussed the considerations leading to a specification of the maximum clock rate at which a synchronous system can be reliably clocked. Generally, we are interested in using these ideas the other way around; that is, given the required clock rate for a system, how do we design the system? For a synchronous system, this maximum clock rate places a constraint on the speed of the logic used (i.e., its maximum propagation delays and flipflop setup time) and on the number of levels of gating permitted, allowing a trade-off between these two factors.

In the more general case of a system designed with one of the variety of clocking schemes discussed in the last section, we shall find that a few key ideas can be applied to determine the maximum clock rate. First, consider the effect of asynchronous design on the maximum clock rate of a single-phase system. This is very similar to the case of synchronous design. Now, however, we must account for the effect of the rippling of flipflop outputs in response to a clock input. This is illustrated in Fig. 5-41a, where, for proper operation, an asynchronous binary counter must settle out to 000 (after three flipflop propagation delays), these settled-out variables must propagate through two

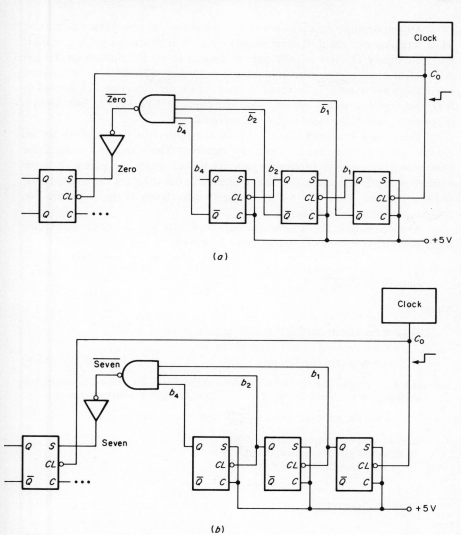

Fig. 5-41 Two examples of the effects of asynchronous circuitry on maximum clock rate. (a) System sees the effect of the asynchronous circuitry; (b) system is oblivious to the presence of asynchronous circuitry.

levels of gating to form the variable *zero*, and finally this must be permitted to sit at the set input long enough for the flipflop to set up before the next clock transition C_0 occurs.

An opportunity to capitalize on the simplicity of asynchronous circuitry while retaining the speed of synchronous circuitry is illustrated in Fig. 5-41b. If the 3-bit binary counter is used only as a scaler to set the flipflop on the left every eight clock times, then it does not make any difference to the system operation what number is detected in the counter. By detecting 111 instead of 000, the flipflops settle out (in counting from 110 to 111) in *one* flipflop propagation delay—the same as in synchronous design.

These two examples illustrate how appropriate it is to define for an asynchronous system the *r levels of rippling*. This concerns only those asynchronously coupled flipflops which are looked at by the gating. It is the number of flipflop propagation delays which can occur before the inputs to the gating settle out. Thus Fig. 5-41a represents three levels of rippling while Fig. 5-41b represents only one level.

A specification for the maximum clock rate for a system employing *single-phase asynchronous clocking* can now be made:

$$f_{max \text{ (MHz)}} = \frac{1,000}{T_{min \text{ (ns)}}} \tag{5-1}$$

where

T_{min} = r x maximum flipflop propagation delay
    $+ n$ x maximum gate propagation delay
    $+$ worst-case flipflop setup time $\tag{5-4}$

Example 5-9 Determine the maximum clock rate of the circuit of Fig. 5-41a, assuming it is implemented with series 54/74 TTL master-slave *JK* flipflops and NAND gates.

First, we might summarize the logic timing characteristics:

Maximum flipflop propagation delay = 40 ns
Maximum gate propagation delay = 19 ns
Worst-case flipflop setup time = 20 ns

Then

T_{min} = 3 x 40 + 2 x 19 + 20 = 178 ns

and

f_{max} = $\frac{1,000}{178}$ = 5.6 MHz

Example 5-10 Repeat Example 5-9 for the problem of Fig. 5-41b.

T_{min} = 1 x 40 + 2 x 19 + 20 = 98 ns

and

f_{max} = $\frac{1,000}{98}$ = 10.2 MHz

The maximum clock rate for a system employing *single-phase pseudo-synchronous clocking* can best be determined by considering Fig. 5-38. Any response to a pseudosynchronous clock pulse that feeds back to the gates which generate these pulses must settle out before C^* goes high again. Otherwise, as was mentioned in Sec. 5-11, a spurious clock pulse may occur. As a result, we must satisfy *two* requirements: that imposed by Eqs. (5-1) and (5-4) for *all* variables in the system and an additional requirement for the variables which help generate the pseudosynchronous clock pulses. If C^* is a square wave (so that it equals 1 for exactly one-half clock period), then we must satisfy

$$\frac{T_{min}}{2} = \text{maximum propagation delay for a gate generating a}$$
pseudosynchronous clock pulse
$$+ \ r' \times \text{maximum flipflop propagation delay}$$
$$+ \ n' \times \text{maximum gate propagation delay} \qquad (5\text{-}5)$$

where r' and n' are defined as before but are applied only to the signal paths leading back to the gates which generate the pseudosynchronous clock pulses. $T_{min}/2$ is used because these signals must settle out in one-half clock period or less. A higher clock rate could be obtained by narrowing C^* to less than one-half of the clock period.

The use of *multiple-phase system clocking* combines the ideas discussed so far in order to specify a maximum clock rate. For example, the clocking scheme implied by Fig. 5-39 requires changes resulting from the clock transition C_0 to be settled out by

1. The beginning of C_2 for variables which will be ANDed with C_2 in order to generate a pulse for presetting purposes
2. The beginning of C_3 for variables which will be ANDed with C_3 for similar purposes
3. One flipflop setup time before the next clock transition C_0, for all other variables

The maximum clock rate must be restricted to the minimum of the three values determined by these three criteria.

A somewhat different situation is presented by the clocking scheme illustrated in Fig. 5-40. There the variables in each subsystem which feed into the other subsystem must be settled out early enough for the set and clear inputs in the other subsystem to set up. With the two clock phases shown, $T_{min}/2$ is available for this settling to occur. Each subsystem is also constrained so that *all* variables settle out within one flipflop setup time less than T_{min}, the same as in any single-phase asynchronous system. Whichever of these constraints on the minimum clock period is the larger determines the maximum clock rate.

PROBLEMS

5-1 Synchronous sequential circuits Is each of the circuits shown in Fig. P 5-1 a
synchronous circuit? Explain.

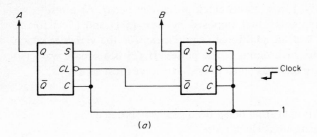

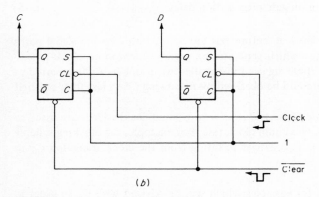

Fig. P 5-1

5-2 Transition maps Construct transition maps for each flipflop in each of the following
synchronous sequential circuits:

    (a) A 4-bit binary counter.

    (b) An 8421 BCD code counter (one decade).

    (c) An 8421 BCD code down counter (one decade).

    (d) A 3-bit self-stopping binary counter which counts in binary up to seven but
which does not count back to zero, rather staying in state 7.

    (e) A self-starting scale-of-five scaler which counts in the sequence shown in Fig. P 5-2.

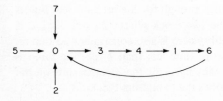

Fig. P 5-2

Each number is the decimal equivalent of the scaler's contents, expressed as a binary number ABC. (The scaler is *self-starting* in the sense that regardless of what state it is in when power is turned on, it will get into the scale-of-five count sequence.)

5-3 Synchronous counter design with RS flipflops Using RS flipflops (with single set and clear inputs) and NAND gates (not having dot-AND/OR capability), design a minimum-cost
  (*a*)   4-bit binary counter
  (*b*)   8421 BCD code counter (one decade)

5-4 Flipflop types A flipflop satisfies the experimentally determined input-output table shown in Fig. P 5-4. Together with the presence or absence of small circles, label set and clear inputs and Q and $\overline{Q}$ outputs in as many ways as possible to make this look like
  (*a*)   A *JK* flipflop
  (*b*)   A set-overrides-clear flipflop

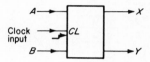

		Before clock transition		After clock transition	
A	B	X	Y	X	Y
L	L	L	H	H	L
L	L	H	L	L	H
L	H	L	H	H	L
L	H	H	L	H	L
H	L	L	H	L	H
H	L	H	L	L	H
H	H	L	H	L	H
H	H	H	L	H	L

Fig. P 5-4

5-5 Generalized input equations Illustrate the eight possible input-output conditions (similar to Fig. 5-8) for the DDT flipflop shown in Fig. P 5-5, which looks like a delay flipflop if $DT = 0$ and a toggle flipflop if $DT = 1$. The corresponding generalized input equations are difficult to express. What is the difficulty? How would you design with DDT flipflops?

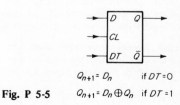

$Q_{n+1} = D_n$ if $DT = 0$

Fig. P 5-5 $Q_{n+1} = D_n \oplus Q_n$ if $DT = 1$

5-6 Synchronous counter design Can a synchronous 3-bit binary counter be constructed solely with 1-bit shift registers and NAND gates? Explain.

5-7 Synchronous counter design with *JK* flipflops Using series 54/74 TTL master-slave *JK* flipflops (sensitive to 1 to 0 transitions and having single set and clear inputs), together with NAND gates (not having dot-AND/OR capability), obtain input equations and show a minimum-cost implementation for each of the counters below:

(*a*)   The counter of Prob. 5-2*a*
(*b*)   The counter of Prob. 5-2*b*
(*c*)   The counter of Prob. 5-2*c*
(*d*)   The counter of Prob. 5-2*d*
(*e*)   The counter of Prob. 5-2*e*
(*f*)   The counter with transition maps shown in Fig. P 5-7*a*.
(*g*)   The counter with transition maps shown in Fig. P 5-7*b*.
(*h*)   The counter with transition maps shown in Fig. P 5-7*c*.

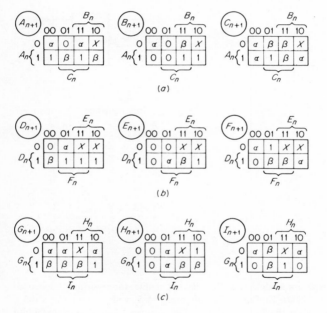

Fig. P 5-7

5-8 Synchronous counter design with *JK* flipflops Consider the *pseudorandom binary noise generator* shown in Fig. P 5-8. By constructing the transition map for flipflop *A* (a *JK* flipflop) and using its set and clear inputs more powerfully than as a 1-bit shift register, simplify the circuit as much as possible. Use NAND gates, if necessary.

5-9 Synchronous design with different flipflop types Obtain as simple input equations as possible for a flipflop with each of the transition maps shown in Fig. P 5-9 if the flipflop is each of the following types: *RS*, *JK*, set-overrides-clear, clear-overrides-set, toggle, delay.

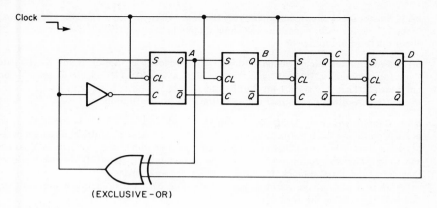

Fig. P 5-8

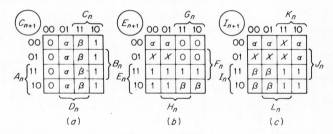

Fig. P 5-9

5-10 Transition maps for circuits with inputs Construct transition maps for each flipflop in each of the following synchronous sequential circuits:

(a) A 3-bit *gated binary counter* which counts when an enable input $E = 1$ and does not count when $E = 0$.

(b) A 3-bit *synchronously clearable binary counter* which counts if $R = 0$ and clears to 000 if $R = 1$.

(c) A 2-bit Gray-code up-down counter which counts up when $U = 1$ and counts down when $U = 0$. (This counter is commonly used to drive a bidirectional stepping motor.)

(d) The implementation in time of the iterative circuit represented by the flow diagram shown in Fig. P 5-10, with input I, output F, and states A and B. Also show the Karnaugh map for $F_n = F_n(I_n, A_n, B_n)$.

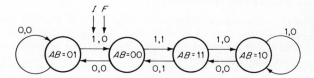

Fig. P 5-10

5-11 Synchronous circuit design using JK **flipflops** Using the same flipflops and gates as in Prob. 5-7, derive input equations and show minimum-cost implementations for each of the circuits defined in Prob. 5-10.

5-12 Synchronous circuit design Using a set-overrides-clear flipflop B and NAND gates, show the minimum-cost circuitry needed to shift a variable A (available in asserted form only) into B. That is, make a 1-bit shift register.

Hint: As always, construct the transition map for the flipflop.

5-13 Counter structure Using JK flipflops and the structure shown in Fig. P 5-13, is it possible to define the iterative block B (with general inputs c, u, and b and general output c^*) so as to implement a gated up-down binary counter which does not count if count = 0 and which otherwise counts up if up = 1 and counts down if up = 0? If your answer is yes, then define the iterative block. If your answer is no, then explain.

Hint: Write out the count sequence and try to define first an up counter and then a down counter having this structure.

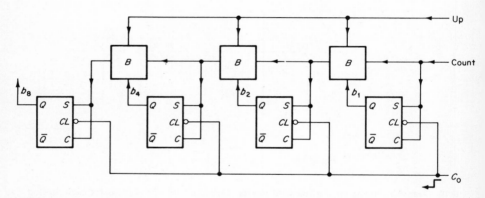

Fig. P 5-13

5-14 Synchronous counter structure (*a*) What 5-bit binary number A should be added to any 5-bit binary number B to form $B + 1$?

(*b*) What 5-bit binary number S should be added to any 5-bit binary number B to form $B - 1$ (neglecting the sixth bit of the result)?

(*c*) Design as simple a circuit as possible with one Boolean input I and five outputs forming A for one value of I and S for the other value.

(*d*) Using this circuit plus five full adders plus five delay flipflops to hold the number B, design a 5-bit up-down binary counter.

5-15 Scaler design Using JK flipflops (with a single set and clear input) and no extra gating, design each of the following synchronous scalers. Are your designs "self-starting?" That is, will the scalers count from any states not included in the count sequence to a state in the count sequence?

　　(*a*)　　Scale-of-two
　　(*b*)　　Scale-of-three
　　(*c*)　　Scale-of-six

5-16 Scaler design If scalers having the following periods are paralleled, what will the resulting period be?

(a) $p_1 = 3$ $p_2 = 4$
(b) $p_1 = 4$ $p_2 = 6$
(c) $p_1 = 3$ $p_2 = 6$
(d) $p_1 = 2$ $p_2 = 3$ $p_3 = 5$
(e) $p_1 = 2$ $p_2 = 3$ $p_3 = 4$

5-17 Maximum clock rate (a) If an *RS* flipflop is characterized by a setup time of T_S ns, a release time of T_R ns, and a propagation delay of T_D ns, then write an expression for its *worst-case maximum toggling rate* (in megahertz) such that it will toggle back and forth reliably if this pulse rate is applied to the clock input. (In order to have it toggle, the set input is tied to $\bar{Q}$ and $C = Q$.)

(b) Check a manufacturer's data for an *RS* flipflop to see if the listed maximum toggling rate is the same as that calculated by this means.

5-18 Maximum clock rate Given *RS* flipflops (all of one type), is the worst-case maximum toggling rate higher, lower, or the same as the worst-case maximum shift rate? Explain in terms of appropriate circuits and flipflop timing characteristics.

5-19 Maximum clock rate Several different logic lines can be characterized (more or less accurately) by substituting different values of X into the following relations:

Maximum gate propagation delay = X ns
Maximum flipflop propagation delay = $3X$ ns
Maximum flipflop setup time = $2X$ ns
Maximum flipflop release time = $\frac{1}{2}X$ ns

If a synchronous system is to be designed and the number of levels of gating will be constrained to be 10 or less, then what must X be in order to assure a maximum clock rate of at least 1 MHz?

5-20 Maximum allowable clock skew (a) What does it mean if the maximum release time for a flipflop type is negative?

(b) If all the other characteristics of two flipflop types are the same except that one has a positive maximum release time while the other's is negative, then which has the larger maximum allowable clock skew?

(c) Is it good to have a large maximum allowable clock skew? Why?

5-21 Maximum allowable clock skew Consider a system designed with a mixture of the following two flipflop types which both have clock inputs sensitive to 0 to 1 transitions:

	Min propagation delay (ns)	Max release time (ns)
Flipflop type A	20	10
Flipflop type B	30	5

Is the maximum allowable clock skew determined by a type A driving a type A, a type A driving a type B, or what? Show the circuit and timing diagram corresponding to the critical case. What is the maximum allowable clock skew?

5-22 Asynchronously coupled counters Consider a 16-bit asynchronous binary counter constructed as shown in Fig. 5-25. If each flipflop propagation delay is 20 ns, then it will take 320 ns for this counter to settle out as it rolls over from all 1s to all 0s. Speed up this settling time (using NOR gates if necessary and minimizing cost) by redesigning the counter with asynchronously coupled synchronous binary counters so as to (*a*) Decrease the maximum settling time to 160 ns

(*b*) Decrease the maximum settling time to 80 ns

5-23 Asynchronously coupled scalers Given the two scalers with the count sequences shown in Fig. P 5-23, show the simplest asynchronous coupling and the connection to the clock in order to obtain the desired combined count sequence shown. Assume flipflop clock inputs are sensitive to 0 to 1 transitions. Do not design each individual scaler, but simply show its outputs and clock input.

Individual scaler count sequences				Desired combined count sequence			
A	*B*	*C*	*D*	*A*	*B*	*C*	*D*
0	0	0	0	0	0	0	0
0	1	0	1	0	1	0	0
1	0	1	1	1	0	0	0
0	0	1	0	0	0	0	1
		0	0	0	1	0	1
				1	0	0	1
				0	0	1	1
				0	1	1	1
				1	0	1	1
				0	0	1	0
				0	1	1	0
				1	0	1	0
				0	0	0	0

Fig. P 5-23

5-24 Asynchronously coupled counters Consider the *hours and minutes* counter used in a digital watch and built with flipflops whose clock inputs are sensitive to 1 to 0 transitions. Assume all outputs are available in both asserted and negated form. Also assume that each digit of hours and minutes is coded as a binary number, giving

$$H_{20}H_{10}H_8H_4H_2H_1M_{40}M_{20}M_{10}M_8M_4M_2M_1$$

(*a*) Break the design down into an asynchronously coupled chain of counter stages, as shown in Fig. P 5-24 in which each counter stage includes as few of the variables as possible. Show this breakdown and the variables in each counter stage. As an example of the considerations involved, will M_1 count correctly if it changes state every time the clock emits a pulse? And will the remaining stages to the left count correctly if they are told to count each time M_1 changes from 1 to 0 or from 0 to 1?

(*b*) In the case of each counter stage, is there a flipflop in the stage adjacent to it on the right which can be used as a source of clock input transitions? If so, then show the connection. If not, then using minimum-cost NAND gating, generate an appropriate clock transition. (What must the gating do?) Do not design the individual synchronous counter stages themselves.

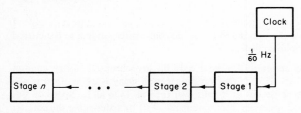

Fig. P 5-24

5-25 Pseudosynchronously coupled counters Design the *hours and minutes* counter of Prob. 5-24 pseudosynchronously using (fast) NAND or NOR gates to generate the pseudosynchronous pulses.

5-26 Pseudosynchronously coupled counters Reconsider the design of the 16-bit binary counter of Prob. 5-22 and, by using the best possible combination of synchronous, asynchronous, and pseudosynchronous techniques, speed up the maximum settling time of the counter as required below. Use NOR gates, if necessary, and minimize cost. Decrease the maximum settling time to

(a)   160 ns   (c)   40 ns
(b)   80 ns   (d)   20 ns

5-27 Disc memory address counter by pseudosynchronous design The disc memory shown in Fig. 4-16 and described in Sec. 4-8 requires an address counter which derives its clock input from the *bit clock* and which uses the *origin clock* to direct clear it to its zero position. Design this address counter, using the flipflops of Fig. 4-9a and either NOR or NAND gates, as follows:

(a) Design a 4-bit asynchronous binary *bit* counter $b_8 b_4 b_2 b_1$.

(b) Design the scale-of-33 *word* counter, with the count sequence shown in Fig. P 5-27, in two parts (which will be coupled together pseudosynchronously): A 5-bit asynchronous binary counter $w_{16} w_8 w_4 w_2 w_1$ and a w_d bit (which equals zero only for the first count of this word counter).

(c) Design a 5-bit asynchronous binary *sector* counter $s_{16} s_8 s_4 s_2 s_1$.

(d) Drive the counters pseudosynchronously with narrow positive pulses derived from the bit clock, which also puts out narrow positive pulses. The bit counter counts once for every bit-clock pulse. The word counter counts once as the bit counter rolls over from 15 to 0. The sector counter counts once as the word counter rolls over from 63 to 0.

(e) Direct clear the counter to all 0s with a pulse of correct polarity derived from the origin clock, a positive pulse occurring once per cycle of the complete counter and between bit-clock pulses.

Word counter count sequence

Counter state	W_d	W_{16}	W_8	W_4	W_2	W_1	
0	0	0	0	0	0	0	← First word of sector
32	1	0	0	0	0	0	⎫
33	1	0	0	0	0	1	
34	1	0	0	0	1	0	
35	1	0	0	0	1	1	
36	1	0	0	1	0	0	
37	1	0	0	1	0	1	
38	1	0	0	1	1	0	⎬ 32 data words
39	1	0	0	1	1	1	
40	1	0	1	0	0	0	
•••	•	•••	•	•••	•	•••	
62	1	1	1	1	1	0	
Count sector ⎧ 63	1	1	1	1	1	1	⎭
counter ⎩ 0	0	0	0	0	0	0	

Fig. P 5-27

5-28 Direct presetting of flipflops (*a*) For the circuit shown in Fig. P 5-28, show a timing diagram for $P1, \ldots, P8$ so as to transfer the contents of C into D, B into C, A into B and X into A. Assume the availability of both positive and negative pulses, each of which lasts for an entire clock interval. Minimize the total number of clock intervals needed.

      (*b*) If D is connected to X, is there any way to transfer D into A as well as C into D, B into C, and A into B? For example, if we start with $ABCD = 1010$, can we end up with $ABCD = 0101$? If so, show the timing diagram. If not, explain.

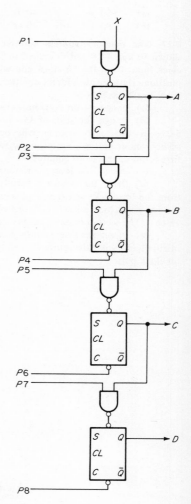

Fig. P 5-28

5-29 Single-phase synchronous clocking Suppose it is decided to implement a certain system by using single-phase synchronous clocking in order to speed up its operation. The system has previously been implemented using multiple-phase synchronous clocking. That implementation used only *JK* flipflops (and NAND gates), with all clock inputs tied to one clock phase. The other phases were used solely for two-step presetting into these flipflops. How would you proceed to redesign the circuitry if you wished to leave the implementation unchanged, except for converting the presetting operations? Show an example and discuss any changes required in the timing associated with presetting.

5-30 Single-phase asynchronous clocking The circuit shown in Fig. P 5-30 has been designed to do its job properly if it is entirely synchronous, as shown. Will the circuit work correctly if the (expensive) synchronous binary counter is replaced with a (cheap) asynchronous binary counter? Explain your answer, assuming the clock rate is not particularly fast.

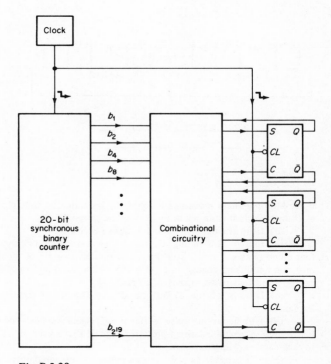

Fig. P 5-30

5-31 Single-phase pseudosynchronous clocking For a system using flipflops sensitive to 0 to 1 transitions on their clock inputs, explain

   (*a*) Why the pseudosynchronous clock pulses should be negative pulses.

   (*b*) Why the pseudosynchronous clock pulses should occur during the last half of the system clock period rather than the first half. Also, what determines when the system clock period begins (and ends)?

5-32 Single-phase pseudosynchronous clocking. Using the flipflops and gates of Prob. 5-7 plus fast NOR or NAND gates for the pseudosynchronous gating, design a minimum-cost circuit to generate the pseudosynchronous waveforms C_0, C_{0A}, and C_{0B} for Prob. 4-18.

   Hint: For a scale-of-24 scaler, note that $24 = 3 \times 2 \times 2 \times 2$.

5-33 Single-phase pseudosynchronous clocking Using the flipflops and gates of Prob. 5-7 plus fast NOR or NAND gates for the pseudosynchronous gating, design a minimum-cost circuit to generate the pseudosynchronous waveforms C_{0A} and C_{0B} and the variable S from C_0 in Prob. 4-19.

5-34 Two-phase clocking Consider the circuit shown in Fig. P 5-34. After $m + n$ clock periods (that is, $m + n$ 0 to 1 transitions on both C_0 and C_1), will the contents of the shift registers be the same as initially? (Assume arbitrary initial contents.) Explain your answer and whether it depends on the values of m and n.

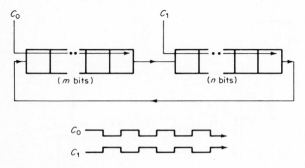

Fig. P 5-34

5-35 Multiple-phase clocking In order to generate the four clock phases shown in Fig. 5-39 the two circuits shown in Fig. P 5-35 are proposed.

   (*a*) Using the logic of Prob. 5-7, design each circuit.

   (*b*) Construct a timing diagram for each, showing C^*, the flipflop outputs and the four clock phases. For the asynchronous counter, exaggerate the delay between the change in b_1 and resulting change in b_2. Do any of the resulting waveforms (C_0, C_1, C_2, or C_3) exhibit a spurious pulse, as shown? Explain.

   (*c*) Do any of the C_i outputs of the Gray-code circuit exhibit spurious pulses? Explain.

   (*d*) Will a spurious pulse matter if a C_i signal is used as the clock input to a flipflop? If it is used to generate a direct presetting signal? If it is used on a flipflop set or clear input? In each case, explain your answer.

   (*e*) Is it possible to get spurious pulses on any gated outputs from any *unit-distance-code* counter (which changes only 1 bit at a time)? Explain.

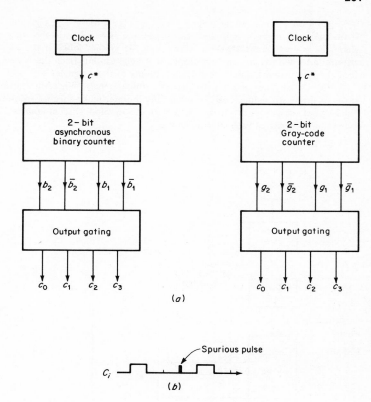

Fig. P 5-35

5-36 Multiple-phase clocking Using the flipflops of Fig. 4-9a plus NAND gates and a clock which emits a single-phase square-wave output, design the complete circuit, including all timing circuitry, to implement Prob. 4-18. Use either one- or two-step direct presetting on the JK flipflops instead of doing it synchronously. Label the signal which can be used as the system clock for clocking the rest of the system (which will feed an input into the shift register and take an output from it). Minimize cost, figuring one flipflop is equivalent to 10 gate leads.

5-37 System clocking In this problem, we wish to make the magnetic core memory of Figs. 4-19 and 4-20 look like eight parallel 1,024-bit clocked shift registers clocked at 330 kHz. The proposed organization is shown in Fig. P 5-37. The scale-of-four scaler generates the initiate waveform required in Fig. 4-20. The scale-of-two scaler generates the system clock rate C_0 with which all operations in the rest of the system are clocked. It also causes the core memory to alternate read and write cycles. The scale-of-1,024 scaler is clocked once for each read-write cycle. The intent is to read out of a memory location, then write new information into it, and then not come back to it again for 1,024 read-write cycles. Assume the circuitry and the system using it will be implemented with the logic of Prob. 5-7, and minimize the cost of the implementation.

(a) Construct a timing diagram for C_X, C_A, initiate, C_0, C_B, and mode. Indicate where the core memory is in the read mode and where it is in the write mode. Indicate where the address input changes. Note when the system looks at the eight core memory outputs and when the core memory looks at the eight inputs from the system. Are there any clock skew constraints which must be met for any of these signals?

(b) Design the circuitry to generate these signals. Wherever legitimate, use asynchronous design to reduce cost. In generating initiate, make sure no spurious pulses occur. Discuss your design of the initiate pulse with this in mind. Discuss your use or avoidance of asynchronous design at each step of the way.

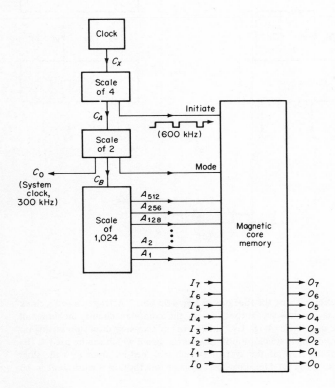

Fig. P 5-37

5-38 Maximum system clock rate—single-phase asynchronous clocking Using the TTL logic of Example 5-9, we wish to examine the trade-off possible between levels of gating and levels of rippling in a single-phase asynchronously clocked system. If we are required to clock the system at a 5-MHz rate, then show all possible combinations of maximum number of levels of gating and maximum number of levels of rippling which satisfy this clock rate.

5-39 Maximum system clock rate—single-phase pseudosynchronous clocking Using the TTL logic of Example 5-9, we wish to examine the *two* trade-offs possible between levels of gating and levels of rippling in a single-phase pseudosynchronously clocked system. Assume that C^* propagates through the pseudosynchronous clock signal gating with a maximum propagation delay of 5 ns. Also assume that C^* is a square wave. If the system is to be clocked at 5 MHz, then show all possible combinations of r' and n' in Eq. (5-5) and compare these with the other constraint on r and n which also must be met (and which was found in Prob. 5-38).

5-40 Maximum system clock rate—multiple-phase clocking A system which uses separate clock phases for direct presetting and clearing has its maximum reliable clock rate determined by the worst-case among several constraints. Why is it that the constraints involving direct presetting and clearing do not depend on the flipflop setup time?

REFERENCES

For the original treatment of the transition-map approach to sequential circuit design, see M. P. Marcus, "Switching Circuits for Engineers," chap. 19, Prentice-Hall, Inc., Englewood Cliffs, N.J., 1962, 1967.

For more insight into the specific test circuits and test procedures used by an integrated-circuits manufacturer in specifying the timing characteristics of logic elements, see the manufacturer's integrated-circuits catalogs.

6
Organization of
Digital Systems

6-1 A CHOICE OF STRUCTURES

Any digital system can be implemented in a variety of ways. However, one design choice which the designer should consider from the outset is whether or not to organize the system around a general-purpose digital computer. A starting point toward this decision concerns the estimated cost (or, perhaps more properly, the estimated payoff) of the system. With small computers available for $5,000 to $10,000 or less, it would be absurd to ignore the benefits of organizing the system around such a computer if the estimated cost of the system is many times this amount.

There is one major constraint which can rule out the organization of the system around a specific computer. The *data rates* imposed by the input and output devices may be difficult to meet. For example, a system which must continuously process serial data arriving over a communication channel at a 1 Mbit/s rate cannot handle this information bit by bit if it executes instructions only every 2 μs. On the other hand, perhaps the processing can be organized so that a special-purpose input circuit processes bits in groups of 8 or 16 bits while the computer takes these processed groups (every 8 or 16 μs) and completes the processing on them. Consequently, before ruling out the use of a computer, it is worth considering not only the I/O data rates involved but also whether the preprocessing of input data (or the postprocessing of output data) in a special-purpose circuit will not alleviate the problem.

Another data-rate problem which may appear to rule out the use of a computer concerns the implementation of the algorithms involved in meeting the system requirements. For example, consider a system which must drive and coordinate the motion of two antennas so that the intersection of their beams follows some well-defined path in space. The motions may be rather slow in terms of computer-output requirements. However, the program which implements the coordinate transformations involved in the problem may require more time than is permitted in order to generate output data at the rate required. One solution to this problem might be to replace relatively slow multiply-and-divide software routines by fast multiply-and-divide hardware. This hardware can be coupled to the computer just like any other peripheral device, accepting inputs from the computer and generating outputs which are taken back to the computer. An even faster solution to the problem would be to implement in hardware the entire coordinate transformation process using some especially efficient algorithm. Again, this hardware might be treated by the computer like any other peripheral device.

Thus far we have discussed two reasons related to required data rates which might lead us away from organizing a system around a general-purpose computer. Another more fundamental reason dominates the decision for many small, simple digital systems. Here the lowest-cost implementation may be achieved with a special-purpose system structure. A broad class of examples arises in instrumentation. The flurry of activity by the many manufacturers of digital voltmeters and digital multimeters is a response to this stimulus. Another is represented by averaging and correlating systems which accept an input signal and which, after sampling and conversion to digital representation, carry out a simple algorithmic process on that data. The net result is the generation of an output (at a much lower data rate) in which repetitive components of the input data are enhanced and nonrepetitive components are virtually eliminated.

As the cost of general-purpose computers continues to drop, more and more of these applications will be designed around small computers rather than with special-purpose structures. Several reasons for this shift are explored in the remainder of this section. One reason is that the system design is simplified to three steps:

1. The interfacing of input and output devices and perhaps auxiliary memory devices
2. Perhaps augmenting the computer with special-purpose units which implement certain algorithms in order to meet data-rate requirements
3. Meeting the system specifications through programming (software)

Some systems are especially well suited for being organized around a computer because either they include much decision making or else they require a variety of things to be done one after another. This decision making and sequencing is a "bread and butter" job for a computer. In contrast, a special-purpose system tends to yield either an expensive but versatile structure or a less expensive but virtually unchangeable structure, as we shall see when we discuss *mode circuitry* in Secs. 6-2 and 6-5.

Regardless of the complexity of the algorithms which must be implemented by the system, a general-purpose computer has the capability of implementing them. Generally speaking, they are easier to design and debug through the software of a computer than through a special-purpose structure. The questions which arise revolve around the *time* required, as imposed by I/O data rates, and the *storage* required, as determined by the skill of the programmer in meeting the needs of the problem. As mentioned previously, if this time requirement cannot be met, then implementing a portion of an algorithm in hardware may resolve it.

Many times it pays to organize a system around a computer because uncertainties exist in the system specifications. The changes which result as these uncertainties become resolved are much easier to handle in the software of a computer than in the hardware of a special-purpose structure. This occurs in systems which are intended to *evolve*. For example, if some new ideas are to be applied to the problem of extracting information from voice waveforms, perhaps a system should be built and some preliminary data gathered and processed before tying the system down to a fixed structure. In this way, successes can be built upon and weaknesses eliminated. Another example occurs where the system is likely to be modified eventually in order to upgrade its performance or to increase its convenience. This modification will almost certainly be easier in the software of a computer than in the hardware of a special-purpose structure.

In documenting a system so that it can be understood by the user, the system organized around a computer has a large head start over that using a special-purpose structure. The computer has already been described by the manufacturer. Describing the I/O interfacing is simplified because both the computer and the I/O devices are well understood and documented. Finally the software can be flow-diagrammed and described, using all the standard descriptive techniques available to programmers.

From the user's viewpoint, the documentation of a system built with a special-purpose structure is likely to appear much more complex. As with the computer-organized system, the user must first understand what the system is trying to do and the algorithms being used. But then he must also understand how the system is organized and the function of each subsystem. Since each subsystem is generally a *sequential* circuit, this understanding and the understanding of the interconnected subsystems are vastly complicated by the interactions of these subsystems as time progresses.

The same reasons which simplify the documentation of a computer-organized system also simplify the diagnostic testing 'of the system if it malfunctions. The computer itself can be tested using a diagnostic routine supplied by the manufacturer. Furthermore, simple diagnostic routines can be prepared for the I/O interface circuitry and any algorithms implemented in hardware. This permits the computer to be used not only as the heart of the system but also as its own diagnostic tester. When a special-purpose structure malfunctions, first the logic boards and then the wiring between boards can be checked using computer-aided diagnostic testing. This should be no more difficult than for the computer-organized system. However, if this computer-aided diagnostic testing has not been prepared for the system, the alternative of manual troubleshooting is a great deal more time-consuming because of the system's irregular structure.

In conclusion, we have many incentives to organize systems around a computer. However, we still need the ability to design *special-purpose structures*, for these are used in a variety of circumstances:

1. For the design of small, simple systems where cost prohibits the use of a computer
2. For the design of systems where the data rates are higher than can be handled by a computer
3. To implement preprocessors into a computer and postprocessors from a computer in order to satisfy data-rate problems which cannot be met by the computer alone
4. To implement algorithms in hardware for use as an adjunct to a computer in order to meet the data-rate requirement for the processing of data

6-2 SPECIAL-PURPOSE STRUCTURES

Special-purpose systems using single-phase clocking can be usefully described in terms of the structure shown in Fig. 6-1. A more general structure would include several clock phases to permit the direct presetting of flipflops. However, that structure is a simple extension of the structure shown here. Figure 6-1 illustrates the two major parts of a special-purpose system structure:

1. The data processing circuitry
2. The timing and mode circuitry

The *data processing circuitry* includes input devices such as multiplexers, analog-to-digital converters, switches, and keyboards. It includes output devices like stepping motors, digital-to-analog converters, and displays of various types. It includes data storage devices like core memories or long shift registers if they are appropriate to the problem. Finally, it includes whatever structures are most

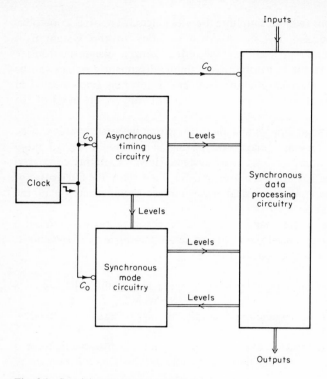

Fig. 6-1 Special-purpose system structure.

appropriate for implementing the algorithms which will take the system inputs and generate the system outputs.

The *timing and mode circuitry* serves much the same role for this special-purpose system structure as the *program* serves for a general-purpose computer. That is, it sequences all of the operations of the data processing circuitry. *Timing circuitry* sequences those operations which are functions of time only. An example of this would be the implementation of an algorithm where certain operations have to be done one after another. The timing circuitry might simply be an asynchronous binary counter which is in state 0 when operation begins. The data processing circuitry is controlled by levels coming from this binary counter, so that when the first clock transition C_0 occurs, the circuitry responds to those things which are enabled when the binary counter is in state 0. When the next clock transition occurs, the circuitry responds to those things which are enabled when the binary counter is in state 1, and so forth. If the operations have to repeat after every n clock periods, then instead of using a binary counter, we would use a scale-of-n scaler.

A variation on this structure again uses single-phase clocking but also employs pseudosynchronous design in order to simplify the timing. Consider the following example.

Example 6-1 We are given a synchronous analog-to-digital (A/D) converter which converts a voltage input to a 5-bit sign plus two's complement number in the five clock periods following that clock period when the level input *initialize* equals 1. Develop a system structure and its timing diagram which will repetitively generate the average of four successive conversions.

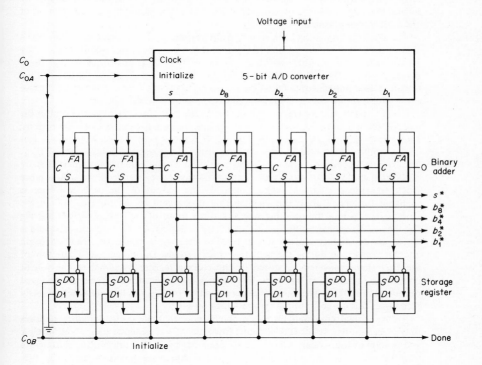

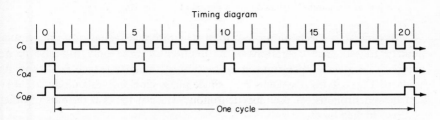

Fig. 6-2 A/D converter and averager.

A *parallel* structure for carrying this out is shown in Fig. 6-2. (The corresponding serial structure is considered in Prob. 6-1 at the end of the chapter.) The structure here assumes that all initializing, for the 7-bit storage register (made up of switched-input delay flipflops) as well as the A/D converter is done synchronously. If in actuality these initializing operations employed direct presetting, the only modification required would be to use a multiple-phase clock to generate presetting pulses in the middle of the appropriate clock periods.

Since four 5-bit sign plus two's complement numbers are to be added together, the result may require 7 bits for its representation. This has necessitated the use of a 7-bit storage register and a 7-bit binary adder. It has also required that the 5-bit A/D-converter output be represented as a 7-bit number. This can be done simply by letting the three most significant bits of the 7-bit representation equal the sign bit of the 5-bit representation.

To form an average, the sum must be divided by four. This can be done for a sign plus two's complement number, just as it can be for a binary number, simply by moving the binary point two places to the left. (This is analogous to dividing a decimal number by 100 by moving the decimal point two places to the left.) In the circuit, this is implemented by taking the averaged output $s*b_8^*b_4^*b_2^*b_1^*$ from the five most significant bits of the 7-bit sum, discarding the fractional remainder.

To follow the timing, note that the flipflops in the A/D converter and in the storage register are specified as being sensitive to negative-going clock transitions; thus, the only time the A/D-converter output changes is on the negative-going edges of C_0, while the storage register changes only on the negative-going edges of C_{0A}. The system operation begins with the transition at the end of clock period 0 by initializing the A/D converter and clearing the storage register to 0. After four more clock transitions (that is, during period 5) the output of the A/D converter is available for use. During this clock period it is added to the number "0" in the storage register and the resulting sum sits at the input of the storage register waiting for the negative-going transition of C_{0A} (at transition 5). At this transition the sum is stored in the storage register and the A/D converter is initialized, ready to begin another conversion during the next five clock periods. During period 20 the sum of the first three conversions, stored in the storage register, is added to the fourth conversion, available at this time from the A/D converter, and forms the averaged output $s*b_8^*b_4^*b_2^*b_1^*$. The negative-going transition of C_{0B} can be used synchronously to transfer this output into the system which uses it.

As a final comment on this problem, note that the timing circuitry requires only a scale-of-five scaler (taken from Appendix A3) to generate the period for C_{0A} and a scale-of-four-scaler, which counts once for each C_{0A} transition, to generate C_{0B}. One possible circuit (using scalers given in Appendix A3) is shown in Fig. 6-3. An alternative circuit would use C_0 to clock both scalers, generating C_{0B} as the output of the parallel scalers having a period of 5 x 4 = 20.

In general, a special-purpose system structure will include not only timing circuitry to sequence operations as a function of time only but also *mode circuitry* to sequence operations as a function of the *data* as well as of time. As shown in Fig. 6-1 for a system using single-phase clocking, this mode circuitry must be synchronous (or pseudosynchronous) since it looks at outputs of other circuitry clocked by C_0.

While timing circuitry is best described using a timing diagram, mode circuitry is best described using the flow diagrams of Sec. 2-12. The inputs are

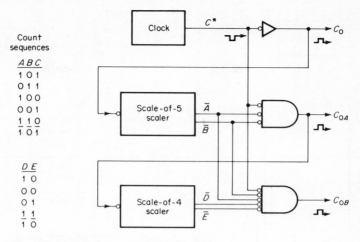

Count
sequences

$A B C$
1 0 1
0 1 1
1 0 0
0 0 1
1 1 0
1 0 1

$D E$
1 0
0 0
0 1
1 1
1 0

Fig. 6-3 Timing circuitry for Example 6-1.

functions of variables in the data processing circuitry and of time, derived from the timing circuitry. The mode circuitry generates circuit outputs which the data processing circuitry uses to sequence its operations. It also goes from state to state during successive clock transitions. To illustrate these ideas, consider the following example.

Example 6-2 Design a simple digital combination door lock. The output, when the combination is worked correctly, will be a 5-V signal *open door* which operates an *electric strike* mounted in the door jamb in place of the regular strike. When this electric strike is energized, it pulls out of the way of the latch on the door, permitting the door to open. The combination door lock input is a single illuminated pushbutton switch mounted on the door jamb or the outside wall. Assuming a combination of 3-6-5, the lock is to be operated as follows:

1. The switch is depressed until the light comes on (within 4 s).
2. The light will stay on for 4 s during which time the switch must be depressed exactly three times.
3. The switch will turn off for 4 s during which time the switch must be depressed exactly six times.
4. The light will come on again for 4 s during which time the switch must be depressed exactly five times.
5. If these four things have been done correctly, then during the next 4 s the electric strike will be energized and the door unlocked.

In general, the most difficult step in carrying out a digital design consists of breaking down the problem so as to obtain as simple a configuration for the data processing circuitry as possible. Figure 6-4 illustrates one possibility. Note that this system has two clocks: the 0.25-Hz clock C_0, which clocks the mode circuitry every 4 s, and the pushbutton switch, which clocks the binary counter. The latch on the

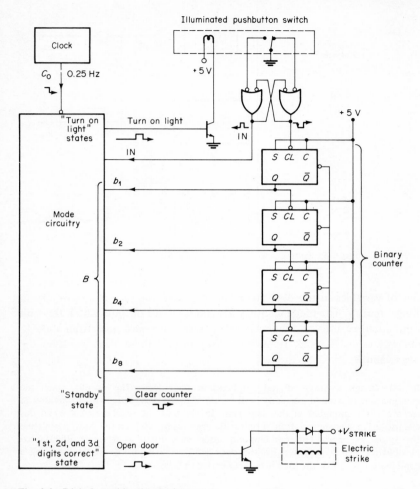

Fig. 6-4   Digital combination lock.

output of the switch does two things. It removes the effect of any contact bounce, which might otherwise give more than one transition per push of the button. In addition, it provides a fast transition independent of the relatively slow switch closure, which is satisfactory for clocking the 4-bit binary counter.

    The intent of this circuit is to begin the combination with the binary counter cleared to $B = 0$ and with the mode circuitry sitting in the *standby* state, shown at the bottom of the mode-circuitry flow diagram of Fig. 6-5. As long as IN = 0 during each C_0 transition, the mode circuitry remains in the standby state. However, when someone depresses the switch and holds it down until a C_0 transition occurs, then the mode circuitry reads IN = 1 and goes to the *start* state, shown at the top of the mode-circuitry flow diagram. While in this state, the light is turned on. Now, if the switch is depressed three times, the binary counter will count up to three ($B = 3$).

When the next C_0 transition occurs, the mode circuitry will go to the *first digit correct* state. If the switch had been depressed any other number of times, the mode circuitry would have gone to the *first digit incorrect* state. During the next 4 s, while the light is off, the pushbutton is supposed to be depressed six times. This will count the binary counter up to $B = 3 + 6 = 9$.

This operation continues until the *first, second, and third digit correct* state is reached (if the combination is worked correctly). While in this state, the electric strike is energized (through a transistor switch in order to provide sufficient current and with a diode across the strike coil to protect the transistor from an inductive surge when the transistor is turned off). At the next C_0 transition, the mode circuitry goes back to the standby state.

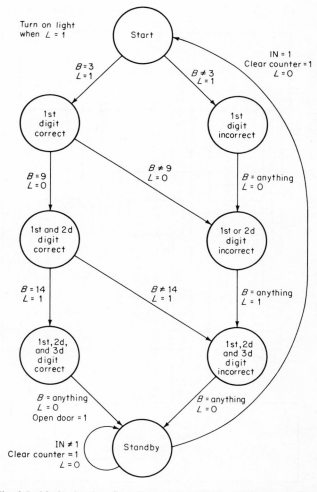

Fig. 6-5 Mode-circuitry flow diagram for digital combination lock.

The implementation of this mode circuitry utilizes the same procedure as discussed in Chap. 2. However, since this *iterative circuit* will be iterated in time, we can simplify the circuitry to some extent by using JK flipflops for the state variables and transition maps to simplify their input equations. Figure 6-6 illustrates one way in which the implementation can be broken down. The function F is introduced so that the transition maps for the A, B, and C flipflops (used to define the eight states of Fig. 6-5) will be functions of only the four variables A_n, B_n, C_n, and F_n instead of the eight variables $A_n, B_n, C_n, IN_n, b_{1n}, b_{2n}, b_{4n}$, and b_{8n}.

As was discussed in Chap. 2, the state assignment chosen has a large impact on the resulting design. The state assignment shown in Fig. 6-7a was selected rather arbitrarily. However, two criteria were used in selecting it. First, the minimum number of flipflops possible (three) is used. Second, in going from one state to the

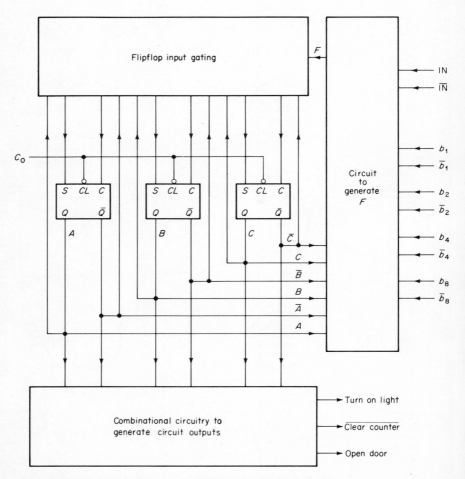

Fig. 6-6   Breakdown of mode circuitry for digital combination lock.

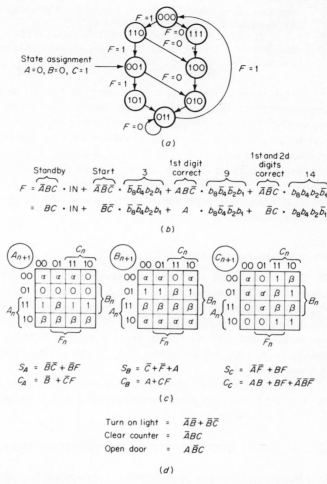

Fig. 6-7   Design of mode circuitry for digital combination lock. (a) State assignment and definition of F; (b) simplification of F; (c) transition maps and input equations using JK flipflops; (d) decoding of states for data processing circuitry.

next, as many flipflops were made to change as possible. This is done in order to have as few 1s and 0s in the transition maps as possible, thus introducing many don't cares into the set and clear functions for each flipflop.

Figure 6-7a also defines the function F which is expressed in Fig. 6-7b. Noting that the role of F is to distinguish between the two branches out of a state, we see that we have four states which require this distinction. The other four states serve as don't care conditions in the implementation of F. For example, if $ABC = 111$, then, regardless of the value of F, the next state of the mode circuitry is $ABC = 100$. These don't cares result in the final equation for F.

The transition maps for the JK flipflops shown in Fig. 6-7c are derived directly from Fig. 6-7a. Finally, the circuit outputs are obtained as in Fig. 6-7d in order to control the data processing circuitry.

This example illustrates a point made in the last section concerning the implementation of a system which involves much decision making and sequencing. Although this is a simple job for a computer, it is arduous, even for a system as simple as this, when implemented in a special-purpose structure. Furthermore, a slight change in the specifications for the system causes drastic changes in this mode circuitry. In Sec. 6-5, we shall have more to say about this problem and shall consider some more flexible structures. Nevertheless, this problem represents a prominent difficulty in the design of special-purpose system structures.

6-3 PIPELINE ORGANIZATION

In this section and the next, we shall consider two extremes of system organization. The organization discussed in this section is extremely fast at the expense of much hardware. That discussed in the next section is extremely economical of hardware at the expense of speed. In both cases, these approaches are useful when they repeatedly apply a specific algorithm to large arrays of numbers. This may form a subsystem in a larger system, or it may stand alone as a complete system.

To provide some perspective for the applications of pipelining, large systems have been organized around pipeline implementations of each of the following algorithms:

1. Fast Fourier transforms for assorted signal processing applications (see Fig. 1-16).
2. Floating-point vector operations. One application is to the processing of large quantities of seismic signals for oil and mineral exploration.
3. Correlation-function evaluation, again for various signal processing applications.

For the implementation of some algorithm (to be applied to extensive arrays of numbers), the pipeline approach breaks the algorithm down into a sequence of steps. The implementation of this sequence of steps uses *synchronizing registers*, defined in Fig. 6-8. A premium is placed on obtaining a circuit for this synchronizing register which has extremely low propagation delay as well as small size and low cost. The pipeline structure then takes the form shown in Fig. 6-9. Data are fed into the pipeline at the top, processed as they are clocked down the pipeline, and extracted at the bottom. Each step of the algorithm is implemented as one or more of the stages shown.

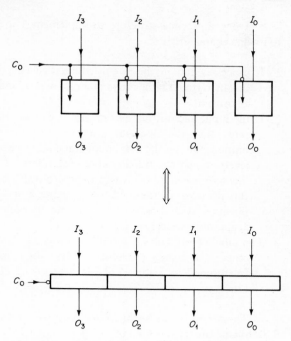

Fig. 6-8 Symbolism for a synchronizing register.

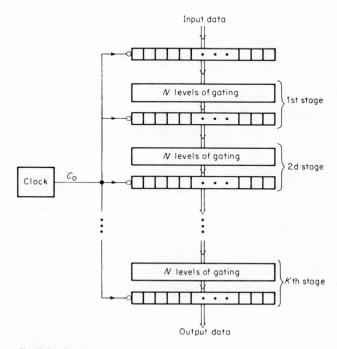

Fig. 6-9 Pipeline organization.

Using a pipeline structure to implement a specific algorithm provides the following characteristics:

1. It processes data at the rate at which it accepts data on the input (or emits it on the output) rather than at a rate dependent upon the complexity of the algorithm.
2. If the input and output are organized so as to provide the necessary high data rates, then the clock rate can be increased up to the point at which it is limited only by the maximum clock rate of a synchronous system having n levels of gating. Furthermore, regardless of the algorithm being implemented, n can be decreased to an arbitrarily small value ($n \geqslant 1$). However, this decrease is attended by an increase in the number of stages in the pipeline, with less processing done in each stage. Consequently, more synchronizing register bits are needed.
3. The pipeline effectively uses all of its gating 100 percent of the time. In this sense it is highly efficient. On the other hand, it permits the trade-off (mentioned in 2 above) of speed versus number of synchronizing register bits.

These points can be illustrated with the two pipeline implementations of a 3-bit binary adder, as shown in Fig. 6-10. The two numbers

$$A = a_4 a_2 a_1 \quad \text{and} \quad B = b_4 b_2 b_1$$

are added to form the sum

$$S = A + B = s_4 s_2 s_1$$

In Fig. 6-10a, the numbers are added in one stage. If we assume that the two outputs of each full adder are implemented with three levels of gating, then this circuit has nine levels of gating because of the carry propagations. In contrast, Fig. 6-10b illustrates a structure in which each stage has only three levels of gating. Consequently, it can be clocked with a higher clock rate, which is all-important in a pipeline system.

The whole philosophy of pipelining is to let the length (i.e., the number of stages) of the pipeline grow as it will but to push the clock rate up to some suitably high rate by

1. Using synchronizing registers and gates with extremely short propagation delays
2. Designing *all* stages with n levels of gating or less, where n is some suitably small number

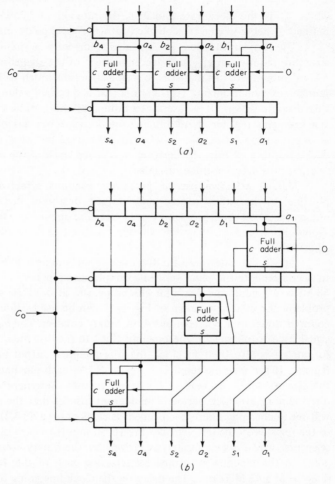

Fig. 6-10 Two pipeline implementations of a 3-bit binary adder. (*a*) Lower rate, less expensive implementation; (*b*) higher rate, more expensive implementation.

The size of the data arrays to be processed must be long relative to the number of stages in the pipeline for this philosophy to be worthwhile. Then, although it may take a reasonably long time T_d to execute the algorithm on any one set of data, this time will be only a small fraction of the total processing time T_p for all of the data. This total processing time will be

$$T_p = \frac{N-1}{f_0} + T_d$$

where f_0 is the clock rate and N is the number of *bytes* of data. A *byte* is defined as being whatever is clocked into the pipeline during each clock period.

The implementation of an algorithm with a minimum-cost pipeline structure requires an efficient decomposition of the algorithm. A good first step toward minimizing total cost is to seek a structure which will minimize the total number of synchronizing register bits (for a specified value of n). In achieving this decomposition, it is useful to note that the output of each bit of each synchronizing register at any time represents a specific variable. It can be used as an input to the gating not only of the next stage but of *any* stage. In order to take advantage of this, the designer must keep track of the temporal and spatial relationships between these variables.

Making effective use of pipelining requires effective coupling of the pipeline to its input source and output destination. If these consist of sequential-access bulk-storage devices like disc memories, then the input data should be stored in successive storage locations in the order required by the algorithm.

Often, the data rate of a disc memory may appear to be insufficiently fast to accommodate the pipeline. For example, the pipeline might be clocked at a 48-MHz rate while the disc's bit clock operates at a 3-MHz rate. To resolve this problem, the circuitry shown in Fig. 6-11 can be used. Here a 48-MHz clock is counted down in a synchronous 4-bit binary counter. The b_8 output is a 3-MHz signal used to phase-lock the pipeline clock to the disc memory's bit clock. This b_8 output is also used to clock the disc memory output into a synchronizing register. If the pipeline requires bytes of B bits each pipeline clock period, then the disc memory must read $16\,B$ bits of data into the synchronizing register each disc memory bit-clock period. This register insures that the register on the right will see unchanging inputs each time it is clocked (at a 48-MHz rate). The output of the register on the left provides the 16 bit inputs to each of B 1-out-of-16 data selectors, whose *select* inputs are driven by the binary counter. Thus each bit going to the pipeline is formed by selecting each of the 16 bits into its data selector at a 48-MHz rate. The delay on the clock line going to the synchronizing register on the right is included in order to compensate for the delays through the counter and the data selector. This insures that the register will see stable inputs when it is clocked. It might be derived from the propagation delay through a few gates.

Transferring data back into the disc memory from the output of the pipeline can be accomplished by shifting each output bit into a 16-bit shift register (at the pipeline rate). These bits can then be transferred once every 16 pipeline clock times into a synchronizing register (at a 3-MHz rate) which is then stored in the disc memory.

Some real-time pipeline systems avoid I/O problems completely. The input may come from a transducer or an array of transducers, which provide the high data rate that necessitated the pipeline structure in the first place. The output,

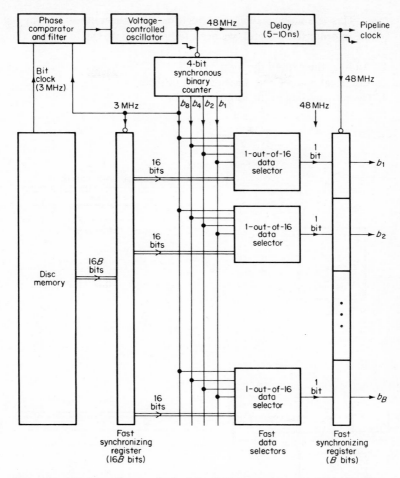

Fig. 6-11 Matching the output of a "slow" disc memory to the input of a fast pipeline.

on the other hand, may have a substantially reduced data rate, permitting it to be treated by any one of a number of conventional means. This would be true if the algorithmic process being implemented included an averaging, correlation, or convolution process. Any of these condense a flood of input into a trickle of output.

6-4 SERIAL ORGANIZATION

This form of organization is extremely suitable for implementing iterative algorithms in time. The key element in serial organization is the *recirculation loop*. This is simply a long shift register with the output feeding back to the input. In order to be useful, we need to be able to do the following things:

1. Address the data in the loop
2. Insert data into and extract data from the loop
3. Operate on data in the loop

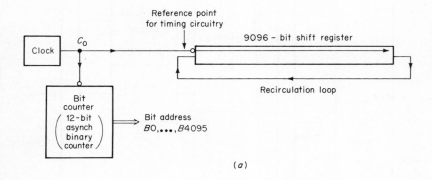

(a)

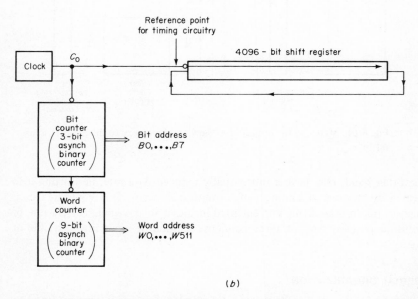

(b)

Fig. 6-12 Recirculation loop addressing. (a) Bit-organized recirculation loop; (b) word-organized recirculation loop.

The addressing of a 4,096-bit recirculation loop, bit by bit, is illustrated in Fig. 6-12a. The *reference point for timing circuitry* at the input to the shift register indicates the location of the bit which is addressed by the *bit counter*. For example, when the bit counter is in state $B35$, then the input to the long shift register might be considered to be the 1-bit variable $X(35)$ in the array of variables $X(0), \ldots, X(4,095)$. Because the counter and the shift register recycle every 4,096 clock periods, every time the bit counter is in state $B35$, $X(35)$ is at the input of the shift register.

Often it is useful to organize the recirculation loop into words, as illustrated in Fig. 6-12b. Here, every time the bit counter is in state $B0$, the 0th bit b_0 of some word $X(i)$ is available at the input to the shift register. Bit b_0 of word $X(0)$ is available when the counters are in state $W0 \cdot B0$.

We may wish to store two arrays of 8-bit words

$$X(0), X(1), \ldots, X(255)$$

and

$$Y(0), Y(1), \ldots, Y(255)$$

in the recirculation loop with the intention of operating on corresponding words in the two arrays. If these are stored in the recirculation loop as shown in Fig. 6-13a, then we need *two* 2,048-bit shift registers in order to access the bits of corresponding words at the same time. For example, when bit b_0 of $X(0)$ is at the reference point (address $X \cdot W0 \cdot B0$), then bit b_0 of $Y(0)$ is at the input to the other shift register.

The *labeling* of the states in the address counters is meant to imply *when* each counter is counted as well as the names of bits, words, and arrays. Thus in Fig. 6-13b, the array counter is counted as the bit counter rolls over from $B7$ to $B0$. Similarly, the word counter is counted as the array counter rolls over from Y to X. Consequently, when bit b_0 of $X(0)$ is at the reference point (address $W0 \cdot X \cdot B0$), bit b_0 of $Y(0)$ is at the input to the short shift register. Eight clock periods later, the address is given as $W0 \cdot Y \cdot B0$, putting bit b_0 of $Y(0)$ at the reference point. At this same time, bit b_0 of $X(0)$ is 8 bits into the long shift register while bit b_0 of $X(1)$ is at the input to the short shift register. This interlacing of the words of the two arrays (rather than grouping all of the words of each array together, as in Fig. 6-13a) permits the use of only one long shift register rather than two while still permitting simultaneous access to corresponding words of the two arrays. (Instead of interlacing words, we might interlace bits, as shown in Fig. 6-13c. With this storage configuration, every other bit is a bit of the same array.)

Data can be serially inserted into a recirculation loop as in Fig. 6-14. If we wish to replace the contents of the word $X(87)$ in the recirculation loop with the

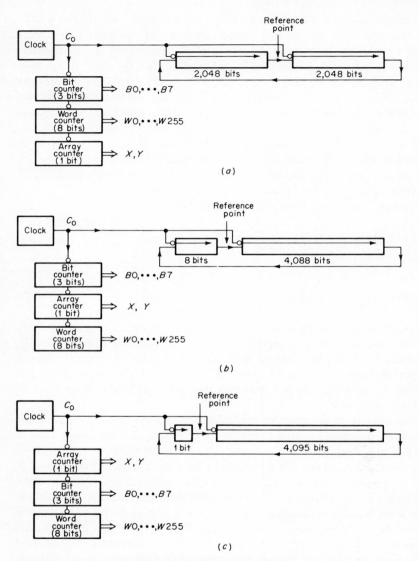

Fig. 6-13   Alternative storage configurations for two arrays of words. (*a*) Arrays not interlaced; (*b*) arrays interlaced by words; (*c*) arrays interlaced by bits.

contents of the 8-bit shift register on the left, we need only let the switch $SW = 1$ during $W87$. The previous contents of word $X(87)$ can be serially read out at the same time from the output of the long shift register. Since there are no bits of delay between the output of the long shift register and the reference point (when $SW = 0$), this serial output is addressed identically to the data at the reference point. That is, bit b_0 of word $X(87)$ is on the output during $W87 \cdot B0$.

Parallel input and output to a recirculation loop is shown in Fig. 6-15a. This is illustrated on 4-bit words using direct presetting and clearing and a multiple-phase clock with the waveforms C_0, C_1, and C_2 shown. To load $b_3 b_2 b_1 b_0$ into word $X(56)$, it is only necessary to let

Preset = $W56 \cdot B0 \cdot C_2$

Similarly, to read out the contents of word $X(56)$ in parallel, we can look at $b_3^* b_2^* b_1^* b_0^*$ during $W56 \cdot B0$. A weakness of using direct presetting is that we cannot read in and read out simultaneously. However, by using another clock phase, we can read out on C_1 and read in on C_2. This problem is eased with switched-input delay flipflops as we revert to the simplicity of a single-phase synchronously clocked system. Figure 6-15b illustrates the system configuration. Note that the reference point has been moved 1 bit to the left. This permits synchronous read in and read out of a word, say, word $X(56)$ during $W56 \cdot B0$.

Thus far, we have discussed addressing data, inserting data, and extracting data in a recirculation loop. Some *data buffering* applications use a recirculation loop for no more than these things. It permits the collection of data at a slow rate and the output of this collected data in a fast burst. Some communication systems use this in order to increase the efficiency of the communication channel. It can also be used to build a preprocessor to a computer if the computer is bogged down by the bookkeeping activities involved in collecting data from many input devices. The recirculation loop might collect input data from many devices over 1-s intervals and then insert this into the computer during 1 ms every second. Alternatively, as a postprocessor tied to the output of a computer, it can be swiftly loaded with a great deal of data and then this data

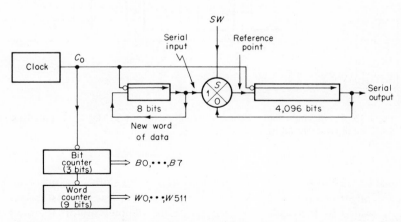

Fig. 6-14 Serial input to and output from a recirculation loop.

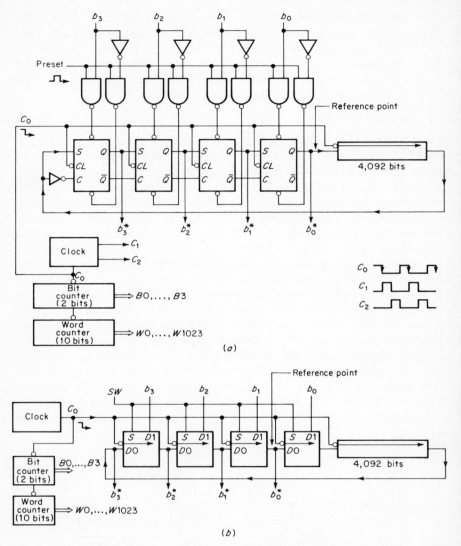

Fig. 6-15 Parallel input-output for a recirculation loop. (*a*) Using direct presetting; (*b*) using switched-input delay flipflops.

can be used to run many relatively slow devices. In a process-control application, this might be 64 stepping motors controlling 64 valves. The postprocessor might be loaded in 1 ms and then used to run the stepping motors for the following 10-s interval.

A recurring question which will arise as we proceed concerns the number of *accessible bits* required in order to carry out a certain operation. Referring back to the previous example of Fig. 6-15, where we had 4,096 bits in the recirculation loop, we needed 4 accessible bits outside of the long shift register in order to read in (or out) 4-bit words in parallel. In designing a system, this can be taken into account one operation at a time. The final system design will then evolve with the minimum number of accessible bits required. However the long shift register is implemented, this will help minimize cost since these bits are less expensive than distinct flipflops (the incremental cost of adding a few bits in a delay line is zero!)

In contrast to data buffering, *data processing* applications manipulate the data in the recirculation loop. We shall consider how several operations can be carried out on data in a recirculation loop, and then we shall discuss how these can be combined to carry out iterative algorithms. The operations we shall discuss are

1. Data shifting
2. Simple arithmetic operations

One common shifting operation consists of continuously collecting data into an array

$$X(511), \ldots , X(1), X(0)$$

where $X(0)$ is the most recent word of data collected and $X(511)$ the oldest. If these words are arranged *most recent word first* in the recirculation loop, then the circuit of Fig. 6-16 will insert the new data $b_7 \ldots b_0$ into $X(0)$, shift everything over one word, and discard the oldest word every N recirculations.

An extension of this occurs where there are two arrays of data. Perhaps one array

$$X(255), \ldots , X(0)$$

is being updated in order to keep a continuous scan on the last 256 samples of some variable. The other array

$$Y(255), \ldots , Y(0)$$

might be storing the results of a previous calculation which is being used in conjunction with a digital-to-analog converter to provide a continuously refreshed oscilloscope display. In this case, the updating of the X array must shift that data while leaving the Y array alone. Figure 6-17 illustrates this case. Again, it is assumed that the X array is arranged most recent word first. The circuit works as follows.

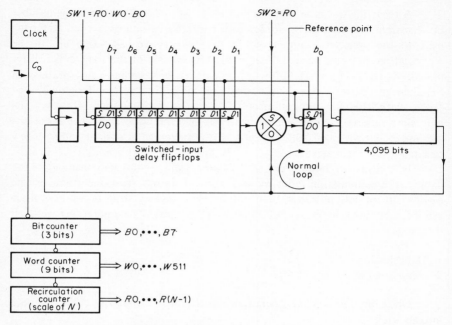

Fig. 6-16 Periodically updated array of words.

As the recirculation counter rolls over from $R(N-1)$ to $R0$, the reading in of the new $X(0)$ value is begun, as shown in Fig. 6-17b. This figure shows the data as it is (in effect) when the address counter reads $R0 \cdot W0 \cdot X \cdot B0$. It also shows the shift register input-output connections as they are during this clock period and the following seven clock periods. At the end of this time, the data is located as shown in Fig. 6-17c. The old value of $X(0)$ has been shifted into the 8-bit shift register on the left, while the new value of $X(0)$ has been shifted into the first 8 bits of the long shift register. Now $Y(0)$ must follow the new $X(0)$ into the long shift register, while the old value of $X(0)$, which will be the new value of $X(1)$, simply recirculates in the 8-bit shift register. Thus it will still be there, as shown in Fig. 6-17d, when $Y(0)$ has been completely shifted into the long shift register. It then follows $Y(0)$ into the long shift register. At the end of recirculation $R0$, the shifting has been completed.

Carrying out arithmetic operations serially on numbers expressed in sign plus two's complement code or in binary code is greatly facilitated by the fact that the algorithms can be implemented bit by bit. To illustrate what is involved, we shall consider the example of serial up-down counting. The key element in the process is the *serial operator*, which actually implements the algorithm. It accepts input data and generates output data subject to appropriate control

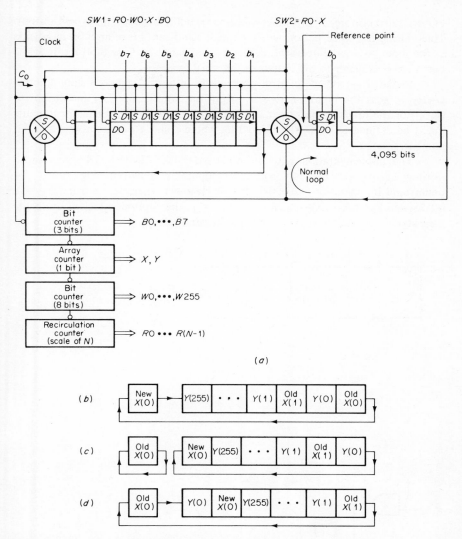

Fig. 6-17 Updating one array while leaving another untouched. (*a*) System; (*b*) data at $R0 \cdot W0 \cdot X \cdot B0$; connection for next eight clock periods; (*c*) data at $R0 \cdot W0 \cdot Y \cdot B0$; connection for next eight clock periods; (*d*) data at $R0 \cdot W1 \cdot X \cdot B0$; connection for next eight clock periods.

inputs. Furthermore, it introduces no bits of delay between input and output. Thus during the clock period when the least significant bit of an 8-bit number is at the input to a serial operator, the least significant bit of the 8-bit result of the operation is available at the output of the serial operator.

Included among the control possibilities of a serial operator should be the ability to *pass* the input on to the output unchanged and *clear* the output to zero. For the up-down-pass-clear serial operator of Fig. 6-18a, the control inputs might be defined as shown in Fig. 6-18b, where Z and X each represent an n-bit number.

The implementation with an AND gate, EXCLUSIVE-OR gates, and a flipflop having direct preset and clear inputs is shown in Fig. 6-18c. To understand its operation, note first that if clear = 1, then $\overline{\text{clear}}$ = 0 and Y_K = 0; otherwise, $Y_K = X_K$. Also, as long as pass = 1, the flipflop is locked up in the clear state, forcing Q to 0. And as long as $Q = 0$, $Z_K = Y_K$.

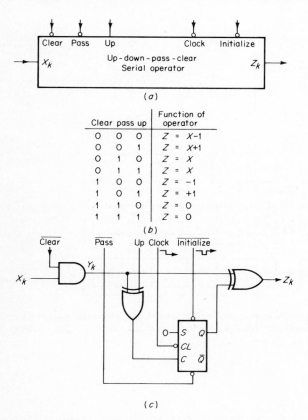

(a)

Clear	pass	up	Function of operator
0	0	0	$Z = X-1$
0	0	1	$Z = X+1$
0	1	0	$Z = X$
0	1	1	$Z = X$
1	0	0	$Z = -1$
1	0	1	$Z = +1$
1	1	0	$Z = 0$
1	1	1	$Z = 0$

(b)

(c)

Fig. 6-18 Up-down-pass-clear serial operator for sign plus two's complement numbers. (a) Form of serial operator; (b) definition of control inputs; (c) implementation.

The algorithm for counting up, which can be verified with a few examples, is

$$Z_K = \overline{Y}_K \quad \text{up to and including the first time } Y_K = 0$$
$$ = Y_K \quad \text{thereafter}$$

This is implemented by making pass = 0 and up = 1 for the duration of the *word time*, that is, while Y_K equals the bits of the number to be counted up. *Initialize* presets the flipflop in the middle of the initial clock period of counting with

Initialize = $B0 \cdot C_2$

where $B0$ comes from the bit counter while C_2 is the clock phase used for presetting. As long as this flipflop is set, $Z_K = \overline{Y}_K$ as required initially. The flipflop will remain set as long as $Y_K = 1$. During the clock period when Y_K first equals 0, the flipflop will still be set, and so Z_K will still equal $\overline{Y}_K$. However, the flipflop's clear input equals 1 during this clock period and will clear to 0 at the end of the clock period, making $Z_K = Y_K$ for all subsequent clock periods.

The algorithm for counting down is

$$Z_K = \overline{Y}_K \quad \text{up to and including the first time } Y_K = 1$$
$$ = Y_K \quad \text{thereafter}$$

The only change in the circuit for counting up or down is the clear input to the flipflop, which is now equal to Y_K. Consequently, it detects the first time $Y_K = 1$.

The use of this serial operator in a recirculation loop is illustrated in Fig. 6-19. It is particularly useful in an application requiring many counters, each of which must be counted up or down once per recirculation. With the 8-bit words shown, each counter can count (up or down) 127 counts without overflowing. This unit might be cleared during recirculation $R0$. Then starting at $R1 \cdot W0 \cdot B0$, the control inputs *pass, up,* and *clear* can be set as desired for counting word $W0$. These must remain constant for the duration of $W0$. For each successive word, they are changed as appropriate for that counter. After one recirculation (at $R2 \cdot W0 \cdot B0$) each of the 512 counters has been accessed once. This might continue until the recirculation counter reaches $R127$, at which time the counter contents are used by the system employing this unit.

More involved algorithmic processes use combinations of the techniques discussed here. The serial operator (several useful examples of which are given in Appendix A3) must be tailored to the algorithm, shifting of the data may be needed, and, of course, the data must be inserted and extracted from the recirculation loop. A valuable aid in designing the timing so that data bits go where they should go is to make a sequence of "snapshots" of all shift registers and interconnections, just as was done in Fig. 6-17b, c, and d.

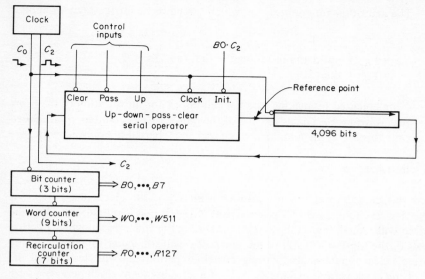

Fig. 6-19   Recirculation loop employing a serial operator.

6-5 TIMING AND MODE CIRCUITRY

In Sec. 6-2, we saw how the mode circuitry for even a simple problem could become difficult to handle. In this section, we will consider several structures which can be used to implement timing circuitry and mode circuitry. These greatly simplify the efforts of the designer, provide ease of change in an already designed system, and lead to clarity of system organization.

Often in designing timing circuitry, we only need a scale-of-n scaler such as one of those given in Appendix A3. For example, one of the *bit counters* used in the last section to keep track of the bits of each word need only be a scale-of-eight scaler if the word length is 8 bits. The fact that the scaler may not count in binary is irrelevant since we shall only be ANDing flipflop outputs together to form bit counter outputs like $B0$. Furthermore, we may not need to implement more than one or two outputs like $B0$. Note that the *word counter*, which must be counted as the bit counter rolls over from $B7$ to $B0$, can use as its clock source either the leading edge of $B0$ or the trailing edge of $B7$, providing asynchronous design is sufficiently fast. Alternatively, the word counter can be pseudosynchronously clocked, using a pulse derived by ANDing $B7$ with the clock signal $C*$ used for this purpose.

On occasion, we need to use all of the states of a timing counter for a variety of purposes. Rather than AND the asserted and negated flipflop outputs together over and over again to form these counter outputs, we can use the *ring counter* shown in Fig. 6-20a. This is simply a small recirculation loop containing a single 1. When the system is initialized, we might direct preset one flipflop while the remainder are direct cleared in order to achieve this state. Because it is not self-starting, this implementation of a ring counter will cause the system using it to malfunction if an extra 1 ever inadvertently enters the recirculation loop.

The circuit of Fig. 6-20b illustrates a self-starting ring counter. To show this, note that if $B0 = 1$, then when the clock transition occurs, $B0$ will return to the 0 state. On the other hand, if $B1, B2$, or $B3$ equals 1, the set input on the $B0$ flipflop will equal 0 and so $B0$ will remain in the 0 state when the clock transition occurs. This clears out the shift register until $B0, B1, B2$, and $B3$ all equal 0. Whether or not the last flipflop $B4$ contains the 1 which it should contain, on the next clock transition $B0$ will be set to 1. Thus, we achieve the single 1 and four 0s which we desire.

An alternative way to implement a scale-of-*n* timing counter plus all of its decoded outputs uses a (self-starting) scale-of-*n* scaler, together with one or more of the MSI one-out-of-eight decoders† shown in Fig. 6-21a and defined in Fig.

†Also called a *data distributor* or a *demultiplexer*.

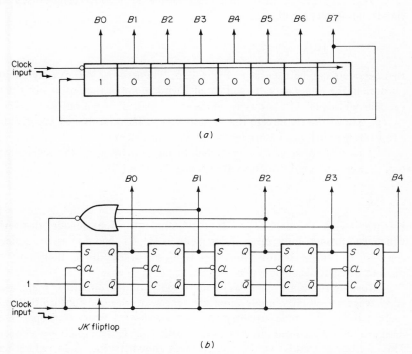

(a)

(b)

Fig. 6-20 Ring counters for achieving decoded outputs. (*a*) Ring counter; (*b*) self-starting ring counter.

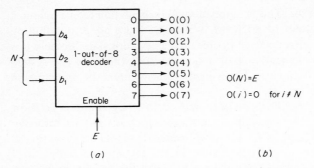

$$O(N) = E$$

$$O(i) = 0 \quad \text{for } i \neq N$$

(a)   (b)

Fig. 6-21 One-out-of-eight decoder. (a) Symbolic representation; (b) Boolean representation.

6-21b. For a scale-of-n timing counter in which n is equal to 8 or less, one decoder can be coupled to the three flipflop outputs of a scale-of-n scaler, as in Fig. 6-22a. Then, by considering the count sequence of the scaler, the outputs of the decoder can be appropriately selected and labeled so as to occur in sequence.

If n is greater than 8, then more than one decoder can be used. In the simple, common case of

$$9 \leqslant n \leqslant 16$$

two decoders can be used as in Fig. 6-22b. Whenever $b_1 = 1$, exactly one of the outputs in the upper decoder will equal 1 while none of the outputs of the lower decoder will equal 1. Conversely whenever $b_1 = 0$, all of the outputs will equal 0 except one of the outputs in the lower decoder. The fact that b_1 is derived from a separate parallel scaler is irrelevant to this implementation.

This procedure can be extended to larger n by using the scheme of Fig. 6-23, using as many decoders as are needed. However for

$$17 \leqslant n \leqslant 24$$

it is worthwhile to select as inputs to the one-out-of-four decoder two variables which go through only *three* states (such as 00, 01, and 11) as the scaler goes through its entire count sequence. If this can be done, then only three one-out-of-eight decoders will be needed.

Just as there are good ways to simplify timing circuitry, there are also good ways to simplify mode circuitry. One way uses one flipflop to represent each state of the mode circuitry. At the expense of many flipflops, an easily designed, easily changed circuit results. Furthermore, the modes are all decoded. This method depends on the equivalences shown in Fig. 6-24, which can be implemented with *RS* or *JK* flipflops and gates. As an example, Fig. 6-25 shows the implementation of the mode circuitry for the digital combination door lock whose flow diagram is shown in Fig. 6-5.

Another good, versatile implementation of mode circuitry is shown in Fig. 6-26. It uses n delay flipflops to store the present state of the system so that generating the next state requires generating only the n inputs to the n flipflops. By doing this and by using as few flipflops as possible, the read-only memory (ROM) will have the minimum possible number of outputs.

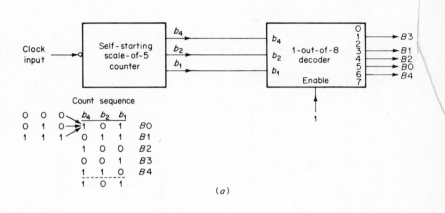

(a)

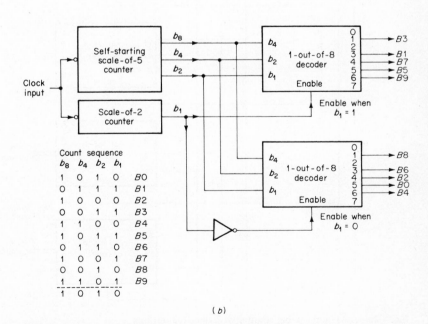

(b)

Fig. 6-22 Timing counters with decoded outputs. (a) Scale-of-five counter; (b) scale-of-10 counter.

Except for generating outputs to the data processing circuitry, the cost of this implementation is independent of the state assignment. This eliminates what is otherwise a difficult design decision. Furthermore, the states can be decoded using one-out-of-eight decoders configured as in Fig. 6-22 or 6-23. If the number of states to be decoded is between 17 and 24, then by making state assignments using the binary numbers

$$00000 \leqslant b_{16}b_8b_4b_2b_1 \leqslant 10111$$

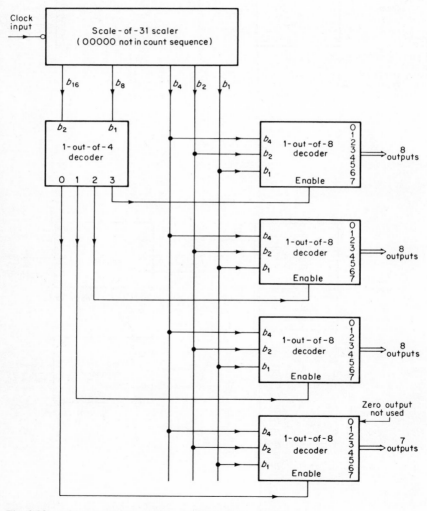

Fig. 6-23 A 31-state timing counter with decoded outputs.

Flow diagram   Circuit

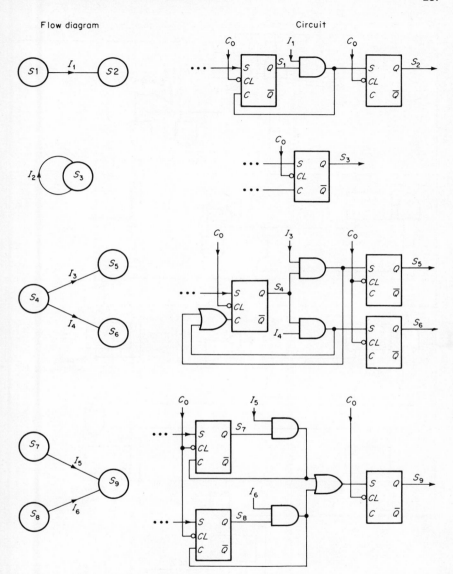

Fig. 6-24 Equivalences for designing simple mode circuitry.

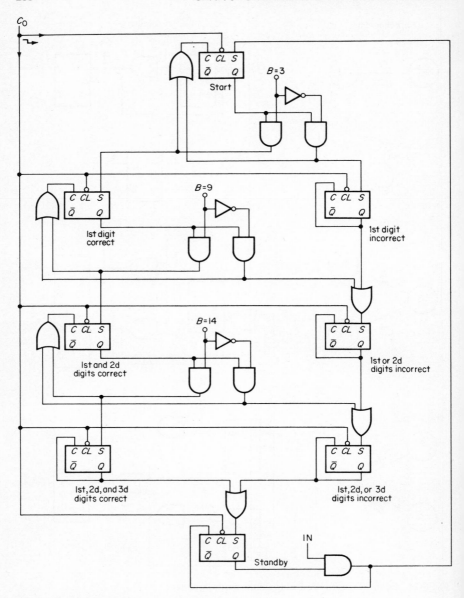

Fig. 6-25   Mode circuitry for digital combination lock.

only 3 one-out-of-eight decoders are needed to generate the outputs. In this case b_4, b_2, and b_1 are decoded in these decoders while b_{16} and b_8 go to the one-out-of-four decoder to generate the three *enable* inputs to the 3 one-out-of-eight decoders. If the number of states is between 33 and 64, this same technique can again be applied so as to use as few decoders as possible. Now b_{32}, b_{16}, and b_8 go to a one-out-of-eight decoder which generates the enable inputs to the other decoders.

This approach to the design of mode circuitry has much to recommend it. It provides simplicity for the designer. It uses a minimum number of building blocks, all in a very regular arrangement. The system can initially be built with a read-write magnetic core memory and debugged. When a properly working design has been achieved, the core memory can be replaced with a (cheaper) ROM for production purposes.

6-6 SMALL-COMPUTER CHARACTERISTICS

Our rationale for describing some of the characteristics of small computers is solely related to the *speed* and *memory* requirements of the systems which will

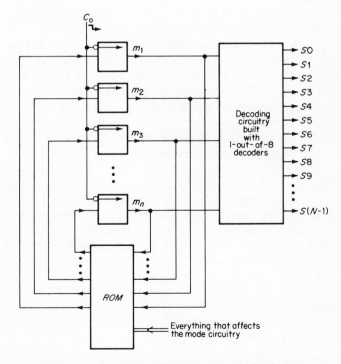

Fig. 6-26 Mode circuitry implemented with a read-only memory.

use these computers. This is so because any computer will do any job, given sufficient time and memory (in one form or another). Consequently, we shall consider those characteristics which differentiate the computers of different manufacturers and which have a bearing on these two factors.

Our concern about memory requirements for a dedicated small computer begins when we exceed the minimum core memory size available in the computer (typically $4K$, or 4,096 words). Our caring peaks each time we approach the limit of another quantum of core memory ($8K$, $12K$, etc.) or as we approach the decision of backing up the core memory with a magnetic disc or tape unit.

The concern about the speed of a computer which is to be dedicated to a specific process is whether it can do the job directly. If it cannot handle the input (or output) data rate, then either the computer must be augmented with a suitable preprocessor (or postprocessor) or else a different, more powerful computer must be used. If it cannot handle the throughput rate because of the complexity of the data processing, then again either the computer must be interfaced with appropriate hardware which will speed up this processing (such as hardware multiply/divide circuitry) or it must be replaced by a more powerful computer. For many dedicated computer applications, neither speed nor memory pose a problem. In such a case, the discussion of this section is academic since any computer will do the job directly.

In designing a small computer, a manufacturer has the immediate problem of deciding on a *word size*. In striving to produce a low-cost, competitive computer, he has a strong incentive to select a short word size. On the other hand, to facilitate the speed of processing instructions, it is desirable to have most instructions contained in a single word. The more bits there are in each of these instruction words, the more powerful each instruction can be. Having powerful instructions bears on both of our desired ultimate objectives. First, fewer instructions are needed to implement a given process, resulting in reduced memory requirements. Second, with each instruction requiring its own execution time, fewer instructions mean that the process can be executed faster.

One of the most popular and most enduring small computers ever built is Digital Equipment Corporation's PDP-8 series, shown in Fig. 6-27. This machine has met a wide variety of applications with a relatively short 12-bit word size. The more recent trend in small computers has been toward a 16-bit word size. This not only permits much more powerful instructions, but it also allows two 8-bit *bytes* of data to be stored in a single word. This may provide a significant advantage in terms of memory requirements for systems which include interfacing to devices such as perforated tape or magnetic tape units that deal in 8-bit bytes or to input devices that quantize measured variables into 8 or less bits.

Another factor which affects the speed of a computer in carrying out a process is the execution time of its instructions. Many small computers have an

Fig. 6-27 A 12-bit computer, the PDP-8/E. (*Digital Equipment Corp.*)

"average" instruction execution time of roughly two times their memory cycle time. Since memory cycle times typically vary between 1 and 3 μs from one manufacturer's small computer to another's, this (by itself) represents a 3:1 difference in their speeds.

A factor which bears directly on the ease of programming a computer, as well as on the speed and memory requirements, is the specific character of its *memory addressing*. Memory addressing variations arise since an instruction must be able to specify both the operation to be performed and the location of the data word upon which it should be performed. With a 4K memory, specifying the location of any of these 4K words directly would require 12 bits. In a 16-bit machine, this would leave only 4 bits with which to specify the variety of instructions desired.

Virtually all small computers permit data to be addressed in any of several modes. Several bits of an instruction are used to specify which of these *addressing modes* will be used. Then some other bits of the instruction, the *address bits* D, will be interpreted according to which addressing mode is specified. Some commonly used addressing modes follow.

Page zero addressing specifies address 2^D at the beginning of the core memory. If D is 8 bits long, this permits the addressing of words 0 to 255 of the core memory.

Present page addressing divides memory into 256-word "pages" (if D is 8 bits long) and uses D to specify the address within the page from which the present instruction was taken.

Relative addressing treats D as a signed number and adds it to the address from which the present instruction was taken.

Base register addressing does the same thing except to an address stored in a base
register (whose contents can be controlled by other instructions).

Indexed addressing adds the contents of an index register to the address
otherwise specified by one of the above addressing modes (yielding, for
example, *indexed page zero* addressing). Some computers permit the index
register to be automatically incremented or decremented, allowing
efficient operation when operating with sequential memory locations.

Direct or *indirect* addressing is often used in conjunction with one of the
above modes. Direct addressing uses the contents of the address specified
by D as data. Indirect addressing uses these contents to specify the address
of another word whose contents will be used as the data. With 16 bits, this
permits addressing any memory location (up to 64K words). Furthermore,
many powerful software addressing techniques can be translated into
simple, indirectly addressed instructions.

In a system employing a dedicated computer, the programmer's job is to
arrange the addresses of successive instructions and data so that the sequencing
of instructions proceeds smoothly. If speed becomes critical, he may work to
reduce the number of instructions which employ a relatively slow addressing
mode by changing it to a faster mode. If storage becomes critical, he may change
as many indirectly addressed instructions to directly addressed instructions as
possible since the former require two memory locations per instruction (while
adding an extra memory cycle time to the instruction execution time). The
choice of a computer having good alternative memory addressing modes thus
becomes valuable for both speed and memory requirements.

The instruction set of the computer can have a significant bearing on the
speed of the computer for a specific job. For example, if the job involves many
byte manipulations on 8-bit bytes and if these bytes must be stored two to a
data word in order to fit everything into the available memory, then a computer
which can handle these 8-bit bytes directly will be significantly faster than one
which cannot.

Another example of the power which can be built into an instruction set is
given by the *two-address* arithmetic instructions of Data General Corporation's
NOVA computer shown in Fig. 6-28. These instructions permit any one of four
accumulators to be used as the source for each operand, storing the result back
in one of them. Furthermore, each arithmetic instruction is really a combination
of several *microinstructions*. Thus the basic ADD instruction has 256 variations.
Two bits of the instruction determine the source or the value of an initial carry
into the addition. Two more bits determine whether or not to shift the result of
the addition, and, if so, how much. Three more bits cause the computer to skip
the next instruction if one of seven possible tests on the sum is met. Finally, one
bit determines whether the result should be retained. Processes involving many
arithmetic operations can achieve significant time and memory savings if a
computer is used having these two-address, multipurpose instructions.

Fig. 6-28 The NOVA computer. (*Data General Corp.*)

All small computers accept and emit data using *programmed data transfers* in conjunction with an *interrupt and priority system*. (They may also use a *direct memory access* channel, which will be discussed later, for faster data transfer.) A programmed data transfer operates under the control of a computer routine to transfer words of data between memory and a peripheral device—one word at a time. The maximum rate of transfer depends on how involved the program is which controls this data transfer, but a typical rate might be 30,000 words/s. This rate is significantly lower than the rate determined by the memory cycle time alone because of the need to incorporate the program into the interrupt and priority system.

The interrupt and priority system is vital to the computer because while each input or output device may not need to be serviced often, it may need to be serviced quickly after it is ready. Otherwise, faulty operation can occur resulting in lost information. For example, a magnetic tape unit, whether it is being written into or read out of, may require transferring a byte of information every 100 μs. This is slow enough to permit the computer to carry on another program between transfers. After each instruction of this other program is processed, the computer automatically looks for an interrupt signal. If the tape unit is not ready yet, the computer goes on and processes another instruction. When the tape unit finally is ready, the interrupt signal causes the computer to

1. Store the contents of all registers which will be used by the interrupt routine
2. Determine what I/O device generated the interrupt signal (and invoke some priority mechanism if several devices have done this simultaneously)
3. Service that I/O device
4. Restore the contents of all registers stored in step 1 in order to return control to the interrupted program

A vital question in selecting a computer for a specific application is how quickly the computer can begin data transfer after receiving an interrupt signal (assuming it has priority). This must be fast enough to handle any I/O devices which will use programmed data transfers. Some computers implement their interrupt and priority system in hardware, some in software. The worthiness of the actual implementation and organization of this system is perhaps best measured by the interrupt response time which results. This, in turn, bears directly on the data rate which can be expected for programmed data transfers.

For faster response time and higher data transfer rates, most small computers provide a *direct memory access* (DMA) channel, at least as an option. This is used to provide a fast, intimate coupling between the computer and (usually) a disc memory for the mass transfer of a large block of data. Rather than go through the interrupt routine of a programmed data transfer for each word transferred, a DMA channel uses only one memory cycle for each word transferred. A typical way in which a DMA channel is used consists of three steps:

1. When the computer is ready to transfer a block of data between core memory and a disc, it transfers initializing information to the DMA interface between the computer and the disc memory. This includes the first address in the block for both the core memory and the disc memory. It also includes the number of words in the block. Finally, it includes the direction of transfer and a command to begin. The computer then continues with its other tasks, leaving the DMA channel to fend for itself.
2. The DMA interface waits for the first address of the block to appear on the disc memory. When it does, it signals the computer. Then, at the completion of the computer instruction being processed, the computer's operation is suspended for one core memory cycle. The DMA channel steals control of the core memory for this cycle, transferring one word between the first core address in the block and the disc memory. At the completion of this cycle, the computer continues its operation, unaware that a transfer has taken place.
3. When the entire block of data has been transferred, the DMA interface stops any further transfer. It signals the computer of this completion through a normal interrupt. Now the computer can make use of the new data in core if the transfer has been into the computer. Or it can use the space made available in core if the transfer has been the other way.

Because of this *cycle-stealing* property of a DMA channel, it gives to the device using it the highest priority of any I/O device. In effect, it overrides the normal priority structure in the interrupt system.

An extremely powerful and versatile small computer organization for interacting with a variety of peripheral devices is exemplified by Digital

Equipment Corporation's PDP-11 computer shown in Fig. 6-29. It has three features which provide this I/O power:

1. The central processor, memory, and all peripheral devices are connected to each other through a common bus. This bus consists of 56 signal lines, including 16 data lines, 18 address lines, 13 priority transfer lines, and 9 control lines. All but 5 of these 56 signal lines are bidirectional, permitting signals to flow into and out of each device. Each device is addressed like a core memory location; its address is just made higher than any core memory address.

2. A flexible interrupt and priority system permits any device to seize control of the bus at the completion of any instruction by the central processor or any transfer of a word of data on the bus. The device seizing control need only have a higher priority than any other device simultaneously requesting control. In seizing control, this device causes the central processor to set aside what it was doing and begin a service routine written to meet the needs of this device. The device in control of the bus can directly transfer information to or from any other device on the bus. This means that all devices have a DMA channel available to them.

3. Instructions and the computer organization are tailored to the job of quickly recognizing an interrupt signal of highest priority, storing the state of the central processor, and quickly getting to the service routine for the interrupting device. Regardless of its priority, a device (which is not preempted by a higher-priority device) will cause the central processor to be fetching the first instruction of its service routine 7.2 μs after the interrupt signal is accepted by the central processor. If a data transfer is

Fig. 6-29 The PDP-11 computer. (*Digital Equipment Corp.*)

made directly, as with a DMA channel, control of the bus will be seized within 3.5 μs and data can be transferred every 1.2 μs.

Because one interrupt can preempt another, the computer is also efficiently organized to *nest* superimposed interrupts. Thus while a device is being serviced, it can be interrupted by a higher-priority device, and that device by an even higher-priority device. As the servicing of each device is completed, the computer picks up where it left off on the next highest-priority device.

In concluding this section, it is worth recalling the point made at the very beginning of the section. That is, given sufficient time and memory, any computer can do any job. If a system can be organized around an unsophisticated small computer, the main advantage which might accrue from using a more powerful computer is ease of programming. Furthermore, if sufficient time and memory are available, some of the programming conveniences of the more powerful computer (like index registers) can be simulated as subroutines in the less powerful computer.

6-7 INTERFACING A SMALL COMPUTER

Interfacing between a small computer and any one of several I/O devices using a programmed data transfer involves two functions:

1. Transferring each word of data between the computer and the selected I/O device
2. Synchronizing when both the computer and the device are ready to make the transfer by means of the interrupt and priority system

Both of these functions are implemented partially within the computer, through software and hardware, and partially through the hardware of the interface circuitry. The details of the portion implemented within the computer can vary quite a bit from one computer to another and can have a significant bearing on the interrupt response time and the transfer data rate. Similarly, the details of the portion implemented in the interface circuitry will vary from computer to computer. However, there is enough similarity to warrant our discussion of a "typical" structure.

The structure discussed will be somewhat rudimentary in order to highlight the main points of interfacing. An excellent follow-up to this discussion would be to obtain the user's manual and the interface manual from the manufacturer of a specific computer. These will describe in detail the interaction between the programming of both I/O instructions and interrupt routines and the implementation of them by the computer. They will also provide an exact understanding of what is required of the interface as well as some examples interfacing between the computer and typical I/O devices.

   The interface circuitry for an I/O device is connected to the computer
through an *I/O bus*, as shown in Fig. 6-30. If the computer has a 16-bit word
length and if it can be connected to any of 2^6 = 64 I/O devices, then the I/O bus
will typically consist of:

1. Sixteen bidirectional *data* lines $\overline{D15}, \ldots, \overline{D0}$ (labeled in negated form $\overline{D15}$
   because when the variable $D15 = 1$, the data line is pulled low)
2. Six *device-selection* lines from computer to devices $DS5, \ldots, DS0$
3. *Computer-to-device control* lines
4. *Device-to-computer control* lines

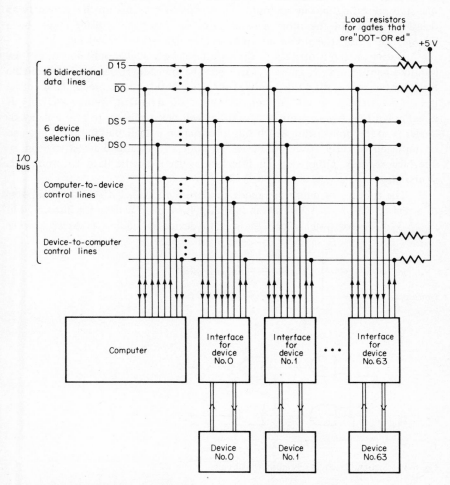

Fig. 6-30 Typical I/O interconnections for devices using programmed data transfers.

Signals on the control lines from the computer synchronize all transfers of data on the data lines, start and stop device operations, and control the interrupt and priority system. Signals on the control lines from a device permit the device to request a program interrupt, indicating that the device is ready for a data transfer.

During an output operation, data typically flow from an accumulator in the computer to a register in the interface. The interface register is used on output simply to provide availability of the data to either the interface or the device for a period which is longer than the few hundred nanoseconds during which the transfer is made. If the register does no more than this, then it is conveniently implemented with the *strobed latches* shown in Fig. 6-31. These commonly available integrated circuits are nothing more than flipflops which use one-step presetting and no ac input. The symbolism points up the similarity to delay flipflops. In the more general case, the interface register might be a counter. Data might be preset into the counter using direct presetting.

During an input operation, the data need be available only during the few hundred nanoseconds it takes to carry out the transfer. If the data are available for a longer period than this, perhaps for a few hundred microseconds, then the interrupt system can signal the computer when the data first become available. If it is known that higher-priority operations will never pile up to give a delay of longer than the time during which this information is available, then the data can be inputted directly from the device without any intermediate storage in an interface register. Otherwise, an interface register can be used to insure this availability.

The transfer of data from an accumulator $(A15, \ldots, A0)$ in the computer to a register $(X15, \ldots, X0)$ in the interface for a specific device is illustrated in Fig. 6-32. The computer selects the specific device by loading its *device number*

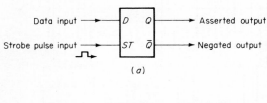

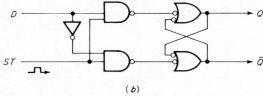

Fig. 6-31 Strobed latch. (*a*) Symbol; (*b*) circuit.

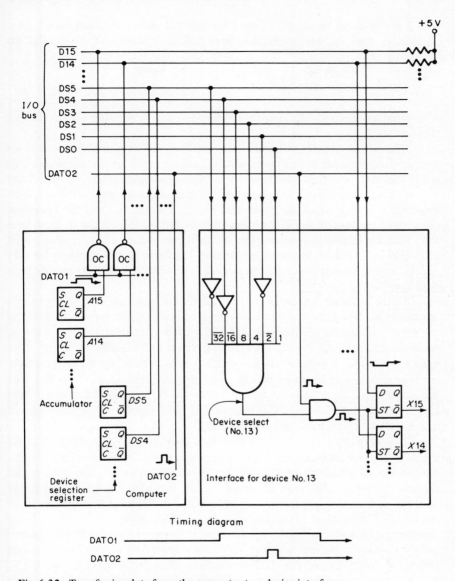

Fig. 6-32 Transferring data from the computer to a device interface.

into a device-selection register. This is transmitted to the interface circuitry for all devices over the device-selection lines (DS5, . . . , DS0). Thus for selecting device 13

DS5 . . . DS0 = 001101

The interface circuitry for device 13 decodes this, generating a *device select* signal.

The actual transfer is initiated by strobing the data onto the data lines using the data output control pulse DATO1 shown in the timing diagram of Fig. 6-32. The gates which do this have open-collector outputs (signified by OC and described in Sec. 3-10). This permits the data lines to be shared, through dot-ORing, among all of the input and output operations. Only the operation using the data lines at any given moment is permitted to pull any of these lines low. With the circuit shown, any bits of the accumulator $(A15, . . . , A0)$ which are equal to 1 will cause the corresponding data lines to go low when DATO1 occurs. The remaining bits, which are equal to 0, will block DATO1 leaving their data lines high.

In the interface for device 13, each data line might go to the D input of a strobed latch. The data is strobed into the latch with a pulse formed by ANDing the other data output control pulse DATO2 with device select. DATO2 is timed, as shown in Fig. 6-32, so that the resulting strobe pulse occurs while the other signals are stable. Because of the propagation delays caused by the gating of any of these signals, it is necessary that the data lines and device-select lines be stable for some extra time both before and after DATO2 occurs, as shown in the timing diagram of Fig. 6-32. This insures that the D input on each strobed latch is stable when its strobe-pulse input occurs.

In general, the output instruction for a computer may be able to transfer the data from any one of several accumulators $A, B,$ or C in the computer to any one of several registers $X, Y,$ or Z in the device interface. To transfer the contents of any one of three accumulators, the instruction specifies which one of three data output control pulses DATO1A, DATO1B, or DATO1C is to be generated. This strobes the appropriate accumulator on to the data lines (with the timing of DATO1 in Fig. 6-32). To select the proper device-interface register, the computer also generates one of the three narrow data output control pulses DATO2X, DATO2Y, or DATO2Z (having the timing of DATO2 in Fig. 6-32). The interface circuitry uses these to generate the strobe-pulse inputs to the strobed latches making up each register.

Often another narrow output control pulse DATOP is generated, which occurs after DATO1 begins and before DATO2 occurs. This is useful for the two-step presetting of the data lines into a flipflop register, as shown in Fig. 6-33. The DATOP pulse is ANDed with device select to form a pulse which direct presets all flipflops. Then DATO2 is ANDed with device select and with

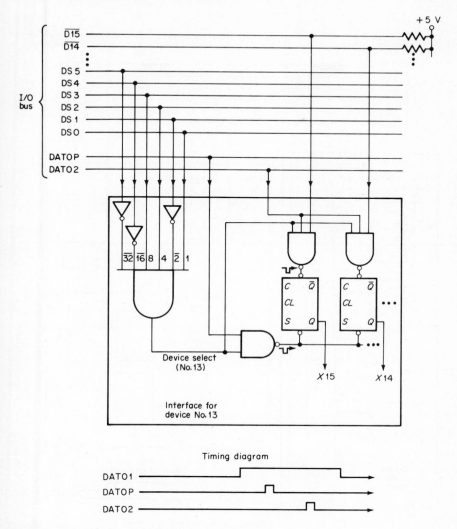

Fig. 6-33 Two-step presetting of a device interface register.

each data line, in turn, to form the direct clear inputs to each flipflop. Consequently, if a data line is low, corresponding to a 1 in the accumulator of the computer, then the corresponding flipflop in the device interface will be set at the time of DATOP but not cleared again at the time of DATO2.

The transfer of data from a register in the device interface to an accumulator in the computer is illustrated in Fig. 6-34. After setting up its device-selection register, the computer transmits a data input control pulse

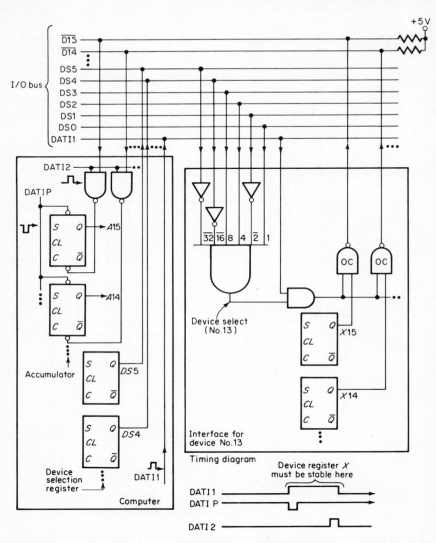

Fig. 6-34 Transferring data from a device interface register to an accumulator in the computer.

DATI1 to the interface circuitry for all devices. The selected device uses this to generate a pulse to strobe the contents of $X15, \ldots , X0$ onto the data lines of the I/O bus. The computer then presets the accumulator which will receive this data to all 1s, using the narrow pulse DATIP shown in Fig. 6-34. Finally, after the data lines have stabilized, they are strobed into the direct clear inputs on the flipflops of the accumulator using DATI2. This presetting and then (possibly) clearing is done because the data lines carry data in inverted form.

Thus far, we have discussed the I/O circuitry involved in the transfer of data between the computer and the interface circuitry for a device. These "data" may be actual data, as when the computer outputs the coding for a letter which is to be printed by a teletypewriter. Alternatively, they may be control information for the device, such as a command to a teletypewriter to print or to execute a carriage return. In either case, the transfer is handled in the manner discussed previously. The difference lies in *what bits of information* are placed in an accumulator before an output instruction is executed and *which register* this information is transferred to in the interface circuitry. In the case of device control information, this "register" may simply be several flipflops or one-shots.†

†Defined in Appendix A2.

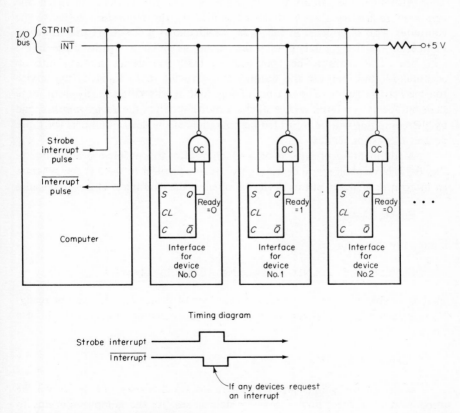

Fig. 6-35 Rudimentary interrupt system.

Turning now to the development of a typical interrupt and priority system, consider the rudimentary interrupt system shown in Fig. 6-35. Each device interface includes a *ready* flipflop. When the device is ready to be serviced by the computer (either to accept or to transmit information), the ready flipflop in its interface circuitry is set. Then when the computer is ready to be interrupted, it will transmit a *strobe interrupt* pulse to all device interfaces using the control line of the I/O bus designated STRINT. The computer will be ready to do this after executing each instruction providing its *interrupt enable* flipflop is set. (This flipflop, which is set or cleared under program control, permits the computer to ignore all interrupt requests.) If, when this strobe interrupt pulse occurs, any of the device interfaces are ready to be serviced (such as that for device No. 1 as shown), then the $\overline{INT}$ line on the I/O bus is pulled low. This is done by the output of one (or more) of the open-collector NAND gates shown in each device interface as in Fig. 6-35. Pulling $\overline{INT}$ low generates an interrupt signal in the computer which initiates an interrupt routine.

Although the circuit of Fig. 6-35 permits the devices to signal the computer requesting service, it does not identify the requesting device to the computer. This is resolved in Fig. 6-36, which shows a device putting its device number on the first six data lines of the I/O bus as well as a negative pulse on the $\overline{INT}$ line. This permits the computer to load this device number into an accumulator and then use this number to get to the first address of the service routine for the device. The scheme of Fig. 6-36 works satisfactorily until more than one device requests service at the same time. Then the *device number* read by the computer will be a garbled combination of the device numbers for those devices requesting service.

A rudimentary priority system which resolves this problem is illustrated in Fig. 6-37. Now of all *ready* devices, only the one farthest to the left can generate an interrupt signal and put its device number on the data lines. This is so because

Enable 13 = 1

if and only if

Enable 12 = 1 AND device No. 12 is not ready

That is, enable 13 = 1 if all devices to the left of device No. 13 are not ready. Now if device No. 13 is ready, it will cause an interrupt to occur. It will also cause

Enable $K = 0$ for all $K > 13$

Although this simple priority system insures that only one device will be recognized at a time, now a new problem arises. As the computer begins to

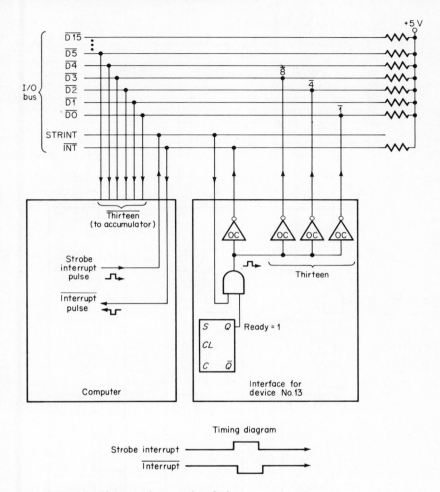

Fig. 6-36 Identifying an interrupting device.

service the device having highest priority, it needs to disable the interrupt signal coming from that device. It also needs to disable all lower-priority devices. On the other hand, all higher-priority devices must be left enabled. Then, any time they become ready, they can interrupt the service routine for the device being presently serviced.

One way in which some computers resolve this problem is by means of *priority masking*. Each device is assigned to one of 16 *priority groups*. These are not initially ranked. However, two devices assigned to the same priority group will have the same priority, and one cannot interrupt the other. Now assume that device No. 13 is assigned to priority group 5. When this device makes an

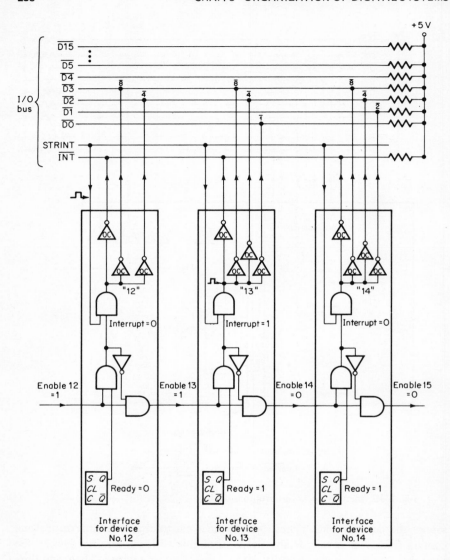

Fig. 6-37 Rudimentary priority system.

interrupt, the first thing the service routine in the computer does is to read this device's *priority mask* out of memory and into an accumulator. As seen in Fig. 6-38, this mask might be set up to disable all devices in priority groups 11, 10, 5, and 1. The remaining devices are to be left enabled so that they may interrupt the service routine for device No. 13.

15	14	13	12	11	10	9	8	7	6	5	4	3	2	1	0
0	0	0	0	1	1	0	0	0	0	1	0	0	0	1	0

Fig. 6-38 Priority mask.

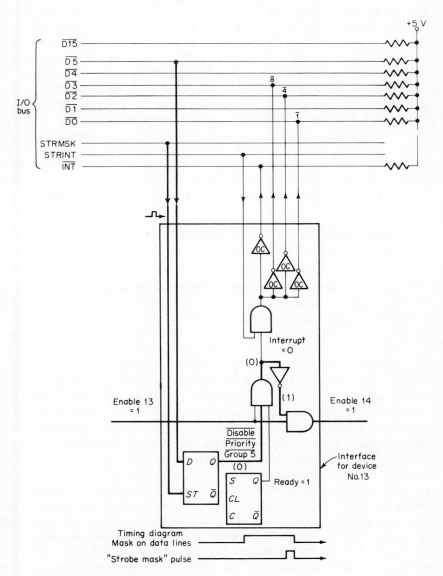

Fig. 6-39 Setting priorities with a mask.

To implement priority masking involves a simple augmentation of the rudimentary priority system shown in Fig. 6-37. The augmented priority system is illustrated for the interface circuitry of device No. 13 in Fig. 6-39. A strobed latch has been added with its D input tied to data line $D5$ on the I/O bus. This puts device No. 13 into priority group 5. The output of this strobed latch is labeled "Disable priority group 5" because if bit 5 of the priority mask has a 1 in it, then data line $\overline{D5}$ will equal 0 when it is read into the strobed latch. This is transferred to the output of the strobed latch and causes the interrupt circuitry to ignore the ready signal. To complete the augmentation, another computer-to-device control line $STRMSK$ is added to the I/O bus. A *strobe mask* pulse is generated by the computer with the timing shown to strobe the selected mask bits (bit 5 in this case) into the strobed latch of every device interface.

This development has described the approach to an interrupt and priority system used in some computers. Since such systems are by no means standardized, this system should perhaps not be called "typical." On the other hand, it illustrates the kinds of problems which arise in any system. It also illustrates the point that interface circuitry can be designed in two parts:

1. The data transferring and device control circuitry
2. The interrupt and priority system

For a given computer, the latter part of the design has already been worked out by the computer manufacturer and only needs to be implemented. These two parts of the design interact only in the *ready* flipflop, which is set and cleared by the device control circuitry and monitored by the interrupt and priority system.

One final point (which will be developed in general in Chap. 7) concerns the synchronization of the ready signal. The exact moment at which the device becomes ready for a data transfer will generally be determined by the dynamics of the device and will not be synchronized to the computer's instruction execution cycle. If the ready flipflop were permitted to change at this exact moment, it might catch the computer in the middle of its interrupt-interrogating cycle and lead to ambiguous results. This can be easily avoided with the circuit of Fig. 6-40. The flipflop on the left is set when the device is actually ready. This is loaded into the ready flipflop on the trailing edge of the strobe interrupt pulse (on the STRINT control line of the I/O bus). Although this means that the computer must wait through the execution of another instruction before becoming aware of the interrupt, this also provides time for the chain of enable K signals shown in Fig. 6-37 to settle out. Notice that this is now entirely synchronized. When the strobe interrupt pulse occurs, it will see a completely stable set of interrupt signals in the device interfaces. Finally, the *unsynced ready* flipflop is cleared by the service routine for the device.

The discussion up to this point has been concerned with programmed data transfers. The use of a direct-memory-access (DMA) channel is an extension of

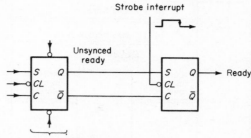

Fig. 6-40   Obtaining a ready signal which is synchronized to the computer.

this discussion. It is an interesting extension because, as it is often used, each data transfer on the DMA channel is free of program control. Furthermore, it goes unnoticed by the central processor. As was mentioned in the last section, using the DMA channel for block transfers of data is *set up* using programmed data transfers into the DMA channel interface. This interface may be incorporated as a standard feature of the computer's hardware, it may be available as an option, or it may require implementation by the user.

In some computers, data is transferred between the central processor and the core memory on the I/O bus. This bus might then be configured to handle the core memory addresses as a (large) extension of the device numbers. Alternatively, the central processor and the core memory might transfer data on a separate *memory bus*. In either case, a computer configured with a DMA channel will provide terminals for connecting a peripheral device so as to transfer data into and out of core memory.

The function of the DMA channel interface during data transfer can be understood by considering the signals involved, shown in Fig. 6-41. Recall that the function of the DMA channel is to provide fast servicing to a peripheral device like a disc memory for a block transfer of data. Consequently each time the device is ready to transfer data to or from its next memory address, it must signal the DMA channel interface with an (unsynchronized) ready signal. Using a circuit similar to that of Fig. 6-40, the interface might synchronize this to the computer's operation with the *leading* edge of the strobe interrupt pulse (on the STRINT control line of the I/O bus). This permits the interface to signal the computer with a DMA channel request before either another instruction or an interrupt is initiated. In so doing, it "steals" the next memory cycle, stalling what the computer was doing for that one cycle. The computer connects the core memory's address input to the interface, its data input or output to the peripheral device, and executes a read cycle or a write cycle (depending on the core memory in/out control from the interface).

Toward the end of the memory cycle, when the core memory no longer needs its memory address input, another pulse from the computer (labeled

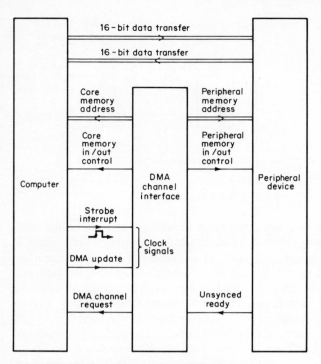

Fig. 6-41 Signals involved in a DMA channel during data
transfer.

"DMA update" in Fig. 6-41) updates the interface. It does this by counting a
core memory address counter and a peripheral address counter up one and by
counting a block-length counter down one. When the block-length counter has
been counted to zero, further DMA channel request signals are inhibited and an
interrupt signal is sent to the computer using the programmed data channel's
interrupt and priority system. The service routine for the interface will then
ascertain that the data transfer has been completed.

Before leaving Fig. 6-41, note that the interface is clocked by a two-phase
clock, using strobe interrupt and DMA update. Here is a good example of a
device which uses each of these to clock the ac inputs on some of the flipflops.
This does not introduce confusion since it is readily apparent which flipflops
must be clocked by each clock phase.

6-8 AUGMENTING A SMALL COMPUTER

Earlier in this chapter, we stated that any computer can do any job if it is
neither speed- nor memory-limited. In the case that it is speed-limited, we

mentioned several ways in which the computer might be augmented in order to speed up I/O data rates or data processing rates. In this section, we shall consider two examples which illustrate this augmentation.

Example 6-3 Design a preprocessor which will take the outputs from eight incremental shaft-angle encoders, accumulate the changes on their outputs over 10-ms intervals (more or less), and then, through programmed data transfers, send these changes to a computer. Assume each encoder will not change at a rate in excess of 10,000 quanta/s.

To carry out this design, use the series 54/74 TTL logic elements shown in Fig. 6-42, together with whatever MSI circuits are convenient. The only gates having open-collector outputs are those driving the I/O bus. (The relative costs of the elements, as measured by the dimensionless *cost units* shown, represent a somewhat arbitrary weighting between number of gate leads and actual device cost.)

This preprocessor will reduce the input data rate from the eight encoders by as much as 800:1 when compared with interrupting the computer for each quantum change of each encoder. For this to be a valid approach to the problem, we assume that a 10-ms sampling interval is sufficiently fast to meet the system requirements. Presumably the fine quantization, which results in this high data rate, is needed to provide good static accuracy.

Each encoder is configured as shown in Fig. 6-43. The gearing on the input translates a convenient process variable quantum size into the quantum size of the encoder. The incremental encoder and its *synchronous decoder* are described in detail in Chap. 7. In essence, they provide outputs which are synchronized to the clock input (which must exceed 10 kHz in order to avoid missing any quanta changes). Each time the encoder crosses a quantum boundary, the outputs of the synchronous decoder duly note the change and its direction during the following clock period, as shown in the truth table and timing diagram associated with Fig. 6-43.

When data are transferred into the computer, the accumulated number of quanta changes for each encoder may be as large as

$$\pm 10 \ \frac{\text{quanta}}{\text{ms}} \ \times 10 \text{ ms} = \pm 100 \text{ quanta}$$

If this is accumulated as a sign plus two's complement number, we shall require (at least) *8 bits* in order to insure that overflow will never occur.

Now in order to plan the interface, we shall assume a 16-bit-word-length machine. Then, by packing two 8-bit numbers into each word, we can read the data into the computer every 10 ms with the following instructions in the preprocessor service routine:

DATA IN (16 bits from preprocessor to accumulator in computer)
STORE ACCUMULATOR (in memory)
DATA IN (second word)
STORE ACCUMULATOR
DATA IN (third word)
STORE ACCUMULATOR
DATA IN (fourth word)
STORE ACCUMULATOR

To do this we shall set up the first 16-bit word so as to be ready when the first DATA

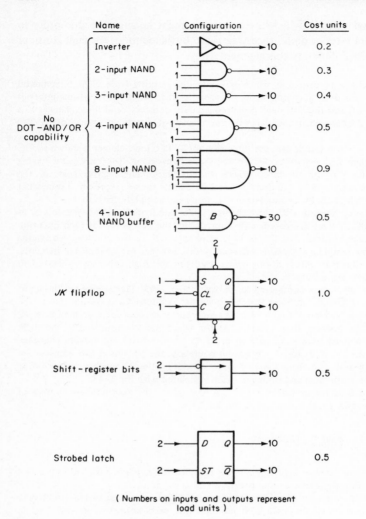

(Numbers on inputs and outputs represent
load units)

Fig. 6-42   Series 54/74 TTL logic—loading rules and cost criterion.

IN instruction occurs. As each successive DATA IN instruction occurs, we shall have
the corresponding word ready to be transferred. To be specific, we shall assume that
the DATA IN plus the STORE ACCUMULATOR instructions take roughly 10 μs.

The collection of data in the preprocessor is conveniently organized around a
64-bit recirculation loop and the up-down-pass-clear operator discussed in Sec. 6-4.
This configuration, shown in Fig. 6-44, will be modified shortly to account for the
outputting of the data to the computer. Our only accommodation to that operation at
this point is to make two 8-bit *word times* take less than 10 μs. With the clock rate of
3.2 MHz shown, these two word times will actually take 5 μs.

During each 2.5-μs word time W_i, the two one-out-of-eight data selectors connect the *change* and *CW* outputs of synchronous decoder No. *i* to the $\overline{pass}$ and the *up* inputs of the serial operator. Thus, if that decoder is registering a change for its encoder, the corresponding counter will be counted once, either up or down. Since the synchronous decoders are clocked once per recirculation, every encoder change is counted. The bit, word, and recirculation counters can be designed synchronously, asynchronously, or pseudosynchronously as needed in order to meet the timing requirements.

The transfer of the accumulated data to the computer is carried out during recirculation $R0$, which occurs approximately every 10 ms. Note in Fig. 6-44 that the serial operator is "cleared" during $R0$. However, as shown in Fig. 6-18*b*, this serial operator can still be used to count the contents of each counter up or down one count, starting from zero, if the corresponding synchronous decoder indicates that a change has occurred. Consequently, the transfer of the data will not interfere with the correct monitoring of the incremental encoders.

The circuitry to execute this transfer is block-diagrammed in Fig. 6-45. An interrupt request is initiated when the address counter reaches $R0 \cdot W0 \cdot B0$. At this same moment, the clock is stopped. Since bit 0 of word 0 sits at the input to the serial operator, words 0 and 1 are in the last 16 bits of the shift register. These 16 bits will be transferred into the computer when it executes its first DATA IN instruction.

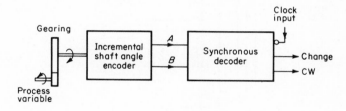

Change	CW	Meaning
O	O	No change
O	1	No change
1	O	Changed 1 quantum counterclockwise
1	1	Changed 1 quantum clockwise

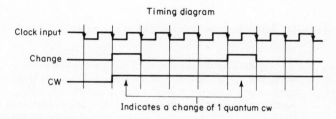

Indicates a change of 1 quantum cw

Fig. 6-43 Encoder-decoder configuration.

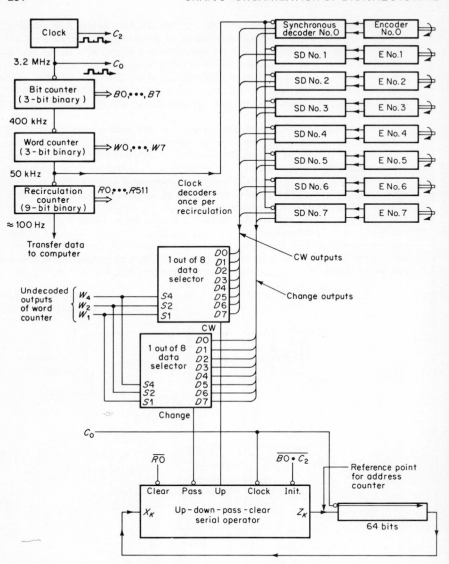

Fig. 6-44 Accumulation of encoder data in a recirculation loop.

Following the generation of the interrupt request, the preprocessor stops and waits. For correct system operation, this wait plus the transfer of the contents of the eight counters to the computer must not exceed 100 μs (1/10 kHz). When the computer acknowledges the interrupt, the preprocessor service routine will execute its first DATA IN instruction, putting a pulse on the DATI1 line of the I/O bus. This is ANDed with the *device select* signal to form a *transfer data* pulse which puts the 16 data bits on the data lines of the I/O bus. The trailing edge of this pulse (which occurs after the data has been transferred) is also used to start the clock again.

The clock now emits 16 C_0 pulses, at which point address $R0 \cdot W2 \cdot B0$ is detected, stopping the clock again. Words 2 and 3 are now in the 16 accessible bits, waiting for the next DATI1 pulse. In this way all eight words are transferred, two at a time, to the computer.

The implementation of this data transfer circuitry is shown in more detail in Fig. 6-46. In both the controlled clock and the interrupt request circuitry much of

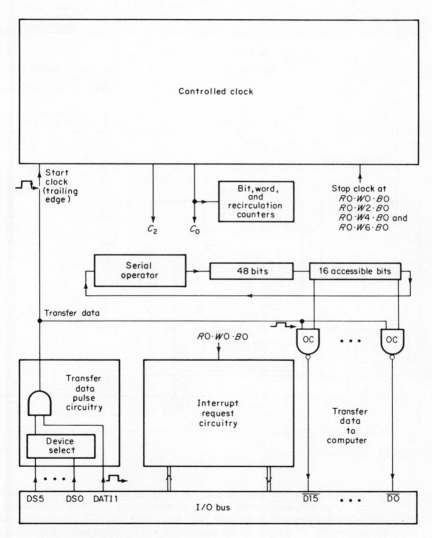

Fig. 6-45 Overview of data transfer circuitry.

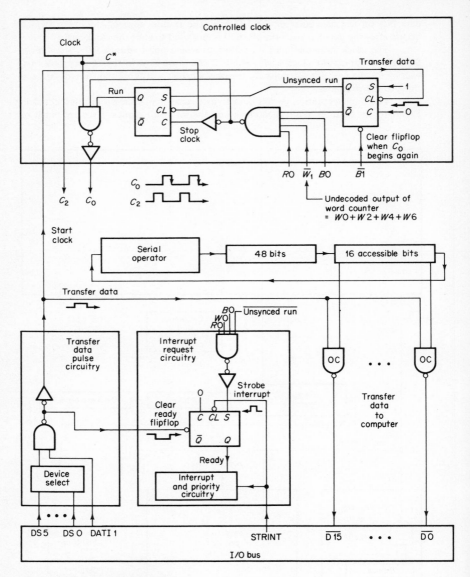

Fig. 6-46 Data transfer circuitry.

the complication which arises is there in order to insure proper operation even though the preprocessor's clock and the computer's clock are not synchronized to each other. Looking first at the controlled clock, note that the C_0 output is stopped by enabling the clear input on the *run* flipflop and by simultaneously blocking the gate which forms C_0. It is started again after the trailing edge of the transfer data pulse causes the *unsynced run* flipflop to set. The next C^* transition sets the run flipflop and permits the generation of C_0 pulses again. This method of controlling the C_0 output insures against cutting it on or off in the middle of a pulse, which could cause unreliable operation.

The interrupt request circuitry begins its operation as the address counter counts to $R0 \cdot W0 \cdot B0$ and stops. The trailing edge of the next strobe interrupt pulse will set the ready flipflop. The following strobe interrupt pulse will cause an interrupt signal to be transmitted to the computer (if no higher priority activity is going on). The ready flipflop is direct cleared again when the DATA IN instruction is executed.

In concluding this example, we should reiterate a point made earlier. Although this represents one way to organize the preprocessor, it is not the only way. However, it does take advantage of the iterative operations involved by employing serial organization. The reader might wish to consider alternative implementations and compare costs using the cost criterion of Fig. 6-42, together with some appropriate cost unit equivalents for any MSI circuits used.

Example 6-4 For the following problem, discuss a design approach which might be used but stop short of carrying out the detailed design. Consider the design of an array processor which uses the direct memory access (DMA) channel to find the largest number L and its address Y in an array of values

$$X_0, \ldots, X_{n-1}$$

stored in the core memory between addresses N and $N + n - 1$. Assume the numbers in the array are expressed in sign plus two's complement form.

The array processor will organize the DMA channel in much the same way as it was organized to handle block transfers of data in the last section. Thus it will be set up using programmed data transfers. Once set up and its operation initiated, the array processor will run on its own until its operation has been completed. At that time, it stops making DMA channel requests and instead makes an interrupt request. The service routine for the array processor, called up by the interrupt, transfers the results of the array processor back to the computer and lets the computer then continue on its way.

Since full-time use of the DMA channel will usurp complete control of the computer, the question arises whether there are any circumstances warranting interruption of this array processor. If there are any input or output devices which must be serviced on demand, then we must organize the array processor to honor these. We shall assume that while the computer will ignore an interrupt request in favor of servicing a DMA channel request, nevertheless the interrupt request signal still exists on the $\overline{\text{INT}}$ line of the I/O bus. Then it can be used by the array processor, setting a flipflop which blocks any further DMA channel requests. The interrupting device can then take over control of the computer through its service routine. Upon completion of its activity, the computer can execute a DATA OUT instruction to the array processor clearing the flipflop, which will again permit it full access to the DMA channel.

Operation of the array processor is initiated with three DATA OUT instructions to three separate *registers* in the processor:

1. Load the address N of the first element in the array into a binary *up* counter in the processor. This counter will provide the memory address.

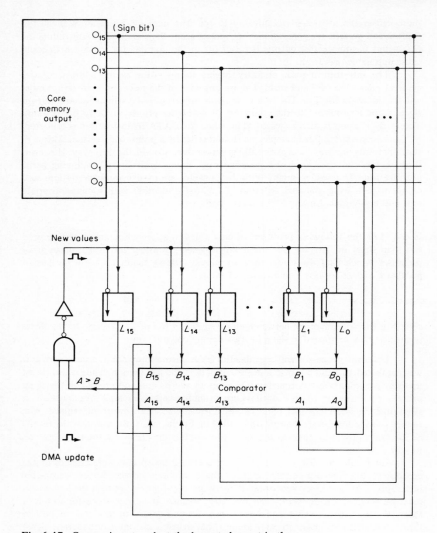

Fig. 6-47 Comparison to select the largest element in the array.

2. Load the number of elements in the array *n* into a binary *down* counter in the processor. The processing will be done when this counter equals zero.
3. Put a 1 in bit 15 of an accumulator and load it into a *start* flipflop in the processor.

As long as the *start* flipflop is set, the array processor will carry out one comparison per memory cycle, comparing the largest number found so far $L_{15}\cdots L_0$ with the contents of the present memory address $O_{15}\cdots O_0$. This is illustrated in Fig. 6-47. The sign bits are shown switched so that a negative number (with sign bit = 1) will not look larger than a positive number (with sign bit = 0). It is assumed that the *DMA update* pulse occurs late enough in the memory cycle for the circuit to have settled out before its trailing edge. Then the *new values* pulse will replace the contents of $L_{15} \cdots L_0$ by $O_{15} \cdots O_0$ if the latter were larger. Otherwise, it will leave it alone. The new values pulse is also used to store the present memory address in a register $Y_{15} \cdots Y_0$.

After each comparison, the two binary counters are counted (if start = 1) in order to move on to the next element in the array and to determine whether or not the processing has been completed. At the completion of the processing, the two registers $L_{15} \cdots L_0$ and $Y_{15} \cdots Y_0$, will be read into the computer with two DATA IN instructions. Consequently, they must be interfaced to the I/O bus.

Controlling the *start* flipflop and the interrupt and priority circuitry leads to much the same considerations as were discussed in the last example. The timing is somewhat simplified because all signals are derived from the computer and are therefore all synchronized.

The completion of the design is highly dependent upon what signals are actually available from the computer and their timing interrelationships. A valuable exercise would be to carry this design to completion for a specific computer.

PROBLEMS

6-1 Special-purpose structures Show a serial system structure and a timing diagram for implementing Example 6-1. Use only one full adder. Define all (otherwise undefined) circuits and signals used and explain the operation of your system.

6-2 Special-purpose structures As will be discussed in the next chapter, a stepping motor plus its synchronous decoder-driver circuitry permits an output shaft to be rotated a precisely controlled amount. Each step might give 1/200 of a revolution. Furthermore, the error in each step does not accumulate, so that 200 steps give precisely one revolution of the shaft.

The purpose of this problem is to improve on the performance of a single stepping motor by a factor of 13. This will be done by combining three motors plus differential gearing plus digital circuitry, as shown in Fig. P 6-2. The result will be a *superstepper,* in effect, which still takes steps at the same rate (say, 100 steps per second) but for which the step size can be any integral number of quanta between 13 quanta *CW* and 13 quanta *CCW*. For this to be practical, the *accuracy* of each step of each motor must be something like one twenty-sixth of its step size or better. This characteristic is provided by some stepping motors.

Each motor is driven by a synchronous decoder-driver which is clocked continuously at a 100-Hz rate. The state of the two inputs *CW* and *CCW* during each clock period determine whether the motor will step and in which direction it will step when the next clock transition occurs, as follows:

CW	CCW	Operation at next clock transition
0	0	Don't step
0	1	Step one step *CCW*
1	0	Step one step *CW*
1	1	Don't step

The differential gearing shown between the outputs of the three stepping motors Θ_1, Θ_3, and Θ_9 and the output shaft of the *superstepper* Θ_0 provides an output-shaft rotation

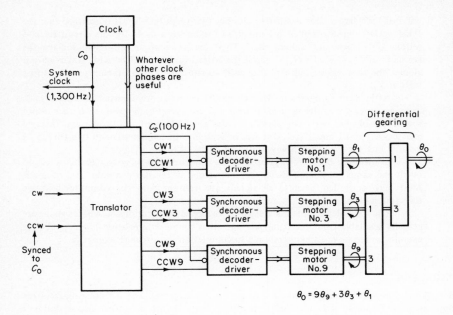

$$\theta_0 = 9\theta_9 + 3\theta_3 + \theta_1$$

Binary coded ternary code

I	A +9	B -9	C +3	D -3	E +1	F -1	← Weights
5	1	0	0	1	0	1	
4	0	0	1	0	1	0	
3	0	0	1	0	0	0	
2	0	0	1	0	0	1	
1	0	0	0	0	1	0	
0	0	0	0	0	0	0	
−1	0	0	0	0	0	1	
−2	0	0	0	1	1	0	

⋮

Fig. P 6-2

of

$$\Theta_0 = 9\Theta_9 + 3\Theta_3 + \Theta_1$$

where $\Theta_i = 0, +1,$ or -1 for $\Theta_1, \Theta_3,$ and Θ_9.

Using the logic shown in Fig. 6-42 and minimizing cost, design the translator shown.

Hint: An up-down counter which counts in the binary coded ternary code shown might be used to accumulate the inputs to the translator over each 0.01-s interval.

6-3 Special-purpose structures We wish to control two binary outputs and monitor two binary inputs in each of two remote stations from a monitor and control center, as shown in Fig. P 6-3. These inputs and outputs might be represented by switches and lights, where each switch in the monitor and control center controls a corresponding light in one of the stations. Similarly each light in the center is controlled by a corresponding switch in one of the stations.

In order to simplify the interconnections between these three locations, only two wires are to be used. One is a clock line C_0 going from the center to both stations. The other

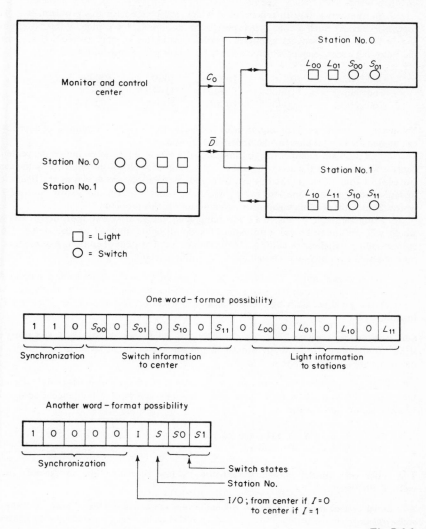

Fig. P 6-3

is a bidirectional data line, $\overline{D}$. This latter line is normally high. Any of the locations can pull the line low using the dot-OR connection of a gate having an open-collector output (just as will be done on a computer's bidirectional I/O bus).

Information must be transmitted over the data line in words, where each bit of the word has its own meaning (such as turn off light No. 0 at station No. 0). A synchronizing problem arises because each station must somehow determine when words begin. One way in which this is often done is to use a separate channel to transmit a synchronizing pulse which occurs between words and which could be used by each station to initiate operation on a new word.

An alternative way to synchronize, which will be used for this problem, is to use a *comma-free code*. Such a code synchronizes the stations to the center by the pattern of 1s and 0s in the code itself. As examples of some possibilities of comma-free codes, consider the following codes, each of which consists of the four code words shown:

Code No. 1:	10	100	1000	10000
Code No. 2:	110000	110001	110100	110101
Code No. 3:	10000	10001	10010	10011

No matter how the words of any of these codes are alternated, the beginning of a new word can be detected by looking for the underlined pattern.

This problem requires the transmission of 4 bits of information out of the center (to control four lights in the stations) and the reception of 4 bits of information by the center (to control four lights in the center). Two code possibilities are shown in the figure. One updates the system in one long word, while the other requires the transmission of four words. Some other coding might prove even better for this problem.

Using the logic of Fig. 6-42 and minimizing the total system cost, design a system which will continuously and automatically keep all lights updated on the status of their corresponding switches. Describe your coding and your system operation. Assume that the *time* required to complete each update cycle is unimportant.

6-4 Pipeline organization Restructure the circuit shown in Fig. P 6-4 using a maximum of only three levels of gating between synchronizing registers. Determine the maximum clock rate for the pipeline, both before and after restructuring, in terms of T_G, T_R, and T_{SU} (nanoseconds).

6-5 Pipeline organization Develop the circuitry, analogous to Fig. 6-11 and using any signals found there, to load the output of a pipeline clocked at 48 MHz back into a disc memory with a bit-clock rate of 3 MHz.

6-6 Serial organization Show the serial organization of 16 x 3 x 100 bits of data organized into three 100-word arrays X, Y, and Z with 16 bits in each word. Simultaneous access must be available to the following bits:

    (a)   Bit b_i of $X(k)$, $Y(k)$, and $Z(k)$
    (b)   All 16 bits of any word

The serial organization shown should use as few accessible bits as possible in the recirculation loop.

6-7 Serial organization (a) Using a full adder plus associated circuitry, design the *add-pass serial operator* shown in Fig. P 6-7. It should add two sign plus two's complement numbers together bit by bit if a control input add = 1 and should simply pass one of the inputs on to

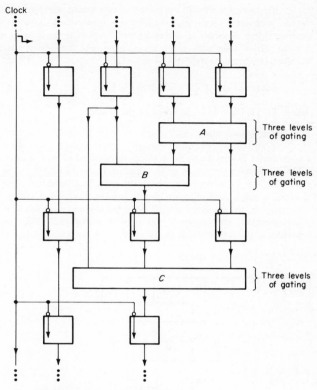

Clock

A {Three levels of gating

B {Three levels of gating

C {Three levels of gating

T_G = Maximum gate propagation delay
T_R = Maximum register propagation delay
T_{SU} = Worst-case register setup time

Fig. P 6-4

the output if the control input add = 0. That is,

$$Z = X + Y \quad \text{if add} = 1$$
$$= X \quad \text{if add} = 0$$

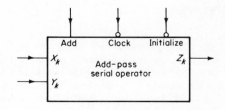

Fig. P 6-7

(*b*) Design a serially organized circuit which will store two arrays X and Y of 16-bit words, each array consisting of 128 words. The circuit should be capable of adding together corresponding numbers in the two arrays, replacing the X array with the sum obtained. Use a recirculation loop with as few accessible bits in the loop as possible. Explain the operation involved in forming

$$Z(k) = X(k) + Y(k) \qquad \text{for } 0 \leqslant k \leqslant 127$$

where $X(k)$ is the kth 16-bit word of the X array.

6-8 Serial organization Using one iterative block B, together with switched-input delay flipflops and other circuitry, design a recirculation loop which will recirculate each of one-hundred twenty-eight 8-bit words unchanged or which can be used to replace all of the 8-bit words with the result of the operation shown in Fig. P 6-8. The control of this latter operation is to be implemented with the switch on the delay flipflops and whatever timing is needed. A single control input *operate* is to be designed so that if operate = 1 for a complete recirculation, the contents will be operated upon as required in the figure. If operate = 0 for a recirculation, the contents will remain unchanged. (This example is typical of many algorithmic processes where an iterative block must manipulate several bits simultaneously.)

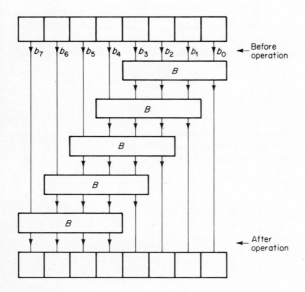

Fig. P 6-8

6-9 Timing counter (*a*) Using the logic and cost criterion of Fig. 6-42, design a minimum-cost asynchronous eight-state bit counter with only one decoded output labeled $B0$. The flipflops should settle out, in counting into the $B0$ state, within one propagation delay. Also the $B0$ output must not exhibit spurious pulses.

(*b*) Is there any advantage to be gained by replacing the asynchronous counter with a synchronous counter? Explain.

6-10 Timing counter with decoded outputs Using the scale-of-seven scaler given in Appendix A3 and a one-out-of-eight decoder, design a *bit* counter with all output states decoded. Label the output states $B0, \ldots, B6$.

6-11 Timing counter with decoded outputs Using the approach of Fig. 6-23, design a scale-of-21 *word* counter with all output states decoded. Label the output states $W0, \ldots, W20$. Show the count sequence of the scale-of-21 scaler used (which must be self-starting, synchronous, and minimum cost).

6-12 Mode circuitry (a) If the mode circuitry for the digital combination lock were organized as shown in Fig. 6-26, how many delay flipflops would be needed?

(b) How many inputs and outputs would be required of the ROM? (Assume that no gating is done on any inputs like b_1, requiring them to be used directly.) How many bits of storage does this imply for the ROM?

(c) If a function F is first generated, as in Fig. 6-6, then how many inputs, outputs, and bits of storage are required of the ROM?

(d) Using an MSI data selector, as in Sec. 3-14, design the circuitry for this function F.

6-13 Memory addressing Consider a dedicated computer which has its program stored in the first 2,048 memory locations and requires arrays of data to be stored in the next 2,048 memory locations. If these arrays must be repetitively processed, then discuss the benefits and liabilities of each of the addressing modes discussed in Sec. 6-6 for this application. In particular, consider the problem of repeatedly reading instructions out of the lower-numbered addresses of the memory which operate on data in much higher addresses. Consider also the problem of repeatedly addressing successive elements of the arrays of data.

6-14 Programmed data channel interfacing Interface a 10-digit keyboard (digits 0 to 9) into a computer. Assume the keyboard outputs consist of 10 single-pole, single-throw (normally open) switches ($D0, \ldots, D9$) which will provide an uncoded output to the computer. For simplicity, these will be put on bits 0 to 9 of the I/O bus data lines.

The keyboard also includes a double-pole, double-throw switch (STROBE) that changes state if any of the keyboard digit switches have been depressed. It does so *after* the contacts of the digit switch have stabilized into the closed position.

The interface should provide one interrupt and one data transfer per closure of the STROBE switch. Assume the computer structure of Sec. 6-7.

6-15 Programmed data channel interfacing A low-cost analog-to-digital and digital-to-analog converter facility can be added to a computer by interfacing two components to it. These are a D/A converter module (a combinational circuit) and a voltage-comparator integrated circuit. The voltage comparator compares two inputs and puts out either of two logic levels (like 0 or 3 V) on a single output line. This output depends on which input is the larger. Any voltage difference exceeding the threshold (like 1 mV) will provide an unambiguous, clamped output of 0 or 3 V.

To use this facility it is necessary to be able to transfer the contents of an accumulator in the computer to a register in the converter interface using a DATA OUT instruction. This might be a 10-bit register connected to a 10-bit digital-to-analog converter. The voltage on the output of the D/A converter might be proportional to the sign plus two's complement number in the register.

Besides providing an analog output, the D/A converter output also goes to one input on the comparator. The other input is the analog voltage input to be converted to digital form. The output of the comparator is transferred to the sign bit of an accumulator (on data line $\overline{D15}$ of the I/O bus) whenever a DATA IN instruction is executed for this facility. The conversion of an analog voltage to its digital representation is then carried out under program control by the following sequence of instructions in a manner described in Chap. 7:

LOAD ACCUMULATOR (with an approximation to the converted number)
DATA OUT (to D/A converter)
DATA IN (from comparator output)
TEST SIGN BIT
LOAD ACCUMULATOR (with a better approximation)
. . . .

Design the interface using the logic of Fig. 6-42 (plus gates with open-collector outputs to drive I/O bus lines). Does the operation of this facility require it to have interrupt capability?

6-16 Programmed data channel interfacing (a) Design an interface between a single input of 0 or +3 V (which might represent the state of a set of contacts in some relatively slow process) and the computer. Every time this input changes in either direction, an interrupt request must be made. The service routine will then read out the state of this switch onto the $\overline{D15}$ data line of the I/O bus.

(b) A process must be monitored by keeping track of 32 Boolean inputs (from 32 pairs of contacts), each with its own interrupt and each putting its bit of data on the $\overline{D15}$ data line of the I/O bus. Does the repetition of this job provide any opportunities for simplifying the circuitry over the alternative of using 32 of the circuits designed in (a)?

(c) Again a process must be monitored by keeping track of 32 Boolean inputs. Now, however, only one interrupt will be sent to the computer (from one interface for all 32 inputs). In response to a DATA IN instruction in the service routine for this interface, the unit will transmit a 5-bit binary number on data lines $\overline{D4}, \ldots, \overline{D0}$ saying which input changed. It will also transmit the state of this input on $\overline{D15}$. Design this interface. Make sure the interface will not send erroneous results to the computer if two inputs change simultaneously. It should first interrupt for the one and then for the other, or some such operation.

6-17 DMA channel interfacing A DMA channel designed to accept one device is to be shared by two devices. Develop and explain the circuitry which might be used to establish priority and control data transfer between core memory and the appropriate device.

6-18 Preprocessor The designs shown in Fig. 6-44 and 6-46 have glossed over the problem of satisfying the loading rules for the logic elements used. Show modifications which might be made to satisfy these. Discuss any constraints on the modification in order to meet clock skew requirements.

6-19 Preprocessor The interrupt request circuitry shown in Fig. 6-46 has a ready flipflop, which is enabled when

$$R0 \cdot W0 \cdot B0 \cdot \overline{\text{unsynced run}} = 1$$

The unsynced run input is included in order to keep the ready flipflop from being set immediately after being direct cleared and before $R0 \cdot W0 \cdot B0$ has a chance to change to 0. Briefly discuss why this is a problem. Show typical timing diagrams of the important signals and their interrelationships.

6-20 Preprocessor Taking the 3.2-MHz clock rate of Example 6-3 into account as well as the uses to which the address counter is put, design a minimum-cost but reliable address counter (bit, word, and recirculation counters). What is the worst-case timing constraint which this counter must meet? Assume the timing characteristics of Fig. 5-16 and 5-18 for the logic elements.

6-21 Preprocessor The preprocessor of Example 6-3 accepts data from eight synchronous decoders which, in turn, accept unsynchronized data from eight incremental encoders. Each of the synchronous decoders actually consists of circuitry configured as shown in Fig. P 6-21. Restructure the design shown in Fig. 6-44 by putting the one-out-of-eight data selectors on the A and B outputs of the incremental encoders instead of on the Change and CW outputs of the synchronous decoders. However, be sure that the outputs of the data selectors are synchronized (clocked into delay flipflops) before they are used. Using the cost units of Fig. 6-42, determine the net change in the preprocessor's cost.

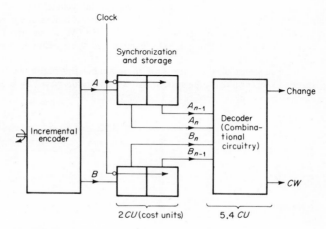

Fig. P 6-21

6-22 Array processor Using a programmed data transfer to initiate and terminate its operation, a *display generator* might use a DMA channel to provide continuous refreshing of a waveform on an oscilloscope. The waveform is represented by the 256 words in locations 3840 to 4095 of memory. Each word consists of two 8-bit numbers which are used to drive two 8-bit D/A converters (combinational circuits) in the display generator. The outputs of these converters go to the vertical and horizontal axes of an oscilloscope.

In order to tie up the computer as little as possible this display generator moves from one point to the next after every N instructions have been executed. It does so by transferring the next word in the array from memory to a register which drives the D/A converters. By making N equal to 8 or 16, the efficiency of the computer for doing its other jobs will hardly be impaired. Notice that this interlacing of display-generator operations with normal operations permits the array to be updated, under program control, even while it is being displayed.

Using the logic of Fig. 6-42, the computer structure of Sec. 6-7, and minimizing cost, design the display generator and describe its operation.

6-23 Array processor (*a*) How would you modify the design of the display generator of Prob. 6-22 so that it will display four waveforms simultaneously, each having the same 256-point resolution?

(*b*) How would you modify the design so that only one of these four waveforms is ever displayed at a time, the choice being under program control?

REFERENCES

An excellent presentation of the strengths, characteristics, and organization of pipeline systems is given by L. W. Cotten, Circuit Implementation of High-Speed Pipeline Systems, *Proceedings, 1965 Fall Joint Computer Conference*, pp. 489–504. Multiple-phase clocking can afford significantly higher throughput rates, as is discussed by the same author in Maximum-Rate Pipeline Systems, *Proceedings, 1969 Spring Joint Computer Conference*, pp. 581–586.

The organization of a specific pipeline processor is developed by H. Groginsky and G. Works, A Pipeline Fast Fourier Transform, *1969 EASCON Convention Record*, pp. 22–29.

Pipelining, as an approach to high-speed general-purpose computing, merits comparison with highly parallel systems. Two supercomputers, the pipeline STAR computer (of Control Data Corporation) and the parallel ILLIAC IV (of the University of Illinois), are compared by W. R. Graham, The Parallel and the Pipeline Computers, *Datamation*, April 1970, pp. 68–71.

The considerations involved in matching the requirements for a computer to the specifications of a real-time system are extensively discussed by S. Stimler, "Real-Time Data-Processing Systems," McGraw-Hill, New York, 1969.

7
System Input-Output Considerations

7-1 ACTUATION

The function of many digital systems is to control something. For many other digital systems, control plays a subordinate role but is nevertheless a part of the system.

One very simple actuator for affecting control of most on-off devices is the *transistor switch*, shown in Fig. 7-1a. When the input V_1 goes high, the transistor is turned on into saturation so that almost the entire voltage V_{cc} appears across the on-off device, actuating it. In contrast, when V_1 goes low, the transistor is cut off, causing its three terminals to be open-circuited with respect to each other. With its bottom terminal open-circuited, the on-off device is turned off.

Often, as shown in Fig. 7-1b, a light driver includes an extra resistor R_2, which passes a small current through the light even when it is turned off. This increases the light's *off* resistance significantly, reducing the sudden surge of current on the ground line when an entire bank of lights is turned on.

The driver for an inductive device like a relay, a winding of a stepping motor, or the actuator of a printing mechanism is often configured as in Fig. 7-1c. The resistor R_3 is used to turn the transistor off harder when V_1 goes low. In addition, the diode permits the current in the inductive device to turn off

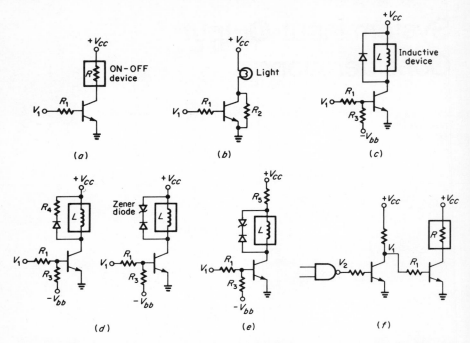

Fig. 7-1   Transistor switches. (*a*) Basic transistor switch; (*b*) light driver; (*c*) inductive load driver; (*d*) inductive load drivers having faster turn-off; (*e*) inductive load driver having faster turn-on and turn-off; (*f*) cascaded transistor switches.

gently instead of abruptly when the transistor is turned off. These modifications are made to protect the transistor from excessive power dissipation during switching and from voltage breakdown during turn-off due to an inductive voltage surge.

Although the circuit of Fig. 7-1*c* will drive any inductive device, often the performance of the device can be significantly improved if the current can be turned on and off faster. Thus a stepping motor can be made to step faster and a printer can be made to print at a higher rate.

One of the modifications shown in Fig. 7-1*d* is often used to speed up *turn-off* of the current in the inductive coil. Turn-off is accelerated by dissipating energy in either R_4 or the Zener diode. The Zener permits the breakdown voltage of the transistor to be approached more closely than R_4 does. Also, it kills the current at a constant (maximum) rate. In contrast, the current in the R_4 circuit peaks close to the same maximum rate, and then its rate decays exponentially.

The circuit of Fig. 7-1*e* adds a resistor R_5 to speed up *turn-on* of the current. To do this V_{cc} must be increased so that in the steady state the inductive load sees its rated voltage. Increasing V_{cc} and R_5 together in this way, in effect, increases the *source resistance* seen by the load. In the limit with infinite source resistance (i.e., if the load were supplied from a switched current source) the current buildup would be instantaneous. The trade-off involved in increasing R_5 is the power dissipated in R_5 and the increased power required of the V_{cc} power supply.

In many cases, the device current is sufficiently large so that V_1 cannot be driven directly from a gate output. Figure 7-1f shows a transistor switch driven by an inverter whose sole function is to provide current gain, permitting a lower value of R_1 than a gate output can drive.

Sometimes when finer control is required than can be achieved with normal on-off operation, this finer control can be obtained while still retaining the simplicity and power efficiency of a transistor switch. By using fast, time-averaged switching, we can obtain proportional temperature control of a gyro in an inertial guidance system, as shown in Fig. 7-2. The duty cycle T_1/T_2 can be controlled digitally with a counter to provide heat input to the gyro directly proportional to the error between the desired and actual temperatures. Furthermore, the thermal response of the heater winding will smooth the input to its average value of

$$\frac{T_1}{T_2} V_{cc}$$

Direct digital control of shaft position can be efficiently achieved with a *stepping motor*, such as that shown in Fig. 7-3. With the many manufacturers who provide them, stepping motors are available having a broad range of torque ratings, without gearing, from a fraction of an ounce-inch for small instrumentation stepping motors up to hundreds of pound-inches for large units. They are

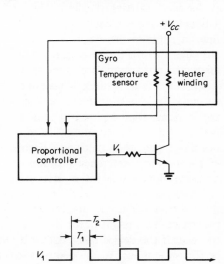

Fig. 7-2 Time-averaged switching for fine control of a variable.

Fig. 7-3 Stepping motor. (*The Superior Electric Co.*)

also available in a broad range of step sizes, without gearing, from 90 down to 0.45° per step. With the addition of gearing, an arbitrary trade-off between high sweep rate and high resolution and torque is possible.

In many applications, use is made of the fast start-stop capability of a stepping motor. As long as the dynamic torque of the load does not exceed that available from the motor, it can be started and stopped "on a dime." Typical stepping rates for various motors operated in this fashion are on the order of 100 to 400 steps/s, with high performance motors providing up to 1,200 to 2,000 steps/s. If the motor is gently accelerated up to its maximum stepping rate and decelerated to a stop, it can generally reach a speed of two to four times that specified for starting and stopping on a dime and still not miss a step.

Another useful feature of stepping motors is the accuracy of their stepping. For example, consider the motor shown in Fig. 7-3 which steps 200 steps/revolution. If it is stepped exactly 400 steps clockwise, it will turn exactly two revolutions. Then, if it is stepped 400 steps counterclockwise, it will return to its exact starting position. This happens because the motor is essentially a 100-pole ac motor. Each step position is defined by the response of a permanent magnet rotor to the magnetic field pattern set up by the stator. Consequently, although there is some error in the exact position held at each step position, this error does not accumulate as the motor steps along.

These two features of fast starting and stopping and of accurate stepping account for the use of stepping motors in a wide assortment of *positioning* applications. Digital plotters, numerically controlled machine tools, positioning systems for remote manipulators and large antennas all use stepping motors to position a pen, tool, or device. Each position corresponds to a discrete number of steps from a reference position. For example, if each step of the motor is translated into a 0.001-in motion, then moving 0.125 in means taking 125 steps.

An *incremental control system* such as this possesses the deficiency that if steps are ever missed, the system will be in error by that number of steps thereafter. This might occur if a large inertial load is accelerated or decelerated too fast, if the device being driven by the motor runs into a stop or an obstacle, or if power is lost to the counters in the system which keep track of absolute position (by counting steps). In many applications, such a malfunction may occur so rarely or with so little consequence that the simplicity of stepping motor positioning overrides this drawback.

If a positioning system must run continuously for long periods of time, it may be able to take advantage of this low-cost, incremental control provided only that it has some way to re-reference itself automatically and indicate whenever stepping errors have been detected. One way to do this consists of mounting a switch in the middle of the travel of the positioning system in such a way that its closure will pinpoint one specific step position. If the total travel contains around 16,000 steps, the switch might indicate position $2^{13} = 8,192$. When the switch closure occurs, the counter keeping track of absolute position should be at 8,192. If it is not, it can be direct preset to this number at the same time that an error signal is generated.

Stepping motors are often used in *closed-loop position-control or rate-control systems* because of their excellent dynamic characteristics. The absolute position might be measured with a binary or BCD shaft-angle encoder in order to avoid the problems of incremental control just discussed. If the desired position (stored in a register) and the actual position (available from the encoder) are compared, the stepping motor can be stepped until the error is zero. The device to be positioned must receive smaller steps from the stepping motor than the encoder measures in order to insure that the position of zero error can always be reached. This approach to closed-loop control provides excellent response without stability problems. When zero error is reached, the motor stops stepping and the device stops.

One interesting opportunity made possible with stepping motors is *electronic gearing*, as shown in Fig. 7-4. The speed of the system can be increased or decreased easily by changing N. Also the *gear ratios* can be easily changed by varying the other scalers. The use of stepping motors in this application provides the same *phaselocking* between output shafts as is achieved through gearing, but it does so with a great deal more flexibility than is possible through conventional gearing.

Stepping motors are driven by switches, but the exact switching cycle depends on the specific motor used. The motor shown in Fig. 7-3 is reasonably typical in its driving circuitry. It uses a *bifilar wound* stator, as shown schematically in Fig. 7-5. The two vertical bifilar windings avoid the problem of having only one vertical winding in which the current must flow in either direction. Switching the current through one winding in either direction is difficult to achieve with transistor switches. In contrast, the bifilar windings permit current to be turned on (or off) in one winding while it is turned off (or on) in the other.

The resistors R_1 and R_2 can be left out of the circuit of Fig. 7-5 for simplicity. Their function is to optimize the dynamic response of the motor, as discussed in conjunction with Fig. 7-1. Each transistor switch shown in Fig. 7-5

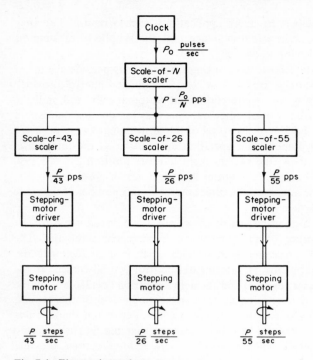

Fig. 7-4 Electronic gearing.

is assumed to have a large enough current gain to be turned on into saturation when the gate driving it goes high. The diode bias insures that a transistor will be cut off hard when the gate driving it goes low.

The actual sequencing of switching operations to make the motor step through four steps in a clockwise direction is illustrated in Fig. 7-6. Each step is shown as 90 electrical degrees. For the 100-pole motor, this corresponds to the $1.8°$ step seen on the output shaft. The count sequence for G_2 and G_1 is seen to be that of a 2-bit Gray code. Consequently, to make the motor step one step clockwise, it is necessary to make $G_2 G_1$ count up to the next Gray-code number. To go counterclockwise one step, $G_2 G_1$ must be counted down one count. The design of the up-down counter needed to drive a stepping motor is considered in Prob. 7-5 at the end of the chapter.

Many devices provide an output quantity proportional to an input voltage or current. One example is a dc motor whose direction and speed depend on the sign and magnitude of an input current. Another is a hysteresis clutch such as that shown in Fig. 7-7. This is a device which is used, as shown in Fig. 7-8, to drive a load with a torque T which is proportional to an input current I.

Significantly, the torque transmitted by a hysteresis clutch is virtually independent of the speed of either the load or the ac motor.

To drive such devices, we can use a low cost *digital-to-analog* (D/A) *converter* to provide a voltage or current proportional to a digital input. With the advent of high-performance integrated-circuit components, these D/A converters are being built by many manufacturers with ever-improving performance specifications and dropping costs. An example of a low-cost 12-bit D/A converter is shown in Fig. 7-9. It converts a 12-bit sign plus two's complement input (from DTL or TTL logic) into a bipolar output voltage proportional to the input and between ± 10 V.

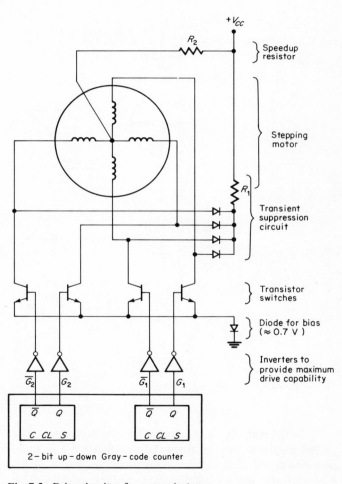

Fig. 7-5 Drive circuitry for a stepping motor.

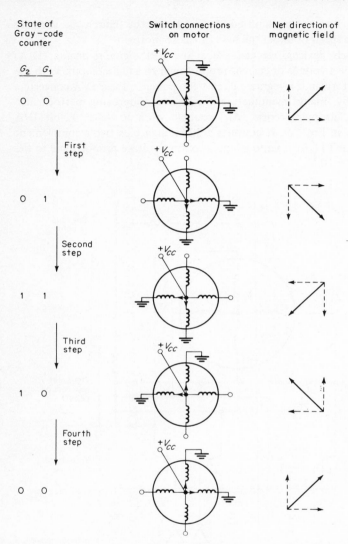

State of
Gray-code
counter

G_2 G_1

0   0

First
step

0   1

Second
step

1   1

Third
step

1   0

Fourth
step

0   0

Switch connections
on motor

Net direction of
magnetic field

Fig. 7-6 Switching sequence for stepping.

In general, the technology available makes 8- to 12-bit D/A converters (either binary or two to three digits of BCD) commonplace. Lower resolution does not save a manufacturer appreciable cost, while higher resolution presses a manufacturer toward significantly costlier circuits. The circuit of a D/A converter is combinational. Furthermore, the settling time of the output in response to a change on the input is fast. For example, the time for the

Fig. 7-7 Hysteresis clutch. (*Magtrol, Inc.*)

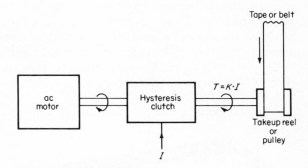

Fig. 7-8 Controlled torque drive.

Fig. 7-9 Twelve-bit digital-to-analog converter. (*Redcor Corp.*)

converter in Fig. 7-9 to reach 99.975 percent of its final value is 10 μs. Higher-performance units provide settling times of less than 100 ns while only increasing the cost by a factor of 3 to 5.

The output of a D/A converter is typically limited to 5 or 10 V (plus or minus) and 2 to 10 mA, which is hardly enough to drive any device other than an oscilloscope·(for a display). However, this problem is readily resolved using a *programmable power supply*, such as the low-cost modular supply shown in Fig. 7-10. This specific supply will accept the unipolar output of a D/A converter as an input and generate a unipolar dc voltage of up to 7 V (at a maximum of 2 A) which is proportional to this voltage and has an arbitrary proportionality factor. Alternatively, it can be connected to generate a unipolar dc current of up to 2 A (at a maximum of 7 V) proportional to the input voltage, again with an arbitrary proportionality factor. With a regulation of 0.05 percent, it will hold the output to within the resolution of a 10-bit D/A converter. And with *operational amplifier* control, the input-output relationship will be virtually constant.

In general, programmable power supplies will provide voltages up to several thousand volts and currents up to 100 A (but not in the same supply!). To obtain a bipolar output of $\pm$ 10 V, the most straightforward approach is to use a fixed −10-V supply in series with a programmable 0- to 20-V supply. The output of a unipolar D/A converter can be used to control the latter supply. With a 10-bit converter, an input of

1000000000

Fig. 7-10 Programmable modular power supply. (*Kepco, Inc.*)

can be set up to put out exactly 0 V. Furthermore, if the sign bit of a sign plus two's complement number is inverted, it will provide the needed input to this 10-bit binary converter with the unipolar output.

7-2 DISPLAY

Most digital systems have some form of information display. The display associated with a control system on a jet fighter provides information to the pilot so that together he and the control system can optimize their combined performance. In a more passive role, a display can provide the operator of an automated warehouse with the location and movement of a stacking crane as it stores and retrieves material. Thus, its performance can be checked and the cause of a malfunction easily discovered. A display is sometimes used to provide the entire output of a system. The diagnostic instrument which provides a doctor with an averaged or correlated biomedical waveform is an example of a system with this emphasis on the display.

A digital-to-analog converter is sometimes used in conjunction with an oscilloscope to provide a display of a waveform. This use of a D/A converter places greater constraints on the performance of the converter than is required when it is used in a control application. It is important that the output increase monotonically as the input increases. While monotonicity is implied by the typical linearity tolerance of one-half of the least significant bit, temperature and aging have hurt the performance of enough converters to cause this to be a real concern. Fortunately, the excellent matching and temperature-tracking capabilities of the MSI integrated-circuit components used in more recent converters tend toward eliminating this problem.

Another problem of the past which will probably give way to MSI components manifests itself in the form of *glitches* on the output waveform. These are spikes which occur as the output changes from certain values to others. For example, if the input changes from 0111111111 to 1000000000 and if the transistor switches in the converter turn off faster than they turn on, then there will be a moment when the input appears as 0000000000. This will put a large negative spike in what might otherwise be a smoothly changing waveform.

The settling time mentioned in the last section becomes important here because the time interval between samples displayed on the scope must not be significantly shorter than this time. For example, a recirculation loop might employ a glass delay line and be clocked at 10 MHz. It may contain an array of 10-bit words which must be displayed one after another to yield a desired waveform on the scope. Every microsecond one word can be transferred in parallel out of the loop and into a register which provides the input to the D/A converter. If the settling time of the converter is short relative to 1 μs, then whatever switching transients occur will not dominate the display.

A final consideration for using a D/A converter to provide a scope display centers on the sampling and the quantization which tend to make the waveform appear granular. This can be smoothed out using a lowpass filter whose cutoff frequency is somewhat lower than the sampling rate but higher than the highest components in the waveform being displayed. Often a simple RC circuit is all that is needed.

For the display of a limited amount of information, incandescent lights are often used. They can either show the status of portions of a system or display binary numbers. Often, where a status signal is supposed to be followed by a response from an operator, an illuminated pushbutton switch provides a convenient, *human engineered* means of preventing the wrong response from being made accidentally. Such a switch is illustrated in Fig. 7-11. Its light and its switch are electrically unrelated, permitting them to be used in all the unconstrained ways open to separate switches and lights.

If a system uses just a few lights, it would be convenient to use lamps which can be operated from a power supply already available, perhaps the +5-V supply used for DTL or TTL logic. However, if the transistor switch used to turn the light on and off has a saturation voltage of 0.7 V, then a proper choice of lamp would be one of 4.3 V or higher. Using a standard 6 or 6.3 V light may be satisfactory, but the light emitted will be significantly less than 4.3/6 or 4.3/6.3 of its normal brightness.

An alternative solution for this case and a general solution where many lights are used is to provide a separate power supply for these lights. A low-cost supply having much poorer regulation and ripple characteristics than would be used for logic is excellent here. In fact, a transformer and a rectifier might be perfectly satisfactory. The lamps will then light up by an amount determined by the rms value of the rectified (but not filtered) waveform across them.

When numbers must be used by an operator, displaying them in binary form is not very satisfactory. Any one of a variety of decimal displays can be used. The general problem of selecting a decimal display includes

1. Choosing the display device itself
2. Obtaining a decoder-driver to accept a coded input like 8421 BCD code and control the device with transistor switches (this is likely to be a standard IC for the more popular display devices)

Fig. 7-11 Illuminated pushbutton switch.
(*Dialight, Inc.*)

Fig. 7-12 Complete decimal display using six NIXIE tubes. (*Burroughs Corp.*)

3. Mounting the device, perhaps with a front bezel and a polarizing filter
4. Powering the device

Complete units which resolve choices 1, 2, and 3 all at once are available using a variety of technologies. Figure 7-12 illustrates one of these. Powering such a unit generally involves supplying one voltage for the display devices (such as the +200 V for those of Fig. 7-12) and +5 V for the decoding logic if it is DTL or TTL. Low-cost supplies are readily available for the purpose of meeting the specific voltage and current requirements of all display devices.

Systems organized around a small computer can profit from all the effort which the industry has expended on developing versatile I/O devices. One of the most useful and versatile devices for a dedicated, real-time system requiring much man-machine interaction is the *display terminal*, which is a cathode-ray-tube (CRT) monitor and a keyboard input. The unit, shown in Fig. 7-13, can display up to 1,998 characters. Queries or status information can be provided by the system and responded to by the operator. Furthermore, the choices open to the operator under specific circumstances can be flashed on the screen. From a human-engineering standpoint, this contrasts very favorably with the control panel faced by the operator of a complex system in the past. No longer must he interact with the system through a maze of lights, meters, switches, and dials which encompass every conceivable thing the system can do at any time. All this information is still available, but it is sequenced to him a step at a time. Each step contains only that information needed so that he can make the necessary decision.

A feature of some display terminals is especially useful for this type of interaction. Selected data presented by the system can be *protected* so that it cannot be changed by the operator. This prevents the operating procedures for the system from being inadvertently destroyed.

Fig. 7-13 Display terminal with capacity for 27 lines, each having 74 characters. (*Hazeltine Corp.*)

Fig. 7-14 Graphic display terminal. (*Tektronix, Inc.*)

Some systems are better described with a *graphic display terminal* such as that shown in Fig. 7-14. This permits the system to be described to the operator not only with characters but also with arbitrary figures. All of the opportunities for powerful man-machine interaction previously mentioned are available here, together with the clarity of graphics. Thus, for the automated warehouse mentioned earlier, the layout of the warehouse might be displayed showing the present position of the stacking crane. Or for a process-control system, process variables and their limits can be shown in the form of bar graphs drawn on the CRT.

Cost is one major obstacle to the complete domination of the display-terminal field by units with graphic capability. These units typically cost at least three times as much as a unit not having graphic capability. On the other hand, many systems are so much more costly in their entirety than the cost of a graphic display terminal that its use is easily justified. For other systems, the required system performance may be virtually unattainable without graphic capability.

A major consideration when designing a system around a display terminal is the amount of memory required to store all of the messages which will ever be displayed. For character messages, it is necessary not only to store the messages themselves but also the format information saying how this information should be displayed on the display terminal. This information is typically stored in exactly the same form as it is originally generated. Each message is composed on the keyboard by depressing a succession of character-generating keys and control keys (like the *carriage return* key). Since each key has associated with it a code word, each message is stored in the computer as a string of code words, generally using the 7-bit ASCII† code shown in Fig. 7-15.

To estimate how much memory will be required to store the messages desired, the messages can be typed out and the number of key strokes counted (including those for control keys). Using a 16-bit-word-length machine, these can be packed two to a word. This is especially convenient if the instruction set includes byte-manipulating instructions for handling the two 8-bit halves of a word separately.

A sophisticated graphic display terminal, such as that shown in Fig. 7-14, will accept character data from the computer in the same coded form and will generate the characters from this code. The graphics capability can require either much data storage or much computer time unless the terminal includes a linear interpolation mode which will accept the end points of a line and construct a

---

†Pronounced *as'-key*. This is the American National Standard Code for Information Interchange, X3.4-1968. This is a widely accepted code sponsored by the American National Standards Institute and adopted as a federal information processing standard. A copy of the complete standard may be purchased from American National Standards Institute, 1430 Broadway, New York, N.Y. 10018.

b_7 b_6 b_5 →				Column	0 0 0	0 0 1	0 1 0	0 1 1	1 0 0	1 0 1	1 1 0	1 1 1
b_4	b_3	b_2	b_1	Row	0	1	2	3	4	5	6	7
0	0	0	0	0	NUL	DLE	SP	0	@	P	`	p
0	0	0	1	1	SOH	DC1	!	1	A	Q	a	q
0	0	1	0	2	STX	DC2	"	2	B	R	b	r
0	0	1	1	3	ETX	DC3	#	3	C	S	c	s
0	1	0	0	4	EOT	DC4	$	4	D	T	d	t
0	1	0	1	5	ENQ	NAK	%	5	E	U	e	u
0	1	1	0	6	ACK	SYN	&	6	F	V	f	v
0	1	1	1	7	BEL	ETB	'	7	G	W	g	w
1	0	0	0	8	BS	CAN	(	8	H	X	h	x
1	0	0	1	9	HT	EM	)	9	I	Y	i	y
1	0	1	0	10	LF	SUB	*	:	J	Z	j	z
1	0	1	1	11	VT	ESC	+	;	K	[	k	{
1	1	0	0	12	FF	FS	,	<	L	\	l	|
1	1	0	1	13	CR	GS	–	=	M	]	m	}
1	1	1	0	14	SO	RS	.	>	N	^	n	~
1	1	1	1	15	SI	US	/	?	O	___	o	DEL

NUL	Null	DLE	Data Link Escape (CC)
SOH	Start of Heading (CC)	DC1	Device Control 1
STX	Start of Text (CC)	DC2	Device Control 2
ETX	End of Text (CC)	DC3	Device Control 3
EOT	End of Transmission (CC)	DC4	Device Control 4 (Stop)
ENQ	Enquiry (CC)	NAK	Negative Acknowledge (CC)
ACK	Acknowledge (CC)	SYN	Synchronous Idle (CC)
BEL	Bell (audible or attention signal) .	ETB	End of Transmission Block (CC)
BS	Backspace (FE)	CAN	Cancel
HT	Horizontal Tabulation (punched card skip) (FE)	EM	End of Medium
LF	Line Feed (FE)	SUB	Substitute
VT	Vertical Tabulation (FE)	ESC	Escape
FF	Form Feed (FE)	FS	File Separator (IS)
CR	Carriage Return (FE)	GS	Group Separator (IS)
SO	Shift Out	RS	Record Separator (IS)
SI	Shift In	US	Unit Separator (IS)
		DEL	Delete

Fig. 7-15 American National Standard Code for Information Interchange (ASCII 68). (*American National Standards Institute.*)

straight line between them. Without this capability, each pattern must be specified point by point either absolutely (specifying the coordinates of each point) or incrementally (specifying a point adjacent to the previous point, in one of eight directions, and whether or not it should be printed). Thus, without a linear interpolation mode, either each point in a plot must be stored absolutely or incrementally or the computer must generate these using an interpolation routine on the end points of lines. The terminal shown in Fig. 7-14 offers all three of these plotting modes. It also is built around a storage display so that only *additions* to the graphic pattern need be generated; that is, the pattern does not need to be refreshed, as does an ordinary cathode-ray-tube display.

The manner in which a display is maintained or refreshed defines limiting characteristics of a terminal. For example, using a storage CRT permits a highly complex pattern to be displayed without the annoying flicker which results if a refreshed CRT is used to display the same pattern. On the other hand, if a deletion is required in the pattern displayed in a storage CRT, the entire pattern must be erased and then regenerated without the portion which was to be deleted. The unit of Fig. 7-14 provides a compromise in the form of a *line buffer* which permits one line of characters at the bottom of the display to be edited with deletions as well as additions while the remainder of the display remains unchanged.

A display terminal with no graphics capability which uses a refreshed CRT generally includes storage and circuitry to handle the refreshing automatically. The terminal shown in Fig. 7-13 is typical in having a variety of editing operations, such as the insertion or deletion of a character or a line. Such operations require storage and refreshing if the computer is not to be brought into the act during editing.

7-3 INPUT SYNCHRONIZATION

A digital system often must accept logic inputs which change at an arbitrary time completely independent of the system clock. In order for the system to read these inputs correctly each and every time, two conditions are necessary. First, the input data must be in a form which is inherently capable of being synchronized to the clock, without ambiguities arising in the information represented. Second, when designing the read-in circuitry, we must take advantage of this capability by synchronizing correctly.

An example illustrating input data which is incapable of always being read into a system correctly is shown in Fig. 7-16. If we consider a device having a shaft whose position we would like to monitor, then by attaching a 7-bit binary encoder, we can read the position of this shaft as some binary number between 0000000 and 1111111. Now, suppose that we are loading this number into a shift register every 100 ms and that the encoder output is changing from 0111111 to 1000000 at some exact instant in which the system is trying to load

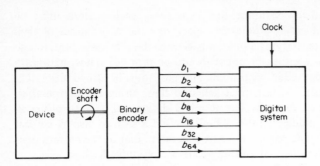

Fig. 7-16   Faulty use of an encoder.

this number into the shift register. Will a bit of the shift register read in the old value, which had been present on its input? Or will it read in the new value? With different setup-release times for the different flipflops, some bits may read the old values while others may read the new values. Whereas such errors will be the exception rather than the rule, nevertheless as designers of the system using this encoder we are helpless to prevent occasional erroneous data input. The problem is not our lack of care in designing shift-register input circuitry but rather the faulty use of the encoder: *More than one bit has been permitted to change at a time, and the time of this change is unsynchronized to the clock.* In the paragraphs which follow, the synchronization of system inputs under a variety of conditions and by a variety of means will be considered.

A device which feeds a *single unsynchronized bit* of information at a time into a system illuminates some fundamental data synchronization problems. A digital tachometer is an example of such a device, emitting a pulse rate proportional to the rate at which its shaft turns. In order for the system to read the pulse rate correctly, we may wish to construct input circuitry which will generate a 1 or 0. Of course, for such a scheme to be successful, we must insure that the clock rate exceeds the maximum rate at which 1s and 0s will ever be generated by the tachometer.

Figure 7-17 illustrates a synchronous decoder for this input and its relation to the rest of the system. The function of the lowpass filter, if needed, is simply to eliminate any hash on the tachometer output which might be interpreted as extra counts. By using the filtered signal R' as a level rather than as a transition, we avoid any need for sharpening up the edges of R'. Also, we are then able to synchronize this level with the clock.

The two 1-bit shift registers in the synchronous decoder serve to synchronize R' and hold the values of R' which existed at the time of the last two clock transitions. If these are ever different, as will happen when R' changes, then the output of the EXCLUSIVE-OR gate will be 1 during that clock period. There is still some ambiguity which can occur if R' is changing at the instant a clock transition occurs. However, the effect of this ambiguity is to cause uncertainty as to *when R* will equal 1, rather than *whether R* will equal 1.

A digital tachometer exemplifies a device which is inherently capable of error-free synchronization. Nevertheless, it is possible, through careless design, to throw away this capability, as shown in Fig. 7-18. In this circuit, the unsynchronized input R' is permitted to generate *two* unsynchronized variables, namely, the two shift-register inputs. All that is needed for the circuit to err in its function is to have R' change just prior to the occurrence of the clock transition. Then $SR1$ will see the new value of R', whereas $SR2$ will see a function of the old value because of the propagation delay through the EXCLUSIVE-OR gate. Consequently, neither during this clock period nor during the next one will R equal 1; this quantum change from the tachometer has been lost forever.

Many devices feed a *number of unsynchronized bits* of information into a system during any one clock period. There are several ways of avoiding the

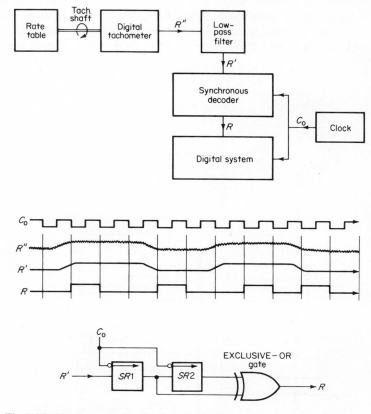

Fig. 7-17 Synchronous decoder for a single bit.

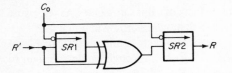

Fig. 7-18 Unsatisfactory circuit.

problem that arose with the binary encoder mentioned previously. One common way is to *code information with a unit-distance code* so that as the information changes, only 1 bit changes at a time. This technique is commonly used in incremental encoders for which direction sensing is required. Figure 7-19 illustrates an incremental encoder having a rotating disc which incorporates a single track of alternating insulated and conducting areas tied to ground. The brushes are spaced so that only one will cross a quanta boundary at a time, giving rise to the unit-distance coding of quanta changes represented by the voltage truth table. This figure also indicates the operation of one possible synchronous decoder having a *change* and *CW* output. We may expect ambiguity occasionally as one of the bits changes just as a clock transition occurs. Although either the old or new value will be read, no error will occur; this ambiguity will only result in uncertainty as to whether the quantum change will be registered

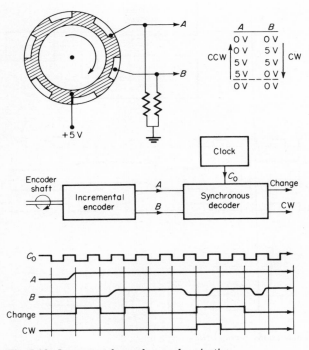

Fig. 7-19 Incremental encoder synchronization.

during one clock period or the next. For the same reason, Gray code, another unit-distance code, is used for encoding shaft-angle position. It provides un-ambiguous synchronization by permitting no more than 1 bit to change at a time.

Another solution to this problem of synchronizing data without error uses a very different approach. Instead of using a code which insures that only 1 bit changes at a time, it uses two outputs per bit, one of which is assured of being unchanging when it is read.

Figure 7-20*a* illustrates a *U-scan brush selection* binary encoder. For clarity, the encoding disc has been straightened out. The output desired is the number along the *read line,* defined by the position of the $B1$ brush (in the case shown, either number 11 or 12). The leading brushes are offset ½ quantum to the right of the read line, while the lagging brushes are offset ½ quantum to the left. This brush selection scheme depends on the fact that if $B1$ is reading a 0, then each leading brush is at least ½ quantum away from a place where its value changes. Similarly, if $B1$ is reading a 1, then each lagging brush is at least ½ quantum away from a change. Consequently, the synchronized output b_1 can be used to select either the lagging or the leading brushes in order to form b_2, b_4, and b_8, as illustrated in Fig. 7-20*b*. Notice that although the value of $B1$ may be ambiguous when it is at a quantum boundary, the resulting binary output will be one of the two numbers separated by that boundary rather than some grossly erroneous number. If the clock rate C_0 is sufficiently fast to insure that the encoder disc does not move appreciably during a clock period, then the scheme shown in Fig. 7-20*c* will insure that the synchronized value b_1 will provide unambiguous decoding of the remaining bits.

The U-scan brush selection scheme solves the problem of providing error-free data synchronization. However, both it and the unit-distance-code approach require that the brushes be aligned to within at least plus or minus ½ quantum of their nominal positions. An extension of the U-scan scheme, called *V-scan brush selection*, permits the brush position tolerances to be increasingly relaxed for successively more significant bits. This is especially valuable when the more significant bits are placed on the inner tracks of an encoding disc. Here the relaxation of the required angular tolerance on these brush positions compensates for the effects of having a smaller radius.

In Fig. 7-21, we see that the brush positions fan out from the read line for successive tracks, with lead n and lag n being positioned away from the read line by an amount equal to one-half the quanta size of the previous track. The brush selected for each track determines the value for that track along the read line. Consequently, its output can be used in the same way that $B1$ on the read line in U-scan is used to determine which brush to select on the next track. That is, if $b_k = 0$, then lead $2K$ is selected; if $b_k = 1$, then lag $2K$ is selected. Or, in the form of an equation:

$$b_{2k} = b_k \cdot \text{lag } 2K + \bar{b}_k \cdot \text{lead } 2K \qquad\qquad (7\text{-}1)$$

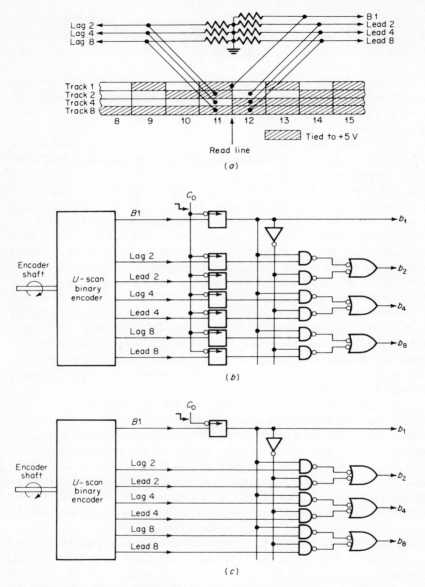

Fig. 7-20 U-scan brush selection. (*a*) Encoder brush positions; (*b*) synchronization and brush selection; (*c*) simplified synchronization and brush selection.

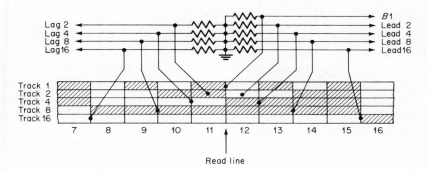

Fig. 7-21 V-scan brush positions.

Each of the techniques discussed so far has required that when an unsynchronized output changes, it does so in a very constrained way. The more general case is typified by the problem of interfacing a device which is clocked by its own clock into a computer. A specific example occurs during the parallel transfer of successive words of data from a disc memory into a computer. In going from one word to the next, any number of bits may change. Furthermore, this change is unsynchronized to the clock. As was mentioned in conjunction with interfacing in Sec. 6-7, the device can generate a *ready* signal which equals 1 all the time except just before and just after the unsynchronized output changes. By transferring data when ready = 1, the receiving device is assured that the inputs will be unchanging during the transfer. The disc memory bit clock, mentioned in Sec. 4-8, was timed to serve as a ready signal since the data of the disc changed *between* successive bit clock pulses.

This method of synchronization is not used in conjunction with encoders. The reason it is not can best be illustrated by considering what the required encoder pattern would look like, shown in Fig. 7-22. The encoder includes a ready bit which equals 1 only when the brushes on the other tracks are nowhere near a quantum boundary. Correct transfer of data out of the encoder is assured if ready = 1. The disadvantage of this approach to synchronization is the unavailability of the data when ready = 0. Until the encoder shaft moves, its output will continue to be unavailable.

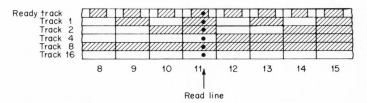

Fig. 7-22 Encoder with a ready bit.

7-4 TRANSDUCTION

A system whose function is to monitor the state of a process and perhaps control it relies heavily on the transduction of these state variables into digital form. A particularly simple transduction occurs with *switch contacts*. Sometimes a variable is encoded with 1 bit (*go-no go*) in order to indicate when the variable exceeds an allowable limit or that a specified operation has been completed. For example, a simple thermostat closes a pair of contacts when the temperature drops below a specified limit. Or, in an automatic bottle-filling operation, a microswitch indicates that a bottle is in place and that it can now be filled. To convert the state of such switch contacts into Boolean variables which can be used by a digital system, we might use a circuit configuration such as that shown in Fig. 7-23.

A real-life problem arises because noise is often capacitively or inductively coupled to the cable leading from the process being monitored to the digital system doing the monitoring. Since the signal is a high-level two-valued signal, a simple *RC* filter located in close proximity to the digital system will smooth out the noise.

Another real-life problem arises if these Boolean variables change at times which are unsynchronized to the system clock. If one of these Boolean variables is used as an input to two (or more) places in the system, then problems can arise when the input changes just before the clock transition occurs. One input may see the old value of the Boolean variable while the other sees the new value. The solution, of course, is to synchronize the input to the clock using the techniques discussed in the Sec. 7-3.

A system organized around a computer may need to scan the Boolean inputs from many switch contacts. Then inputs can be multiplexed using a data selector of the type discussed in Sec. 3-14. For more inputs than one data selector can handle, data selectors with *enable* inputs (which force the output to equal 0 if the enable input equals 0) can be combined as in Fig. 7-24.

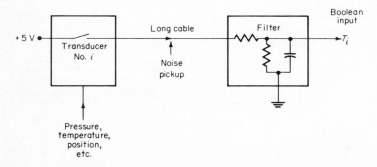

Fig. 7-23 Obtaining a Boolean input from switch contacts.

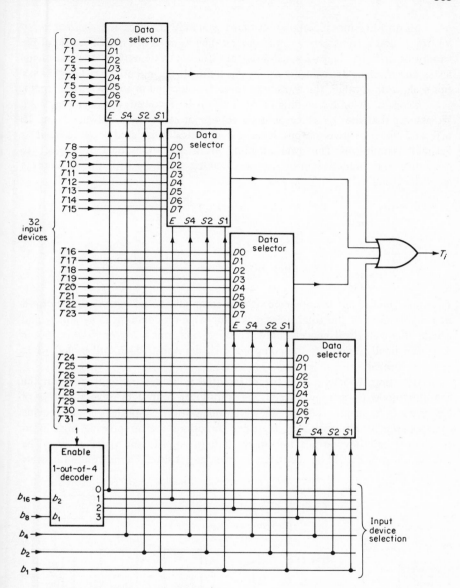

Fig. 7-24 Multiplexing many Boolean inputs.

Monitoring more complex systems generally involves the *acquisition of low-level signals* from a variety of sources. This is an art in itself because of the variety of different factors which arise in different systems. For one, the signal levels out of many transducers are in the millivolt range, perhaps 10 or 100 mV full scale. For another, the transducers are often located in a noisy environment.

To gain an understanding of what might be involved, consider Fig. 7-25. We assume that the transducer emits a voltage of somewhere between 0 and 10 mV and that its two output leads are electrically isolated from ground, a desirable condition. The cable leading from the transducer is subject to capacitive and inductive noise pickup, making the inputs to the differential amplifier equal to:

$$e_1 = e_1{}_{\text{transducer} \atop \text{output}} + \text{common-mode noise} + \frac{\text{differential noise}}{2}$$

$$e_2 = e_2{}_{\text{transducer} \atop \text{output}} + \text{common-mode noise} - \frac{\text{differential noise}}{2}$$

The noise picked up is expressed as two components: *Common-mode noise* is that component of the total noise picked up which is common to e_1 and e_2 and which, therefore, will cancel out when $e_1 - e_2$ is formed. *Differential noise,* on the other hand, represents the component of the noise which will be left when $e_1 - e_2$ is formed.

By using shielded cable, the differential noise can be kept small but the common-mode noise may exceed the transducer output by several orders of magnitude. A major role of the instrumentation amplifier is to provide *common-mode-noise rejection*. Its other functions are to provide high input impedance and low output impedance and to amplify the signal $e_1 - e_2$. The differential gain should be accurately known, and it should amplify the full-scale

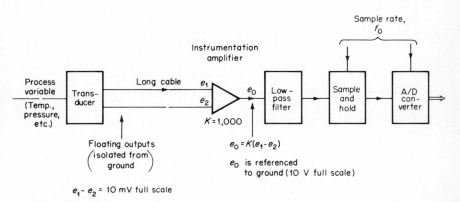

Fig. 7-25 Acquisition of a low-level signal.

input of 10 mV to the full-scale range of the analog-to-digital (A/D) converter (or somewhat less).

The lowpass filter is included in Fig. 7-25 to eliminate any signal or differential noise components above one-half the sampling rate imposed by the A/D converter. Otherwise, the sampling process will make these components look like lower-frequency components in the signal, confusing the interpretation of the signal. Actually since nonideal filters are used, it is typical to use a filter with a cutoff frequency of perhaps $f_0/5$. Sometimes, no filtering at all is needed because of the lowpass characteristics of the signal and noise or the input cable.

The sample and hold circuit insures that the sampling will occur at equal intervals of $1/f_0$. As we shall see shortly when we discuss A/D conversion, the conversion to a 10-bit number may require 10 clock periods. If the input is changing during the conversion, then the final result will be equal to what the input was during any one of these clock periods. This can cause the sampling period to vary significantly from period to period when the conversion time is an appreciable portion of the sampling period. On the other hand, if a sample and hold circuit is introduced, it samples the input at equally spaced sample intervals, holding these values constant for each conversion.

Under certain circumstances either the lowpass filter, the sample and hold circuit, or both may be omitted. The sample and hold circuit may provide negligible benefit if the conversion time is much shorter than the sampling interval or if the input does not change appreciably during the conversion. In general, the inclusion of both the lowpass filter and the sample and hold circuit assume that the processing requires, in some sense, a signal from which the original signal can be reconstructed. If this is not true, then again these components might be omitted. For example, suppose successive periods of a noisy waveform are averaged together in order to average out the noise. Then, in general, leaving off the lowpass filter and the sample and hold circuit will not change the average waveform but only the rate of convergence toward it.

The general problem of multiplexing inputs from several transducers can be handled as shown in Fig. 7-26. This uses N instrumentation amplifiers to normalize the full-scale output of each transducer to the A/D converter's full-scale input. Even if the output of the transducer has the same full-scale value as that of the A/D converter, an instrumentation amplifier with unity gain is still useful in order to reject common-mode noise. The multiplexer transfers the selected analog input on to its output.

The last step in the process of converting any of several analog inputs to digital form is the actual A/D conversion. As was indicated in Prob. 6-15, a high-speed A/D converter requires two components—a D/A converter and a voltage comparator—plus the sequencing of the conversion process. The common method used to carry out the conversion is the *successive-approximation* method. This method is used in the 10-bit A/D converter shown in Fig. 7-27.

To understand this method, consider first the analogous method of weighing an unknown weight in the range of 0 to 63 oz to within 1 oz by using a

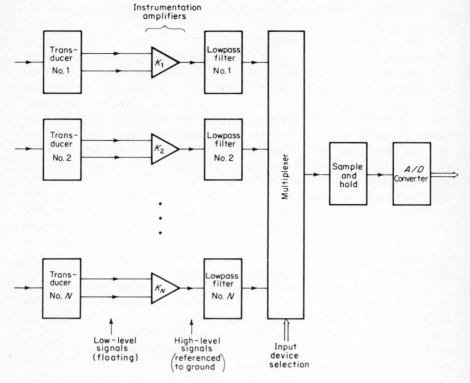

Fig. 7-26 Acquisition of many low-level signals by multiplexing.

balance scale as in Fig. 7-28. The unknown is put in one pan, and then a sequence of different weights is placed in the other, at each step noting which side is the heavier. The unknown weight W can be determined as a 6-bit binary number

$$W = b_{32} b_{16} b_8 b_4 b_2 b_1 \ \text{oz}$$

using the six measurements shown. Thus, if W is larger than 32 oz, then b_{32} will equal 1; if not, then b_{32} will equal 0. To find out which is the case, W is balanced against a 32-oz weight. The outcome shown in Fig. 7-28a indicates that W is less than 32, and so

$$W = \underline{0} \ \_ \ \_ \ \_ \ \_ \ \_$$

Since W is less than 32 oz, the 32-oz weight is removed and a 16-oz weight added, as in Fig. 7-28*b*. Now W is greater than 16, and so

$$W = \underline{0}\ \underline{1}\ \underline{\ }\ \underline{\ }\ \underline{\ }\ \underline{\ }$$

The next test is made leaving the 16-oz weight on the scale and adding an 8-oz weight. In general, at each step of the procedure, the weight added on the previous step is either left on or removed, depending on whether the unknown weight was greater or less than the known weights. But in either case, a weight equal to the next smaller power of two is added to the pan of known weights on a trial basis.

The analogous operation of measuring a voltage between 0 and 63 mV with a successive-approximation A/D converter is illustrated in Fig. 7-29. The voltage comparator is analogous to the pointer on the balance scale, telling whether e_1 is larger or smaller than e_2 at each step. Similarly, the D/A converter produces a voltage analogous to the known weights at each step. The comparison of the unknown input e_1 and the D/A converter output e_2 at each step produces a Boolean variable C_n, which becomes one of the bits of the digital output. The control circuitry for this 6-bit converter carries out the required sequence of

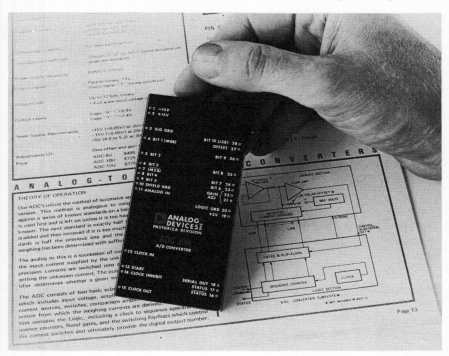

Fig. 7-27 Ten-bit A/D converter. (*Analog Devices, Inc.*)

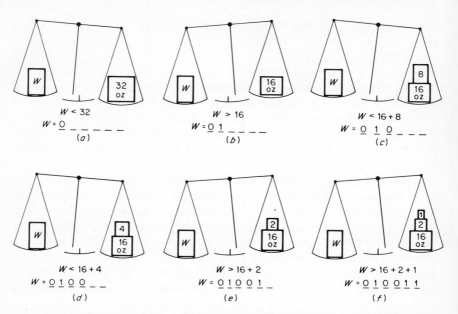

Fig. 7-28 Weighing an unknown weight by successive approximations. (*a*) First weighing; (*b*) second weighing; (*c*) third weighing; (*d*) fourth weighing; (*e*) fifth weighing; (*f*) sixth weighing.

events in seven clock periods. It can be speeded up to six clock periods (if an unsynchronized output bit causes no harm) by taking b_1 from C_n during the sixth clock period.

An A/D converter which converts an input between 0 and 10 V into a 10-bit binary number operates on the same principle but with scale factors adjusted to fit the range. Thus, a 5-V input produces an output of

1000000000

Similarly, a 12-bit 8421 BCD converter might also be adjusted to the range of 0 to 10 V. A 10-bit sign plus two's complement converter might be adjusted to the range of −10 to +10 V.

This problem of acquiring low-level signals from a variety of sources has been presented here in terms of the various components involved. The configuration required for a specific system varies considerably from one application to another. Consequently, the companies which manufacture components of the types discussed here are also, almost invariably, in the systems business. That is, they interconnect and package the components needed for a specific system so that it is only necessary to plug in inputs and use the digital output. An example of such a data acquisition unit is shown in Fig. 7-30.

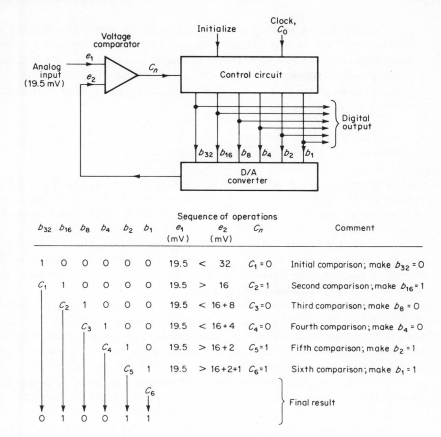

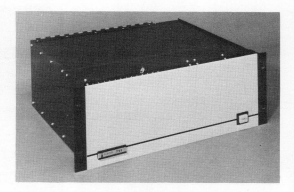

Fig. 7-29 Six-bit successive approximation A/D converter.

The figure 7-29 contains the following table for "Sequence of operations":

b_{32}	b_{16}	b_8	b_4	b_2	b_1	e_1 (mV)	e_2 (mV)	C_n	Comment
1	0	0	0	0	0	19.5	< 32	$C_1 = 0$	Initial comparison; make $b_{32} = 0$
C_1	1	0	0	0	0	19.5	> 16	$C_2 = 1$	Second comparison; make $b_{16} = 1$
	C_2	1	0	0	0	19.5	< 16 + 8	$C_3 = 0$	Third comparison; make $b_8 = 0$
		C_3	1	0	0	19.5	< 16 + 4	$C_4 = 0$	Fourth comparison; make $b_4 = 0$
			C_4	1	0	19.5	> 16 + 2	$C_5 = 1$	Fifth comparison; make $b_2 = 1$
				C_5	1	19.5	> 16 + 2 + 1	$C_6 = 1$	Sixth comparison; make $b_1 = 1$
					C_6				
0	1	0	0	1	1				Final result

Fig. 7-30 Flexibly configured data acquisition system. (*Redcor Corp.*)

Thus far in this section, we have discussed the simple transduction of two-valued inputs via switch contacts. We have also discussed the more involved transduction of multivalued inputs, from an analog transducer to a low-level analog voltage and on through a low-level data acquisition unit to a digital quantity. In the remainder of the section, we shall consider two other types of transduction for multivalued inputs:

1. Linear and shaft-angle encoders
2. Pulse-rate and frequency-generating transducers

The last section presented an overview of the two approaches used to provide reliable readout from encoders. These are the use of a unit-distance code and the use of a brush-selection scheme (U-scan and V-scan). As was indicated there, unit-distance codes form the basis for incremental encoders. An interesting example is the linear incremental optical encoder shown in Fig. 7-31, which provides a resolution of 10,000 quanta/in over a length of up to 48 in. By driving a seven-decade up-down BCD code counter with its output, the measuring system shown has been obtained.

An incremental encoder will be significantly lower in cost than an absolute encoder having the same resolution because of its inherent simplicity. Often a *zero-reference* output is included in order to provide automatic error detection and correction capability. Thus each time the zero-reference point is crossed, the counter which counts quanta changes can be checked and initialized to its reference value. A typical low-cost optical incremental shaft-angle encoder might have 1,000 to 10,000 quanta/revolution. More exotic incremental encoders of this type improve on this resolution by almost two orders of magnitude!

When discussing absolute encoders, *low cost* and *optical* tend *not* to go together. The low-cost encoders are *brush encoders*, which use a commutator

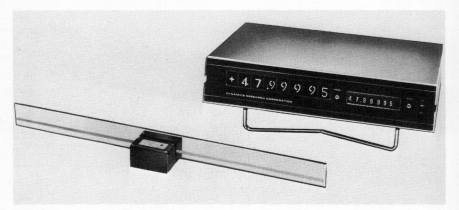

Fig. 7-31 High-resolution, linear incremental encoder. (*Dynamics Research Corp.*)

Fig. 7-32 Eight-bit Gray-code encoder. (*Singer-Librascope*.)

having a conductor-insulator pattern to which electrical contact is made with small brushes. Typical resolutions are 2^7–2^{10} quanta/revolution in encoders having outside diameters of 1 to 3 in. Figure 7-32 illustrates an 8-bit Gray-code encoder having an outside diameter of 1.750 in. Its commutator is shown in Fig. 7-33.

Fig. 7-33 Commutator used in the Gray-code encoder of Fig. 7-32. (*Singer-Librascope.*)

Because they require all brushes to be aligned to within ± ½ quanta or better of their nominal position, encoders employing unit-distance codes or U-scan brush selection are limited to

1. Brush encoders
2. Single-turn encoders

In contrast, V-scan brush selection permits increasingly relaxed tolerances for the brushes of the more significant bits. In the case of a binary encoder, the brush on track 2^n must be aligned to its nominal position $\pm 2^{n-2}$ quanta. This permits multiturn encoders in which one commutator is geared to another. With V-scan brush selection, correct readout is easily obtainable in spite of the inevitable backlash in the gearing between the encoders. Using this technique, an encoder for 2^{15} quanta spread over 2^7 revolutions is easily attainable. V-scan brush selection also makes possible unambiguous readout from an 8421 BCD code encoder. Although the tolerances are somewhat more constrained within each decade, the principle is the same. Thus the tolerance requirements relax by a factor of 10 from decade to decade.

The use of optical techniques permits far greater resolution than is possible with brush encoders. This has been indicated in the discussion of optical incremental encoders. Here again the state of the art permits resolutions of 2^{18} to 2^{20} quanta/revolution. However, typical values are 2^8 to 2^{14} quanta/revolution. This improved resolution over that attainable with a brush encoder comes at a cost. Not only is the basic encoder more costly, but also the low-level voltage outputs require amplification. Thus a 10-bit V-scan optical encoder requires 19 amplifiers, while a 10-bit V-scan brush encoder requires none. Furthermore, it is possible to build diodes and extra tracks into the brush encoder. Then the brush-selection circuitry requires only a flipflop on the least significant bit to provide synchronization to the system clock. The rest of the brush selection is resolved with the internal diode circuitry in this *self-selecting V-scan* encoder.

Some transducers emit a pulse rate or a frequency proportional to the transduced variable. One example of this is the *turbine flow meter*, illustrated in Fig. 7-34, used to measure liquid flow rate in a process-control system or in a liquid-blending system. As liquid flows past, it causes the turbine to turn with an angular velocity which is linearly related to flow rate. By imbedding a magnetic material in the tip of one or more of the turbine vanes and using a variable-reluctance pickup, a pulse rate is generated which is exactly proportional to the angular velocity. Typical accuracies attained in this way are 0.1 to 1 percent over the range from 10 to 100 percent of rated flow. Both viscosity and density have only minor effects on the transduction.

The pulse rate can be converted to an absolute quantity by counting pulses per unit time. Alternatively, it can be converted using one of the pulse-rate

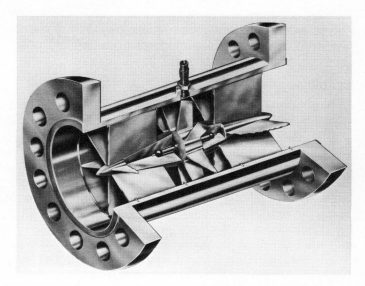

Fig. 7-34 Cutaway view of a turbine flow meter. (*Halliburton Services.*)

algorithms discussed in the next chapter. In fuel blending systems, the pulse rate is often not converted at all but rather is manipulated directly as a pulse rate to achieve the control desired. Since the time integral of flow rate gives liquid quantity, the pulses can be counted to obtain a number proportional to liquid quantity.

The *quartz thermometer* shown in Fig. 1-3 is a fine example of the effective transduction of temperature to frequency. Normally, quartz crystals are used to build oscillators which emit a stable frequency in spite of variations in the circuit, including temperature. In the quartz thermometer, the quartz crystal is cut along a plane which yields an oscillator whose frequency changes slightly with temperature. However, that slight change is highly linear and highly stable. By putting the quartz crystal into a probe, temperatures can be measured, the cycles of the oscillator counted over a fixed time interval, and the resulting number displayed in a decimal display. This results in a thermometer which can measure temperatures in either Centigrade or Fahrenheit over the temperature range -80 to $+250°C$ and with a resolution of $0.0001°C$. For temperature *difference* measurements made over a short interval of time, this fine resolution provides an accuracy of $0.0002°C$! The absolute accuracy depends upon the range involved, being better than $0.1°C$ in the range 0 to $100°C$.

In general, transducing a variable to frequency with high stability and (less importantly) with high linearity can provide *unusually* accurate transduction. This is true because highly stable time bases (i.e., oscillators) are available having accuracies far exceeding those available for almost any other measurable quantity. Counting a specific number of periods of this *time-base* oscillator's output provides the highly accurate time base. This time base can then be used to convert the transducer's output frequency to an absolute quantity.

7-5 DATA INPUT

In this section, *data input* will refer to man-to-machine inputs, since we previously discussed data derived through transduction of physical variables.

In the last section, we considered how switch contacts could be used to generate a Boolean input to a system. The same approach can be used here. Using a double-pole, double-throw switch, a variable can be presented in both asserted and negated form, as in Fig. 7-35. If the switch is sufficiently far removed from the logic to make noise pickup a problem, the simple filters shown can be included, locating them close to the logic.

This switch configuration provides satisfactory operation as long as the switch is used to set up the system *before* operation begins. However, if the switch is to be changed *during* system operation, then its output should be synchronized to the clock, using the techniques of Sec. 7-3.

Sometimes a switch input is used as a clock source itself. In general, if a system has two unsynchronized clock sources, it will operate incorrectly from time to time. Consider when one clock's transition occurs just before the other's, causing several variables to change. The circuitry responding to the other clock may see the old values of some of these variables and the new values of some others. The solution, of course, is to synchronize the slower clock to the faster one. If the rates of the two clocks vary so that sometimes one is faster and sometimes the other, then a third clock can be introduced which is faster than either of the two. Then each of the original clocks can be synchronized to the third.

The digital combination lock, discussed in Sec. 6-2, exemplifies a system using two unsynchronized clocks, one of which is generated from a switch. In Fig. 6-4, the mode circuitry is clocked by C_0, using the unsynchronized inputs IN, b_1, b_2, b_4, b_8. In Fig. 6-6, we see that all of these inputs are used to determine the single variable F which affects the input gating to the flipflops. Since the changes in F are not synchronized to the C_0 clock, the opportunity arises for its value to be misinterpreted if it changes just before the C_0 transition

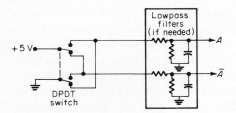

Fig. 7-35 Use of a double-pole, double-throw switch to generate a variable in both asserted and negated form.

occurs. Some flipflops might respond to its old value (say, $F = 0$) while others to its new value ($F = 1$).

The worst-case risk is that the flipflops will inadvertently go to the state which opens the door, namely,

$$ABC = 101$$

as shown in Fig. 6-7d. Looking at the input equations in Fig. 6-7c, we can pursue this question of whether the mode circuitry could ever get to this state from any of the other states (besides $ABC = 001$), given that $F = 0$ in some equations while $F = 1$ in others. If this is possible, we might do well to redesign the circuit, synchronizing the two clock sources to a faster clock.

The use of a latch to generate a sharp transition and eliminate the effects of switch-contact bounce was illustrated in Fig. 6-4. If the switch is located some distance from the logic, again a simple filter might be used on each input to the latch.

Sometimes a switch is used to steer a presetting pulse to either the direct preset or the direct clear input to a flipflop. This is illustrated in Fig. 7-36, which shows a 4-bit shift register being preset with the number set on four switches. Again, this can introduce synchronizing problems unless the switches are set up before system operation begins and then left unchanged thereafter. An example of this use of switches is given in Appendix A3 for the design of a scale-of-N counter, where N is set into the system on switches.

Sometimes the contents of a register or a counter are compared for equality with the contents of a switch bank. A connection serving this purpose is shown in Fig. 7-37. For decimal inputs to a system, *thumbwheel switches*, such

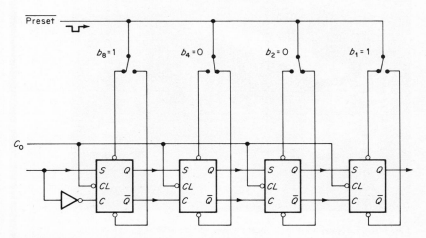

Fig. 7-36 Using switches to steer a presetting pulse.

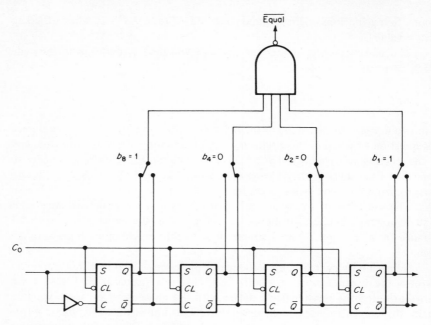

Fig. 7-37 Use of switches for comparison.

Fig. 7-38 Cutaway view of a thumbwheel switch assembly. (*Electronic Engineering Co. of California–EECo.*)

as those shown in Fig. 7-38, provide ease and versatility. These come in a variety of sizes and styles, with or without illumination. Electrically, they also are available in a variety of forms. The switch connects a *common* terminal to any of several other terminals, depending on the coding.

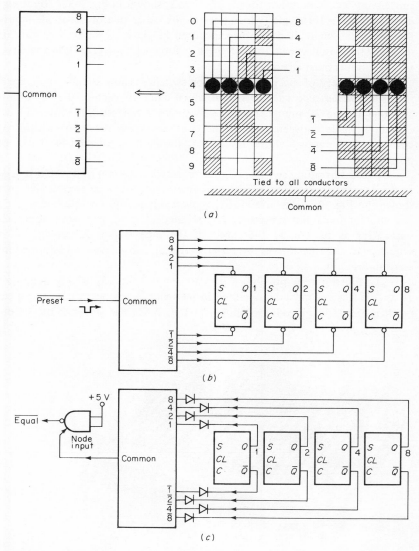

Fig. 7-39 Thumbwheel switch symbolism and circuitry. (*a*) Symbolism; (*b*) presetting circuit; (*c*) comparator circuit using DTL gate.

The thumbwheel switch configuration shown in Fig. 7-39*a*, designated "8421 BCD code with complement," is particularly useful for BCD code operations. Its use for presetting a register is a straightforward application of the technique shown in Fig. 7-36 and is illustrated in Fig. 7-39*b*. In contrast, its use for comparison, analogous to the scheme of Fig. 7-37, is complicated by having a single *common*. A solution to this problem is shown in Fig. 7-39*c*. By using the *node* input to a DTL gate (which goes to the other side of the diode inputs on the gate), the eight diodes shown are used in place of the normal gate input diodes. The switch selects four of these as inputs to the gate. For equality, the selected inputs must all equal 1.

The variety of special-configuration switches is almost endless. Figure 7-40 shows a *crossbar-type selector switch* which connects each of the 20 outputs to any one of the 20 inputs. Figure 7-41 shows a *card-reading switch* in which contact is made between each of the contacts below the inserted card to the corresponding contact above the card if the card is punched in that contact position.

The card-reading switch is useful to *set up* a system to do what it is going to do. In contrast, a *standard eight-channel perforated-tape reader*, such as that shown in Fig. 7-42, is useful for *sequencing* many operations, where the sequence is fixed but arbitrarily complicated. The speed of this approach to sequencing is limited by the speed of the tape reader. Assuming the same sequence is to be performed over and over again, the tape can be formed into a continuous loop.

To illustrate one possibility for carrying out this sequencing, suppose that 18 on-off devices must be operated in sequence. Each operation can be coded (with a nonstandard code) as shown in Fig. 7-43. The states of the 18 on-off

Fig. 7-40 Crossbar-type selector switch. (*Cherry Electrical Products Corp.*)

Fig. 7-41 Card-reading switch. (*Hickok Electrical Instrument Co.*)

devices during each operation are indicated by the presence or absence of a hole in the 18 positions labeled $S_1, \ldots, S_{18}$. Each operation takes up a *block* of three successive characters on the tape with a 1 (a hole) in channel 7 indicating the last character in a block. A 1 in channel 8 indicates the beginning of the entire sequence of operations, so that the sequence can be started and stopped on this character.

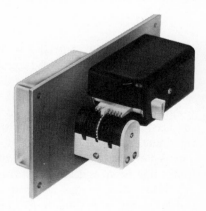

Fig. 7-42 Perforated-tape reader. (*Computer Mechanisms Corp.*)

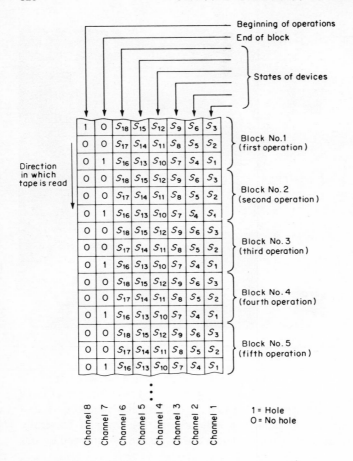

Fig. 7-43 Format for tape to implement sequencing operations.

The sequence controller is illustrated in Fig. 7-44. The outputs to the on-off devices are all disabled except at *end of block*, at which time the tape reader and shift registers present the data required for each on-off device. The function of the digital control is to read out successive blocks of data by advancing the tape to the next *end of block*. To do this, the tape reader is advanced for each character with one *advance tape* pulse of the proper amplitude and duration. (The duration of the pulse can be conveniently obtained with a *one-shot* circuit which will generate a fixed pulsewidth pulse from a transition, as described in Appendix A2.)

This example has assumed that all devices would be on-off devices. However, there is nothing restricting eight of the bits from driving an 8-bit D/A converter, or some other multiple-input device. Consequently, this illustrates a general technique for sequencing *any* operations where the sequence required can be specified a priori. If this is not the case and the sequencing depends on results obtained along the way, then the sequencing operation becomes a good candidate for a small computer.

Thus far in this section, we have viewed data input devices which are particularly well suited for special-purpose structures. For systems organized around a dedicated small computer, several possibilities exist. In some systems, once the operating program is loaded (perhaps as a read-only memory), the computer may never look at anything but transduced inputs from then on. In effect, the computer has been buried in a system and it asks nothing directly of an operator. Some systems configured in this way use a blank front panel for the computer. The system controls may be mounted separately and may consist of those few lights and switches needed by the operator to start and stop the system.

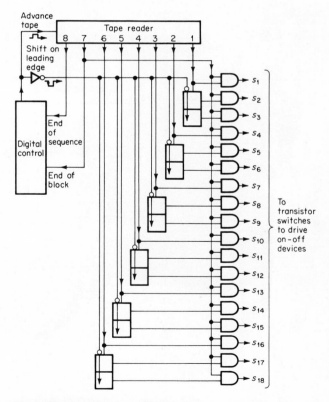

Fig. 7-44 Sequence controller circuitry.

Other systems may require a varied array of initializing data before beginning operations. In this case, the long-popular and low-cost Teletype ASR 33, shown in Fig. 7-45, can be used. Virtually every small computer provides an interface to this teletypewriter. It can input data from either keyboard or punched tape and can output data on the typewriter or by punching tape.

Finally, for systems requiring constant man-machine interactions, display terminals provide the highly human-engineered possibilities discussed in Sec. 7-2. Graphic display terminals offer not only the alphanumeric input possibilities of a keyboard but also various means for entering graphic data directly onto the CRT. For example, alongside the terminal of Fig. 7-14 is shown a *joystick* for moving a point around on the CRT "by hand." The *track-ball* ball-to-digital encoder shown in Fig. 7-46 is built around two incremental encoders. As the ball

Fig. 7-45   Teletype^R 33 ASR (automatic send-receive) terminal. (*Teletype Corp.*)

Fig. 7-46 Track-ball ball-to-digital encoder. (*Singer-Librascope.*)

is rotated by hand, these encoders generate X- and Y-axis outputs which can be used to move a marker about on the display.

To be effectively used, these devices require a great deal of interaction between the graphic-display console and the computer. Not only does this tie up extensive amounts of computer time, but also the software ties up extensive amounts of memory.

PROBLEMS

7-1 Switching inductive loads The winding of a certain inductive device should be turned on with 10 V, causing 0.5 A to flow through the winding. The winding can be approximately modeled by a 20-Ω resistance in series with a 100-mH inductance. Evaluate the performance of the three circuits of Fig. 7-1c and d in turning off the 0.5-A current to one-fifth this value by sketching the current waveform versus time for each circuit, subject to the following assumptions. The transistors and diodes are ideal switches with no voltage drop across them when turned on and no current flow through them when turned off. When the Zener is conducting, its voltage drop is independent of the current through it. R_4 and the Zener voltage should be selected so that the transistor's collector voltage peaks to exactly 20 V.

7-2 Switching inductive loads (*a*) Using the same inductive load and assumptions as in Prob. 7-1, together with the circuit of Fig. 7-1e, sketch the load current as it is switched on if $R_s = 0$. Determine the time T_1 it takes for the current to build up to four-fifths of its rated value.

(*b*) Determine appropriate values of V_{cc} and R_s to cut this time in half. Make sure that V_{cc} and R_s are constrained so that the steady-state load current is still 0.5 A.

7-3 Time-averaged switching The proportional controller shown in Fig. 7-2 includes a bridge circuit, amplifier, and 6-bit analog-to-digital converter to convert the resistance of the temperature sensor into a digital error. If the actual temperature is below the desired temperature, then the digital number is proportional to this error, coded in binary code. If the actual temperature is above the desired temperature, the number is binary zero.

Using the logic of Fig. 6-42 and minimizing cost, design the remainder of the proportional controller of Fig. 7-2. Select the clock rate so that T_2 equals 0.1 s. Explain your design, using whatever block diagrams and timing diagrams will clarify this explanation.

7-4 Stepping motors A closed-loop position controller is to be designed as follows. A 10-bit binary number is preset into a 10-bit shift register to indicate the desired position of a shaft. (The timing and circuitry for this presetting as well as the source of the number will not concern us here.) The actual shaft position is encoded with a 10-bit Gray-code encoder.

(*a*) Using serial conversion of the Gray-code number to binary and serial comparison of the desired and actual numbers, generate the *CW, CCW*, and clock inputs needed by a stepping motor's synchronous decoder-driver, as defined in Prob. 6-2. These should be updated every 0.01 s. With this input, the stepping motor will drive the shaft toward zero error.

(*b*) Using the logic of Fig. 6-42, design a minimum-cost system. Explain its operation with the help of a timing diagram.

7-5 Stepping motors For each input format specified below, design a minimum-cost synchronous decoder for a stepping motor. It should have a 2-bit Gray-code output, a clock input, and the following level inputs:

(*a*) The *CW* and *CCW* inputs defined in Prob. 6-2

(*b*) A *step* input (defined such that the motor steps whenever step = 1 and doesn't step whenever step = 0) and a *CW* input (which determines the direction of stepping)

7-6 D/A converter (*a*) Why is the settling time for a 10-bit binary D/A converter specified as the time for the output to settle to 99.95 percent of its final value?

(*b*) How should the settling time for an 8-bit 8421 BCD code D/A converter be specified?

7-7 D/A converter At the end of Sec. 7-1, it was suggested that inverting the sign bit of a sign plus two's complement number would provide a useful input to a binary D/A converter. What purpose does this inversion serve?

7-8 D/A converter Assume zero settling time for a 10-bit binary D/A converter. If it were driven by an asynchronous binary counter which was counted up from 0 to 1023 at a 5-MHz clock rate, then what would be the extent of the deviation of the resulting ramp voltage from the ideal because of *glitches*? Assume 20-ns flipflop propagation delays. Illustrate the scope pattern for the worst-case glitch. At what count does this occur?

7-9 Light display A bank of 14-V lights receives its power from the full-wave rectified output of a multitap rectifier transformer, as shown in Fig. P 7-9.

(*a*) Assuming zero voltage drop in conducting rectifiers and turned-on transistor switches, what should the transformer output voltage be in order that the lights will see an rms voltage of 14 V?

(*b*) Assuming a fixed voltage drop of 1.0 V in each silicon rectifier and a drop of 0.5 V in a transistor switch, what should the transformer output voltage be? Draw a sketch of the waveforms involved. Also note the definition of the rms value of a voltage

$$V_{\text{rms}} = \left[\frac{1}{T} \int_0^T v^2 \, dt \right]^{1/2}$$

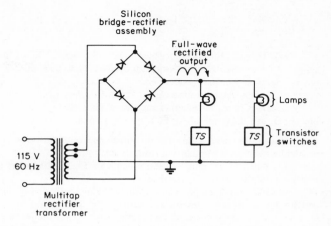

Fig. P 7-9

7-10 Graphic display terminals Consider the number of programmed data transfers required to generate a rectangle on the display of Fig. 7-14, which displays points on a grid of 1024 by 742 points. The coordinates of the corners of the rectangle are (200,100), (200,600), (300,600), and (300,100). Absolute coordinates are to be transferred between the computer and the terminal using one transfer per absolute coordinate. On the other hand, incremental commands take 4 bits each and are transferred four at a time.

(a) Using the terminal's linear interpolation mode, how many data transfers are needed to plot the rectangle?

(b) Using the terminal's absolute point plotting mode, how many data transfers are needed?

(c) Using the terminal's incremental plotting mode, how many data transfers are needed?

7-11 Incremental encoders We found that the circuit of Fig. 7-18 could miss a quantum change under certain circumstances. Can it pick up extra quantum changes (above what it should detect) under other circumstances? If so, what are the circumstances?

7-12 Incremental encoders Using the logic of Fig. 6-42 and minimizing cost, complete the design of the synchronous decoder of Prob. 6-21 by designing the combinational circuit to generate the *change* and *CW* outputs. Does the 5.4 cost units shown for this circuit represent the cost for a poor design, a good design, or a "pipe-dream" design?

7-13 Incremental encoders What is the minimum reliable clock rate for a synchronous decoder if the incremental encoder which feeds it has a maximum output rate of 1,000 quanta/s?

7-14 Incremental encoders One liability of an incremental encoder is that if a quantum change ever erroneously goes undetected from one clock period to the next, that error will upset the system performance from then on. Will a similar long-term error result if one of the output bits changes $0 \to 1 \to 0$ within one clock period, thus going undetected? Explain.

7-15 Gray-code encoders As discussed in Sec. 2-9, an n-bit Gray code can be converted to an n-bit binary code with the following algorithm:

$$b_n = g_n$$
$$b_k = g_k \oplus b_{k+1}$$

(a) Using 1-bit shift registers and two-input EXCLUSIVE-OR gates, design a synchronous decoder for the output of an 8-bit Gray-code encoder, so that a synchronized (error-free) binary output is obtained.

(b) Is it necessary to use eight 1-bit shift registers, or is it possible to use less? Explain.

(c) Does it matter whether the Gray code is first synchronized and then converted to binary? Or can these operations be reversed? Explain.

7-16 U-scan encoders Using U-scan brush selection, the leading and lagging brushes are nominally positioned ½ quantum from the read line.

(a) With the synchronization scheme of Fig. 7-20b, what tolerance on these brush positions will still insure correct readout?

(b) With this same synchronization scheme, is there any minimum clock rate below which the readout may exhibit gross errors?

(c) With the scheme of Fig. 7-20c, assume that the leading and lagging brushes are aligned to within ¼ quantum of the nominal position and that the encoder output rate will never exceed 1,000 quanta/s. What is the minimum clock rate above which correct readout is assured?

7-17 U-scan encoders If the circuit in Fig. 7-20b is modified, in order to reduce the number of 1-bit registers required, by first decoding and then synchronizing, will correct readout be assured? Explain.

7-18 V-scan encoders If a V-scan encoder has a maximum output rate of 1,000 quanta/s and lead k and lag k are aligned to within $k/8$ quantum, then the minimum clock rate (above which synchronization with correct readout is assured) depends on the synchronization and brush-selection circuit used. What is the minimum acceptable clock rate corresponding to each approach shown in Fig. P 7-18?

7-19 Synchronizing Boolean inputs In synchronizing the 32 Boolean inputs shown in Fig. 7-24, is it necessary to synchronize each input separately or can the 1-bit output of the multiplexer by synchronized instead (saving 31 delay flipflops)? Or is it unnecessary to synchronize at all? Explain which of the three procedures provides minimum-cost, reliable read-in of the information. If any of the procedures is unreliable, give an example illustrating how it could provide faulty operation.

7-20 Low-level data acquisition Many transducers convert a physical quantity to a resistance. Strain gages, load cells (for measuring force), and resistance thermometers represent some examples. Generally, the full-scale range of the transducer's input produces a small fraction of change from the nominal resistance value. In order to convert the resistance change into a (more or less) proportional voltage with reasonable sensitivity, a bridge circuit is generally used, as shown in Fig. P 7-20. Sometimes all four legs of the bridge vary with the input (as in the case of a strain gage), and sometimes only one leg varies. In the figure, assume that at the minimum value of the transduced input, the transducer output $R_{\text{transducer}}$ is equal to the fixed resistance R_0.

(a) Determine the sensitivity of the bridge circuit

$$\frac{\Delta e_x}{\Delta R_{\text{transducer}}}$$

where $\Delta R_{\text{transducer}}$ is a small deviation from the minimum value R_0. If the reference voltage

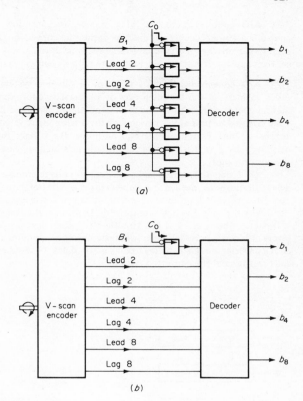

Fig. P 7-18

is 10 V and if the resistance of the transducer changes 1 percent over its full-scale range, then what will be the maximum value of e_x?

(b) The sensitivity relationship above is nonlinear. Compare the value found by taking a derivative with the values obtained using $\Delta R_{\text{transducer}}$ equal to these values: $0.01R_0$, $0.03R_0$, $0.1R_0$.

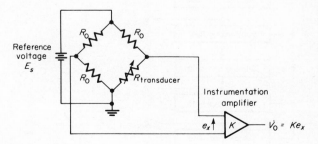

Fig. P 7-20

7-21 A/D conversion In the text, it was asserted that if the input to a successive approximation A/D converter changes during the conversion, then the converted output will correspond to what the input was at some time during the conversion. Is this really true? If so, then explain. If not, then demonstrate with a counter example.

7-22 A/D conversions In this problem, a pipeline system organization will be used in order to increase the sampling rate of a successive approximation A/D converter. Assume that an *analog shift register* has been constructed as shown in Fig. P 7-22, with sample and hold circuits to pass along samples of the analog input satisfactorily and with satisfactory accuracy. Thus, for all intents and purposes, the voltage on the A_{n-9} output during the present clock period is the same as the voltage which appeared on the A_n output nine clock periods previously.

(*a*) Using this analog shift register, 10 voltage comparators, 10 D/A converters, and delay flipflops as needed to implement the control circuitry, develop a pipeline A/D converter which will produce a new 10-bit conversion every clock period.

(*b*) If a single voltage comparator, D/A converter, and control circuitry combination is capable of being clocked at a 10-MHz rate, producing converted outputs at a 1.0-MHz rate (every 10 clock periods), then what are the corresponding characteristics for the pipeline A/D converter designed in (*a*)? How much delay occurs between the input to the analog shift register and the converted output?

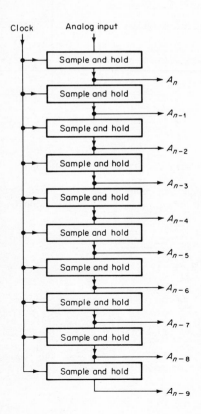

Fig. P 7-22

7-23 A/D conversion What modification, if any, must be made to the procedure developed in Sec. 7-4 in order to convert an analog voltage input into a three-digit 8421 BCD code number?

7-24 Optical encoders (a) In order to gain a feel for the tolerances involved in constructing an optical encoder having 2^{18} quanta/revolution, determine the angle (in seconds of arc) corresponding to one quantum.

(b) If the track for the least significant bit of this encoder is 1 ft in diameter, then what is the width of 1 quantum?

(c) The elevation angle of a telescope mounted on top of the Empire State Building in New York City is to be measured with this encoder. Now the tip of the torch on the Statue of Liberty, 5½ miles away, is sighted in the cross-hairs of the telescope. If the elevation angle is dropped exactly 1 quantum, how far down the Statue of Liberty have the cross-hairs moved?

7-25 V-scan encoders How should the brushes be positioned on a two-digit 8421 BCD code encoder so that V-scan brush selection will provide correct readout under all circumstances and so that the tolerance on each nominal brush position is a maximum? Illustrate your brush positioning with a figure analogous to Fig. 7-21.

7-26 Data inputs In view of the potential problems for the digital combination lock mentioned in Sec. 7-5, redesign the circuit by deriving all clocking signals from a 16-Hz clock. Except for synchronizing the switch input and for deriving the 0.25-Hz clock rate for the mode circuitry, leave the circuit otherwise unchanged if possible. Use the logic of Fig. 6-42 and minimize the cost *change*.

7-27 Switches for presetting Show a circuit for presetting a three-digit 8421 BCD code down counter from a three-decade thumbwheel switch consisting of three of the units shown in Fig. 7-39.

7-28 Switches for comparison Show a circuit for comparing the contents of a three-digit 8421 BCD code up counter with the contents of a three-decade thumbwheel switch consisting of three of the units shown in Fig. 7-39. Use diodes and as few DTL gates as possible.

7-29 Sequencing of operations What modification is needed in the sequencer described by Fig. 7-43 and 7-44 in order to drive 300 binary outputs during each operation?

REFERENCES

For a discussion of the design of transistor switches, read J. Millman and H. Taub, "Pulse, Digital, and Switching Waveforms," secs. 6-7 to 6-18, McGraw-Hill, New York, 1965.

For an excellent presentation of specific stepping-motor types and their principles of operation, see T. Baasch, Understanding Digital Stepping Motors, *Electronic Products,* August 1970, pp. 99–105.

The structure and characteristics of an instrumentation amplifier, that vital element in low-level data acquisition, are well developed by T. Cate, Op Amps or Instrumentation Amplifiers? *EEE,* August 1970, pp. 52–57.

The considerations involved in design of A/D and D/A converters are thoroughly developed in the book by D. Hoeschele, "Analog-to-Digital/Digital-to-Analog Conversion Techniques," Wiley, New York, 1968.

To discover the capabilities and operating characteristics of a variety of I/O devices, obtain data sheets and application literature from their manufacturers. Who makes what can be determined from a guide to products and their manufacturers like *EEM* or *Electronics Buyers' Guide.*

8
Algorithmic Processes

8-1 GENERAL CHARACTERISTICS OF ALGORITHMIC PROCESSES

In this chapter, our interest will center not only on specific algorithms but also on the *structure* of these algorithms. We shall be concerned with the implications which this structure has on the implementation of the algorithm. Because of this emphasis upon structure, we shall consider examples of useful algorithms which illustrate a variety of structures.

Describing an algorithm can be done in several ways. If the algorithm manipulates integers, then the algorithm can be expressed in terms of operations on these integers. The description can take the form used to express algorithms in a book on numerical analysis.

Many of the algorithms we shall discuss are very bit-oriented. To express them as manipulations on integers would tend to gloss over features important to the implementation. We shall present such algorithms by beginning with a description, in words, of the problem and how the algorithm resolves it. Then we shall usually develop the algorithm as a combinational circuit so that all variables, as well as the relations between them, are evident at once. Our intent is not to encourage combinational implementations of these algorithms. Rather, it is to present a clear picture. Once this picture is understood, the actual implementation can take a variety of forms. If the algorithm is iterative or has its iterative aspects, then the structure and timing needed to iterate in time will be reasonably apparent. Furthermore, if several approaches are possible (as with the implementation of a two-dimensional iterative circuit), then this view of the combinational implementation will make the other possibilities apparent.

For the sake of clarity, these bit-oriented algorithms will be presented in scaled-down form. Thus, while an algorithm implemented on 3- or 4-bit numbers is probably not useful as it stands, it can be most easily understood in this form. The extension to larger numbers will be passed off as one of the steps which must be taken in the implementation of the algorithm.

8-2 CODE CONVERSION

In Chap. 2, we discussed the problem of converting Gray code to binary code. We found that the problem could be resolved with a one-dimensional iterative algorithm.

The problem of converting from one BCD code to another is simplified in the sense that each digit can be handled separately. Thus Fig. 8-1 illustrates the structure of a three-digit converter from 8421 BCD code to excess-three BCD code. The implementation might actually be designed as a combinational circuit

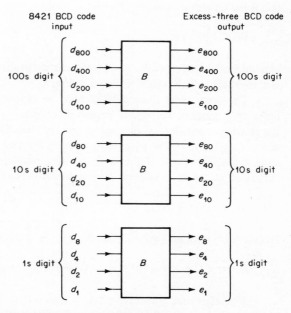

Fig. 8-1 Conversion between BCD codes.

having this structure. The iterative block B might be an MSI circuit specifically designed for this purpose. Alternatively, the circuit might be designed with NAND gates, simplifying the implementation with the techniques of Chap. 3. As another alternative, advantage can be taken of similarity between the analytic expressions for the two codes. The B block can be implemented with a 4-bit binary adder by adding binary three to each input digit.

Each of these possibilities can be implemented serially by iterating in time, a digit at a time. Furthermore, the last alternative above indicates that the algorithm for converting between these two specific BCD codes can be implemented bit by bit. This is particularly convenient if the numbers to be converted are available serially, least significant bit first, perhaps in a recirculation loop.

An iterative structure for converting, bit by bit, either way between numbers expressed in 8421 BCD code and excess-three BCD code is illustrated in Fig. 8-2. The iterative block is a full adder. To convert from 8421 BCD code to excess-three BCD code,

0011 0011 0011

is added to the input; that is, binary three is added to each digit. To convert the other way, we would like to subtract binary 3 from each digit. Alternatively, we can add binary 13 to each digit and neglect the resulting carry. (To check that this is so, try some examples.) Or we can add

1100 1100 1100

plus an initial carry of one and let the carries propagate between digits. It is this last approach which is implemented in Fig. 8-2.

The conversion from a BCD code to binary code is often useful at the input to a system. Perhaps a person must insert numbers into the system on thumbwheel switches or through a display console. One way to carry out this conversion involves the successive division by two of a number expressed in a *hybrid number* form. In this form, the number will have an integer part expressed in the BCD code and a fractional part expressed in binary code. Thus

$$N = (096)_{10} . (101)_2$$

represents N with an analytic code having the following analytic relationship:

$$N = 0 \times 10^2 + 9 \times 10^1 + 6 \times 10^0 + 1 \times 2^{-1} + 0 \times 2^{-2} + 1 \times 2^{-3}$$

The algorithm for converting a three-digit BCD number $D_{100}D_{10}D_1$ to binary code begins with the BCD number being expressed in the hybrid number

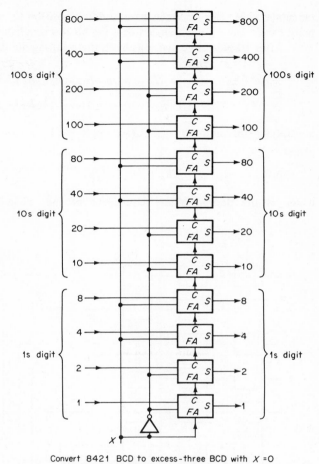

Convert 8421 BCD to excess-three BCD with X = O
Convert excess-three BCD to 8421 BCD with X = 1

Fig. 8-2 Bit-by-bit BCD code conversion.

form

$$N = (D_{100}D_{10}D_1)_{10} .(0000000000)_2$$

Now N is successively divided by two 10 times. Each division requires the division of the BCD part by 2 and the binary part by 2. Dividing the BCD part by 2 can be handled digit by digit using a *halver*, defined in Prob. 2-30. Dividing the binary part by 2 is accomplished by moving the number to the right by one place. Whenever the decimal part is an odd integer, division by 2 leaves a remainder of ½. This results in a 1 in the first position to the right of the decimal point (or *decinary* point?) since this is the bit position having a weight of ½.

After 10 successive divisions by 2, the resulting number is

$$\frac{N}{2^{10}} = (000)_{10} . (b_{512}b_{256}b_{128}b_{64}b_{32}b_{16}b_8b_4b_2b_1)_2$$
$$= \qquad . (b_{512}b_{256}b_{128}b_{64}b_{32}b_{16}b_8b_4b_2b_1)_2$$

Multiplying this number by 2^{10} (accomplished by shifting the binary point 10 places to the right) gives

$$N = b_{512}b_{256}b_{128}b_{64}b_{32}b_{16}b_8b_4b_2b_1$$

which is the desired binary equivalent of the original BCD number. The

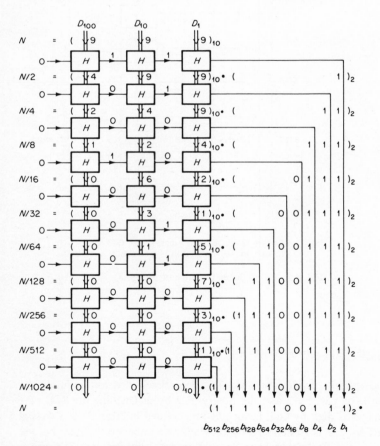

Fig. 8-3 Decimal to binary conversion by successive divisions by two.

Fig. 8-4 Equivalence for an 8421 BCD code halver when $r = 0$.

complete algorithm is illustrated in Fig. 8-3 for the number 999. The iterative block H is the halver of Prob. 2-30.

It is interesting to note that this two-dimensional iterative process can be understood in another way. Instead of looking upon each horizontal row as $N/2^k$, each vertical column can be looked upon as a hybrid number of the form

$$N \times 10^k = (b_{512} b_{256} b_{128} b_{64} b_{32} b_{16} b_8 b_4 b_2 b_1)_2 \, . (D_{100} D_{10} D_1)_{10}$$

Three successive multiplications by 10 achieve the conversion. Viewed in this way, what does each iterative block do?

Looking at this conversion algorithm iterated entirely in space vividly points out its two-dimensional iterative structure. The implementation of the algorithm in any of a variety of forms can be easily obtained, using this combinational representation as a guide. In contrast, if the algorithm were presented solely in terms of algebraic manipulations on hybrid numbers, only one implementation would be immediately obvious: iteration horizontally in space and vertically in time. This illustrates the point made in the previous section.

Notice that this algorithm is independent of the BCD code employed—until the halver is implemented. If the circuit were actually to be implemented as a combinational circuit, the array could be reduced to a triangular array since those halvers can be removed which have nothing but zeros on their inputs and outputs. Furthermore, for 8421 BCD code, the equivalence of Fig. 8-4 provides the reduced three-digit converter shown in Fig. 8-5.

This same hybrid-number approach can be used to carry out binary to decimal conversion. Now, however, we begin with

$$N = b_{512} b_{256} b_{128} b_{64} b_{32} b_{16} b_8 b_4 b_2 b_1$$

$$\frac{N}{2^{10}} = . (b_{512} b_{256} b_{128} b_{64} b_{32} b_{16} b_8 b_4 b_2 b_1)_2$$

$$\frac{N}{2^{10}} = (000)_{10} . (b_{512} b_{256} b_{128} b_{64} b_{32} b_{16} b_8 b_4 b_2 b_1)_2$$

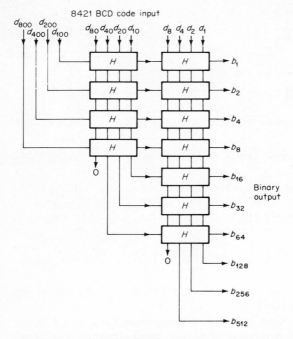

Fig. 8-5   Three-digit BCD to binary combinational converter.

If we assume that the input is the binary equivalent of a number less than 1,000, then 10 successive multiplications by two will yield

$$N = (D_{100}D_{10}D_1)_{10}.(0000000000)_2$$

or

$$N = D_{100}D_{10}D_1$$

The complete algorithm is illustrated in Fig. 8-6 (for the number 999) as a two-dimensional iterative array. The iterative block D is the doubler of Prob. 2-29. Again, the combinational implementation may actually be desired. If 8421 BCD code is used, then the equivalence of Fig. 8-7 will result in the simplified circuit of Fig. 8-8 for numbers less than 1,000.

The circuitry for the 8421 BCD code doubler and halver can be reduced from five-input, five-output circuits to four-input, four-output circuits by recognizing (back in Probs. 2-29 and 2-30) that

$$d_1^* = c \qquad \text{for the doubler}$$
$$r^* = d_1 \qquad \text{for the halver}$$

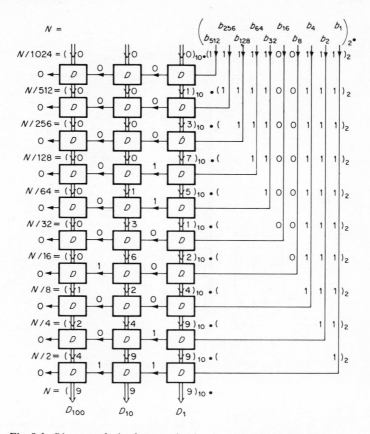

Fig. 8-6 Binary to decimal conversion by successive multiplications by 2.

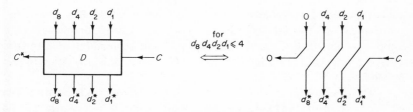

Fig. 8-7 Equivalence for an 8421 BCD code doubler.

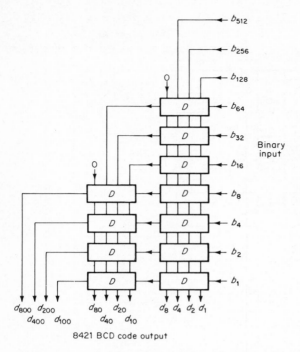

Fig. 8-8 Three-digit binary to BCD combinational converter.

Because of the broad application of these algorithms, these (reduced) iterative blocks have been implemented as MSI circuits. Both the (reduced) doubler and the (reduced) halver have been implemented in the same MSI circuit with a four-input, eight-output read-only memory (Motorola's MC4001).

Another code-conversion algorithm of interest is the conversion between a sign plus binary magnitude code and a sign plus two's complement code. If the number to be converted is positive, it requires no change since positive numbers are expressed in the same way in both codes. On the other hand, if the number is negative, then regardless of which of the two codes it is represented by, the other code is obtained by forming the two's complement of the number part, leaving the sign bit unchanged. This is illustrated in Fig. 8-9, where the two's complement is formed by first forming the one's complement (i.e., by complementing all bits except the sign bit) and then adding one to the result with a string of half-adders. A serial version of this algorithm is given in Appendix A3.

The conversion between sign plus 8421 BCD magnitude code and sign plus ten's complement (8421 BCD) code again requires no change for positive numbers. For negative numbers, the ten's complement of the number part must be formed, leaving the sign bit unchanged. The ten's complement can be formed by first forming the nine's complement and then adding one.

Alternatively, the conversion can be carried out using binary number operations which will lead to the desired BCD result. If a digit D is expressed as

$$D = d_8 d_4 d_2 d_1$$

then the nine's complement of D can be expressed as

Nine's complement of $D = 1001 - d_8 d_4 d_2 d_1$

where the expression on the right represents the binary subtraction of D from 9. Now note that simply complementing each of the bits is equivalent to forming the binary difference between 15 and the digit:

$$\bar{d}_8 \bar{d}_4 \bar{d}_2 \bar{d}_1 = 1111 - d_8 d_4 d_2 d_1$$

Consequently, the nine's complement of a digit can be expressed as

$$\begin{aligned} \text{Nine's complement of } D &= 1001 - d_8 d_4 d_2 d_1 \\ &= 1111 - d_8 d_4 d_2 d_1 - 0110 \\ &= \bar{d}_8 \bar{d}_4 \bar{d}_2 \bar{d}_1 - 0110 \end{aligned}$$

A binary subtractor can be used to implement this expression.

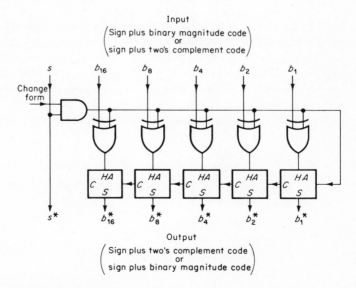

Fig. 8-9 Conversion between sign plus binary magnitude code and sign plus two's complement code.

The use of a binary adder to form the nine's complement can be justified as follows.

$$\text{Nine's complement of } D = \bar{d}_8\bar{d}_4\bar{d}_2\bar{d}_1 - 0110$$

But this is equivalent to

$$\text{Nine's complement of } D = \bar{d}_8\bar{d}_4\bar{d}_2\bar{d}_1 + 1010 - 10000$$

since

$$0110 + 1010 = 10000$$

Now, since $d_8d_4d_2d_1$ represents the 8421 BCD coding of a digit, it follows that

$$\bar{d}_8\bar{d}_4\bar{d}_2\bar{d}_1 + 1010 \geqslant 10000$$

Consequently, the nine's complement of a digit can be formed by complementing each bit, adding 10, and throwing away the carry.

Forming the ten's complement of a three-digit number, using binary addition, requires more than simply forming the nine's complement of each digit and adding one. If the units digit is zero or if the units and ten's digits are both zero, then the corresponding digit(s) in the ten's complement should be zero also. Forming the nine's complement of the units digit and adding 1 will yield 1010 instead of the desired 0000. One form of the correct algorithm is listed in tabular form in Fig. 8-10. This proceeds by complementing all bits if the sign bit is 1 (and if *change form* = 1). Then either 11, 10, or 1 is added to this result, depending on which digits were initially equal to zero. Note that if a digit had initially been equal to zero, it would be complemented to 1111. Adding one to this would result in 10000, which equals zero if the fifth, or carry, bit is neglected. The complete number conversion algorithm is shown in Fig. 8-11.

D_{100}	D_{10}	D_1	Add to $\bar{d}_{800}$ $\bar{d}_{400}$ $\bar{d}_{200}$ $\bar{d}_{100}$	Add to $\bar{d}_{80}$ $\bar{d}_{40}$ $\bar{d}_{20}$ $\bar{d}_{10}$	Add to $\bar{d}_8$ $\bar{d}_4$ $\bar{d}_2$ $\bar{d}_1$
X	X	Not zero	1 0 1 0	1 0 1 0	1 0 1 0 +1
X	Not zero	Zero	1 0 1 0	1 0 1 0 +1	0 0 0 0 +1
Not zero	Zero	Zero	1 0 1 0 +1	0 0 0 0 +1	0 0 0 0 +1

$$\binom{\text{Do not let carries propagate}}{\text{between digits}}$$

Fig. 8-10 Algorithm for forming the ten's complement of a three-digit number $D_{100}D_{10}D_1$.

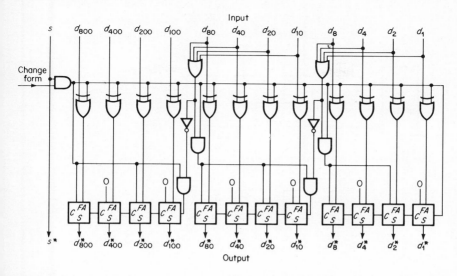

Fig. 8-11 Conversion between sign plus 8421 BCD magnitude code and sign plus ten's complement (8421 BCD) code.

8-3 ARITHMETIC ALGORITHMS

The *addition* of two binary numbers, or two sign plus two's complement numbers, was discussed in Chap. 2 and 3. There it was found that these numbers can be added using a one-dimensional iterative array of full adders. Sometimes this circuit is modified in order to reduce the settling time of the adder, so that the system can be clocked at a higher rate. A *look-ahead carry* adder is designed to do just this. Instead of generating each carry as a function of the previous carry, the carry input to each bit position is generated more directly so as to reduce the number of levels of gating. Because these look-ahead carry adders are widely applicable, they have been implemented as MSI circuits.

The addition of two 8421 BCD code numbers can be developed around binary adders. As long as the binary sum of two digits and a carry input is less than 10, the BCD representation of the sum is the same as the binary sum. However, if the binary sum is 10 or greater, then the binary result must be modified in order to achieve the correct result. By constructing a truth table of each possible binary sum and its corresponding representation as a BCD code number, it is found that the correction can be made by adding 6 to the binary result whenever that result is 10 or greater. This is illustrated for one decade in Fig. 8-12. It is shown with eight full adders although the full adder in the lower-right-hand corner can be removed and the full adder in the lower-left-hand corner can be replaced by a half-adder. The representation with eight full adders

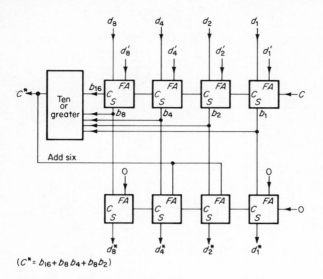

$(C^* = b_{16} + b_8\,b_4 + b_8 b_2)$

Fig. 8-12   One decade of an adder for 8421 BCD code numbers.

is useful if the circuit is to be implemented by iterating entirely in time since the iterative block will then be a full adder. The modification required for adding two three-digit sign plus ten's complement numbers is shown in Fig. 8-13. Each decade adder in Fig. 8-13 is the circuit of Fig. 8-12.

An arithmetic operation which is useful in a variety of circumstances is *multiplication by* -1. For a sign plus magnitude code, this simply requires complementing the sign bit. However, if zero is defined only with a sign bit of 0, then the coding of zero must be left unchanged by the operation. For sign plus

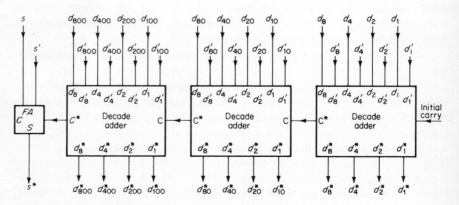

Fig. 8-13   Three-digit sign plus ten's complement adder.

two's complement numbers, multiplication by -1 is closely related to the process previously discussed for conversion between sign plus binary magnitude code and sign plus two's complement code. Now however, the two's complement of the number *and* its sign is formed. This is implemented in Fig. 8-14a by first forming the one's complement and then adding 1. The simplification shown in Fig. 8-14b is obtained by replacing the half-adder on the right (for which one input is always equal to one) by a simplified circuit which gives the same outputs.

The algorithm for the multiplication of a sign plus ten's complement (8421 BCD) code number by minus one is likewise closely related to the algorithm for converting between sign plus magnitude code and sign plus ten's complement code. One approach is to complement the sign bit, form the nine's complement of each digit, and add one to the result (using an 8421 BCD code adder). A more direct approach involves modifying the code conversion algorithm depicted in Fig. 8-11 in a way analogous to the modification of Fig. 8-9 to obtain Fig. 8-14a. The result is shown in Fig. 8-15. This can be simplified by replacing the full adders which have a 0 input by half adders.

The algorithm for binary *subtraction* using full subtractors was developed in Prob. 3-28. In this section, we shall organize the algorithm around full adders

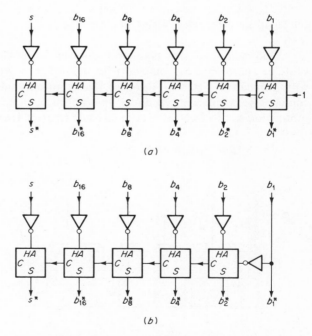

Fig. 8-14 Multiplication of a sign plus two's complement number by -1. (*a*) Iterative implementation; (*b*) simplified circuit.

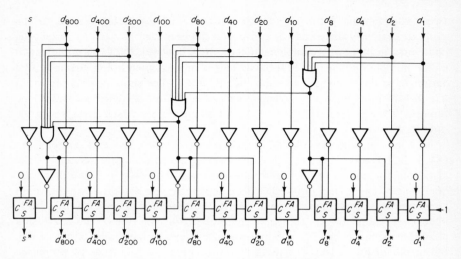

Fig. 8-15 Multiplication of a sign plus ten's complement (8421 BCD) number by −1.

and apply it to sign plus two's complement numbers. This can be achieved by multiplying the subtrahend by −1 and adding the result to the minuend. Thus, the algorithm becomes a simple modification of Fig. 8-14a and is shown in Fig. 8-16.

Subtraction of sign plus ten's complement (8421 BCD) code numbers could be approached by combining the *multiplication by −1* circuit of Fig. 8-15 with the adder of Fig. 8-13. However, this approach would pile complexity upon complexity, where a more direct approach is actually possible. Consider the subtraction of two 8421 BCD code digits, M (minuend) and S (subtrahend):

$$M - S = m_8 m_4 m_2 m_1 - s_8 s_4 s_2 s_1$$

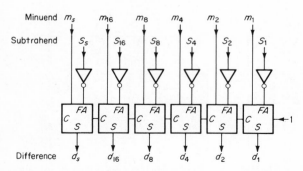

Fig. 8-16 Subtraction of sign plus two's complement numbers.

Now complementing the bits of S gives

$$\overline{s_8}\,\overline{s_4}\,\overline{s_2}\,\overline{s_1} = 1111 - s_8 s_4 s_2 s_1$$

where the expression on the right represents a binary subtraction. Consequently,

$$M - S = m_8 m_4 m_2 m_1 + \overline{s_8}\,\overline{s_4}\,\overline{s_2}\,\overline{s_1} - 1111$$
$$= m_8 m_4 m_2 m_1 + \overline{s_8}\,\overline{s_4}\,\overline{s_2}\,\overline{s_1} + 0001 - 10000$$

This says that $M - S$ can be formed through the binary addition of $m_8 m_4 m_2 m_1$, $\overline{s_8}\,\overline{s_4}\,\overline{s_2}\,\overline{s_1}$, and 1. If the addition overflows (i.e., if a 1 results in the fifth-bit position), then the first 4 bits provide the correct representation for the difference as an 8421 BCD code digit. On the other hand, if the addition does not overflow, then the subtrahend digit was greater than the minuend digit and two things must be done:

1. This result must be corrected
2. A borrow must be propagated to the next digit position by not adding the extra 1 into that addition

A result of 1111 should be 1001, 1110 should be 1000, and so forth. This can be corrected by adding $11001 - 1111 = 1010$ to the result and neglecting the carry which occurs. The complete circuit for three-digit sign plus ten's complement (8421 BCD) code numbers is shown in Fig. 8-17. It is shown

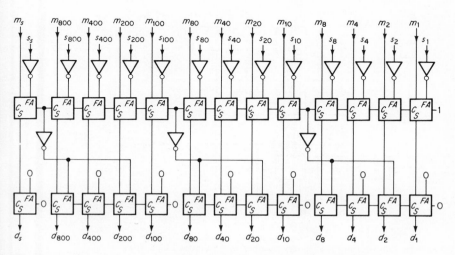

Fig. 8-17 Subtraction of sign plus ten's complement (8421 BCD) code numbers.

iteratively, using a full adder in each block. If it were implemented combinationally, the full adders with one or two 0 inputs could be simplified.

The algorithm for the *multiplication* of two binary numbers can be developed by analogy with decimal multiplication. As always, our intent in developing the algorithm as a combinational circuit will be to present a clear picture of the variables involved and their interrelations. The actual implementation can then take a variety of forms, with this combinational circuit used as a guide to their design. If we consider the multiplication of 3-bit numbers

$$A = a_4 a_2 a_1 \quad \text{and} \quad B = b_4 b_2 b_1$$

then we can begin by multiplying A by b_1, adding the result to zero to form the first partial product P_1. Note that

$$A \times b_1 = \begin{cases} A & \text{if } b_1 = 1 \\ 0 & \text{if } b_1 = 0 \end{cases}$$

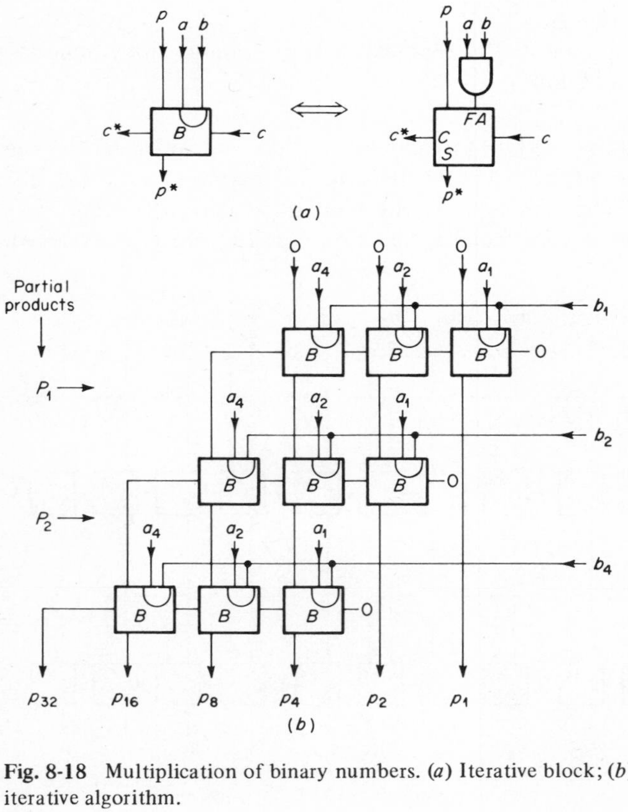

(a)

(b)

Fig. 8-18 Multiplication of binary numbers. (a) Iterative block; (b) iterative algorithm.

Next $A \times b_2$ is formed, shifted one place to the left and added to P_1 to form the second partial product P_2. Continuing with b_3 yields the final result. The complete algorithm is shown in Fig. 8-18.

The multiplication of signed numbers is straightforward if the numbers are expressed in sign plus binary magnitude form. Then the magnitudes are multiplied as in Fig. 8-18 while the sign bits are EXCLUSIVE-ORed to obtain the sign bit of the product. In contrast, the multiplication of numbers expressed in sign plus two's complement form is more involved.

To understand this, consider the analytic representation of two 5-bit sign plus two's complement numbers:

$$A = -16a_s + 8a_1 + 4a_4 + 2a_2 + a_1$$
$$B = -16b_s + 8b_8 + 4b_4 + 2b_2 + b_1 \tag{8-1}$$

where a_s and b_s are the sign bits. In order to carry out the multiplication and obtain the result in sign plus two's complement code, care must be taken in keeping the signs involved in the multiplication straight. To do this, we need to recall

1. How to multiply a sign plus two's complement number by 2^k
2. How to express an n-bit sign plus two's complement number as an $(n+1)$-bit number

We shall do the first with the following example:

        $(+4)(01101) = 0110100$
        $(+4)(11101) = 1110100$

Furthermore, we can express multiplication by -2^k as follows:

        $(-4)(01101) = (-1)(0110100)$
        $(-4)(11101) = (-1)(1110100)$

The general rule, which these examples follow, says that multiplication by 2^k of a number expressed in sign plus two's complement form can be implemented by shifting the number k places to the left (while filling in the vacated bit positions on the right with zeros). This rule is identical to the corresponding rule for binary numbers.

Extending an n-bit number to an $(n + 1)$-bit number requires that the new sign bit be the same as the old sign bit. Otherwise the number is left unchanged. This is illustrated by

        $01101 = 001101$

and

$$11101 = 111101$$

We are now ready to tackle the problem of multiplying the two sign plus two's complement numbers A and B given in Eq. (8-1). One approach is to multiply the multiplicand A by each term in the analytic expression for B. This will give five sign plus two's complement numbers, one of which must be subtracted from the sum of the others. The correct result will be produced as long as the partial products are extended sufficiently so that correct addition can be carried out. That is, if the sum of two 5-bit numbers requires a 6-bit result, then we should extend the 5-bit numbers to 6-bit numbers before carrying out the addition.

An interesting approach which avoids these *erroneous overflow* considerations is *Booth's algorithm.*[†] The multiplier

$$B = -16b_s + 8b_8 + 4b_4 + 2b_2 + b_1$$

is reexpressed as

$$B = -16(b_s - b_8) - 8(b_8 - b_4) - 4(b_4 - b_2) - 2(b_2 - b_1) - (b_1 - 0)$$

Each of the terms in brackets will be +1, 0, or −1. Furthermore, whenever an operation is called for (i.e., the term within the brackets is +1 or −1), its sign will be changed from the previous operation. For example, if the multiplier is

$$b_s b_8 b_4 b_2 b_1 = 11001$$

then this calls for the following operations on A:

$-(b_1 - 0) = -1$	*Subtract A from zero to form P_1*
$-2(b_2 - b_1) = +2$	*Add $2A$ to P_1 to form P_2*
$-4(b_4 - b_2) = 0$	$P_3 = P_2$
$-8(b_8 - b_4) = -8$	*Subtract $8A$ from P_3 to form P_4*
$-16(b_s - b_8) = 0$	$P_5 = P_4$

This alternation of additions and subtractions always insures that the partial product will require no more bits than the number being added to it (or subtracted from it) requires. The structure of the algorithm for 3-bit numbers is

[†]A. Booth and K. Booth, "Automatic Digital Calculators," 3d ed., pp. 52–55, Butterworth, London, 1965. (Or see Y. Chu's book referenced at the end of this chapter.)

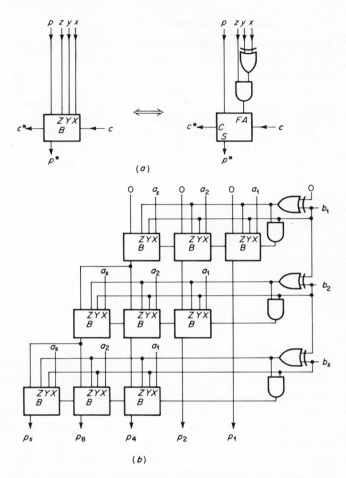

Fig. 8-19 Booth's algorithm for the multiplication of sign plus two's complement numbers. (*a*) Iterative block; (*b*) iterative algorithm.

shown in Fig. 8-19. The gating before each full adder determines whether addition, subtraction, or no change will take place.

The algorithms for other arithmetic operations like division and logarithmic and trigonometric conversions will not be discussed here. However, the development of a certain algorithm may be the key step in the development of a system. Thus, the development of an efficient (and proprietary) algorithm for converting back and forth between numbers and their logarithms provided the competitive edge to Wang Laboratories and their desk-top calculators for years.

8-4   PULSE-RATE ALGORITHMS

Many processes use digital information in pulse-rate form. Thus an input to a system may be a frequency or pulse rate. This may come from a turbine flow meter (like that shown in Fig. 7-34) or some other transducer that obtains a pulse rate (or frequency) proportional to the magnitude of another physical variable. Alternatively, the input may be the stable frequency of a crystal oscillator. This is done to derive other frequencies in frequency synthesizers, where the desired frequency is dialed into the system on thumbwheel switches. The stable 60-Hz frequency of the power line is similarly used to obtain a *real-time* clock in a computer. An interrupt is generated every sixtieth of a second so that a service routine will accumulate counts into seconds, minutes, and hours.

On the output of a system, a pulse rate may be used to drive a stepping motor at a desired rate so as to turn a shaft at a corresponding angular velocity. Or it may be used to generate a pulse rate proportional to an error signal in a feedback control system. The *time-averaged switching* scheme of Fig. 7-2 could have obtained its proportional control signal v_1 in this way.

In this section, we shall discuss rate synchronization, rate division, rate multiplication, rate addition and subtraction, rate comparison, and rate conversion to absolute form.

By *rate synchronization*, we mean the process of synchronizing an arbitrary frequency, or pulse rate, to a clock. This was discussed in general terms in Sec. 7-3 and more specifically, as far as we are concerned here, in the discussion surrounding Fig. 7-17. The synchronous decoder discussed there generated an output which equaled 1 whenever the input changed state. In the problem discussed here, the output of a device may need amplifying, filtering, and diode clipping in order to provide a signal large enough to cross the threshold voltage of the logic and yet not so large as to exceed the maximum input voltage limits of the logic. If the synchronized output should be equal to 1 only once per period of the input (instead of twice, as the circuit of Fig. 7-17 provides), then instead of EXCLUSIVE-ORing the outputs of the two delay flipflops, we can AND the Q output of one of the delay flipflops with the $\overline{Q}$ output of the other. However, the synchronizing clock rate C_0 must still be high enough to insure that all (unsynchronized) 1s and 0s will be detected by at least one clock transition. In general, this means that the clock rate C_0 must be at least two times the maximum input rate.

Rate division is the general process of obtaining a synchronized rate R^* which is related to another synchronized rate R by

$$R^* = \frac{1}{D}R$$

where D is an integer. Rate division can be implemented in a special-purpose structure using a scale-of-D scaler which is clocked with R. R^* is then obtained by ANDing together asserted and negated outputs of the scaler so as to pick out one state in the scaler's count sequence. If the scaler is the asynchronously designed scale-of-N scaler of Fig. A3-1 in Appendix A3, then spurious pulses can be avoided on the output (while still obtaining a pulse which is synchronized to the clock on both edges) by gating out state 1 $(000 \cdots 001)$. For an output rate which is inversely proportional to the number N set on thumbwheel switches, the scale-of-N scaler need only be built around an 8421 BCD code down counter, as suggested in Appendix A3.

Rate division in a small computer can be implemented by synchronizing the input in the interface circuitry and generating an interrupt. Then the service routine called up by this interrupt can count a number K down one, compare it against zero, and do nothing until $K = 0$. When $K = 0$, it is set equal to D and an output R^* is generated to the interface circuitry. This procedure generates one output pulse for every D input pulses.

Rate multiplication produces an output rate R^* which is related to an input rate R by

$$R^* = \frac{M}{N} R \tag{8-2}$$

where M and N are integers and M is less than N. Typically N is fixed (and equal to a power of 2 or 10) so that the output rate is proportional to the input rate R and to the multiplier M. Note that, as defined, the output rate will always be less than the input rate.

We shall discuss the following two algorithms for rate multiplication:

1. Accumulator rate multiplication
2. Counter rate multiplication

Every performance feature of the former algorithm is better than the corresponding feature of the latter, as we shall see. However, as a special-purpose structure, counter rate multiplication can be implemented somewhat less expensively.

Accumulator rate multiplication can be organized either with a fixed N (such as 2^{10}) or with an arbitrary N, which we will discuss first. Assume that M and N are both 10-bit binary numbers (and that M is less than N). Then we require an 11-bit accumulator which holds a sign plus two's complement number A. Every time the synchronized input R occurs, the number M is subtracted from A to form

$$A^* = A - M$$

The sign bit of A^* is used as the synchronized output R^*. Thus, whenever A^* goes negative, $R^* = 1$. During the following clock period, N is *added* to A forming

$$A^* = A + N$$

The synchronizing clock rate C_0 must be sufficiently high so that every clock period when $R = 1$ is followed immediately by at least one clock period when $R = 0$. Then this addition of N to A will never interfere with the subtraction of M from A.

That this algorithm will indeed generate an output pulse rate related to an input pulse rate by Eq. (8-2) will be demonstrated with an example, shown in Fig. 8-20. Here each row represents one clock period and R is shown exactly equal to one-third of the clock rate. The actual rate of R is irrelevant as long as it is no greater than one-half the clock rate. Using

$$\frac{M}{N} = \frac{3}{5} = \frac{011}{101}$$

R	A		A^*		R^*
	Sign plus two's complement representation	Sign plus decimal magnitude representation	Sign plus two's complement representation	Sign plus decimal magnitude representation	
0	0 0 0 0	0	0 0 0 0	0	0
0	0 0 0 0	0	0 0 0 0	0	0
1	0 0 0 0	0	1 1 0 1	-3	1
0	1 1 0 1	-3	0 0 1 0	$+2$	0
0	0 0 1 0	$+2$	0 0 1 0	$+2$	0
1	0 0 1 0	$+2$	1 1 1 1	-1	1
0	1 1 1 1	-1	0 1 0 0	$+4$	0
0	0 1 0 0	$+4$	0 1 0 0	$+4$	0
1	0 1 0 0	$+4$	0 0 0 1	$+1$	0
0	0 0 0 1	$+1$	0 0 0 1	$+1$	0
0	0 0 0 1	$+1$	0 0 0 1	$+1$	0
1	0 0 0 1	$+1$	1 1 1 0	-2	1
0	1 1 1 0	-2	0 0 1 1	$+3$	0
0	0 0 1 1	$+3$	0 0 1 1	$+3$	0
1	0 0 1 1	$+3$	0 0 0 0	0	0
0	0 0 0 0	0	0 0 0 0	0	0
0	0 0 0 0	0	0 0 0 0	0	0
1	0 0 0 0	0	1 1 0 1	-3	1

one cycle of rate multiplier

Fig. 8-20 Accumulator rate multiplication with $M/N = {}^3/_5$.

and a 4-bit accumulator A gives the results shown. Note that the value of A repeats itself after every five input pulses on R. Also note that three output pulses occur during this interval. Consequently, at least in this case, the (average) output rate is equal to *exactly* three-fifths of the input rate.

That Eq. (8-2) is satisfied exactly for arbitrary values of M and N (but with M constrained to be less than N) can be demonstrated as follows. First note that A will be between 0 and $N-1$ following an addition of N (after A has dipped negative). Also, for any interval of N input pulses, there are N subtractions of M from A, giving a gross decrease in A (due to these subtractions) of $N \times M$. During this same interval, there must be exactly M additions of N to A so that the net change in A (of $M \times N - N \times M = 0$) will lie in the range between 0 and $N-1$, assuming the interval began with A in this range. Consequently, every N input pulses produce M output pulses, satisfying Eq. (8-2).

Another desirable property of accumulator rate multiplication is the *smoothness* of its output pulse rate. If the input pulse rate R is perfectly smooth (i.e., its pulses are equally spaced), then for many applications it is desirable that its output pulses R^* be as close to equally spaced as possible. With the algorithm developed here, each output pulse occurs during the same clock period as some input pulse. Consequently, with a multiplier like $M/N = {}^3/_5$, it is impossible to have equally spaced output pulses. The best that can be hoped for is that successive output pulses will be no closer together than the integral part of N/M (for example, 1 for $N/M = {}^5/_3 = 1.67$) times the spacing between input pulses. We also desire successive output pulses to be no farther apart than the next larger integer (for example, 2 for $N/M = {}^5/_3 = 1.67$) times the spacing between input pulses. Notice that the example of Fig. 8-20 has this desirable property. Accumulator rate multiplication has this property in general, regardless of the values of M and N.

A third desirable property of accumulator rate multiplication occurs when M and N change during their use. Then

$$\left[R^*\right]_{average} \approx \left[\frac{M}{N}\right]_{average} \times \left[R\right]_{average}$$

in spite of the changes in M and N. That is, if M decreases during the use of the rate multiplier, then the accumulator will accumulate toward negative values at a somewhat slower rate, slowing down the output rate. This property is used in some operational circuits where the multiplier M may be the changing contents of a counter. One example of this will be discussed later in this section when we convert a rate to a number. We shall compare an unknown rate against the output of a rate multiplier, determine which is the higher rate, and use this information to count a counter up or down. The counter contents, in turn, provide the M input to the rate multiplier.

Thus far, our discussion of accumulator rate multiplication has involved an arbitrary value of N. The algorithm is especially amenable to implementation in a small computer, where all of the operations called for (like addition, subtraction, and comparison of sign plus two's complement numbers) are normal computer instructions.

The implementation as a special-purpose structure is greatly facilitated if N is a power of 2. For example, if M is a 10-bit binary number while N is equal to 2^{10}, then the accumulator A can be implemented with 10 bits. The algorithm can be restructured slightly (in order to use full adders instead of full subtractors) by adding in M to A instead of subtracting M from A. The carry output of the most significant bit of the adder is monitored, and when it equals

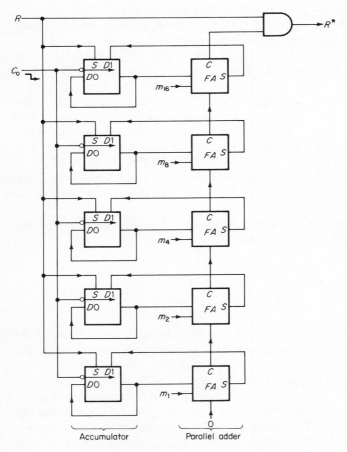

Fig. 8-21   Five-bit accumulator rate multiplier.

1 an output pulse $R*$ is generated. There is no need to do anything with N since its subtraction would not affect any of the bits in the accumulator anyway. It would only affect the sign bit, which is not really needed and thus not included. An example of this structure is shown in Fig. 8-21. Although this is shown using parallel addition, this is a good example of a process where serial addition could be used to advantage in order to use regular delay flipflops plus one serial switch instead of switched-input delay flipflops.

Counter rate multiplication is used only as a special-purpose structure because of its poorer performance characteristics and because it cannot be implemented as easily in a small computer as accumulator rate multiplication can be. Equation (8-2) is implemented with N equal to a power of 2 and M equal to a binary number. Every input pulse R counts a binary counter B up one count. For a 5-bit rate multiplier, the output rates shown in Fig. 8-22 are implemented with the Boolean equations shown. In these equations, the counter contents are denoted by

$$B = b_{16} b_8 b_4 b_2 b_1$$

while the multiplier is denoted, again, by

$$M = m_{16} m_8 m_4 m_2 m_1$$

Rate	Boolean relation between output $R*$ and input R
$R* = \dfrac{16}{32} R = \dfrac{10000}{100000} R$	$R* = m_{16} b_1 R$
$R* = \dfrac{8}{32} R = \dfrac{1000}{100000} R$	$R* = m_8 b_2 \bar{b}_1 R$
$R* = \dfrac{4}{32} R = \dfrac{100}{100000} R$	$R* = m_4 b_4 \bar{b}_2 \bar{b}_1 R$
$R* = \dfrac{2}{32} R = \dfrac{10}{100000} R$	$R* = m_2 b_8 \bar{b}_4 \bar{b}_2 \bar{b}_1 R$
$R* = \dfrac{1}{32} R = \dfrac{1}{100000} R$	$R* = m_1 b_{16} \bar{b}_8 \bar{b}_4 \bar{b}_2 \bar{b}_1 R$

Fig. 8-22 Generation of certain output rates in a counter rate multiplier.

and

$$N = 100000$$

The top relation gates one-half of the input R pulses on to the output (when $m_{16} = 1$) because $b_1 = 1$ one-half of the time as the counter is counted.

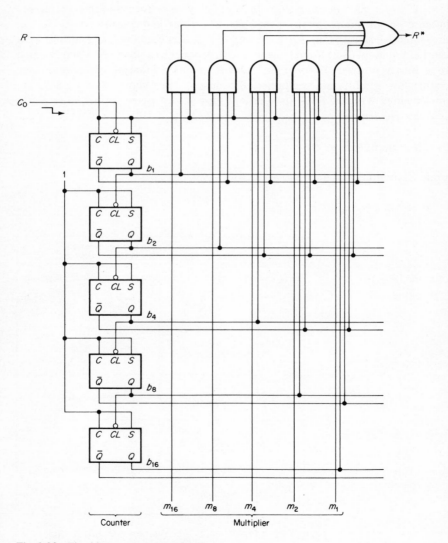

Fig. 8-23 Five-bit counter rate multiplier.

R	B	R^*
0	000	0
0	000	0
1	000	0
0	001	0
0	001	0
1	001	0
0	010	0
0	010	0
1	010	1
0	011	0
0	011	0
1	011	0
0	100	0
0	100	0
1	100	1
0	101	0
0	101	0
1	101	0
0	110	0
0	110	0
1	110	1
0	111	0
0	111	0
1	111	0
0	000	0
0	000	0
1	000	0

One cycle of rate multiplier

Fig. 8-24 Counter rate multiplication with $M/N = {}^3/_8 = {}^{011}/_{1000}$.

Similarly, the second relation gates one-fourth of the input pulses on to the output (when $m_8 = 1$) because $b_2 \bar{b}_1 = 1$ one-fourth of the time as the counter is counted. Notice that none of the states gated on to the output by one of the relations coincides with any state gated on to the output by another of the relations. Consequently, the complete rate multiplier is formed simply by ORing the five relations together, as shown in Fig. 8-23.

To illustrate that counter rate multiplication has its performance deficiencies, note in Fig. 8-24 that the output rate is not always as smooth as would be desired. Thus, with $M/N = {}^3/_8$, we would like to see the spacing between output pulses be never less than every two R pulses nor greater than every three R pulses (since $N/M = {}^8/_3 = 2.67$). However, we find in Fig. 8-24 that the actual spacing of the output pulses is two, two, and four R pulses. For counter rate multiplication with many bits in the counter, the output can be extremely unsmooth for certain values of M. However, the average output rate will satisfy Eq. (8-2) exactly.

If a rate multiplier is to be used operationally so that M changes during its use, then Fig. 8-25 illustrates that the average output rate might not be equal to the average input rate times the average multiplier. In this example, M is equal to binary 3 half of the time and binary 4 half the time. Thus, we would expect to have an average output of

$$R^*_{\text{average}} = \frac{1}{2}\left(\frac{3}{8} + \frac{4}{8}\right) R_{\text{average}}$$

$$= \frac{7}{16} R_{\text{average}}$$

Instead, with M changing when it does

$$R^*_{\text{average}} = 0$$

Although this represents an extreme (and contrived) example, nevertheless, it does illustrate the problem.

Rate addition and subtraction are simply the processes whereby two (or more) synchronized input rates $R1$ and $R2$ are combined to form a synchronized output rate of

$$R^* = R1 + R2$$

or

$$R^* = R1 - R2$$

Obviously, if rate addition is to be successfully implemented, then the synchronizing clock rate C_0 must be higher than $R1 + R2$. Furthermore, if the addition is to be accurate, then whenever input pulses occur on $R1$ and $R2$ during the same clock period, we must not lose one of the pulses (as would happen if we simply ORed $R1$ and $R2$ together to form R^*).

To resolve this problem, we shall assume that the synchronizing clock rate is sufficiently high so that we never have $R1$ (or $R2$) equal to 1 for two successive clock periods. Then by implementing the *Boolean* equation

$$R^*_{n+1} = R1_{n+1} + R2_{n+1} + R1_n \cdot R2_n$$

(where n and $n + 1$ indicate successive clock periods), we can carry out exact rate addition. This is illustrated in Fig. 8-26.

R	B	M	R^*
0	000	100	0
0	000	100	0
1	000	100	0
0	001	011	0
0	001	011	0
1	001	011	0
0	010	100	0
0	010	100	0
1	010	100	0
0	011	011	0
0	011	011	0
1	011	011	0
0	100	100	0
0	100	100	0
1	100	100	0
0	101	011	0
0	101	011	0
1	101	011	0
0	110	100	0
0	110	100	0
1	110	100	0
0	111	011	0
0	111	011	0
1	111	011	0
0	000	100	0
0	000	100	0
1	000	100	0

Fig. 8-25 Counter rate multiplier and an example of its poor performance when used operationally.

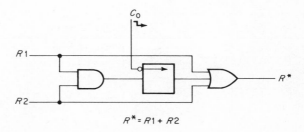

$R^* = R1 + R2$

Fig. 8-26 Rate adder.

In the case of rate subtraction, we need to assume that $R1$ exceeds $R2$. Then, whenever $R2 = 1$, we need to block an $R1$ pulse from reaching the output. Otherwise $R^* = R1$. This can be implemented as shown in Fig. 8-27.

Rate comparison is the process of comparing two synchronized pulse rates $R1$ and $R2$ and determining a Boolean variable G where

$$G = \begin{cases} 1 & \text{if } R1 > R2 \\ 0 & \text{if } R1 < R2 \end{cases}$$

If the two rates are equal, we will let G take on either value. When the two rates are close to each other, the pulses of $R1$ and $R2$ will not generally occur during the same clock periods but rather will alternate with each other. We would like the rate comparator to ignore this alternation of $R1$ and $R2$ pulses and emit a constant value of G—until the faster rate actually becomes the slower rate. Assuming that the two rates are perfectly smooth, the flow diagram of Fig. 8-28a will satisfy this requirement. It will not change the value of the output G until a net surplus of two pulses occurs on one input compared with the number of pulses occurring on the other input. With the state assignment shown in Fig. 8-28a for the state variables X and Y, the transition maps for these variables and the Karnaugh map for G are shown in Fig. 8-28b. The implementation is shown in Fig. 8-29.

As an example of a system tying several of these units together, consider the problem of obtaining a binary number proportional to a synchronized pulse rate $R1$. We will do this by forming a ratio

$$\frac{R1}{R0}$$

where $R0$ is a standard, or reference, rate which is higher than the maximum rate of $R1$. The circuit of Fig. 8-30 shows the reference rate being derived from the

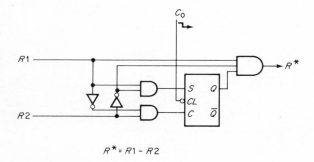

$$R^* = R1 - R2$$

Fig. 8-27   Rate subtractor.

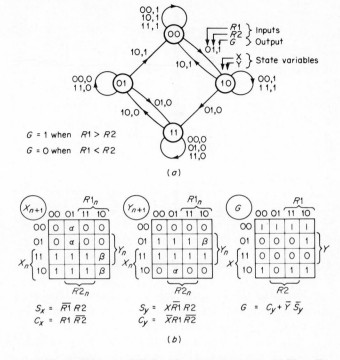

$$G = 1 \text{ when } R1 > R2$$
$$G = 0 \text{ when } R1 < R2$$

(a)

$$S_x = \overline{R1}\,R2 \qquad S_y = X\overline{R1}\,R2 \qquad G = C_y + \overline{Y}\,\overline{S}_y$$
$$C_x = R1\,\overline{R2} \qquad C_y = \overline{X}R1\,\overline{R2}$$

(b)

Fig. 8-28 Definition and design of a rate comparator. (a) Flow diagram; (b) transition and Karnaugh maps.

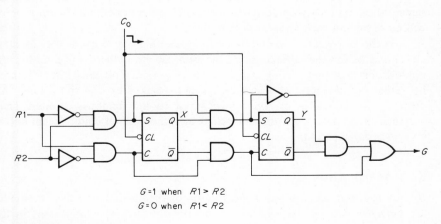

$$G = 1 \text{ when } R1 > R2$$
$$G = 0 \text{ when } R1 < R2$$

Fig. 8-29 Rate comparator.

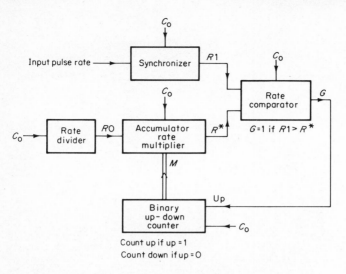

Fig. 8-30 Conversion of a rate to absolute form.

synchronizing clock C_0 through a rate divider. However, it is often useful to obtain the ratio of one rate to another (faster) rate. In this case, $R0$ can be obtained by synchronizing the faster rate.

The rest of the circuit is just a feedback loop which derives a rate

$$R^* = \frac{M}{N} R0 \qquad \text{where } N \text{ is some fixed power of 2}$$

and which compares this R^* rate against $R1$ in order to derive a signal, G. This signal drives the binary up-down counter which generates M in a direction which will make the rate of R^* approach that of $R1$.

If the *loop gain* of the feedback loop is so high as to cause M to oscillate above and below the correct value, the gain can be reduced by counting the up-down counter only during every Nth clock period. This can be implemented by gating out one state of a scale-of-N scaler (clocked by C_0) and feeding this output into an *enable* or *count* level input to the up-down counter. Then although the counter will still be clocked by C_0, it will not count except during every Nth clock period.

8-5 INTERPOLATION

By *interpolation*, we shall mean the process of fitting a straight line or circular arc between two points. The use of interpolation has been important in the numerical control of milling machines. There it has permitted a relatively small amount of information on perforated tape to generate the *profiling* (or *contouring*) motion which produces parts by milling a block of raw stock into a desired shape. It has also permitted the relatively slow data transfer rate of a perforated tape reader to be matched to the high rate of incremental motion along each axis of the milling machine in order to perform profiling at the high rate for which the machine is capable. Operating at any rate which is significantly less than this wastes the profit-making capability of the machine.

Another application of interpolation arises in the use of a graphic display terminal to provide graphic output from a computer. As was discussed in Sec. 7-2, the use of linear or circular-arc interpolation can greatly reduce the data storage within the computer needed to generate desired displays. It can also greatly reduce the time during which the computer is tied up with the data transfers needed to generate these displays—if the interpolator is built into the graphic display terminal or into a postprocessor which is fed by the computer and which drives a graphic display terminal.

Some interpolation algorithms have been developed around rate multipliers. However, their accuracy of interpolation is sensitive to any unsmoothness in the output of the rate multipliers. In contrast, the algorithm presented here provides ideal error characteristics; the error between the actual interpolated position and the desired straight line (or circular arc) is never greater than 1 quantum. In this, the algorithm performs like a stepping motor which holds each step position with some small error. As the motor moves any number of steps, the error does not accumulate. Rather, it always remains a fractional part of a step.

To illustrate our specific task in carrying out straight-line interpolation, Fig. 8-31 provides an example. We will treat the problem as that of interpolating between the origin and some point (XF, YF) in the first quadrant. The

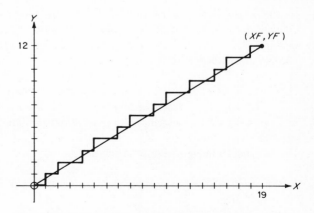

Fig. 8-31 Example of straight-line interpolation from (0,0) to (19,12).

modification needed for any other quadrant involves manipulating the sign bits appropriately for each axis.

The modification needed to go from an absolute point (instead of from the origin) to another absolute point can be handled by giving to the interpolator the *changes* to be made in the position of each axis during interpolation along a line segment. The interpolator can also include counters which hold the absolute position of the interpolated point along each axis. These are counted up or down one count each time the point is interpolated 1 quantum along the corresponding axis. They can also be jumped to a new position (instead of being interpolated there) by direct presetting the new position into the counters.

Any straight line passing through the origin can be expressed as

$$\frac{X}{XF} - \frac{Y}{YF} = 0$$

where the point (XF, YF) is on the line. Alternatively, it can be expressed as

$$YF \cdot X - XF \cdot Y = 0$$

Thus, for the straight line shown in Fig. 8-31, we have

$$12X - 19Y = 0$$

The interpolation algorithm employs an *error function* $F(X,Y)$ defined by

$$F(X,Y) = YF \cdot X - XF \cdot Y \tag{8-3}$$

In this expression, the point (XF, YF) is the final point of the straight-line segment (whose other end is at the origin) along which the interpolation is to take place. Notice that by computing $F(X,Y)$, we keep track of where we are relative to the ideal straight-line segment. Thus

$F(X,Y) > 0$ describes all points below the line
$F(X,Y) = 0$ describes all points on the line
$F(X,Y) < 0$ describes all points above the line

The interpolation algorithm proceeds as follows:

1. Whenever $F(X,Y)$ is greater than zero, increase Y by 1 quantum, leaving X unchanged.
2. Whenever $F(X,Y)$ is equal to or less than zero, increase X by 1 quantum, leaving Y unchanged.

This will carry the interpolated point from the origin to the exact end point specified[†] without ever deviating from the straight line between them by more than 1 quantum.

Although it appears that a multiplication must be performed after each step in order to update the value of $F(X,Y)$ so as to determine what to do next, such is not the case. Note that $F(X,Y)$ is initially equal to zero at the origin. Furthermore, knowing the value of $F(X_n,Y_n)$ at one point (X_n,Y_n), the value of $F(X_{n+1},Y_{n+1})$ at the next point can be determined by computing the *change* $\Delta F(X_n,Y_n)$ and adding this change to the present value. Since

$$F(X_n,Y_n) = YF \cdot X_n - XF \cdot Y_n$$

then

$$
\begin{aligned}
F(X_{n+1},Y_{n+1}) &= YF(X_n + \Delta X) - XF(Y_n + \Delta Y) \\
&= YF \cdot X_n + YF \cdot \Delta X - XF \cdot Y_n - XF \cdot \Delta Y
\end{aligned}
$$

where either ΔX or ΔY equals 1 while the other equals zero. The change $\Delta F(X_n,Y_n)$ can be expressed as

$$\Delta F(X_n,Y_n) = YF \cdot \Delta X - XF \cdot \Delta Y \qquad (8\text{-}4)$$

so that

$$F(X_{n+1},Y_{n+1}) = F(X_n,Y_n) + \Delta F(X_n,Y_n) \qquad (8\text{-}5)$$

Equations (8-4) and (8-5) provide a means for the determination of $F(X_{n+1},Y_{n+1})$ which involves adding YF to $F(X_n,Y_n)$ whenever X is increased by 1 quantum and subtracting XF from $F(X_n,Y_n)$ whenever Y is increased by 1 quantum. If XF and YF are expressed as N-bit binary numbers, $F(X,Y)$ can be expressed as an $(N + 1)$-bit sign plus two's complement number without overflow ever occurring in the calculations.

The complete linear interpolation algorithm is depicted in Fig. 8-32. It is easily implemented within a small computer in order to permit a relatively small amount of data storage to generate extensive displays. Alternatively, it can be implemented in a special-purpose structure. The additions, subtractions, and comparisons can be especially easily implemented in serial form.

Circular-arc interpolation is organized in much the same fashion. An example is shown in Fig. 8-33. Since the equation of a circle centered at the origin is

$$X^2 + Y^2 - R^2 = 0$$

[†]The only exception occurs when the end point is on the Y axis. This exception can be handled by changing the algorithm (for this case only) so as to increment Y, instead of X, when $F(X,Y) = 0$.

the appropriate error function is

$$F(X,Y) = X^2 + Y^2 - R^2 \tag{8-6}$$

which can be computed incrementally as follows:

$$\begin{aligned}
F(X_{n+1}, Y_{n+1}) &= (X_n + \Delta X)^2 + (Y_n + \Delta Y)^2 - R^2 \\
&= X_n{}^2 + 2X_n\,\Delta X + (\overline{\Delta X})^2 + Y_n{}^2 + 2Y_n\Delta Y + (\overline{\Delta Y})^2 - R^2 \\
&= F(X_n, Y_n) + 2X_n\,\Delta X + 1 \quad \text{if} \begin{cases} \Delta X = \pm 1 \\ \Delta Y = 0 \end{cases} \\
&= F(X_n, Y_n) + 2Y_n\,\Delta Y + 1 \quad \text{if} \begin{cases} \Delta X = 0 \\ \Delta Y = \pm 1 \end{cases}
\end{aligned}$$

Thus, it is seen that circular-arc interpolation requires nothing more than

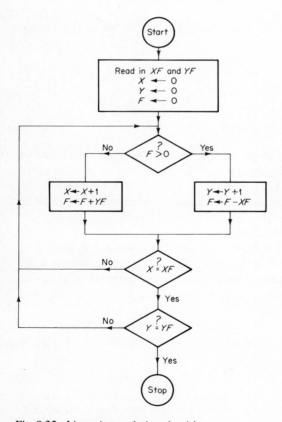

Fig. 8-32 Linear interpolation algorithm.

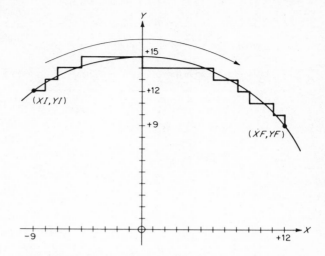

Fig. 8-33 Example of circular-arc interpolation from (−9, +12) to (+12, +9).

additions and subtractions, together with shifting, to implement multiplication by 2. The interpolator is initially loaded with *XI, YI, XF, YF,* and *CW* where

> (*XI,YI*) represents the coordinates of the initial point on the circular arc
> (*XF,YF*) represents the coordinates of the final point on the circular arc
> *CW* is a Boolean variable which, if equal to 1, indicates that the interpolated point is to move clockwise around the circle from the initial point to the final point (if *CW* = 0, the interpolated point is to move counterclockwise)

Implementing the algorithm involves updating the error function $F(X,Y)$, as discussed above. It also involves determining ΔX and ΔY at each step of the way. Since ΔX and ΔY must represent +1, 0, or −1, they can be coded as 2-bit sign plus two's complement numbers as follows:

$$\Delta X = \Delta_{x_S} \Delta_{x_1} = \begin{cases} 01 \text{ means } +1 \\ 00 \text{ means } \ \ 0 \\ 11 \text{ means } -1 \end{cases}$$

$$\Delta Y = \Delta_{y_S} \Delta_{y_1} = \begin{cases} 01 \text{ means } +1 \\ 00 \text{ means } \ \ 0 \\ 11 \text{ means } -1 \end{cases}$$

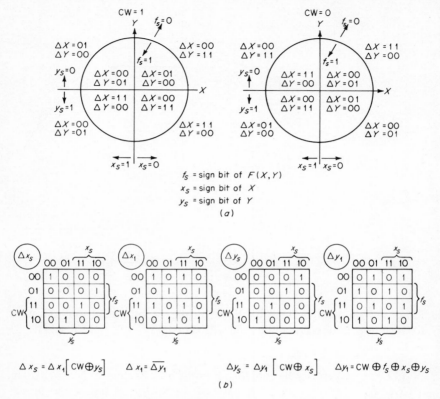

Fig. 8-34 Derivation of equations for the bits of ΔX and ΔY. (a) ΔX and ΔY as functions of CW, f_S, x_S, y_S; (b) Karnaugh maps.

The value of ΔX and ΔY and thus of the four Boolean variables which are used to code them depends upon the Boolean variables CW, f_S (the sign bit of $F(X,Y)$), x_S (the sign bit of X), and y_S (the sign bit of Y). These relationships are shown in Fig. 8-34a. Karnaugh maps for the bits of ΔX and ΔY are shown in Fig. 8-34b. The complete circular-arc interpolation algorithm is shown in Fig. 8-35.

8-6 SIGNAL AVERAGING

A signal waveform which is corrupted by noise can be reconstructed by averaging, provided the waveform is repeated over and over again. Thus, a waveform can be extracted from noise if it is periodic or almost periodic, providing only that the period is known or can be determined. An example arises in a system which monitors the vibration of a rotating machine. The failure of

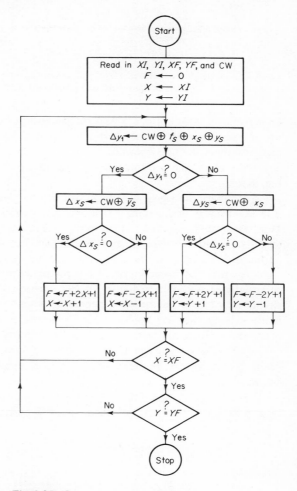

Fig. 8-35 Circular-arc interpolation algorithm.

this machine due to worn bearings or other sources of unbalance can be predicted before the failure actually occurs by analyzing the waveform from a vibration transducer. The component of the waveform whose fundamental frequency is the same as the turning rate of the machine might be corrupted by the vibration of other equipment geared to the machine. By averaging on the fundamental frequency, the waveform which is characteristic of the machine can be extracted.

Another opportunity for signal enhancement by averaging occurs when a waveform repeats itself at irregular intervals and when some characteristic of the signal can be used to align the successive, noisy waveforms. Thus, in spite of a

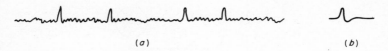

(a)   (b)

Fig. 8-36 Averaging an aperiodic waveform. (a) Aperiodic repeating waveform
having a peak which rises above the noise; (b) averaged signal waveform.

poor signal to noise ratio, a waveform can be averaged if it includes a sharp peak
which rises above the noise, as shown in Fig. 8-36a. By aligning the peaks and
then averaging the noisy waveforms together, the noise will tend to cancel itself
out while the signal reinforces itself, yielding the averaged signal waveform of
Fig. 8-36b.

An aperiodic signal waveform can be completely submerged in noise and
still be retrieved by averaging provided it is *triggered* by a readily available signal.
Thus, the response of the human brain to an aural stimulus (such as the tap of a
mallet on a block of wood) can be seen in an electroencephalogram if successive
responses are aligned to the time of occurrence of the stimulus before averaging.

All three of these opportunities for signal enhancement by averaging can
be structured as shown in Fig. 8-37. For a periodic signal, the trigger-generating
circuit might be a square-wave generator whose frequency is adjusted to the
point where the averaged output is a sharp waveform. Alternatively, a
phase-locked loop might be used to derive the trigger signal from the averaged
output. Or the trigger signal may be derived from a sharp peak in the signal
itself. Finally, it may be derived from another signal which causes the signal to
be averaged.

The averager uses this trigger signal to update a *partial average* formed
from previous waveforms, thus forming a new partial average. The final averaged

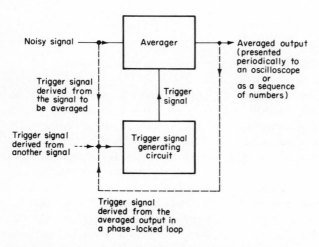

Fig. 8-37 General configuration of an averaging system.

output is obtained by performing this updating many times. To study several possibilities for averaging, we shall define the following waveforms in conjunction with Fig. 8-38:

e *is the present noisy waveform* to be averaged
E is a sampled and quantized version of *e*
A is a sampled and quantized version of the present partial average before it is modified by E

Each sampled and quantized waveform can be described by a sequence of numbers. Thus E may be represented in a digital system as a sequence of one hundred twenty-eight 10-bit sign plus two's complement numbers, where the Ith number is

$$E(I)$$

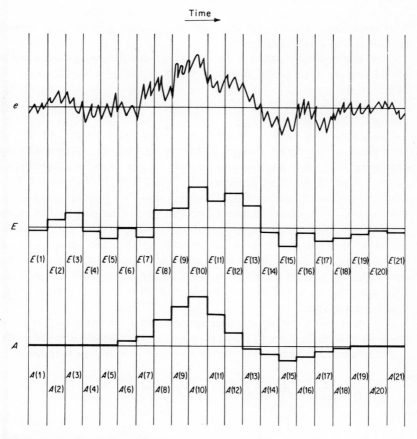

Fig. 8-38 Averaging system waveforms.

Similarly,

$$A(I)$$

denotes the Ith number in the sequence of numbers representing A.

Uniformly weighted averaging is carried out by beginning the partial average at zero:

$$A(I) = 0 \qquad \text{for } I = 1, \ldots, N$$

where N determines the quantization of the average. The average is updated by adding in each new noisy waveform (after aligning it with the average, as discussed above) with

$$A(I) \leftarrow A(I) + E(I) \qquad \text{for } I = 1, \ldots, N$$

This replacement statement says to add $E(I)$ to the present value of $A(I)$ and replace $A(I)$ by this updated value.

If this updating is carried out 2^P times, then the average can be obtained by shifting the final partial average P places to the right. Furthermore, if each sample of the signal $E(I)$ is expressed as a 10-bit number, then by expressing $A(I)$ as a $(P + 10)$-bit number, overflow will never occur while forming the partial averages.

Uniformly weighted averaging gives the same weight to all of the waveforms making up the average. Furthermore, since the average is formed by combining 2^P noisy waveforms into one average waveform, the data rate between input and output is reduced by a factor of 2^P. Sometimes this is an advantage, as when a preprocessor to a small computer presents averaged data to the computer at a rate it can handle, whereas the original data rate might exceed the data processing rate capability of the computer. In other circumstances, the reduction in data rate may be a disadvantage, as when the average waveform is used to provide a visual display on a scope. If a new average is formed at a rate below the eye's flicker rate, the eye will see the changes in the average as a displeasing, jumpy waveform rather than as a smoothly changing, continuously evolving waveform.

Exponentially weighted averaging uses nonuniform weighting of successive noisy waveforms in order to provide an output data rate equal to the input data rate. The algorithm updates the average to form a new average as follows:

$$A(I) \leftarrow \frac{1}{K} E(I) + \frac{K-1}{K} A(I) \qquad \text{for } I = 1, \ldots, N$$

or

$$A(I) \leftarrow \frac{1}{K} [E(I) - A(I)] + A(I) \qquad \text{for } I = 1, \ldots, N$$

The constant K determines the weight of each past noisy input waveform in the present average. For example, if $K = 8$, then the present input waveform is given a weight of

$$\frac{1}{8}$$

the input waveform before it is given a weight of

$$\frac{1}{8} \times \frac{7}{8}$$

the input waveform before that is given a weight of

$$\frac{1}{8} \times \frac{7}{8} \times \frac{7}{8} = \frac{1}{8} \times (\frac{7}{8})^2$$

and so forth. Since the weights decrease as successive powers of some number less than unity ($\frac{7}{8}$ in this case), the averaging is exponential. If K is set equal to some power of 2, the division by K is simplified to a shifting operation for sign plus two's complement numbers.

In many operations, it is difficult to know beforehand how to weight successive waveforms. By using a large value of K, we gain the noise-reducing benefits of having more input waveforms weigh significantly into the average. On the other hand, a small value of K makes the average more responsive to change, thus providing a more dynamic display. In effect, exponential averaging puts a sequence of noisy waveforms through a lowpass filter having a single pole which is determined by the value of K. If K is put under operator control, the trade-off between noise reduction and dynamic response can be tuned to the characteristics of the input signal.

8-7 PSEUDORANDOM BINARY NOISE

White noise, with its flat frequency spectrum, provides a useful abstract concept for many statistical techniques of use in engineering. Because it requires infinite power, and infinite frequency range, it is an unrealizable abstraction. However, for many purposes it can be easily approximated by pseudorandom binary noise.

In Appendix A3, the circuits are given for pseudorandom binary noise generators using any number n of flipflops up to 20. The period of each of these generators is

$$2^n - 1$$

For example, Fig. 8-39b shows the periodic output of the generator shown in

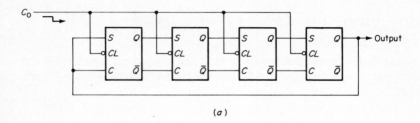

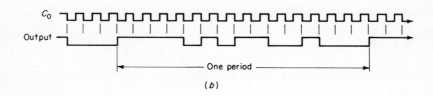

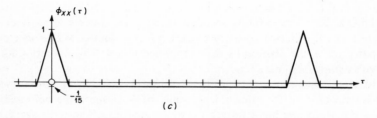

Fig. 8-39 Pseudorandom noise generator and some of its characteristics. (*a*) Pseudo-random noise generator; (*b*) its output; (*c*) its autocorrelation function if the generator output levels are translated from 1 and 0 to +1 and −1.

Fig. 8-39*a*. Since $n = 4$, the period of this generator is 15. A key property of pseudorandom binary noise generators is illustrated by the autocorrelation function shown in Fig. 8-39*c*. In general, the autocorrelation function $\phi_{xx}(\tau)$ of a function $x(t)$ can be expressed mathematically as

$$\phi_{xx}(\tau) = \lim_{T \to \infty} \frac{1}{2T} \int_{-T}^{T} x(t)\, x(t + \tau)\, dt$$

For a periodic function, this simplifies to

$$\phi_{xx}(\tau) = \text{average over one period of } [x(t)\, x(t + \tau)]$$

When $x(t)$ is the pseudorandom binary noise of Fig. 8-39*b*, except with its values changed to +1 and −1 (from 1 and 0), then

$$\phi_{xx}(0) = 1$$

This is true because the amplitude for each clock period +1 or −1 is multiplied by itself when $\tau = 0$ to yield +1. Thus, the average of these squared values is +1. If τ is equal to any integral number of clock periods other than an even multiple of 15 (or $2^n - 1$, in general), then there will be exactly one more clock period when $x(t)$ and $x(t + \tau)$ differ than when they are the same. Consequently,

$$\phi_{xx}(\tau) = -{}^{1}/_{15} \quad \text{when } \tau = \text{any integer other than } 15K$$
$$\text{where } K = 0, 1, 2, \ldots$$

These values are shown in Fig. 8-39c. The noninteger values are simply linear combinations of the adjacent integer values, giving the complete function shown there.

Since the autocorrelation function of white noise is a single impulse at the origin, we see that pseudorandom binary noise can be made to approximate white noise as closely as desired (in the sense of approaching its autocorrelation function) by increasing the value of n as much as is needed. Any autocorrelation functions or crosscorrelation functions which are computed in the process of using pseudorandom binary noise should be computed over an integral multiple of $2^n - 1$ clock periods and need not be computed for any more than $2^n - 1$ values of τ.

An interesting application of pseudorandom binary noise is for the on-line determination of the impulse response of a linear process. As is well known from linear system theory,[†] the impulse response $h(t)$ of a linear system relates the crosscorrelation function

$$\phi_{xy}(\tau) = \lim_{T \to \infty} \frac{1}{2T} \int_{-T}^{T} x(t)\, y(t + \tau)\, dt$$

between the input $x(t)$ and the output $y(t)$ of the system to the autocorrelation function $\phi_{xx}(\tau)$ of the input by

$$\phi_{xy}(\tau) = \int_{-\infty}^{\infty} h(t)\, \phi_{xx}(\tau - t)\, dt$$

This convolution integral yields a particularly simple result when $\phi_{xx}(\tau)$ is an impulse at the origin (as for white noise and as approximated by pseudorandom binary noise). Then

$$\phi_{xy}(\tau) = h(\tau)$$

Consequently, the scheme shown in Fig. 8-40 can be used to determine the

---

[†]J. Truxal, "Automatic Feedback Control System Synthesis," pp. 429–438, McGraw-Hill," New York, 1955.

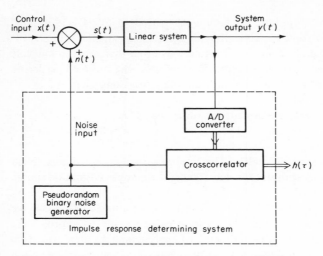

Fig. 8-40 System for determining the impulse response of a
linear system.

impulse response of a linear system. The pseudorandom binary noise signal $n(t)$
is added to the control input $x(t)$ as a sufficiently low-level perturbation to avoid
noticeable disturbance to the system. Assuming that the control input is
uncorrelated to the noise input, it will add no contribution to the crosscorrelation function. The two powerful features of this approach are:

1. The addition of the noise input to the control input is greatly simplified
   because it is two-valued. Its implementation in an electromechanical
   system is thus reduced to a small two-valued linear or angular displacement
   of the control input.
2. The multiplications of normal crosscorrelation are reduced to additions and
   subtractions as the noise input takes on values of +1 and −1.

The use of this approach for determining the impulse response of a linear
system without disturbing the system's normal operation should become
increasingly useful in the future. Its use for the adaptive control of a system
whose dynamic characteristics change relatively slowly but quite severely
represents one application. A more extensive application is in the continuous,
automatic testing of dynamic electromechanical systems to predict malfunctions
before they occur. The deterioration can be isolated, using a computerized
version of this algorithm.

PROBLEMS

8-1 Code conversion If a recirculation loop is used to store 128 three-digit BCD numbers,
then show the structure of a circuit which will use the algorithm of Fig. 8-2 to change each

number from excess-three BCD code to 8421 BCD code or vice versa or leave it alone. Show a timing diagram illustrating the changing of word 0 to excess-three BCD code, while leaving the remaining words unchanged.

8-2 Code conversion A recirculation loop contains five hundred twelve 22-bit numbers. Each number is initially between 0 and 999 coded in binary code. Design as simple a serial operator as possible, using the TTL logic and cost criterion of Fig. 6-42, to convert these binary numbers to three-digit 8421 BCD code numbers in 10 recirculations. At the completion of the conversion, the first 10 bits of each 22-bit number will equal zero while the last 12 bits contain the 8421 BCD code number. Show the complete recirculation loop structure and the timing circuitry (in block diagram form). Describe the conversion and its timing.

8-3 Code conversion Develop the solution to Prob. 8-2 using only 12 bits in each word instead of 22. Intuitively, this might seem to complicate the solution quite a bit. In actuality, does it?

8-4 Code conversion Develop the solution to Prob. 8-2 using 22-bit words again, but completing the conversion in *one* recirculation.

8-5 Code conversion Develop the algorithm for conversion between sign plus excess-three BCD magnitude code and sign plus ten's complement (excess-three BCD) code in a form analogous to Fig. 8-11.

8-6 Arithmetic algorithms Develop the algorithm for the subtraction of sign plus ten's complement (excess-three BCD) code numbers organized around full adders and analogous to Fig. 8-17.

8-7 Arithmetic algorithms In Sec. 8-3 it was demonstrated, by example, that multiplication of a sign plus two's complement number by 2^k can be implemented by shifting the number k places to the left while filling in the vacated bit positions on the right with zeros. Prove that this is true in general by using the analytic expression for a sign plus two's complement number [Eq. (8-1)].

8-8 Arithmetic algorithms Prove the rule given in Sec. 8-3 for extending an n-bit sign plus two's complement number to an $(n + 1)$-bit number.

8-9 Arithmetic algorithms Implement a pipeline structure to evaluate the polynomial

$$a^2 + a(b + c) + bc$$

at the same rate that the adder in Fig. 6-10b produces sums. Assume that inputs a, b, and c are coded as 3-bit binary numbers. Generate an 8-bit binary output. In addition to delay flipflops and to full adders (which have a propagation delay of $2T$ ns between any input and either output), assume that two-input AND gates, two-input OR gates, and inverters are available, each of which has a propagation delay of T ns. Minimize the number of delay flipflops needed.

8-10 Arithmetic algorithms In Sec. 8-3, two approaches were suggested for multiplying sign plus two's complement numbers, but only Booth's algorithm was fully developed (in Fig. 8-19). Show the other approach, implemented on 3-bit numbers (such that a correct product is obtained regardless of the values of the two sign plus two's complement inputs).

8-11 Pulse-rate algorithms An (unsynchronized) source of pulses has a maximum pulse rate of 1,000 pulses/s. However, the pulsewidth of each pulse is 1 to 10 μs.

(*a*) If this rate is synchronized with the approach discussed in Sec. 8-4, then what is the minimum clock rate C_0 which can be used to synchronize these pulses such that no pulses are ever missed?

(*b*) Using the logic of Fig. 6-42, can a slower clock rate be used if each input pulse goes from its normal level of +5 to 0 V and if this is detected by direct presetting a flipflop? If so, then show the circuit and explain how it avoids ever interpreting one input pulse as either zero or two pulses (when the input pulse occurs during the clock's transition). If not, then explain the problem.

8-12 Pulse-rate algorithms In the beginning of Sec. 8-4, it was pointed out that the proportional control signal V_1 in a *time-averaged switching* circuit can be obtained using a pulse-rate algorithm. Should this algorithm be rate addition, rate subtraction, rate multiplication, or rate division? Explain.

8-13 Pulse-rate algorithms If the input to a rate divider is a perfectly smooth (synchronized) pulse rate (i.e., the pulses are equally spaced), is the output rate necessarily perfectly smooth? Explain.

8-14 Pulse-rate algorithms Design a minimum-cost, 10-bit accumulator rate multiplier using a *serial* approach and the logic of Fig. 6-42. Describe the timing involved in your implementation.

8-15 Pulse-rate algorithms Figure 8-25 illustrates that it is possible to get zero pulses out of a counter rate multiplier if M changes during its operation. If the times when $M = 100$ and $M = 011$ are interchanged in Fig. 8-25, then what will the output rate be? Show the figure as it would look with this change.

8-16 Pulse-rate algorithms Develop the flow diagram, transition map, and Karnaugh map for the rate subtractor shown in Fig. 8-27 in a fashion analogous to the development of the rate comparator shown in Fig. 8-29.

8-17 Pulse-rate algorithms The rate comparator of Fig. 8-29 will emit a constant output as long as the synchronized input rates are constant and perfectly smooth regardless of how close one rate is to the other. Is this also true if the synchronized input rates are obtained by synchronizing (unsynchronized) square waves of constant frequency regardless of how close these frequencies are to each other? How might this be proved?

8-18 Pulse-rate algorithms (*a*) Using as few states as possible, show a flow diagram for a rate comparator which will not change the value of its output G until a net surplus of *four* pulses occurs on one input compared with the number of pulses occurring on the other input. This is useful for obtaining a constant output for constant but somewhat unsmooth input rates.

(*b*) What can you say in comparing the dynamic characteristics of this rate comparator with that of Fig. 8-29? Is *hysteresis* a proper term to use in describing these dynamic characteristics? Explain.

8-19 Pulse-rate algorithms If the inputs to the rate comparator shown in Fig. 8-30 were interchanged, how would this affect the performance of the circuit? Explain.

8-20 Pulse-rate algorithms (*a*) Show a system structure for a feedback control loop that will monitor the flow of liquid through a pipe with a turbine flow meter and that will adjust this rate to be proportional to a 10-bit binary number K available in a register (which is either constant or else recirculates, to suit your convenience). The flow rate is to be adjusted by controlling a stepping motor which, in turn, controls a valve.

(*b*) Is there a potential stability problem associated with this feedback loop? If so, then explain, and discuss what might be done to alleviate it.

8-21 Interpolation Using the logic and cost criterion of Fig. 6-42, design a minimum-cost linear interpolator for 10-bit inputs using a special-purpose structure. Assume new values of XF and YF are available on the inputs (in either serial or parallel form) each time the interpolator is ready for them. Generate Boolean outputs ΔX and ΔY which are synchronized to the clock and which equal 1 only during one clock period for each 1-quantum change required.

(*a*) Design the interpolator handling numbers in parallel.

(*b*) Design the interpolator handling numbers serially.

8-22 Interpolation For the purposes of generating graphics on a graphic display terminal, it is useful to extend the development of Sec. 8-5 from straight lines and circular arcs to interpolation along the other conic sections. This is particularly useful where figures on a graphic display terminal will be *rotated* or otherwise manipulated. Determine a suitable error function and discuss its evaluation for interpolation along an ellipse. Can the error function be updated without the use of multiplication if the axes of the ellipse are equal to the X and Y axes used in the calculations? Explain.

8-23 Signal averaging In the beginning of Sec. 8-6, mention was made of isolating the vibration waveform due to one machine from those of other equipment geared to the machine. As an example, consider that for every 256 revolutions of the machine, another piece of equipment goes through exactly 85 revolutions. In forming the average machine vibration waveform, does it make any difference how many periods of the machine waveform go into forming each average (assuming all periods are weighted equally)? Explain.

8-24 Signal averaging For a noisy, periodic waveform having a period of T, uniformly weighted averaging over eight successive periods is closely related to filtering the noisy, periodic waveform with a linear filter having the impulse response shown in Fig. P 8-24.

(*a*) Explain how the output of this filter would progress with time.

(*b*) What is the impulse response of the linear filter for a noisy, periodic waveform having a period of T which is closely related to exponentially weighted averaging with $K = 4$.

(*c*) For a noisy waveform which repeats itself at irregular intervals, why do the approaches of Sec. 8-6 offer a distinct advantage over linear filtering?

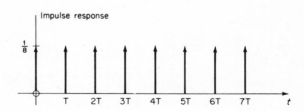

Fig. P 8-24

8-25 Signal averaging Exponentially weighted averaging is to be carried out on successive periods of a noisy, periodic waveform. Express the time constant of the equivalent lowpass filter, discussed at the end of Sec. 8-6, in terms of T, the period of the waveform, and K, the constant which specifies the exponential weighting.

8-26 Pseudorandom binary noise The technique for determining the impulse response of a linear system, shown in Fig. 8-40, requires that the pseudorandom binary noise generator be "tuned" to the dynamics of the linear system. Otherwise its noise output will not look sufficiently like white noise to validate the approach. If the impulse response becomes negligibly small after 1 s and if a 7-bit pseudorandom noise generator is used to determine this response, then the period of the noise generator can be set equal to 1 s.

(*a*) Under these circumstances, what is the effect of the noise generator being periodic?

(*b*) What is the effect of the clock period of the noise generator being finite (instead of zero)?

8-27 Pseudorandom binary noise The purpose of this problem is to investigate the effect of the triangular waveform of the autocorrelation function of pseudorandom binary noise upon the determination of a system's impulse response. Consider a linear system whose impulse response is

$$h(t) = te^{-t}$$

as shown in Fig. P 8-27*a*.

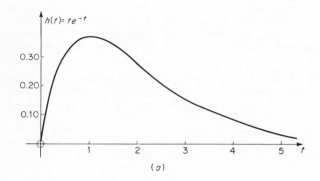

(a)

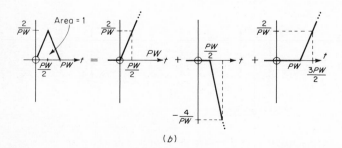

(b)

Fig. P 8-27 (*a*) Impulse response; (*b*) representation of a triangular pulse as three ramp functions.

(a) Evaluate the response of the linear system to a unit impulse at times $t = 0.5$, 1, 2, 4.

(b) Evaluate the response of the linear system to a triangular pulse of unit area at the same four points as in (a) if the pulse width is $PW = 0.4$.

(c) Repeat (b) with $PW = 0.2$.

(d) Repeat (b) with $PW = 0.1$.

Hint: Note that the triangular pulse of unit area and pulsewidth PW can be represented as the summation of the three ramp functions shown in Fig. P 8-27b. Furthermore, the response of this system to a ramp beginning at time T and with slope K is equal to

$$K(t + 2 - T)e^{-(t-T)} u(t - T)$$

where

$$u(t - T) = \begin{cases} 0 & \text{for } t < T \\ 1 & \text{for } t > T \end{cases}$$

REFERENCES

A variety of arithmetic algorithms are clearly presented in Y. Chu, "Digital Computer Design Fundamentals," chaps. 1 and 2, McGraw-Hill, New York, 1962.

An interesting approach to algorithms for division, square root, cube root, and fourth root requires only addition, subtraction, doubling, and halving, and comparison operations. By including squaring as an available operation, an algorithm for obtaining the logarithm of a number is developed. See J. Wensley, A Class of Non-Analytical Iterative Processes, *The Computer Journal*, January 1959, pp. 163–167.

For the developers' view of the interpolation algorithm presented here, see T. Kaiwa and S. Inaba, Latest Japanese Numerical Control Features, *Control Engineering*, October 1961, pp. 88–91.

An excellent introduction to the properties of pseudorandom binary noise as well as a variety of its uses is presented by S. Golomb, "Digital Communication with Space Applications," chap. 1, Prentice-Hall, Englewood Cliffs, N.J., 1964.

The use of pseudorandom binary noise to determine the impulse response of a linear system with an analog crosscorrelator was first suggested by D. Poortvliet, The Measurement of System-Impulse Response by Means of Crosscorrelation with Binary Signals, *Tijdschrift Nederlands Elektronicaen Radiogenootschap*, vol. 28, no. 4, pp. 253–270, 1963 (in English).

The implementation of the algorithm in a special-purpose structure, using a digital crosscorrelator, is developed by O. Williams, System Impulse Response from Digital Crosscorrelation of Additive Input Noise and Output Signal, master's thesis, Georgia Institute of Technology, Atlanta, Ga., April, 1969.

appendix A1
Characteristics of Different
Logic Lines

A1-1 COMPARISON OF DIFFERENT LOGIC LINES

In this appendix, we shall draw the following distinction between a logic *line* and a logic *type*. We shall use the term logic *type* to denote a general structure like TTL (transistor-transistor logic). We will use the term logic *line* to identify one of the several product groups which fall within this general type. Thus, for TTL, five logic lines are Texas Instruments' series 54/74, series 54H/74H, and series 54L/74L, and Sylvania's SUHL I and SUHL II.

In the interests of presenting a meaningful overview of different logic types, we shall go beyond the generalities of the type to comparative data for specific lines which typify the type. The risk of doing this, of course, is to give a more limited view of the capabilities of each logic type than is actually warranted. Thus, the logic line used to typify RTL (resistor-transistor logic) will be Fairchild's standard *medium-power* 900 series. By not listing Fairchild's *low-power* 908 series (each element of which dissipates roughly one-fifth the power of the corresponding medium-power element), it is likely that we shall leave the reader with the impression that RTL dissipates more power than it actually has to dissipate.

382

On the other hand, two logic types are typified by more than one line. In the case of ECL (emitter-coupled logic), this is done to include MECL III, a supremely fast logic, together with MECL II, which is also much faster than representatives of other logic types but which does not exhibit the problems of ultra-high-speed operation to such a marked extent as MECL III. In the case of TTL, the three lines selected provide a view of the breadth of the capability offered in this logic type. This seems worthwhile in view of the trend toward domination of general systems design by TTL.

Selecting a logic line to meet the requirements of a specific system design is often simplified by the constraints of the system. For example, the system might need to interface with a small computer or with any of the many other devices designed mainly with TTL or DTL. If anything but a +5-V logic (like TTL or DTL) is used, it will necessitate the use of *level translators,* which translate voltages corresponding to one logic line to voltages corresponding to the other.

This might be worthwhile where the system to be designed must operate in a high-noise environment. Then, by using a logic line with high-noise immunity, the problem of shielding the system from this noise is simplified. Another situation where a change of logic lines is warranted occurs when a small computer must be augmented to improve the data processing throughput rate. By using a fast logic line, the required algorithm might be implemented serially. This might provide a simpler solution than using a slower logic line together with a parallel implementation of the algorithm.

Selecting a logic line might also be constrained by the ease with which the system can be implemented using the MSI circuits available in certain logic lines. Again, the popularity of TTL has led to a variety of MSI circuits in TTL unequaled by other types of logic.

Another factor in selecting a logic line is cost. For a long time, this has been a prime justification for the use of RTL in a variety of commercial equipment. Again, however, the press of volume in TTL and the consequent high degree of automation in TTL manufacturing is heading it towards price supremacy.

Some systems must operate for long periods on battery power. Under these circumstances a logic line which dissipates significantly less power than other logic lines has a strong point in its favor. Even if power is unlimited, it must be paid for in the cost, bulk, and weight of power supplies and the cost of cooling fans.

Six logic types are characterized in brief (and somewhat oversimplified) form in Fig. A1-1. These are listed in order of relative speed and, more or less, power dissipation. Since relative speed is measured in terms of worst-case maximum flipflop toggling rate, it is worthwhile to recall the rule of thumb given in Sec. 5-6. This says that the maximum reliable clock rate for a system is perhaps one-third of this worst-case maximum flipflop toggling rate. As we saw

Logic type		Specific logic line (second-sourced by many companies)	Relative speed (worst-case flipflop toggling rate) (MHz)	Noise immunity		Logical flexibility		Gate power dissipation at 50% duty cycle (mW)	Power-supply voltage (V)
				Internal	External	Gate fanout capability	Dot AND/OR capability		
CMOS	Complementary metal-oxide semiconductor	RCA COS/MOS	2	Excellent	Good	50	No	3[†] (at 1 MHz)	+10
HTL	High-threshold logic	Motorola MC660 series	2	Excellent	Excellent	10	For some gates	28	+15
RTL	Resistor-transistor logic	Fairchild 900 series	4	Fair	Fair	5	No	12	+3.6
DTL	Diode-transistor logic	Fairchild 930 series	8	Good	Good	7	Yes	14	+5
TTL or T²L	Transistor-transistor logic	Texas Instruments 54L / 74L (Low power)	3	Good *[*]	Good	10	For some gates	1	+5
		Texas Instruments 54 / 74	15			10	For some gates	10	+5
		Texas Instruments 54H / 74H (high speed)	25			10	For some gates	23	+5
ECL	Emitter-coupled logic	Motorola MECL II	70	Excellent	Fair	25	Yes	32	−5.2
		Motorola MECL III	300			7	Yes	240	−5.2

* TTL logic achieves good internal noise immunity only if switching transients on the power supply line are locally suppressed with one 0.01 − μF capacitor per eight integrated circuit packages.

†Power dissipation proportional to frequency down to 2 μW.

Fig. A1-1 Characteristics of different logic lines.

in that section, the price we pay for operating at even this high rate is enslavement to synchronous design and to only a few levels of gating.

In logic design, just as on the highway, "speed kills." The increase in power dissipation with increased speed is only the beginning of the problem. One price paid for using an ultra-high-speed logic like MECL is the need to obey the strict wiring rules specified by the manufacturer. At these speeds, wires look like transmission lines. Wiring rules insure reliable operation in spite of this. However for MECL III, this means the layout of IC packages on a multilayer printed circuit board in order to provide a low-resistance ground plane to keep down cross-talk between adjacent signals and to control strip-transmission-line impedances. Open wiring is limited to lengths of less than 1 in, with severe ringing occurring beyond this length. For longer interconnections, 50-Ω strip transmission lines are required.

By backing off to the slower speed of MECL II, open wiring up to 12 in can be tolerated on a two-sided printed circuit board. Reducing the speed to that of TTL permits wire-wrapped interconnections of up to 10 in. Longer interconnections can be made with a simple twisted-pair cable, grounding both ends of the ground wire. An even further reduction in speed to that of RTL lifts the onus of wiring rules to such an extent that the manufacturers of RTL do not feel compelled to list any.

Speed "kills" when it comes to noise immunity also. It does so because a high-speed flipflop will respond to noise pulses which a slower-speed flipflop will ignore. Thus, the slower-speed flipflop may require a minimum pulse width of 50 ns on a direct preset input in order to be preset. A 25-ns noise pulse will be ignored by this flipflop but responded to by a faster one.

The data on noise immunity in Fig. A1-1 gives some indication of this, However, the strong differences between logic types confuse the picture. For example, MECL exhibits excellent *internal* noise immunity, that is, immunity to noise generated by the MECL circuits themselves. It does so because in changing state, a MECL gate or flipflop causes virtually no change in the current drawn from the power supply—either on a transient or steady-state basis. Consequently, the ground plane and power bus provide a tranquil background for all those fast-moving signals.

In contrast, TTL gates and flipflops make violent demands for current from the power supply each time they switch. They do this because both transistors in the totempole output structure are simultaneously turned on during switching. This places a momentary low-impedance path between the +5 V line and ground. Without the "fix" listed at the bottom of Fig. A1-1, TTL would exhibit poor internal noise immunity.

The propensity of certain logic types to generate their own noise on the power and ground lines is only one factor which contributes to internal noise immunity. Two other factors play a prominent role in the degree of both internal and external noise immunity which a logic type exhibits. These are

1. DC noise immunity
2. 1 and 0 output impedances

The chart shown in Fig. A1-2 gives a quick intuitive view of dc noise immunity. This is done by showing typical values for the 1 and 0 output voltages of a gate together with the typical threshold voltage on the input to a gate. The difference between the 1 output voltage and the threshold voltage gives the *logical 1 typical noise immunity* discussed in Sec. 3-16. It represents the amplitude of a negative noise pulse which will drive the steady-state (or dc) output of a gate down to the threshold voltage. Similarly the difference between the threshold voltage and the 0 output voltage gives the *logical 0 typical noise immunity*.

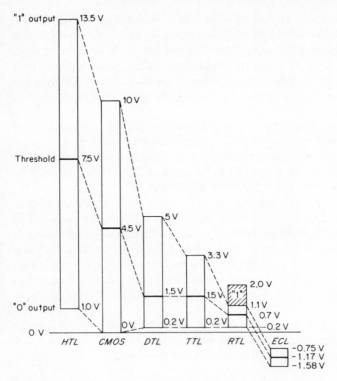

Fig. A1-2 Typical output and threshold voltages for six logic types.

All of the 1 and 0 outputs (except the 1 output for RTL) are shown as a single value. The actual steady-state outputs are quite close to these values either because they are held there by a low-impedance source (as is the case for both outputs of HTL, TTL, and ECL and for the 0 output of DTL and RTL) or because of negligible loading by the circuits driven by the output (as is the case for both outputs of CMOS and for the 1 output of DTL). The 1 output for RTL depends upon the loading, giving roughly the range shown for a fan-out to a number of gate inputs between 1 and 5.

The output impedances shown in Fig. A1-3 also affect the noise-immunity characteristics of a logic type. Figure A1-4 shows a simplified version of the problem. Assume that the output of gate 1 is high when the output of gate 2 changes, as shown in Fig. A1-4b. Because the wire from gate 1 to flipflop A happens to be routed for some distance alongside of the wire from gate 2 to gate B, there is a significant amount of capacitive coupling between the two wires. As $v(t)$ and $r(t)$ drop to 0.2 V and 25 Ω, they will pull v_2 along to about 0.2 V as shown. Since the voltage *across* the capacitive coupling tends not to change instantaneously, v_1 will follow along, exhibiting a negative change of

Logic type	"O" Output impedance (ohms)	"1" Output impedance (ohms)
ECL (MECL II)	15	15
TTL (54/74)	12	140
HTL	35	1,500
RTL	25	640
DTL	25	2,000
CMOS	1,500	1,500

(a)

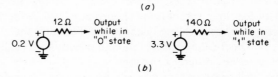

(b)

Fig. A1-3 Typical output impedances for six logic types. (a) Impedances; (b) equivalent output circuits for TTL logic.

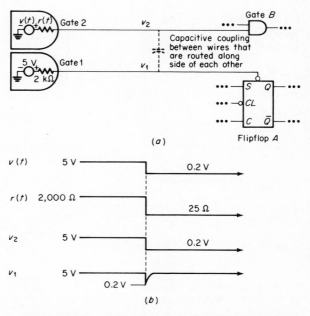

Fig. A1-4 Relationship between output impedance and noise immunity. (a) Circuit; (b) timing diagram.

approximately 5 V (under the idealized conditions shown). Now the *RC* time constant (of approximately 2,000 Ω times the amount of the capacitive coupling) will determine how fast v_1 recovers back to 5 V. With a large amount of capacitive coupling or with a large output impedance, this recovery may be slow enough to provide a pulse which will not be ignored by flipflop *A*. Instead the flipflop will inadvertently be direct preset.

In discussing the effect of low gate output impedance on noise immunity we have neglected other sources of noise such as inductive coupling between wires. We have also treated capacitive coupling as a lumped effect rather than as a distributed effect. Furthermore, there is often strong capacitive coupling to a ground plane. Assuming a constant 0 V on the ground plane, this capacitive coupling sets up a capacitive voltage divider between v_2 and v_1 and ground, as shown in Fig. A1-5. This reduces the amplitude of the pulse picked up on v_1. Although all of these factors tend to complicate the quantitative relationship between low gate output impedance and noise immunity, nevertheless the analysis presented here qualitatively illustrates the nature of the relationship.

One further consideration in selecting a logic line to meet the requirements of a certain system is the logical flexibility of the logic line. Although any logic line will meet any system specifications (if it is fast enough), some lines will

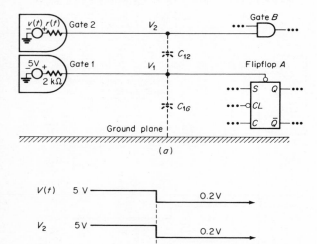

Fig. A1-5 Effect of a ground plane on the amplitude of capacitive pickup. (*a*) Circuit; (*b*) timing diagram.

permit the use of fewer integrated-circuit packages. This will reduce size slightly, may reduce cost, and (perhaps most significantly) permit the system to be clocked at a higher rate because the system can be easily implemented using fewer levels of gating. The quickest measure of this is whether or not a logic line offers dot-AND/OR capability (as indicated in Fig. A1-1). As was seen in Sec. 3-10, this not only reduces the number of gates needed to implement the combinational logic in a system, but it also reduces the number of levels of gating.

Another measure of logical flexibility is given by the *fan-out capability*† of the gates in the logic line (indicated in Fig. A1-1). If the fan-out capability is low, as with RTL, then there will be occasions when buffer inverters (with high fan-out capability) must be introduced to provide drive capability. Some of these might not be needed if a logic line had been used having gates with higher fan-out capability. Since these buffer inverters increase the number of levels of gating in the combinational circuitry, they also decrease the maximum clock rate of the system.

One example of the value of high fan-out capability is given by one special-purpose system used on an aircraft. It is an extreme example because the system is synchronously clocked at one-third the maximum toggling rate of the flipflops and permits only two levels of gating. The resulting system has over 600 ICs. Fifty percent of the gates have an actual fan-out of 6 or more. However, excluding the clock line, only three signals require more than the normal gate fan-out of 10.

Another measure of the logical flexibility of a logic line is the variety of gate types which it includes. For example, one logic line might include only NOR gates, whereas a second line might include NOR, NAND, OR, AND, and EXCLUSIVE-OR gates (as does MECL II). The price paid when using the first logic line instead of the second will be the extra inverters needed to complement those variables which are generated in negated form and are needed in asserted form (or vice versa). Again, a price is also paid in speed because of the extra levels of gating contributed by these inverters.

A1-2 GATE STRUCTURES

One view of the differences in the logic lines of Fig. A1-1 is through the differences in their gate structures. In viewing these, we shall look at the one gate type for each logic line which is most characteristic of the logic line. Thus for RTL, we will consider the NOR gate structure, although this logic line also includes OR, AND, NAND, and EXCLUSIVE-OR gates which are built with combinations of this basic NOR-gate structure. If the normal gates in a logic line have a totempole output structure to provide active pullup to the 1 state,

†The maximum number of gate inputs which can be driven by a gate output.

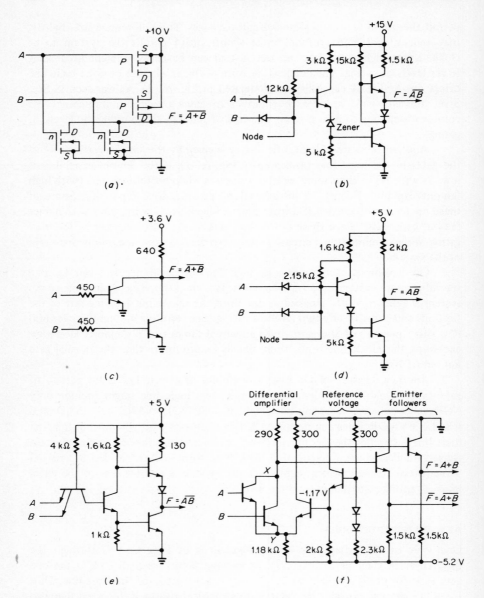

Fig. A1-6 Gate structures for six logic types. (*a*) CMOS gate; (*b*) HTL gate; (*c*) RTL gate; (*d*) DTL gate; (*e*) TTL gate (54/74); (*f*) ECL gate (MECL II).

sometimes the logic line will provide other gates either with the passive pullup of a resistor or with an open-collector output so that dot-AND/ORing can be used. Although we shall not show this modified structure, Fig. A1-1 tells when it is available.

Figure A1-6 illustrates the basic structure of a two-input gate for each of the six logic types. All but the first of these (the CMOS gate) are implemented with monolithic circuits based on bipolar transistor technology. The HTL, RTL, DTL, and TTL gates achieve their low 0 output impedance by using their (bottom) output transistors as switches and driving them into saturation. The ECL gate achieves its high speed largely by keeping its transistors out of saturation, thereby preventing the build-up of stored charge across the base-emitter junction which contributes so much to the propagation delay of *saturated-mode* logic (HTL, RTL, DTL, and TTL).

The input to a DTL gate draws negligible current from the gate which drives it, when the input is high, because of the high inverse resistance of the diode on each input. In contrast, the input to an RTL gate puts a heavy load on the output of the (RTL) gate which drives it, pulling the output down from +3.6 V. This accounts for the difference between the 1 output levels for DTL and RTL gates shown in Fig. A1-2.

The threshold voltage for DTL and TTL gates is significantly improved (i.e., increased) over that for an RTL gate because of the voltage drop across extra semiconductor junctions between the inputs and the base of the lower output transistor. This is carried to an extreme in an HTL gate, where a Zener junction causes an unusually high threshold.

Notice that all of these logic types except ECL and CMOS put very different loads on the power supply, depending on whether the output is high or low. This changing load gives rise to the need for a regulated and filtered power supply and for capacitors distributed throughout a system. Otherwise, the power and ground busses would serve to transmit signals between gates and flipflops when no such transmission is ever desired in this way. As mentioned earlier, the absence of a changing load in the balanced circuitry of an ECL gate contributes to its excellent internal noise immunity. Its low output impedance, in both states, also contributes to this excellent internal noise immunity.

A1-3 GATES AND FLIPFLOPS

In this section, we shall characterize each of the nine logic lines of Fig. A1-1 in terms of the specific gates and flipflops available in each line. This will present a somewhat incomplete picture because

1. Integrated-circuit manufacturers are constantly broadening their logic lines
2. Arrays of gates and flipflops built with medium- or large-scale integration are not included

In addition, we shall generalize somewhat in describing the flipflops available. For example, because of having a limited number of leads (perhaps 14) on an integrated-circuit package, often two flipflops are packaged together with their clock inputs tied together or with their direct clear inputs tied together or with direct preset inputs omitted. These variations will not be described.

The description of a logic line is further confused by its availability in any one of several package configurations and temperature ranges. Figure A1-7 illustrates the four common packages in which a logic line is often made available. The *flatpack* is useful for space-critical applications with a typical size, including leads, of 0.500 x 0.320 x 0.045 in high. It is the most costly package

Fig. A1-7   Package configurations. (*a*) Flatpack; (*b*) TO-5 case; (*c*) ceramic dual-in-line; (*d*) plastic dual-in-line. (*Motorola Semiconductor Products Inc.*)

and the most difficult to handle manually. The *TO-5 case* is a carryover from transistor packaging. With only 8 or 10 leads, its application to digital circuitry is very constrained. The two *dual-in-line* packages provide low cost and ease of handling (either manually or with automatic insertion equipment), and they are available in 14-pin configurations (with 0.750 x 0.300 x 0.200-in-high package). Dual-in-line packages with more pins (16, 24, or more) are especially useful for MSI circuits. The plastic dual-in-line package provides the lowest-cost approach to digital circuitry, but should not be used where humidity is high for an extended period of time or where extreme temperature cycling is a factor.

Integrated circuits are also available in several temperature ranges. Thus RTL is available in a *military* temperature range (-55 to $+125°C$), an *industrial* range (0 to $+100°C$), and a low-cost *commercial* range ($+15$ to $+55°C$). Series 54/74 TTL is available in the two temperature ranges which form the basis for the two series designations. Thus, series 54 ($-55°$ to $+125°C$) is the military series while series 74 (0 to $+70°C$) is the industrial series.

For the figures which follow, several general comments are appropriate. The propagation delays listed represent worst-case values but at $25°C$ only. The propagation delay may be somewhat higher at either or both the upper and lower limits of the temperature range. Furthermore, the propagation delay listed beside a gate or flipflop represents the longer of the two propagation delays which result in a positive transition output and a negative transition output. As was discussed in Sec. 5-6, this leads to a somewhat more conservative figure for the maximum clock rate of a system than reality actually dictates. However, it also provides the simplicity desired here.

The propagation delay is also affected by the capacitive loading on the output of a gate or flipflop. This occurs because the wiring connected to the

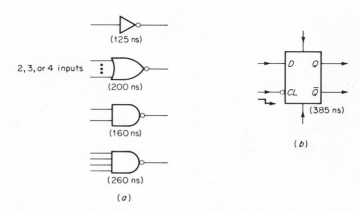

Fig. A1-8 CMOS logic elements. (*a*) Gates; (*b*) delay flipflop. (*Note:* Input impedances $\approx 10^{12} \ \Omega$; output impedances $\approx 1,500 \ \Omega$.)

output is capacitively coupled to ground and to the other wiring. The propagation delay listed in a spec sheet assumes a relatively low value of capacitive loading. If the actual capacitive loading exceeds this value (which it may often do under normal circumstances), the propagation delay will be increased to an extent determined by the output impedance of the gate. Herein

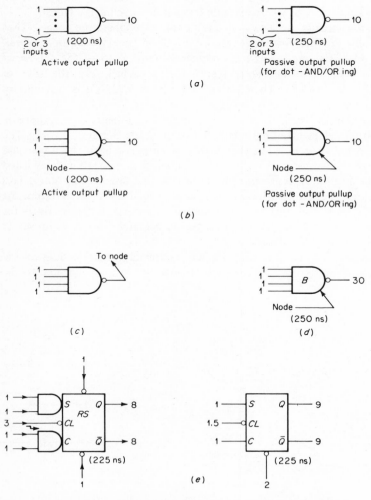

Fig. A1-9   HTL logic elements. (*a*) NAND gates; (*b*) expandable NAND gates; (*c*) expander; (*d*) expandable buffer; (*e*) flipflops.

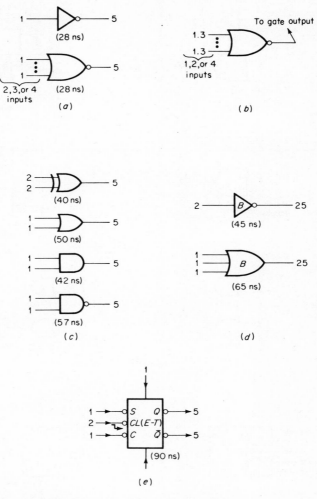

Fig. A1-10 RTL logic elements. (*a*) NOR gates and inverter; (*b*) expanders for NOR gates; (*c*) other gates; (*d*) buffers; (*e*) edge-triggered *JK* flipflops.

lies one great virtue of ECL and TTL, with their extremely low output impedances in both the 0 and 1 states.

Each of the logic lines copes in its own way with the problem of gate *fan-in*, that is, the problem of providing gates with any number of inputs. Looking at the structure of an RTL gate in Fig. A1-6*c*, we see that the fan-in can

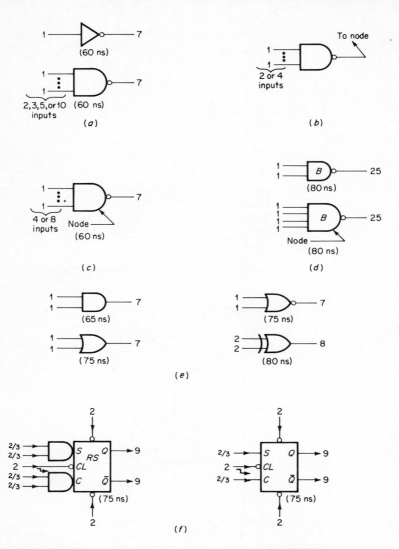

Fig. A1-11 DTL logic elements. (*a*) NAND gates and inverter (with or without open-collector output for dot-AND/ORing); (*b*) expanders; (*c*) expandable NAND gates with or without open-collector output); (*d*) buffers; (*e*) other gates; (*f*) flipflops.

be increased by tying the outputs of two gates together. However, since this results in a net load resistance of 320 Ω (two 640-Ω resistors in parallel), the loading rules are changed. Consequently, the RTL logic line includes *gate expanders*, which are nothing more than gates in which the load resistor has been omitted. By tying the outputs of any number of expanders to the output of a of a gate, the fan-in can be increased as desired.

With DTL and HTL logic the gate expanders are simply diodes which are connected to the *node* input shown in Fig. A1-6b or d. TTL logic is constrained from the use of expanders by its structure. Instead, gates are available having one, two, three, four, or eight inputs. ECL permits use of an expander, but it must be tied into the gate structure at two points (points X and Y in Fig. A1-6f).

In general, a logic line includes *buffers* in addition to the normal gates. These provide the high drive capability needed to drive clock lines and other heavy loads. The nine logic lines are described in Fig. A1-8 to A1-17. Figure A1-15 is included to illustrate that the three TTL logic lines are compatible with each other, requiring only a modification in their loading rules.

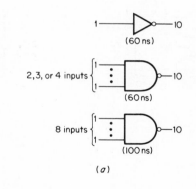

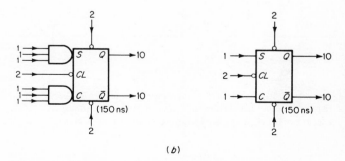

Fig. A1-12 Series 54L/74L TTL logic elements. (*a*) NAND gates; (*b*) master-slave *JK* flipflops.

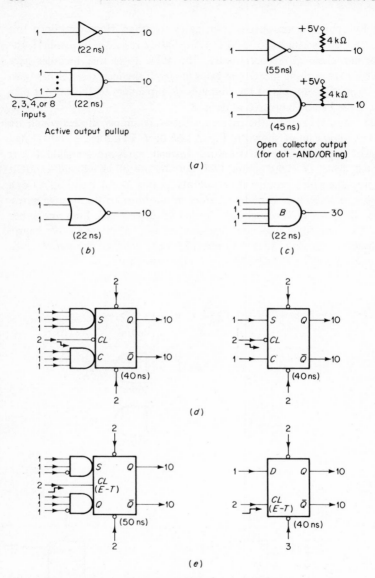

Fig. A1-13 Series 54/74 TTL logic elements. (*a*) NAND gates and inverters; (*b*) NOR gate; (*c*) buffer; (*d*) master-slave *JK* flipflops (sensitive to ⅂ transition; (*e*) edge-triggered flipflops (sensitive to ⌐ transition).

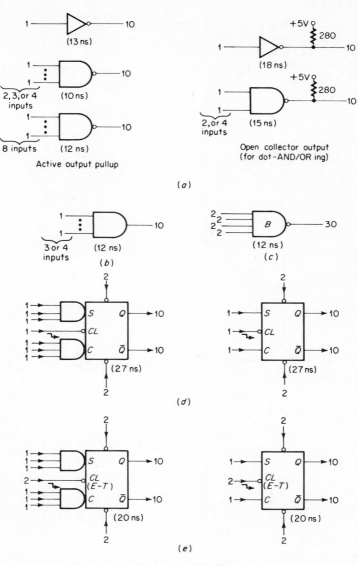

Fig. A1-14 Series 54H/74H TTL logic elements. (*a*) NAND gates and inverters; (*b*) AND gates; (*c*) buffer; (*d*) master-slave *JK* flipflops (sensitive to ⮑ transition); (*e*) edge-triggered *JK* flipflops (sensitive to ⮑ transition).

	Driven		
	54L/74L	54/74	54H/74H
Driver 54L/74L	10	1	1
54/74	40	10	8
54H/74H	50	12	10

Fig. A1-15 Loading rules for mixed TTL logic.

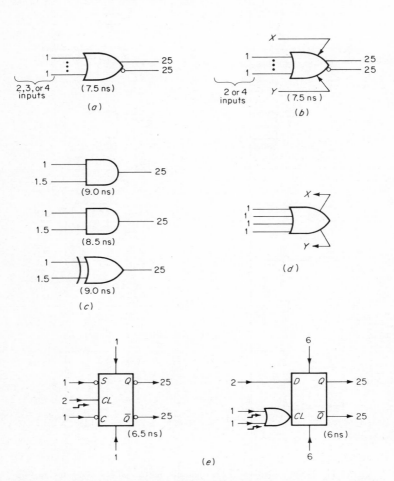

Fig. A1-16 MECL II logic elements. (*a*) OR/NOR gates; (*b*) expandable OR/NOR gates; (*c*) other gates; (*d*) expander; (*e*) flipflops. (*Note:* Propagation delays are specified at a fan-out of 3.)

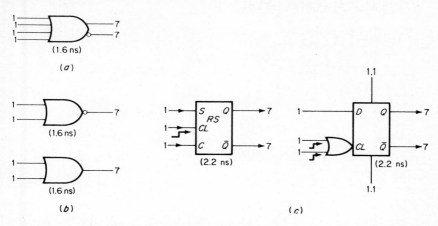

Fig. A1-17   MECL III logic elements. (*a*) OR/NOR gate; (*b*) OR and NOR gates; (*c*) flip-flops. (*Note:* Propagation delays are specified with 50 Ω load.)

REFERENCE

An excellent, in-depth discussion of different logic types, as well as a comparison of these types, is given by L. S. Garrett, Integrated Circuit Digital Logic Families, pts. I, II, and III, *IEEE Spectrum*, October, November, and December 1970.

appendix A2
One-shots

A *one-shot*† is a circuit which accepts a transition at its input and responds with a pulse on its output. Generally, the output pulsewidth can be set to any desired value. Figure A2-1a illustrates the configuration of a typical integrated-circuit one-shot—Fairchild's TTµL9602. The pulsewidth is adjusted by connecting appropriate values of R_x and C_x to the IC as shown. Its input circuitry can be constrained, as in Fig. A2-1b and c, making it sensitive to either a positive or negative transition. The direct clear input terminates the output prematurely.

Because it generates a transition (i.e., the trailing edge of the output pulse) which is unsynchronized to the clock, a one-shot is wisely used in a digital system to solve only a few specialized problems. The most common of these is to generate a relatively long pulse of perhaps 10 to 20 ms, required to drive an electromechanical device. This often occurs in the interface circuitry between a small computer and an electromechanical device driven by it. A DATA OUT instruction may generate a pulse in the interface circuitry of a few-hundred-nanoseconds duration. This is used as the input to a one-shot to generate the long pulse needed to drive the device.

†Also referred to as a *monostable multivibrator*.

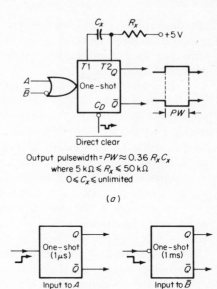

Output pulsewidth = $PW \approx 0.36\, R_x C_x$
where $5\,k\Omega \leqslant R_x \leqslant 50\,k\Omega$
$0 \leqslant C_x \leqslant$ unlimited

(a)

Input to A
$\bar{B}$ = 0 V
C_x = 100 pF
R_x = 20 kΩ
PW = 1 μs

(b)

Input to $\bar{B}$
A = +5 V
C_x = 0.3 μF
R_x = 10 kΩ
PW = 1 ms

(c)

Fig. A2-1 Fairchild's TTμL9602 dual retriggerable resettable one-shot. (*a*) one circuit; (*b*) rising edge triggering; (*c*) falling edge triggering.

Another use of one-shots occurs where the clock for a system is derived from the *bit clock* of a magnetic disc memory. This bit clock serves well for single-phase clocking. However, if three or four clock phases are desired, these cannot be derived in the normal way—from the decoded outputs of a counter driven by a faster clock. Instead, the bit clock can drive a chain of one-shots to obtain these clock phases, as shown in Fig. A2-2. For the reasons which follow in this appendix, this is an undesirable procedure to use in general but one which cannot be easily avoided in this case.

In general, it is worthwhile to give considerable weight to any alternatives to using a one-shot where one seems needed. Over the years, one-shots have gained a reputation among many digital designers as the "black sheep" of the digital family. They have gained this reputation for one reason. So many times the faulty operation of a system has been traced to a one-shot which is blithely generating pulses on its output without corresponding transitions occurring on its input. The one-shot might be inadvertently responding to a *glitch* in the power-supply voltage or on the ground line. Or it might be triggered inadvertently by noise pickup feeding back into the circuit on a wire connected to the output. This latter problem can be avoided by isolating the outputs from the one-shot's timing circuitry with inverters. A third cause of trouble arises when the $R_x C_x$ network, which determines the output pulsewidth, is brought out to a front or rear panel where it can be conveniently trimmed. These components reach right in to the most noise-sensitive part of the one-shot. Consequently, the long leads to the front or rear panel invite trouble in the form of noise pickup.

The revolution in circuit design brought on by integrated-circuit manufacture has yielded great benefits here. Knowing that a successful one-shot design will be used in a variety of applications, there is every incentive to design an IC one-shot which is free of "black-sheep" problems. Thus, the one-shot of Fig. A2-1 is insensitive to noise on an output line. It is insensitive to glitches on the power-supply line. Finally, it lists a specification on the maximum allowable stray capacitance (50 pF) at the timing nodes $T1$ and $T2$, thus providing insensitivity to noise from this vulnerable source.

Even when a one-shot is working correctly, it still has its share of undesirable characteristics:

1. Because a one-shot provides an analog-derived delay (derived from the $R_x C_x$ time constant), the digital system using it is subjected to the *reliability problem* of having either too short or too long a delay for the purpose intended. In contrast, if the required pulse is derived with gates and flipflops from a system clock, then the tolerance on its pulsewidth is equal to the tolerance on the clock rate.
2. In setting up a system which includes one-shots, often the pulsewidths must be aligned by adjusting potentiometers. This *alignment problem* is completely avoided when all pulses are derived with flipflops and gates.

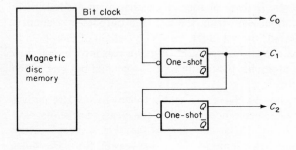

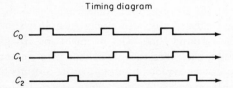

Fig. A2-2 Deriving clock phases with one-shots.

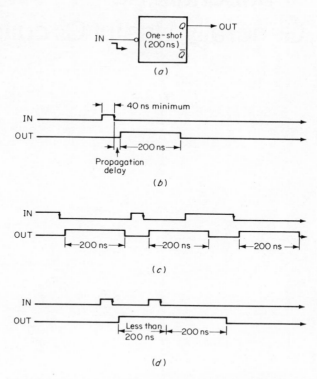

Fig. A2-3   One-shot responses to successive inputs. (*a*) Circuit; (*b*)single pulse input; (*c*) isolated transition inputs; (*d*) retriggering.

3. Often, it is desirable to debug a system by stepping it through its operation one clock pulse at a time. If the system includes one-shots, they may work fine when operations proceed at this slow rate but give trouble at the normal clock rate. This might happen if, at the normal clock rate, the input to the one-shot changes during the output pulse. This might affect the output pulse in a way which was not foreseen by the designer and which is detrimental to the system operation. At the slow rate, the conditions causing the problem are no longer present. In contrast, a system which ties all operations to the clock can be slowed down for debugging. The time relationships between all signals will remain unchanged.

A final point in the definition of a specific one-shot concerns its response to another input in the middle of an output pulse. The TTμL9602 one-shot is *retriggerable*. This means that it will reestablish its timing cycle from the new trigger input. This is illustrated with several examples in Fig. A2-3 for a TTμL9602 one-shot set up with a 200-ns pulsewidth.

appendix A3
Generally Useful Circuits

A3-1 SCALERS AND COUNTERS

In designing digital systems, there is a recurring need for scalers and counters of one period or another. As indicated in Sec. 5-5, the design of simple scalers is not a straightforward problem. Because of this, scalers with various periods are presented in this section. These are developed using the following approaches:

1. Modification of an asynchronous binary counter to obtain any period
2. Tabulation of simple synchronous scalers for periods of 2 to 16
3. Binary and 8421 BCD code counters
4. Tabulation of pseudorandom noise generators (synchronous scalers with period = $2^n - 1$)

For all of these, we shall develop *self-starting* designs which count themselves into the desired count sequence regardless of their initial state. Thus, a scale-of-10 scaler designed around four flipflops might start up, when power is turned on, in any of 16 states. Six of these are not in the count sequence. If the scaler is self-starting, the scaler will count from any of these six states into the scale-of-10 count sequence.

The use of an asynchronous binary counter to obtain any period is attractive because *any* period can be achieved in this way using a simple intuitive approach. Figure A3-1 illustrates the design implemented with typical *JK* flipflops and NAND gates. Its correct operation takes advantage of the fact that in counting down, an asynchronous binary down counter is never momentarily in the zero state as it asynchronously ripples from one state to the next state. Thus, the zero-detecting NAND gate will never generate a spurious pulse which will set the latch circuit at the wrong time. The function of the latch circuit is to hold the number N on the counter during the presetting operation long enough to override the rippling which occurs. This is also the reason why the flipflops must be direct cleared as well as direct preset. Using this same approach, a scale-of-N scaler can be designed with an 8421 BCD code down counter. Thumbwheel switches can be used to preset the counter to N.

For those cases where a simple, low-cost scaler design is needed, Fig. A3-2 illustrates self-starting synchronous scalers with periods from 2 to 16. For simplicity, the clock inputs are not shown, but because the circuits are all synchronous, the clock inputs to the flipflops of each scaler should be tied together and to a clock source. The count sequence for each scaler is shown to the right of its circuit. Each state of the scaler is represented as a binary number.

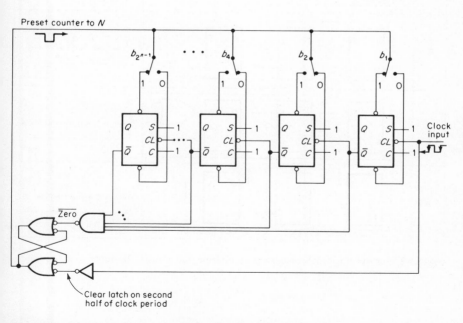

Fig. A3-1 Asynchronous scale-of-N scaler. Circuit operation: (1) Asynchronous binary down counter counts down to zero; (2) NAND gate detects zero and sets latch, which, in turn, presets counter to N where N is set on switches or permanently wired in; (3) latch is cleared.

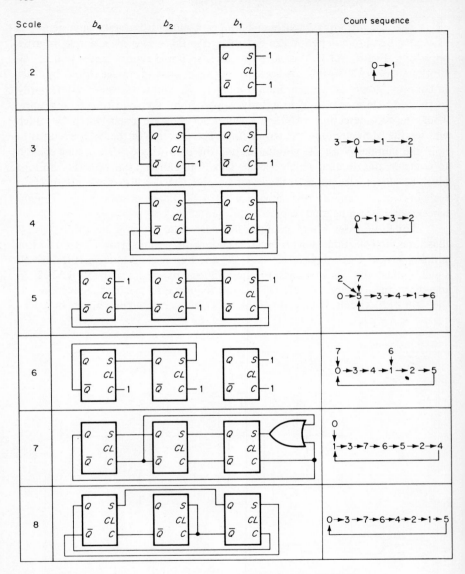

Fig. A3-2 Self-starting synchronous scalers implemented with *JK* flipflops.

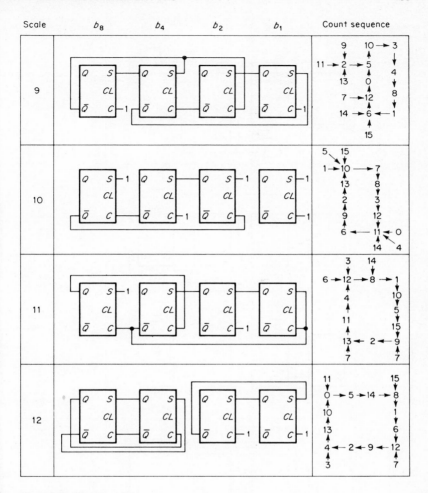

Fig. A3-2 (Continued)

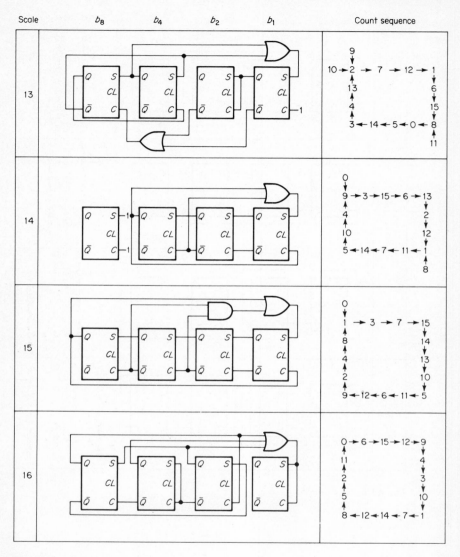

Fig. A3-2 (Continued)

Often a binary counter is needed for one purpose or another in a digital system. Figure A3-3 illustrates several possibilities, including two asynchronous designs and one synchronous design. Figure A3-4 shows a modular design which retains much of the simplicity of asynchronous design while coming close to the speed of synchronous design. The 3-bit module for this design is shown in Fig. A3-4a. If, when the clock transition occurs, the gate input (GI) equals 1, then this module counts; otherwise, it does not. Note that a module tells the module to its left to count (GO = 1) if it is in state 111 and if its gate input = 1. Then, when the clock transition occurs, not only will it count from state 111 to state 000, but the next module will also count. All modules are clocked by a common clock source, and no flipflop in a module receives its transition more than one flipflop propagation delay after the transition of this common clock source. Consequently, the entire counter settles out within two flipflop propagation delays.

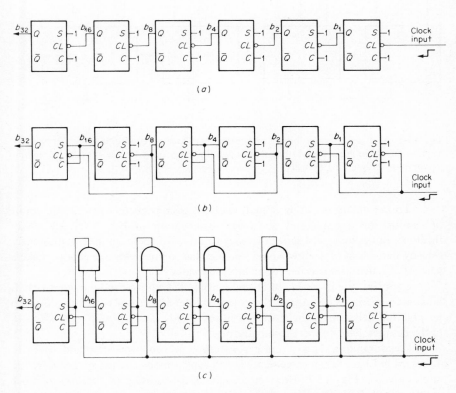

Fig. A3-3 Binary up counter. (a) Asynchronous design; (b) asynchronous design with half the maximum settling time of the circuit in (a); (c) synchronous design.

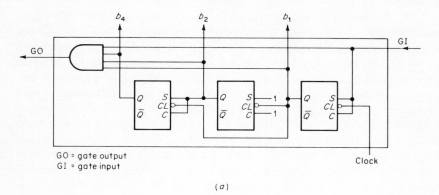

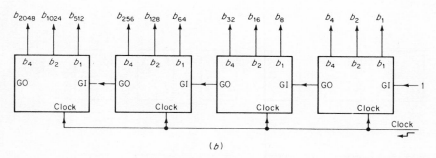

Fig. A3-4   Fast asynchronous binary up counter. (*a*) Three-bit counter module; (*b*) twelve-bit counter whose maximum settling time is two flipflop propagation delays (the maximum gate-output settling time is longer).

To use binary counting operationally, it is convenient to be able to count up, count down, not count, or preset. The circuit of Fig. A3-5 uses delay flipflops, full adders, and serial switches to do all of these things synchronously for any number of bits. How would you use this counter plus one gate to make a scale-of-N synchronous scaler for an arbitrary value of N?

Counting up in 8421 BCD code using the above modular approach is illustrated in Fig. A3-6. Again, the entire counter settles out within two flipflop propagation delays after the clock transition regardless of the number of decades in the counter. This counter is self-starting.

Pseudorandom binary noise generators, whose properties and uses are discussed in Chap. 8, can be generated with synchronous circuits specified by the table shown in Fig. A3-7. These circuits are designed using *JK* flipflops in either of two ways. With the clear input made equal to the set input, it becomes a toggle (*T*) flipflop. On the other hand, with the clear input made equal to the

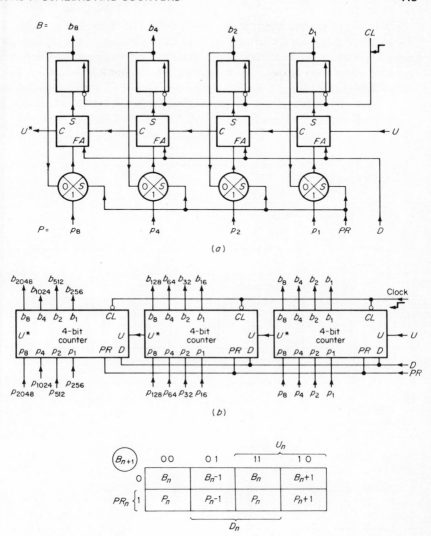

Fig. A3-5 Synchronous presettable up-down binary counter. (*a*) Four-bit counter; (*b*) twelve-bit modular counter; (*c*) operation.

complement of the set input, it becomes a delay (D) flipflop. The toggle input T_n to the flipflop on the left X_n is equal to the output of the flipflop on the right X_1 sometimes EXCLUSIVE-ORed with the output of another flipflop. The required connection is specified in the right-hand column of Fig. A3-7. The use of the data in this table is exemplified for two cases, $n = 5$ and $n = 8$, in Fig. A3-8.

These implementations of pseudorandom binary noise generators using delay and toggle flipflops require less EXCLUSIVE-ORing than the more commonly used implementations[†] which use only delay flipflops. This occurs

[†]See S. Golomb, "Digital Communications with Space Applications," fig. 2.10, Prentice-Hall, Englewood Cliffs, N.J., 1964.

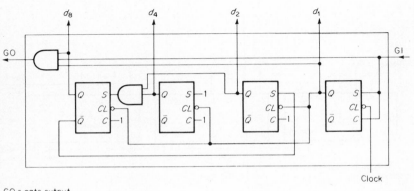

GO = gate output

GI = gate input

(a)

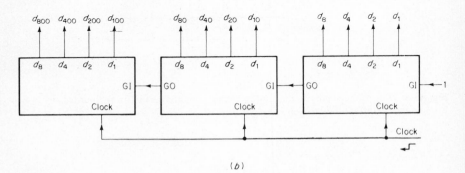

(b)

Fig. A3-6   8421 BCD code asynchronous up counter. (a) Decade counter; (b) three-decade counter (maximum settling time equals two flipflop propagation delays).

n	20	19	18	17	16	15	14	13	12	11	10	9	8	7	6	5	4	3	2	1	Toggle input to nth flipflop
2																			T	D	$T_2 = X_1$
3																		T	D	D	$T_3 = X_1$
4																	T	D	D	D	$T_4 = X_1$
5																T	T	D	D	D	$T_5 = X_1$
6															T	D	D	D	D	D	$T_6 = X_1$
7														T	D	D	D	D	D	D	$T_7 = X_1$
8													T	T	T	T	D	D	T	T	$T_8 = X_1 \oplus X_4$
9												T	T	T	T	D	D	D	D	D	$T_9 = X_1$
10											T	T	T	T	T	T	T	D	D	D	$T_{10} = X_1$
11										T	T	D	D	D	D	D	D	D	D	D	$T_{11} = X_1$
12									T	T	T	T	T	T	D	D	T	T	T	T	$T_{12} = X_1 \oplus X_6$
13								T	T	T	T	T	T	D	D	T	T	T	T	T	$T_{13} = X_1 \oplus X_9$
14							T	T	T	T	D	D	D	D	D	T	T	T	T	T	$T_{14} = X_1 \oplus X_6$
15						T	D	D	D	D	D	D	D	D	D	D	D	D	D	D	$T_{15} = X_1$
16					T	T	T	T	T	D	D	D	D	D	D	T	T	T	T	T	$T_{16} = X_1 \oplus X_{11}$
17				T	T	T	T	T	D	D	D	D	D	D	D	D	D	D	D	D	$T_{17} = X_1$
18			T	T	T	T	T	T	T	T	T	T	T	D	D	D	D	D	D	D	$T_{18} = X_1$
19		T	T	T	T	T	T	D	D	D	D	D	D	T	T	T	T	T	T	T	$T_{19} = X_1 \oplus X_{14}$
20	T	T	T	T	T	T	T	T	T	T	T	T	T	T	T	T	T	D	D	D	$T_{20} = X_1$

Fig. A3-7 Pseudorandom binary noise generators.

because a toggle flipflop implements an EXCLUSIVE-OR function between its input and its output. Thus, if T_n and Q_n represent the input and output of a toggle flipflop during one clock period and if Q_{n+1} represents the output during the next clock period, then

$$Q_{n+1} = Q_n \oplus T_n$$

Since each generator, specified in Fig. A3-7, is a scale-of-(2^{n-1}) scaler, the question arises as to whether these scalers are self-starting. It can be easily checked that, in every case, the one state not included in the count sequence is all zeros and that if the scaler starts in this state, it will remain in this state. Thus, the scalers are not self-starting. Since this is the only state missing from the count sequence, any scaler can be made self-starting by ANDing the negated outputs of every flipflop and using this to direct preset any one of the flipflops.

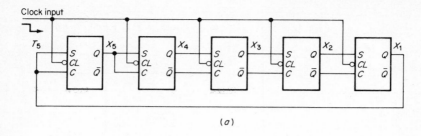

(a)

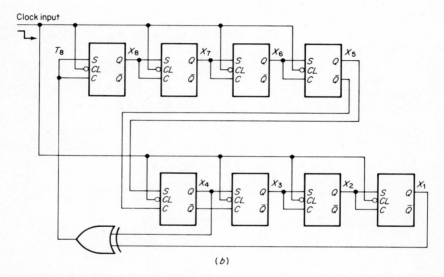

(b)

Fig. A3-8   Examples of pseudorandom binary noise generators. (a) Generator for $n = 5$; (b) generator for $n = 8$.

A3-2   CIRCUITS FOR SERIAL SYSTEM ORGANIZATION

Two useful circuits for serially organized systems are the serial switch shown in Fig. A3-9a and the switched-input delay flipflop shown in Fig. A3-9b. These permit data to be routed synchronously in a system.

The circuits which follow were all designed synchronously and then modified to handle initializing with a separate clock phase C_2. Although this necessitates the generation of more than the one clock phase required of a synchronous system, it simplifies the timing of the initializing operations. Thus, if the serial operator must be initialized to begin an operation on each word in a recirculation loop, then using a separate clock phase for initializing permits initializing when the bit counter is in state $B0$. In contrast, synchronous initializing requires initializing signals to be generated during the previous clock period. For some of the serial operators which follow, the initializing action depends upon the operation to be performed. Since the operation changes with the change of a word, array, or recirculation, this means that the information needed for initializing is conveniently available during state $B0$ and not during the previous clock period.

In this section, we shall consider the following types of serial operations carried out on numbers which appear serially, least significant bit first:

1. Arithmetic operators for numbers coded in sign plus two's complement code
2. Arithmetic operators for numbers coded in sign plus ten's complement (8421 BCD) code
3. Code conversion operators

In Sec. 6-4, we developed an *up-down-pass-clear* serial operator for sign plus two's complement numbers which would count a number up one or down one, which would pass the number unchanged, or which would clear the number to zero. Figure A3-10 illustrates an *add-subtract-up-down-pass-clear* serial

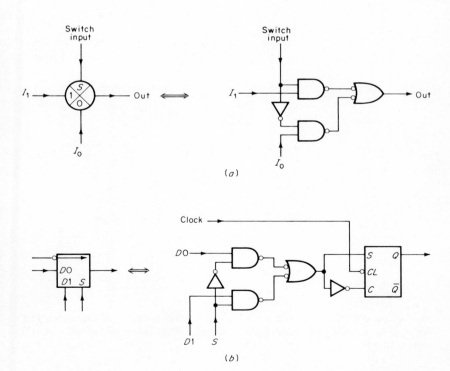

Fig. A3-9 Some equivalent circuits. (*a*) Serial switch; (*b*) switched-input delay flipflop.

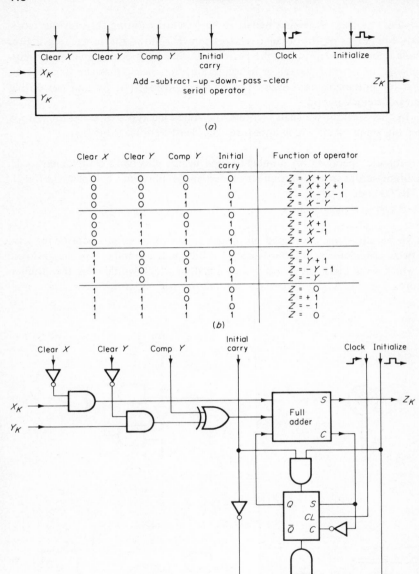

Clear X	Clear Y	Comp Y	Initial carry	Function of operator
O	O	O	O	$Z = X + Y$
O	O	O	1	$Z = X + Y + 1$
O	O	1	O	$Z = X - Y - 1$
O	O	1	1	$Z = X - Y$
O	1	O	O	$Z = X$
O	1	O	1	$Z = X + 1$
O	1	1	O	$Z = X - 1$
O	1	1	1	$Z = X$
1	O	O	O	$Z = Y$
1	O	O	1	$Z = Y + 1$
1	O	1	O	$Z = -Y - 1$
1	O	1	1	$Z = -Y$
1	1	O	O	$Z = 0$
1	1	O	1	$Z = +1$
1	1	1	O	$Z = -1$
1	1	1	1	$Z = 0$

(b)

(c)

Fig. A3-10 An add-subtract-up-down-pass-clear serial operator for sign plus two's complement numbers. (a) Form of serial operator; (b) definition of control inputs; (c) implementation.

operator which will implement any of the operations shown in Fig. A3-10b, depending on the state of the four control inputs during the operation. The circuit performs its various operations by organizing them around a full adder. The function of "Clear X" is to run either X or zero into the top input of the full adder. Similarly, "Clear Y" generates a number W, which is either equal to Y or to zero. "Comp Y" either leaves W alone or complements W bit by bit (i.e., forms the one's complement of W). Depending upon its value, "Initial carry" steers the initialize pulse into either the direct preset or the direct clear input of the flipflop.

Counting X up one is performed by adding zero to X, together with an initial carry of 1. Counting X down one is performed by adding all 1s to X, together with an initial carry of 0. Subtracting Y from X is performed by adding X to the one's complement of Y, together with an initial carry of 1.

The implementation of this serial operator with series 54/74 TTL (or some other logic line) can be simplified with the two equivalences shown in Fig. A3-11. The first equivalence points out that complementing all inputs and outputs of a full adder yields a full adder (which can be verified from the truth table for a full adder). By using these equivalences and permitting some of the control inputs to be given in negated form, the circuit of Fig. A3-12 results.

For sign plus ten's complement (8421 BCD) code counting, the circuit for sign plus two's complement code counting can be augmented and used. The augmentation looks at each digit after it has been counted. If it has been counted up to 10 (1010) or down to 15 (1111), then this digit must be corrected. Also the sign plus two's complement serial operator must be

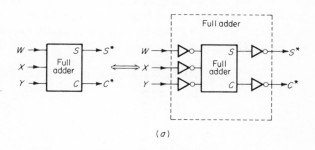

(a)

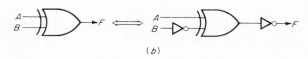

(b)

Fig. A3-11   Two equivalences. (a) Full-adder equivalence; (b) EXCLUSIVE-OR-gate equivalence.

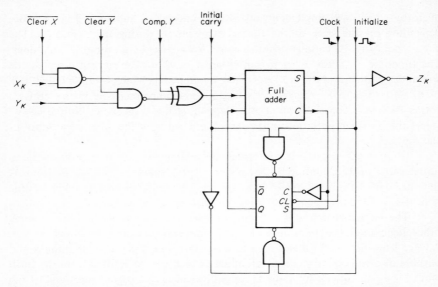

Fig. A3-12 Series 54/74 TTL implementation of the serial operator of Fig. A3-10.

reinitialized in order to count the next digit. The implementation for sign plus three digit numbers is shown in Fig. A3-13, where the control inputs are defined in Fig. 6-18b. Note that whereas the serial operator of Fig. 6-18 has no delay between input and output, this serial operator includes 4 bits of delay between input and output. By using switched-input delay flipflops for these 4 bits, they can be viewed at the end of each digit (when the bit counter is in state $B4$ or $B8$ or $B12$ for three-digit numbers) and if a correction needs to be made, it can be shifted in. These corrections are

$$10 \text{ to } 0 \qquad \underbrace{\boxed{\begin{array}{c|c|c|c}K & L & M & N \\ \hline 1 & 0 & 1 & 0\end{array}} \boxed{X}}_{10} \xrightarrow{\text{shift}} \underbrace{\boxed{X} \boxed{\begin{array}{c|c|c|c}K & L & M & N \\ \hline 0 & 0 & 0 & 0\end{array}}}_{0}$$

$$15 \text{ to } 9 \qquad \underbrace{\boxed{\begin{array}{c|c|c|c}K & L & M & N \\ \hline 1 & 1 & 1 & 1\end{array}} \boxed{X}}_{15} \xrightarrow{\text{shift}} \underbrace{\boxed{X} \boxed{\begin{array}{c|c|c|c}K & L & M & N \\ \hline 1 & 0 & 0 & 1\end{array}}}_{9}$$

Notice that the correction affects only bits L, M, and N. The fifth bit on the right is shown here for clarity. It represents the first bit to the right of flipflop N in the recirculation loop.

Although an *add-subtract-up-down-pass-clear* serial operator for sign plus ten's complement numbers can be developed using a similar approach, this will not be done because of the accumulation of complexity which results. Instead, the ideas involved will be demonstrated with an *add-pass-clear* serial operator.

The circuit of Fig. A3-14 represents a serial version of the 8421 BCD code addition algorithm developed in Chap. 8. The full adder and carry flipflop on the left add each digit of X and Y together serially (if their inputs are enabled) as if they were binary numbers. The result can be anywhere between 0 and 19. When the system timing circuitry's bit counter is in state $B4$, $B8$, or $B12$ (for three-digit numbers), this 5-bit result $b_{16}b_8b_4b_2b_1$ is available in carry, K, L, M, and N. If this number is less than 10, then it represents the correct result and should be left unchanged. The circuitry implements this by leaving all zeros in the lower 3-bit shift register. Then the full adder (and its carry flipflop) on the right will add zero to this result. If, on the other hand, this number is 10 or greater, this will be detected by the Boolean function

$$b_{16} + b_8b_4 + b_8b_2$$

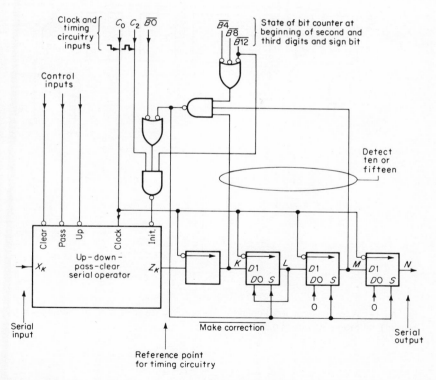

Fig. A3-13 Up-down-pass-clear serial operator for sign plus ten's complement (8421 BCD) numbers.

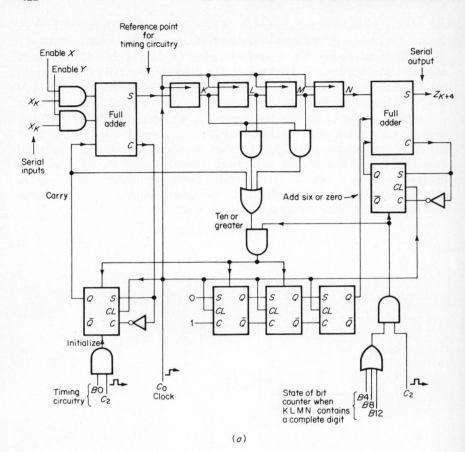

(a)

Enable X	Enable Y	Function of operator
0	0	$Z = 0$
0	1	$Z = Y$
1	0	$Z = X$
1	1	$Z = X + Y$

(b)

Fig. A3-14 Add-pass-clear serial operator for sign plus ten's complement numbers. (a) Circuit; (b) definition of control inputs.

which is implemented as

Carry + KL + KM

If this function is equal to 1, the carry flipflop is direct preset to 1 in order to add one to the next decade. The lower 3-bit shift register is direct preset to 6:

(0)110

This is the correction which must be added to the result of the first binary addition in order to obtain the correct 8421 BCD coded representation.

Again, notice that this serial operator introduces the same 4 bits of delay into the recirculation loop as were introduced by the counting serial operator of

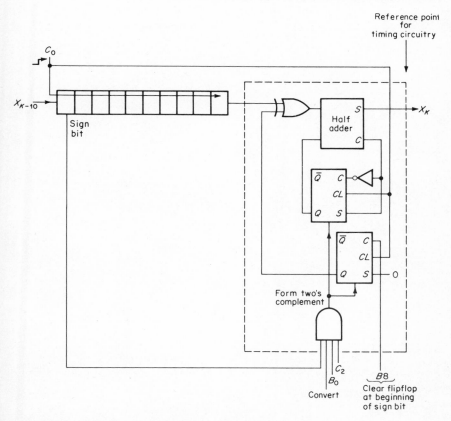

Fig. A3-15 Magnitude-two's complement conversion serial operator.

Fig. A3-13. Consequently, if the recirculation loop were set up to hold 256 sign plus three-digit numbers (256 x 13 = 3328 bits), then 4 of these 3,328 bits would be taken up by this serial operator.

The conversion of a number from sign plus two's complement code to sign plus magnitude code or vice versa is shown in Fig. A3-15, being carried out on 10-bit numbers. Notice that although the operator itself adds no bits of delay to the recirculation loop, it does require access to the sign bit of a number at the same time that its least significant bit is at the reference point. Regardless of whether the conversion is to or from sign plus magnitude code, the algorithm operates as follows. If the sign bit is 0, the number is left unchanged. If the sign bit is 1, then all bits except the sign bit are complemented and one is added to the result. This forms the two's complement of the number, which is what is needed. The sign bit is left unchanged since it is not complemented and since a carry cannot propagate all the way to the sign bit.

appendix A4
System Implementation

A4-1 SYSTEMS ORGANIZED AROUND A SMALL COMPUTER

The implementation of a system organized around a dedicated small computer will generally consist of some or all of the following components:

1. The small computer in a rack-mountable case
2. Circuitry for augmenting the computer's processing capability
3. Interfacing circuitry
4. Input, output, and auxiliary memory devices

Components 2 and 3 can be met within the main frame of the computer itself for many computers and for fairly extensive circuitry. For example, Data General's NOVA computer, shown in Fig. 6-28, has slots for seven 15 x 15 in printed circuit boards, two of which are used by the central processor. The remaining five slots are all wired to the memory and I/O buses. Each memory module of $4K$ words requires one slot. The remaining slots can be used by boards of the type shown in Fig. A4-1 and wired with TTL logic. Each board has room for 96 integrated circuits, which is sufficient for several interfaces.

Fig. A4-1 Interface board for the NOVA computer. (*Data General Corp.*)

A more modular approach is provided by the PDP-11 computer of Digital Equipment Corporation (DEC), shown in Fig. 6-29. DEC has a large line of modules, like the five modules shown in Fig. A4-2, which plug into slots within the computer. A PDP-11 computer configured with 4K words of memory has room within the computer for 44 extra modules. The interconnections are made by wire-wrapping between the connector terminals shown in Fig. A4-2. The variety of modules available extends from flipflops and gates to interfacing modules for address selection and for interrupt control. It also includes low-level data acquisition modules and drivers for switching inductive loads.

If the room available for circuitry within a computer is not sufficient for the system needs, the computer manufacturer may provide a rack-mountable box for holding further circuitry. Alternatively, one of the approaches discussed in the next section can be used.

Systems components which are to be located adjacent to the computer can be mounted along with the computer in a rack like the one shown in Fig. A4-3. These might include a disc memory or a low-level data acquisition unit. If a display-console like that shown in Fig. 7-13 is included in the system, a console such as the one shown in Fig. A4-4 is particularly convenient.

A4-2 SYSTEMS ORGANIZED AROUND A SPECIAL-PURPOSE STRUCTURE

Putting together a system which is organized around a special-purpose structure involves many of the same considerations discussed in the last section. The logic can be implemented in any of several ways. One approach is to use logic modules which plug into wire-wrap connectors. A complete package of modules, connectors, and power supply is available from any of the many companies

Fig. A4-2 System unit holding five modules for the PDP-11 computer. (*Digital Equipment Corp.*)

Fig. A4-3   Rack for holding system components. (*Scientific Atlanta, Inc.*)

which make modules. The package can be configured into a rack-mountable panel having one or two rows of logic modules for small systems or into one or more rack-mountable drawers for larger systems. Figure A4-5 illustrates one of these drawers.

Another approach is to use a dual-in-line packaging panel such as that shown in Fig. A4-6. The panel shown is a *universal* panel which will accept not only the standard 14-pin dual-in-line packages but also the larger dual-in-lines used for medium-scale integration. Alternatively, a panel can be used which is laid out strictly for 14-pin dual-in-lines and for which the power is prewired. With power and ground planes on the top and bottom of the board, this approach provides good noise immunity. The interconnections can be wire-wrapped manually with a wire-wrap gun like that shown in Fig. A4-7.

Fig. A4-4 Console for holding system components. (*Scientific Atlanta, Inc.*)

Fig. A4-5 Implementing a system with logic modules. (*Electronic Engineering Co. of California—EECo.*)

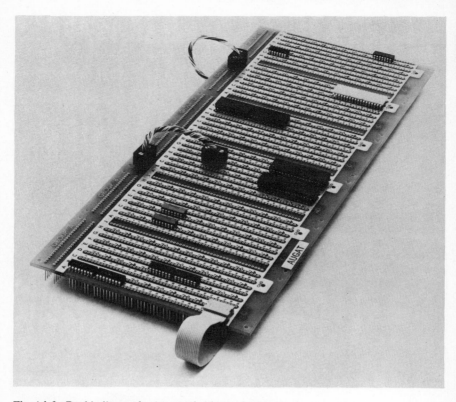

Fig. A4-6 Dual-in-line packaging panel. (*Augat, Inc.*)

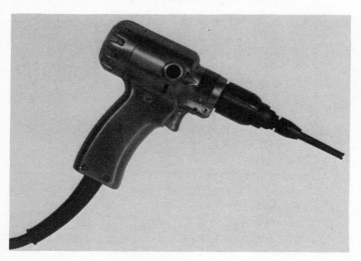

Fig. A4-7 Wire-wrap gun. (*Gardner-Denver Co.*)

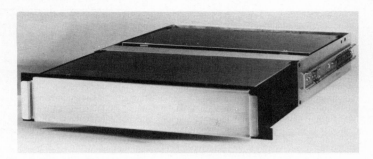

Fig. A4-8 Rack-mountable chassis which holds two dual-in-line packaging panels. (*IFE/Division of Plastic Mold & Engineering Co.*)

For the production assembly of systems, a panel can be automatically wire-wrapped. This service is generally available from the manufacturer of packaging panels or, for a system built with logic modules, from the manufacturer of the logic modules. By providing "carbon-copies" of a working system, automatic wire-wrapping eliminates the large debugging problem associated with manual wiring.

Rack-mounting the circuitry which is implemented on a dual-in-line packaging panel like that of Fig. A4-6 is facilitated with a chassis like that of Fig. A4-8. A variety of configurations permit the implementation of both small and large systems in this manner.

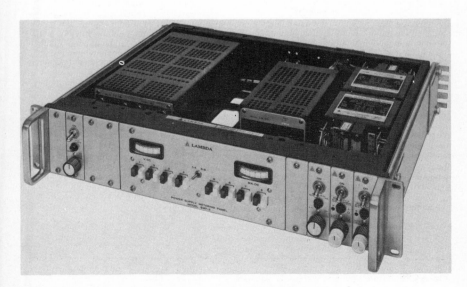

Fig. A4-9 Modular power supply. (*Lambda Electronics Corp.*)

General	
Power supply	Maintain ripple $\leq 5\%$ Maintain regulation $\leq 5\%$ RF bypass supply primary
Decoupling	Decouple every 5 to 10 packages with RF capacitors of 0.01 to 0.1 μF.
Grounding	A ground plane is desirable, especially when the pc board contains a large number of packages. If no ground plane is used, incorporate ground bus around pc board periphery where possible. Make ground bus as wide as possible. Always return both ends of long ground bus to common point (system ground).

Gates	
Data input rise and fall times	Reduce as driver output impedance increases. Should be no greater than $1\mu s$ for $Z_0 \geq 100 \ \Omega$.
Data pulse width	Maintain above 29 ns.
Unused inputs of AND and NAND gates and unused preset and clear inputs of flipflops	Tie directly to $+V_{CC}$ where V_{CC} is guaranteed to *always* be ≤ 5.5 V or Tie to V_{CC} through resistor $\geq 1 \ k\Omega$. Several unused inputs can be tied to one resistor. or Tie to used input of same gate if maximum fanout of driving device will not be exceeded or Tie to unused gate output where unused gate input is grounded.
Unused inputs of NOR gates	Tie to used input of same gate if maximum fanout of driving device will not be exceeded or Tie to ground.
Unused gates	Tie inputs of unused gates to ground for lowest power drain.
Increasing gate/ buffer fan-out	Parallel gates / buffers of same package.
Expanders	Place expanders as close as possible to the gate being expanded and avoid capacitive loading of the expander nodes if switching speed is to be maintained.

Flipflops	
Preset and clear pulses	If clock pulse is present, maintain preset or clear pulse until clock pulse goes low.
Clock pulse	Rise and fall times should be less than 150 ns to improve noise immunity.
Input data	In general, input data of master−slave JK flipflops should not be changed while the clock pulse is high. Consult data sheet for possible exceptions.

Line Driving and Receiving	
Single − wire interconnections	May be used up to approximately 10 in without particular precaution. A ground plane is always desirable. If longer than 10 in, ground plane is mandatory with wire routed as close to it as possible. Use twisted pair or coax for lengths exceeding 20 in.
Coaxial and twisted pair cables	Design around approximately 100 Ω characteristic impedance. Higher impedances increase crosstalk while lower impedances are difficult to drive. (*a*) Coaxial cable of 93 Ω impedance (such as Microdot 293− 3913) is recommended (*b*) For twisted pair, Nos. 26 or 28 wire with thin insulation twisted about 30 turns / foot work well.
Transmission-line ground	Ensure that transmission−line ground returns are carried through at both transmitting and receiving ends.
Resistive pull−up	Use 500 to 1,000 Ω resistive pullup at *receiving* end of long cables for added noise margin and more rapid rise times.
Line termination	Reverse terminate with 27 to 47 Ω at *driving* end in series with the line to prevent negative overshoot.
Gates as line drivers	Drive into only one transmission− line terminated with one gate input. Adverse effects from multiple loads include: (*a*) Erroneous signals due to line reflections (*b*) Long delay times (*c*) Excessive driver loading
Gates as line receivers	Use only one gate input to terminate line. Follow unused input rules for receiver gates.
Flipflops as line drivers	Generally unsatisfactory due to the possibility of collector commutation from reflected signals.
Decoupling	Always decouple driving / receiving devices in addition to normal decoupling. Use 0.1 μF RF capacitors located at V_{CC} and ground pins.

Fig. A4-10   Guidelines for system design with series 54/74 TTL.

Supplying power to a system generally requires several voltages. The logic may use one voltage with a heavy current requirement, lights may use another voltage, while data acquisition circuitry may use several more. These varied requirements are easily met with the modular approach taken by several power supply manufacturers. Figure A4-9 illustrates a rack-mountable unit containing several power supply modules. Everything in this unit is provided on an optional basis, including front panel controls and metering. Even the cables which connect each module to the front and rear panels are available as standard parts.

A4-3 GUIDELINES FOR SYSTEM DESIGN

In using a specific logic line, a variety of practical questions invariably arise. Some of these are resolved by the integrated-circuit manufacturer in the data book on the logic line or in application notes. The companies which manufacture logic modules in printed circuit board form provide another source for this type of information. As an example of the sort of questions which arise and answers to them, consider Fig. A4-10. These are Texas Instruments' guidelines for using their series 54/74 TTL line of logic.[†]

†From H. Bonner, To Optimize TTL Performance, *Electronic Products,* December 1968, p. 52.

appendix A5
Automatic Malfunction Detection

Joseph H. Mehaffey, Jr.
Chief Circuit Design Engineer
Lockheed—Georgia Company

A5-1 SYSTEM DESIGN WITH THE USER IN MIND

Over the past decade, electronic equipment has become increasingly sophisticated. With this sophistication has come increased capability and performance that has caused a revolution in the electronics industry. Progress, unfortunately, has not yielded solutions to all problems. Two of the most elusive solutions have been to the twin problems of reliability and maintainability. Users of complex electronic systems have scant knowledge of the inner workings of machines such as radars and computers. Even such simple devices as electronic counters are a mystery to 90 percent of those who use them in industry. Yet, these same nonelectronically educated individuals must utilize the equipment, detect equipment malfunctions, and make module repairs such as printed-circuit-board replacements.

This broad use of electronic equipment has generated a new burden for the electronic designer. In addition to the usual requirement to design useful and highly reliable equipment, the designer must now plan to alert an equipment operator to an equipment malfunction. One might question whether such malfunction detection is required or even desirable. Let us take an example. Suppose a steel manufacturer is utilizing a small computer to control a strip mill. If the computer or peripheral equipment should develop a malfunction, causing the annealing temperature to become erratic, a large production loss could result before laboratory analysis detected the error. The question then arises, "How can the designer cope with this problem?" The answer lies in designing the equipment in such a way that abnormal behavior can be detected by circuits built into the equipment.

Electronic system designers first resolved automatic malfunction detection by providing totally redundant circuits. In this time-honored technique, each circuit is made redundant, with comparators at critical locations to detect errors between the two redundant channels. An example of this technique for a counter is shown in Fig. A5-1. Flipflops A, B, C, and D are connected identically to flipflops A', B', C', and D', in a redundant channel. Therefore, barring a malfunction, the two redundant channels should always indicate the same count. Should any counter failure occur, it will be detected by one of the EXCLUSIVE-OR gates E, F, G, or H and used to set the *counter failure* flipflop through OR gate I. Therefore, any malfunction of the counter can immediately be brought to the attention of the system operator.

It is obvious that the example cited above is not a very efficient design because of its high parts count. There are few applications which require this "total" approach to malfunction detection. Economic considerations will usually dictate that a bit of ingenuity be used to generate an effective automatic test scheme while maintaining a control on system cost and complexity.

A5-2 APPROACHES TO AUTOMATIC MALFUNCTION DETECTION

Automatic malfunction detection can be approached from three directions:

1. *Built-in test equipment (BITE)* This term is usually applied to circuitry which is included in equipment for verifying normal system operation and is *operator actuated*.
2. *Self-test* This term is applied to circuitry which is included within a system design for verifying normal operation and is usually *operated continuously and automatically without operator intervention*. The example shown in Fig. A5-1 is an example of the self-test concept.
3. *Fault isolation* This term is applied to those built-in test circuits which are included in a system to aid the service personnel in locating a faulty module or circuit card. These circuits are used interactively by the service technician. Depending upon the foresight of the system designer, the data supplied by these test circuits will require a greater or lesser amount of skill and system knowledge to locate a faulty component.

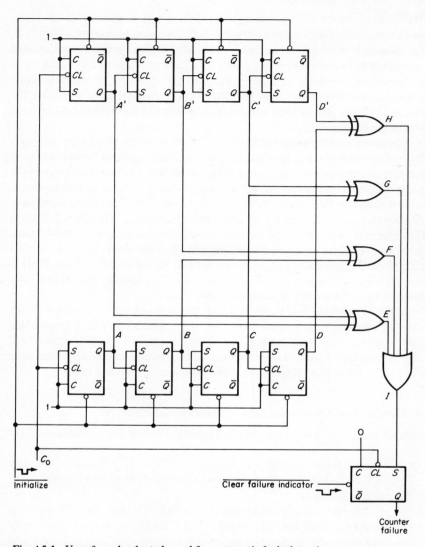

Fig. A5-1   Use of a redundant channel for automatic fault detection.

The use of the above approaches in an economical and effective manner relies almost entirely on the skill and insight of the system designer. To be effective and economical, the concepts of BITE, self-test, and fault isolation *must* be an important consideration in the basic system design. *Add-on* test circuits are almost always ineffective, expensive, or both, and they are always clumsy.

A5-3   AN EXAMPLE OF BITE

Consider the following problem. A radar has a system control counter and a range counter. Verify with a high probability that both counters are functioning properly.

In a radar system, the control counter normally triggers the radar modulator. The RF output to the antenna is used to start the range counter. In this way, any uncertainty inherent in forming the RF pulse is not transferred to the range measurement. The scheme is shown in Fig. A5-2.

The simple addition shown in Fig. A5-3 allows an operator to initiate a BITE test and ascertain with a high degree of accuracy whether or not both counters are operating properly. When the BITE mode is initiated, the range counter is started when the most significant bit of the system control counter goes to the 1 state. N clock periods later the system control counter will be in some state S. State S is selected to occur when the range counter is equal to all 1s. The all-1s state of the range counter is compared with state S of the system control counter using an EXCLUSIVE-OR gate. If these two states do not occur during the same clock period, the *error* output will be set equal to 1. This output might be used to turn on a light. Thus, for an expenditure of very few components, we have achieved a high degree of confidence that both the system control counter and the range counter are operating properly.

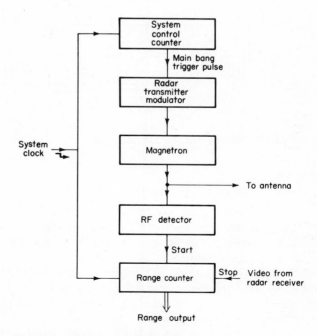

Fig. A5-2 Radar system structure.

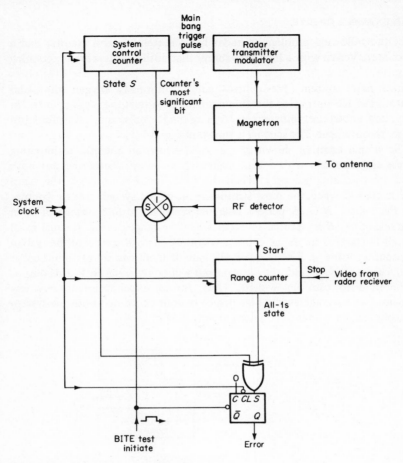

Fig. A5-3   BITE circuitry for the radar system.

A5-4   AN EXAMPLE OF SELF-TEST

As an example of the continuous automatic monitoring inherent in the self-test approach, consider again the problem of Fig. A5-2. Instead of requiring an operator-press-to-test or BITE mode, let us see how we might make the test continuous and automatic.

The range counter in a tracking radar will always have a smaller maximum count than the system control counter. (The system control counter would probably be run at a lower clock frequency than the range counter, but we shall not consider that case here.) If, as shown in Fig. A5-4, we increment a scale-of-256 counter each time the system control counter is equal to all 1s, the all-1s state of this scale-of-256 counter can be used to detect every 256th cycle of the system control counter. We then enable the *self-test control* flipflop when both counters are in the all-1s state. The setting of this flipflop disables the video line from the receiver and prevents it from stopping the range counter. The all-1s state of the range counter is ANDed with the corresponding state of the system control counter. Then, if these two events occur simultaneously, the self-test control flipflop will be reset, thus triggering the retriggerable one-shot. The period of the retriggerable one-shot is normally set to an interval longer than several times 256 times the period of the system control counter. This prevents

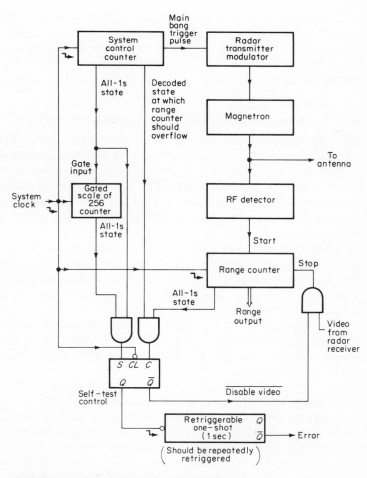

Fig. A5-4   Self-test circuitry for the radar system.

nuisance trips and operator distractions should a momentary transient destroy system synchronization for a short interval. Any time the self-test control flipflop is quiescent (in either state) for a 1-s period, a failure has occurred somewhere in the system and the operator is alerted. Added benefits of this scheme over the one shown in Fig. A5-3 are:

1. Automatic continuous failure monitoring
2. The radar modulator, magnetron, and RF detector are monitored along with the two counters

Note that the cost of the self-test scheme shown in Fig. A5-4 is comparable to the BITE scheme shown in Fig. 5-3.

It should be noted that in this case, ingenuity was the key to obtaining a self-test system having low cost. For all systems, the designer should make maximum use of existing gating and counters in his self-test or BITE design. Often he will find that BITE or self-test is virtually free for the asking if the overall system organization plan included BITE or self-test at the outset.

A5-5 GUIDELINES FOR DESIGNING SERVICEABLE EQUIPMENT

Servicing equipment is a problem of the most severe type to both equipment manufacturers and to users. The owner of a $400,000 numerically controlled machine tool is very upset if his tool is idled for long periods for repair. An airline is quite outspoken if their $12 million aircraft is delayed frequently because the navigation computer is inoperative. The owner of a television set is unhappy if the serviceman spends 10 h isolating a malfunction and charges $70 for the repair.

Unfortunately, electronic equipments are becoming more and more complex at the same time that highly skilled and competent technicians are at a premium. The answer lies in the designer's skill in making his equipment serviceable. There is no use in selling a sophisticated equipment which only the designer can service.

Again, at least half the solution to the serviceability problem lies in the original equipment design. Several features of a digital design contribute to an overall serviceable equipment. Some of the rules for a serviceable digital equipment design follow.

1. *Counters* Use ordinary binary sequences wherever possible (unless servicing will be done with computerized diagnostic test equipment). Gray-code counters are fairly straightforward and are a second best. Stay away from unusual count sequences. A counter that sequences 1, 2, 3, 4, 18, 19, 12, 8, 9, 10, 14, 1, 2, etc., makes a very unusual looking pattern on the oscilloscope and looks broken to the serviceman—even when it is not. Very

little benefit is usually derived by such special sequences and the cost of the few ICs saved will be wasted many times over by the confused serviceman.

2. *If* your counters are not binary or if your logic gating is complex, then your schematic diagram or service literature should include the count sequence of the counters and either truth tables, logic equations, or similar data for the gating. Remember, if your equipment were operating the way you intended, the serviceman would not have the cover off your equipment.

3. Carefully control the layout of the schematic and logic diagrams to insure a clear and logical presentation. There is nothing worse than trying to figure out what is wrong with a counter when it is shown in pieces on three separate drawings.

4. Whenever possible, compartmentalize functional blocks on a single circuit card (or into adjacent sockets of a dual-in-line packaging panel). Try to avoid mixing analog and digital circuits on the same circuit card. Automatic test equipment is much easier to design if a particular card contains all digital or all analog circuits.

5. Bring all flipflop outputs to spare pins on the circuit-board edge connector where feasible. If this is done, automatic equipment capable of locating a trouble almost to the individual integrated circuit is feasible. Functional testing of the card during manufacturing is also easier and *manual* probing of the circuit card during manufacturing troubleshooting will be markedly reduced.

6. Make all circuit boards plug-in. Avoid wired-in boards because they prevent a "check by substitution."

7. Specify certain pins on your circuit cards for each power supply voltage. On any board which does not use a certain voltage, leave the corresponding pin unused. Thus, when the serviceman bypasses your keying scheme (as he is certain to do, maybe with a card extender), maybe he will not get +28 VDC on your +5-VDC logic bus when he plugs the right card in the wrong slot.

A5-6 FAULT ISOLATION

With these guidelines as a starting point, what can the circuit designer do to help the serviceman isolate a system fault? Here, we must define what we mean by *isolate a fault*. A particular equipment may be made of from 5 to 30 circuit cards interconnected with plug-in connectors and a wiring harness. To place the equipment back in service, the usual technique is to locate the defective card, exchange the defective card for a good one, functionally test the equipment, and return it to service.

One might be tempted to conclude here that one simply needs a spare set of cards and a convenient means for functionally testing the overall machine.

Cards can then be substituted until the system performs properly. Indeed, this is a powerful scheme and is used extensively to locate a defective card if a defective card is the culprit. Unfortunately for the circuit designer, most systems interface with the outside world, controlling electronic or, more often, electromechanical devices. The serviceman needs to know if the numerically controlled drill is defective because the digital controller is defective or because a stepping motor is defective.

In this area of system engineering, it is difficult, if not impossible, to make any statements which will be universally applicable. However, there are several methods which appear frequently:

1. *Single-stepping* Almost all digital systems have a clock of some sort. Some clocks are internal, such as in a computer. Other clocks are derived from an external source, such as in an electromechanical event sensor. Trouble in digital equipment most frequently is catastrophic in nature, i.e., it doesn't work! A manually operated single-step switch which allows an operator to execute a sequence of operations step by step and observe the status of the machine at each step is invaluable. Logic circuit and counter operation can thereby be observed at a speed where the human mind can evaluate it in *real time*. For best results, the clock-pulse characteristics of the test pulse (i.e., rise time, width, and fall time) should be identical to the normal system clock. Thus, any aberrations caused by faulty clock shape, overshoot, rise time, or such can be detected.

2. Provide a method of breaking system connections at major interface junctions so that test signals can be easily inserted. As an example, consider a computer printer. A very simple, yet extremely effective method of customer and service technician fault isolation can be provided as shown in Fig. A5-5. The entire logic in the test pattern generator can be assembled on a single 6 x 8 in card and constitutes perhaps 5 percent of the cost of the typical line printer. Yet, this self-contained device provides the customer with the capability of fault isolation to the printer. In addition and equally important, the serviceman can use the fault-isolation circuits as a generator to exercise the printer through its normal operations in a repetitive manner. Therefore, the scheme of introducing test signals into a system at a major system interface where few logic lines are present is seen to be a powerful tool for fault isolation.

3. A fast, effective, and easy-to-use tool for fault isolation is frequently overlooked by the designer. Digital equipment which can be single-stepped through its sequences is an ideal candidate for a *light box*. In this concept, a large number of logic signals are brought out to a connector. This connector is used exclusively for test purposes. Flipflop outputs, major timing and clock busses, outputs of function generators, and system inputs

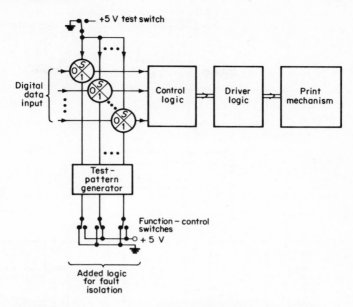

Fig. A5-5   Computer printer with fault-isolation circuitry.

and outputs are brought out, as well as any other important trouble
locating signals.

Often a system (such as the C-5A landing-gear control system) will
have several equipment boxes which are separated (see Fig. A5-6). In these
cases, identical test connectors can be provided on each equipment and a
single test box can service them all. For instance, the C-5A landing-gear
control system includes controls for raising and lowering the landing gear,
kneeling the aircraft in a number of attitudes, steering the aircraft, and
controlling the landing-gear headings to permit crosswind landings. To
control this landing gear requires hundreds of integrated circuits. There are
about 400 wires which interconnect the various controllers with the
hydraulic actuators, proximity switches, ac motors, solenoid valves,
control panels, and similar equipment. The electronic equipment controls
the sequencing of the landing-gear functions and prevents operator
sequencing of the equipment in an unsafe manner. The personnel who
service the landing gear are usually mechanics. These mechanics have only
a rudimentary electrical knowledge. Yet these people are required to
determine which element in a faulty landing-gear system must be replaced.
Therefore, they must be able to determine in an efficient manner the
sequence of operations commanded by the control boxes. The light box
gives immediate access to the proper signals, and the resulting data is easily

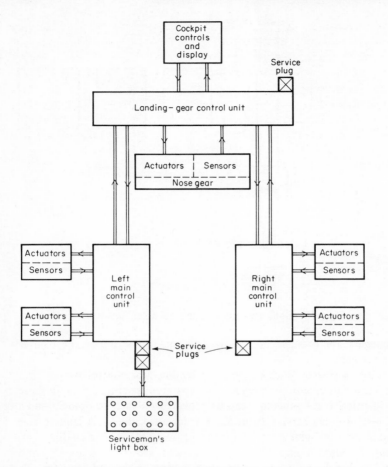

Fig. A5-6 Simplified block diagram of the C-5A landing-gear control system.

interpreted by nonelectronic personnel. As a result, it is not necessary to remove a control box cover and use a voltmeter to determine why a hydraulic actuator will not move. The mechanic simply connects his light box and observes that the landing gear is not properly centered. Many hours of costly troubleshooting are thereby avoided.

A5-7 PROGNOSIS FOR THE FUTURE

Automatic test of both logic and analog circuits under computer control is already widespread. This trend is sure to expand. Some computerized diagnostic test systems can locate a faulty part to the integrated-circuit level. Advances in the techniques of automatic troubleshooting will be made in both software and hardware. Designers are learning to bring sufficient internal signals to the card edge connectors to facilitate automatic fault isolation to the component level. For the logic circuit designer, a major advance will occur in a few years when an integrated-circuit designer incorporates a redundant circuit on his chip with a *light emitting diode* (LED) visible through the integrated-circuit package. EXCLUSIVE-OR gates will determine when the two circuits disagree and will illuminate the LED. By this means, a faulty integrated circuit will announce its sin to the world!

Index

Index